Dominic and Douglas Streatfeild-James have been brothers for as long as they can remember. Quite apart from both answering to a surname that isn't spelled right, they both went to Charterhouse, both had brief careers in the Royal Navy and army respectively (Dominic's considerably briefer and less distinguished than Douglas's) and both spent some time at university (London and Oxford).

Dominic (above, right) and Douglas have lived and travelled extensively in Europe, North America and Asia. In the course of their research for this guide they travelled over 80,000km along the railways of Central Asia and China.

Douglas is currently completing a new guidebook, *China by Rail* (Trailblazer Publications). Dominic is writing and directing documentaries for the Discovery Channel.

Silk Route by Rail
First edition 1993
This second edition 1997

Publisher
Trailblazer Publications
The Old Manse, Tower Rd, Hindhead, Surrey, GU26 6SU, UK
Fax (+44) 01428-607571
E-mail 106101.1611@compuserve.com

British Library Cataloguing in Publication Data
A catalogue record for this book is available from the British Library

ISBN 1-873756-14-3

Editor: Patricia Major
Typesetting: Anna Jacomb-Hood
Cartography and index: Jane Thomas

Printed on chlorine-free paper from farmed forests by
Technographic Design & Print Ltd, Colchester, Essex, UK

SILK ROUTE
BY RAIL

**DOMINIC
STREATFEILD-JAMES**

Second edition researched by

**DOUGLAS
STREATFEILD-JAMES**

TRAILBLAZER PUBLICATIONS

Acknowledgements

From Dominic: Since Doug did all the work this time, he gets most of the thanks. Good job! Well, not bad for an army boy, anyway. There have been accomplices, however: special thanks also go to Simon Richmond, Gavin Hellier, Peter Holdforth, Athol Yates and Richard Brown. As usual, thanks are due to the Thomas family en masse: Bryn, Jane and Patricia; also to Emma for her encyclopedic knowledge of Russian and Chinese current affairs, and to Rollo (that's **three** now). And, belatedly, to Madeleine Stewart, who never got thanked in the first edition – but without whom nothing would have been possible.

From Douglas: Many people have helped with the updating of the guide, and a good few of them have already been mentioned above. Thank you (again) to Neil Taylor of Regent Holidays, Neil Magowan at The Russia Experience and to Jan Passoff and the staff at TGH Moscow for their help.

Along the way thanks to the travellers who helped out with information and were just good company: Tommy Herts; Simon Whitton and Tony Frobisher; Mary and Ronald; Lily; Mike, Fernando and Yew Chin; Beth and Ted Lee at the Manhattan Café in Dunhuang; and Nat and Jodie Stookey. Finally a particularly big thank you to Olia Bakhtiyarova in Tashkent, without whose help I might never have got any further, and to Simon in Beijing for being very, very hospitable for a very long time.

A note on prices in the CIS

Things are changing fast in Central Asia, particularly in the CIS. Rapid inflation means that it would be pointless to give prices in roubles, sum or tenge in this book. Prices in the sections on Russia, Uzbekistan and Kazakhstan are therefore shown in US$; payment should be in the local currency equivalent.

A request

The author and publisher have tried to ensure that this guide is as accurate and up-to-date as possible. Nevertheless things change, prices rise, rail services are extended or cut back, hotels open and close. If you notice any omissions or changes that should be included in the next edition of this book, please write to Dominic Streatfeild-James at Trailblazer Publications (address on p2). A free copy of the next edition will be sent to persons making a significant contribution.

Front cover: Camels were the main means of transport across the lowlands of the Silk Route because of their strength, resilience and ability to survive for prolonged periods with little or no water. This one is pictured in Khiva.

CONTENTS

INTRODUCTION

Mention the Silk Route and most people immediately think of China. This is perfectly natural – silk was first made in China and it was from here that it was originally sent west. Until recently, however, latter-day Silk Route travellers have been unable to penetrate further than Xinjiang Province in the north-west of China, for the border between Xinjiang and the USSR was closed to foreign visitors. From 1986, the Karakoram Pass offered an alternative, so that journeys could be continued south into Pakistan but, in fact, the majority of the Silk Route traffic did not head this way: it went directly west. The gradual disintegration of the USSR and opening up of the CIS have now created new travel opportunities. Further, completion of a rail link from Almaty in Kazakhstan to Urumqi in China has, for the first time ever, made the journey from Central Asia (formerly Soviet Central Asia) into China accessible to the average traveller. This means that Marco Polo successors can not only trek their way across China but can also cross the border and continue west to visit some of the most famous cities of the ancient world. In the last two centuries Western poets and dreamers alike cast their minds eastwards to Samarkand, Bukhara and Xanadu knowing, or at least suspecting, that they would never see the great mystical cities of the East. The trek was just too dangerous; it was not possible. Now it is.

The Silk Route stands for everything that is exciting and exotic about the Far East and some of its stops still maintain the sights which made them famous or notorious. From the walled city of Khiva, where the trade in human slaves ceased only in 1917, the modern traveller moves to the Kalyan Minaret in Bukhara, known as the Tower of Death; skirts some of the greatest deserts of Asia; takes in the natural beauty of the Lake of Heaven near Urumqi; passes the western end of the Great Wall at Jiayuguan; stops at the astonishing decorations of the Mogao Thousand Buddha Caves at Dunhuang....the list goes on.

The rail link between Almaty and Urumqi, opened in June 1992, offers more than simply an alternative to the Trans-Siberian railway. It offers the opportunity of a really challenging, informative trip from west to east and back, for the routes across this part of the world are loaded with historical significance. Currently it is not possible to buy a through ticket from Moscow to Beijing via Kazakhstan but, even if it were, the traveller who did not stop off for a look at some of the cities along the way would be foolish. Virtually every stop suggested in this guide could conceivably constitute the highlight of another trip. Here they are strung together conveniently in the order that they would have been encountered by the former Silk Route travellers.

It is particularly exciting to travel this way at the moment. Mainstream tourism has not had much contact with Central Asia, so the opportunity still exists to visit these ancient sites without encountering truckloads of package holiday devotees. This is particularly so with the great Eastern cities of Bukhara, Samarkand and Khiva, which seem likely to be the next additions to the wealthy jet-set's 'been there' lists.

Throughout history, political upheaval has severed the Silk Route repeatedly but it has always recovered. It is currently more accessible than ever before.

PART 1: PLANNING YOUR TRIP

Routes, costs and making a booking

ROUTE OPTIONS

The fundamental choice, of course, is that of direction. Do you want to start in the Far East and head west, or are you happy to end up in Beijing? At the moment, in order to obtain your visa for Russia and other countries in the CIS, it is necessary to have either an 'invitation' to visit the country (this usually applies to business travellers) or, in the case of tourists, guaranteed hotel bookings. There are ways around this but if you want to play by the rules it may be wise to start in the West, because if for some reason you get held up going the other way your CIS travel arrangements could be jeopardised. Thus this guide takes you from Moscow to Beijing but the information is still valid if you want to head towards, rather than away from, Europe.

There are numerous possibilities for the traveller along this route. Limitations will usually be time, money and independence, and if you have plenty of each of these you are in for a long and exciting trip. For those who are pressed in one or more departments, though, allowances can be made: internal flights are available both in China and the CIS, buses can be quicker and easier than trains, and less interesting stops can be cut out; the choice is yours. Some backtracking may be required to travel the Silk Route entirely by rail, going first from Moscow to Tashkent, since services on the direct Moscow-Urgench route do not currently run regularly.

If you're planning to visit only the Chinese cities on the Silk Route there are two options: there's a direct service from Moscow to Almaty (4057km 77 hours) where you join the Almaty-Urumqi service (1230km, 36 hours). Or you can travel on the Trans-Siberian route from Moscow to Novosibirsk (3335km, 74 hours), transfer to the Turksib line from Novosibirsk to Aktogay (1121km, 25 hours) where you join the Almaty-Urumqi service from Aktogay to Urumqi (1055km, 23 hours).

COSTS

The costs of this trip can vary wildly. Be aware that although various travel companies offer tours to parts of this route, there is no one ticket from Moscow to Beijing via the Silk Route. You will either have to book each sector of the rail journey and each night's accommodation through your travel agent or attempt to obtain tickets for the next leg of your journey wherever you stop. Obviously booking in advance does eliminate the queuing and most of the hassle. It also inflates prices horrendously. Likewise the number of stops you make along the way will affect costs: how many nights' hotel accommodation will you be needing, for example? The whole question of money really pivots around how independent and enterprising you want your trip to be: independent travellers can choose not only how long they want to stay in each place but can also select the best-value hotel when they arrive in a new city. If, however, you have arranged accommodation through Intourist, Uzbektourism, or CITS in China, you can expect to be booked automatically into one of the better hotels in town. In Russia and the CIS, although accommodation isn't cheap, the cheaper (and sometimes friendlier) hotels can be half or even a third the price of the Intourist selection. In China the difference can be greater still: a dormitory bed may cost you £2/US$3 whereas a room in the Holiday Inn will set you back £65/US$100.

Travel costs aren't insubstantial either, and if you book your tickets in advance through a travel agent you can expect them to be higher still. Recent changes in both the CIS countries and in China mean that tourists are now allowed to buy rail tickets for almost the same price that locals pay, but as the distances involved in this trip are vast, the prices still need to be taken into account. A second class ticket from Moscow to Tashkent (a three-day train journey), bought via a travel agent in Moscow, will cost £85/US$127. Although, for convenience, it may be worthwhile getting tickets for CIS countries in advance, buying your own rail tickets in China isn't too daunting and will save you some money. By way of an example of Chinese prices, a ticket from Beijing to Xi'an (a 20-hour journey) will cost from £12/US$18 in 'Hard Seat' to £35/US$53 in 'Soft Sleeper'. See p12 for information on the different classes of rail travel in China and the CIS.

Budget travel

The problem of budget travel in Russia and the CIS is a tricky one. There are no *really* cheap places to stay but if you manage to avoid booking with the various state tourism agencies there are chances to stay in privately-owned hotels which are generally good value. In Moscow and Uzbekistan, homestays with local families are also a possibility. The problem is that in these countries, the 'system' still requires you to have made hotel bookings in advance. Furthermore, although the authorities in Russia don't seem to mind too much, in Uzbekistan the police and immigration authorities may prevent you from going anywhere until you can show them proof of your previous and future movements. You may be required to produce slips from the hotels where you have already stayed, and booking vouchers for the places where you will be staying during the remainder of your visit. Failure to do this will entail a costly visit to the nearest Uzbektourism office to book into state hotels. One solution is simply to avoid places where you are likely to bump into the police. If you're entering the country by train from Russia you may well avoid formal border checks. Equally, if you travel by public bus you stand a good chance of bypassing the police, who seem to keep a closer eye on the railway stations than on the bus stations.

The safer option by far, however, is to accept the inevitable and arrange accommodation in advance for the CIS section of the trip, as this will also ensure that you get your visa without difficulty. Rather than book accommodation through Intourist or Uzbektourism, who will try to put you in expensive hotels, book through one of the UK agencies listed on pp19-20, or through one of the small agencies which are springing up in the countries themselves (see p22). For advice on getting visas see p15; for details of local travel agencies see p19-28.

China, by comparison, is easy. CITS, the state tourist organisation, will sting you if you arrange your trip through them, but since you won't encounter the sort of problems that exist in the CIS there's no need to go near them. Travelling independently will mean that you'll have to get to grips with the Chinese ticket offices, and occasionally that you may have to travel in rather grotty conditions. If you use your initiative, however, you won't have any serious problems. Once you start travelling you'll meet other budget travellers who will pass on the latest money saving tips, and places to stay: the system doesn't take long to get used to.

Hotel accommodation

In the CIS The state tourism authorities in Russia and Uzbekistan, (**Intourist** and **Uzbektourism**) have until recently had a virtual monopoly on accommodation and travel within their countries and have abused it. Rooms in their 'sponsored' hotels, although expensive, will generally be of a fairly low standard, and certainly lower than you might expect for the same amount of money (£30-45/US$50-70 per night) in the West. Increasingly, however, genuinely excellent hotels are springing up in the CIS. These are often termed 'deluxe class', are the products of joint ventures with Western countries, and are very expensive (£65/US$100 or more per night). Alternatives are appearing at the budget end of the spectrum, too; independent companies in Moscow and St Petersburg set precedents in the early 1990s by opening cheap hotels specifically for Western visitors. In both Russia and Uzbekistan, home-stays are also becoming possible; they're still not very cheap, but they are as cheap as you'll get and you have the advantage of getting to live with a local family. The situation as regards homestays, however, is not entirely clear, and it is best to arrange them through an agency, thereby giving some legitimacy to your agreement. Agencies that can help are listed on pp16-17. It is worth remembering that the price for a room in any of the countries dealt with in this book is usually the same whether there are one or two occupants, so bringing a friend makes good financial sense.

In China Standards of accommodation in China are much higher, and in virtually all of the cities in this book Western-standard hotels are available. Prices vary, but for a standard (Holiday Inn type) double room, bank on paying £45-60/US$70-100. In between this and the true budget accommodation there is a complete range of prices and standards available, so that in most places you will be able to find accommodation that suits your pocket. Most of the cheaper Chinese hotels (those that take foreigners) have dormitory rooms, and a bed (typically in a three- or four-bedded room) will cost from £1.20/US$1.80 to £4/US$6.

In many places, if there are two or three of you it will be just as cheap to get a private room. If you are in a four-bedded room which is otherwise empty, do not be surprised when other travellers are sent in to share with you.

Accommodation on the train

A night spent on the train saves you the cost of a night's accommodation, but you should be aware that conditions on the trains running between Central Asian cities can be extremely basic (see p56). Whilst they're OK for the odd night, you might not want to make too many advance bookings for night trains here. Chinese trains, however, are rather more comfortable and the Almaty to Urumqi train is fine.

In the CIS there are three main classes of rail travel:
• **First Class/Soft Class** These are rare; often for those travelling with Intourist. There are four berths with either two or four occupants, depending on how much you have paid.
• **Second Class** Very similar but always with four occupants, which can get a bit crowded, especially if it's hot and your room-mates invite friends in. Most of the fittings will be broken, the windows will be filthy and/or cracked, and don't be surprised to find cockroaches living it up in any food you leave lying around overnight.
• **Third Class** The whole carriage is laid out with bunks but no partitions, much like an Indian Second Class train. They are numbered and may be reserved. It will usually be fairly crowded and very noisy. Keep an especially close eye on your belongings.

In China everyone is 'equal' so the various levels of comfort on trains are not referred to as different classes:
• **Soft Sleeper** These supposedly offer luxury. In effect they are somewhere between Russian First and Second class carriages: laid out for four occupants, with comfy bunks and, most often, air conditioning. Important

to some people is the fact that in Soft Sleeper compartments you can actually turn off the constant music and propaganda broadcasts which are piped throughout the train. Many foreigners, however, prefer Hard Sleeper (see below) as the Soft Sleeper compartments can get a bit claustrophobic when the door is closed, and if you don't hit it off with the others in your compartment, the atmosphere can get rather uncomfortable.

• **Soft Seat** Again for the softies, but this time when the journey is taking place during the daytime. Generally rare, these offer padded seats and the advantage that, unlike hard seat carriages, the number of tickets sold is restricted to the number of seats actually available.

• **Hard Sleeper** The most popular, and thus the most difficult to book. There are no compartments as such but the bunks are partitioned into groups of six – three layers of bunks on each side of the partitioned area. Blankets and sheets are provided. Tickets are generally about two-thirds the cost of a Soft Sleeper.

• **Hard Seat** The cheapest way to get around, and consequently the most packed. Seats face each other and are constructed at such an angle as to render sleep utterly impossible. You will be surrounded by spitting, chain smoking locals who will stare at you for hours at a time. This is by far the most entertaining (and exhausting) way to travel, and it is easy to get seats, although in order to ensure a reserved seat you should book the day before you travel. Be very careful of your possessions – rucksacks may be secured to the overhead luggage racks if you feel uncertain, and securing them at night is definitely a good idea. A Hard Seat will cost you about half the price of a Hard Sleeper.

STOPPING OFF ALONG THE WAY

There is a near-infinite number of possibilities – money, time and interest will all play a part in your decision as to where to stop. The ancient cities in the CIS, notably Khiva, Samarkand and Bukhara, are particularly worth visiting, if only because so few Westerners have actually been there. Get in there before the rush!

For tour-group travellers the decisions will probably be made for you but for budget travellers the story is different: not only will you have more time to spare but you will also be travelling in less comfort, so the stops will give you a chance to rest. This is particularly true in China where Hard Seat rail travel is no party. The journey in this book is conveniently broken up into sections so that apart from the initial Moscow-Tashkent trip, the Tashkent-Urgench leg (or the Moscow-Urgench section if the service is running), and the Kazakhstan- China crossing, none of the others is longer than 21 hours. Train times, numbers and the lengths of each journey are listed in the Moving On section at the end of each city guide. In some places it can be difficult to get hold of train tickets, though, so wherever you visit, make arrangements for your departure and then go sightseeing, rather than vice versa, or you could spend longer than you planned there, waiting for reservations.

Finally, remember that this guide is not definitive; there are many other cities along the Silk Route both in the CIS and in China that are worth visiting. So if you hear about a place that's not included here, go and investigate; the experience of spending a couple of days wandering around a strange town totally bewildered without a guide book is under-estimated – a small dose of confusion and disorientation should be a part of every travel experience.

WHEN TO GO

Bear in mind that most of the routes across the CIS and China skirt around deserts, so that in mid-summer (June, July and August) the heat is fearsome. In Bukhara, on the edge of the Kyzilkum Desert, summer temperatures go up to 40°C, while in Turfan, midway across the Taklamakan on the northern route, it is possible to boil an egg merely by placing it in the sand. (The highest recorded temperature here is 49.3°C/121°F). The good thing about the heat, though, is that it is dry heat, and while this means that you'll die faster if you aren't careful, at least you won't be feeling hot and clammy as you go.

If you don't want to endure this heat, the best time to travel is either in spring or autumn (April-May, or August-September). Of course, if you are going to spend three months on the trip, a reasonable assumption if you plan to stop at every town in this book, you will catch the heat at some point. Beware of early spring or late autumn when temperatures can drop sharply (it snows in Urumqi in October).

It's possible to travel at any time, but remember that just as deserts are hot in the summer, so they get very cold in the winter. One user of this guide who crossed the border from Urumqi to Almaty in February reported that a two-day blizzard in Urumqi was so bad when he visited, that it was pointless even going out of the hotel; sightseeing isn't much fun when you're freezing.

MAKING A BOOKING

With a tour or on your own?

There are two ways of making a booking: the first is simply to arrange a place on one of the package tours (but note that currently there is no single tour which covers the whole trip). This is rather expensive but guarantees you a virtually hassle-free holiday. The second is to book your own accommodation and transport in the CIS through an independent travel agent (see pp18-28) and then make your bookings as you go once you've reached China. Individual travel in China is recommended because accommodation is relatively easy to find there, and because booking in advance will almost certainly involve some contact with the China International Travel Service (CITS). While CITS run some good tours for groups, and are definitely getting their act together in some areas, their service tends to be a bit patchy for individuals, as groups always take precedence.

Many travellers have complained about CITS, so be wary of their promises, as when things go wrong officials tend simply to shake their heads and smile at you. Having said this, China can be one of the more frustrating places to travel through unassisted: people can be very unhelpful, very little English is spoken, and even relatively simple things like buying train tickets can be infuriatingly complex. Basically, if the idea of queuing for three hours for a train ticket and then having to accept a Hard Seat because there are no sleepers appals you, take a tour.

For tours, either of China or the CIS – or both – see pp20-28. For individual travel, the plot thickens.

CIS visas

In the good old days of the USSR, obtaining a visa may not have been easy but the procedure was straightforward. It was necessary to produce Intourist vouchers to prove that you had booked and paid for your trip and that you would be under constant supervision throughout your stay. Since 1990, however, private companies have sprung up to deal with foreign tourists, and partly as a consequence of this, visa regulations have become confused: there is no longer a single source to vet tourists and take care of them when they arrive. To complicate matters further, the newly-independent Central Asian states have taken some time to set up embassies and make their own arrangements for tourists.

In principle, however, the old guidelines apply, and all three of these countries ask to see either proof of bookings with a tour, vouchers for hotel reservations, or a personal invitation. Another vestige of the old system remains common to all three countries: a tourist visa for any one of the countries is valid as a transit visa for up to 72 hours in the others. While 72 hours isn't a very long time, potentially this could be useful: if your passport hasn't been stamped as you cross the border between Central Asian states, you could argue, if stopped, that you've only just arrived. This is no substitute for a proper visa, of course.

Whereas the Chinese visa is easy to get hold of, the visas for Russia, Uzbekistan and Kazakhstan are costly and time consuming to collect, and you may prefer to leave this to your travel agent or to a professional visa service. Be aware that you will need at least six clear months before the expiry date of your passport, a clean page for each visa (except the Russian one) and that you can count on a one to two week wait for each CIS visa. For an update on the latest developments you should check with the travel agents listed on pp16-17, or with a visa agency.

Russia Before being given a visa, it's still necessary to show some kind of proof that you will be taken care of during your stay, and that you won't just wander off. Letters from travel agents stating that they have made bookings at hotels or for transportation on your behalf should be acceptable, but the travel agent or visa service will be the best people to advise on this.

The Russian visa is a separate slip of paper which sits in your passport and is removed when you leave. Cities to which you have been granted access will be printed on the visa and you are not permitted to go anywhere else. In practice there is little that can be done to stop you apart from the fact that hotels should refuse foreigners who don't have the right visas. Certain hotels may accept visitors with non-valid or non-existent visas, but do be warned that you are breaking the law by travelling in a foreign country without the right documentation.

Intrepid independent travellers have managed to get hold of dubious visas by a variety of means and have been trickling into the CIS for a while now. Common examples include business visas for companies that have never existed and dodgy letters of invitation (one guy we met during the initial research for this guide had bought a Russian typewriter and transposed the seal from an out-of-date Intourist document onto a letter inviting him to visit indefinitely). One German even managed to sweet talk his way across the Turkish border and travel through the CIS with no visa at all. Equally, we recently met another guy who was caught in Uzbekistan without a visa, and after a couple of unpleasant days was forcibly put on a train home. The Russians, Uzbeks and Kazakhs tend not to be too ceremonious when they catch a foreigner breaking the law, and at the very least your holiday in that particular country is likely to be over, so it's not worth it.

If you're travelling with a tour, or have prebooked accommodation and transport in Russia, you shouldn't have a problem. For independent travellers, however, there are several places that can help you to get a letter of invitation, and consequently a visa:

• **Travellers Guest House Moscow** (fax +7-095-280 7686 (don't omit the '0' of the 095 code when dialling from outside Russia), e-mail TGH@GLAS.APC. ORG; 10th Floor, Building #50, Bolshaya Pereyaslavskaya St, 129041 Moscow) will not only arrange visa support, but sells train tickets too, and is probably the best place to stay in Moscow if you're looking for budget accommodation (see p112). Visa support for a single entry 25-day visa costs in the region of US$35, and this price increases if you are after a longer period or a multi-entry visa; the charge is payable by American Express credit card.

• **Sindbad Travel** (☎ +7-812-327 8384, fax +7-812-329 8019, e-mail sindbad@ryh.spb.su) at ul 3rd Sovetskaya 28, St Petersburg, Russia, You can also get invitations from their North America partner, **Russian Youth**

Hostels & Tourism (☎ +1-310-379 4316, fax +1-310-379 8420, e-mail 71573.2010@compuserve.com).
• **Russia-Rail Internet Travel Service** (http://www.russia-rail.com/, e-mail russia-rail@russia-rail.com).
• **Passport Travel** (☎ +61-3-9867 3888, fax +61-3-9867 1055, e-mail bmc-cunn@werple.mira.net.au) Suite 11, 401 St Kilda Rd, Melbourne, Victoria, 3004 Australia.
• **G & R International** (☎ +7-095-374 7366, fax +7-095-374 6132, e-mail grint@glas.apc.org), Block 6, Office 4, Institute of Youth, ul Yunosti 5/1, Moscow.
• **IRO Travel** (☎ +7-095-971 4059, 280 8562, fax +7-095-280 7686, e-mail tgh@glas.apc.org), 10th floor, ul Bolshaya Pereyaslavksaya 50, Moscow.
• **Andrew's Consulting** (☎ +7-095-126 9413, 232 3601), Moscow.

Note that your visa will also be checked as you leave the country, and the chances are that you will at the very least be fined if you have the wrong visa or if it's out of date. There may also be a delay which could put you at risk of missing your flight or train. You should be aware that, unlike in some countries, extending your visa isn't necessarily easy. Currently transit visas can be extended once, for up to five days; getting a five day extension costs US$3 and takes 24 hours at the Immigration Office in Moscow (Ul Pokrovka 42, near Kurskaya metro stop). Tourist visas are more difficult to extend, and you'll need a good reason.

Uzbekistan If you are taking an organised tour or have made hotel bookings through a travel agent, getting an Uzbek visa should not be a problem, but for independent travellers who want to make their own arrangements on arrival, getting a visa can be very difficult. Even if you do manage to get a visa without having made any bookings in advance (as we did when researching the update for this guide), there may be problems when you arrive in Uzbekistan, as the immigration authorities and police, should you come across them, will expect to see the requisite booking vouchers (see **Budget travel**, above). Adventurous travellers may still like to try getting a visa independently and working things out on arrival, but it's far easier, safer and less frustrating to make some bookings and get the visa through the proper channels.

If you get to Moscow without a visa for Uzbekistan, you will need to visit the Uzbekistan embassy at Pogorelsky Per 12 (☎ 095-230 0076/1301/0054) although it may take you several days to get the visa. You'll need to leave your passport with them for all this time. Likewise there is an embassy in Almaty (see p165).

As a last resort, there's an immigration office at Tashkent airport (see p155), but there are mixed reports about this place. Here you are likely to be marched down to the Uzbektourism office (in the same terminal) to book your accommodation at massive expense.

Kazakhstan If you are sticking to the route described in this book, you may not need to get a Kazakh visa at all. The chances are pretty good that you will manage to get a ticket for the Urumqi or Tashkent trains within 72 hours of arriving, and thus your valid Uzbek or Russian visa can be used as a 72 hour transit visa. Moreover, since, at the time of writing, there were no passport controls when crossing the border between Uzbekistan and Kazakhstan by train, if you're travelling east it wouldn't matter greatly if you were delayed a day or two: you could claim, if challenged, that you'd only just arrived. This was certainly the advice we were given by the Kazakh embassy in Tashkent, where we were told that our Uzbek visas would suffice and that no one would bother if we were a day or two over the limit. If you want to be certain though, or want to have the flexibility to stay longer in Kazakhstan, you will need to get a separate visa. In the London embassy (see p22) they will expect to see your hotel/tour group booking forms but they may not be so strict at the embassy in Moscow (see p110). If you are travelling from west to east, there is also a friendly and efficiently-run embassy in Tashkent (see p155). If you are travelling from east to west, however, you will need to get your visa well beforehand in Beijing (see p248).

Although there are repeated rumours about the possibility of getting visas in Urumqi or even at the border itself, there is little truth here. You will be turned back automatically from the border if you don't have the right stamp in your passport. The Kazakh Airlines office in Urumqi does give out some visas but for the most part these will be of no use. They will only issue tourist visas if you have proof of your hotel or tour bookings, or a three-day transit visa if you have an air or rail booking to prove that you are moving on within the three days. One traveller we met in Urumqi had been assured by the Kazakh embassy in another country he had recently passed through, that he could get a visa in Urumqi just before he crossed the border. In the event he found that the nearest place he could get a visa was in Beijing. If you're planning to enter Kazakhstan from Urumqi, make sure you have your visa sorted out well in advance.

Chinese visa
Obtaining a Chinese visa is not a problem in most countries where there is a Chinese embassy. Tourist visas generally last one month from the day of entry and are valid for three months. They are usually extendible by one month at any large Public Security Bureau office in China. Note however that Beijing, paradoxically, is a bad place to extend your visa.

MAKING A BOOKING IN BRITAIN

Prices and options change, so the information below is provided for guidance only. Note that almost all of the travel agents listed here will handle visa applications for you if you have booked through them. If you are just looking for flights, try the bucket-seat shops on Earl's Court Rd , in London, or **Aeroflot** (☎ 0171-355 2233) at 70 Piccadilly, London W1V 9HH. There is an **Uzbektourism Office** (☎ 0171-935 1899) in London at 13 Marylebone Lane, W1H 9LG, although they would prefer to book you into hotels than give you advice. By contrast, the **China National Tourist Office** (☎ 0171-935 9787) at 4 Glentworth St, London NW1 5PG, is great; they will certainly advise you to take a tour but they also hand out reams of brochures and travel company literature as well as excellent tourist maps and very useful rail timetables.

• **Regent Holidays** (☎ 0117-921 1711, fax 0117-925 4866, e-mail: 106041.1470@compuserve.com), 15 John St, Bristol, BS1 2HR. This friendly company specialises in independent and small group travel throughout China and the CIS. Whereas all accommodation and rail/air travel can be booked for China, they do not book rail travel in the CIS, dealing only with accommodation and flight arrangements.

• **The Russia Experience** (☎ 0181-566 8846, fax 0181-566 8843, e-mail: 100604.764@compuserve.com), Research House, Fraser Rd, Perivale, Middlesex UB6 7AQ. Specialists in budget travel within the CIS, the Russia Experience are able to book rail tickets within the CIS, tickets for the train between Almaty and Urumqi, and hotels and homestays in Russia. They do not at the moment deal with homestays in Uzbekistan or Kazakhstan but can probably get you into some of the smaller (cheaper) hotels. Although they may be able to help with some onward travel from Urumqi, they do not venture further into China.

• **Intourist** (☎ 0171-538 8600 for tours, ☎ 0171-538 5965 for individual bookings, fax 0171-538 5967, e-mail: info@intourus.demon.co.uk, web-site: http://www.intourus.demon.co.uk), 219 Marsh Wall, Isle of Dogs, London E14 9PD. Intourist also have an office in Manchester at: Suite 2F, Central Buildings, 211 Deansgate, Manchester, M3 3NW (☎ 0161-834 0230, fax 0161-831 7865) and in Glasgow at: 29 St Vincent Place, Glasgow, G1 2DT, Scotland (☎ 0141-204 5809, fax 0141-204 5807). The company you are dealing with here is independent of the larger parent organisation in Russia, and this may have something to do with the rela-tive efficiency you should encounter. It's worth giving them a call if only to see what's on offer: theoretically they should have the best connec-tions. They organise both tours and independent travel throughout the CIS and China. They can book train tickets in Russia, Uzbekistan and Kazakhstan but unfortunately only if you have also booked accommoda-tion or flights through them. Their tour 'Uzbekistan and the Ancient Silk Road' might also be of interest.

• **Progressive Tours** (☎ 0171-262 1676, fax 0171-724 6941, e-mail 101533.513@compuserve.com), 12 Rochester Place, London W2 2BS.

They can organise train tickets including the Almaty-Urumqi link but only if you book accommodation with them. If you get a small group together they may be able to organise a custom tour for you, and this will work out cheaper per person. They do not book for China.

• **The Imaginative Traveller** (☎ 0181-742 8612, fax 0181-742 3045, e-mail 106230.2640@compuserve.com), First Floor, 14 Barley Mow Passage, Chiswick, London W4 4PH. This company specialises in small group tours but is also prepared to make individual travel arrangements, although they don't go into Central Asia.

• **Overseas Business Travel** (☎ 0171-702 2468), 8 Minories, London, EC3N 1BJ. As well as assisting with visas, Overseas Business Travel can arrange accommodation and transport throughout the CIS. An office in Moscow and a representative in Almaty make them well qualified to advise on travel across this part of the route.

• **China Travel Service** (☎ 0171-836 9911, fax 0171-836 3121, e-mail: CTS@ukcts.demon.co.uk, web site http://www.wtgonline.com/cts), 7 Upper St Martin's Lane, London, WC2H 9DL. As well as offering some good standard tours, CTS can tailor individual tours in China to suit the semi-independent traveller's wishes: simply say where you want to go, what you want to see, what class of hotel you want to stay in, and you're off. The helpful staff here offer useful advice on all aspects of Chinese travel. They do not deal with travel in the CIS at all.

• **China Travel Service and Information Centre** (☎ 0171-388-8838, fax 0171-388 8828), 124 Euston Rd , London NW1 2AL. Despite the name, this organisation is a travel agent rather than an information centre; it specialises in tours and tailoring independent travel arrangements.

• **Jasmin Tours** (☎ 01628-531121), High St, Cookham, Maidenhead, Berks SL6 9SQ. Although this company specialise in tours, they will also make independent travel arrangements if required. They currently have several standard tours to China, although none is specifically related to the Silk Route.

Companies specialising in organised tours
• **Voyages Jules Verne** (☎ 0171-616 1000, fax 0171-723 8629, e-mail: sales@VJV.co.uk), 21 Dorset Square, London NW1 6QG. If you want to travel in style, this is the way to go. Their standard Silk Road tour which covered many of the locations dealt with in this book is not currently running but may be reinstated in the next year or two. The 'Beyond the Great Wall' tour covers some of the same ground.

• **Bales Tours** (☎ 01306-885991 for tours, and ☎ 01306-884397 for individual bookings), Bales House, Junction Rd , Dorking, Surrey, RH4 3HL. Bales Tours offer a 20-day 'Journey Along the Silk Road' tour which starts in Pakistan and joins the route described in this book at Kashgar – it's hardly a snip, though, at £2595. They can, however, also make arrangements for individual travellers.

• **Explore Worldwide Ltd** (☎ 01252-319448, fax 01252-343170), 1 Frederick St, Aldershot, Hants, GU11 1LQ. Explore offer several tours in this area including the 12-day 'Ancient Cities of Uzbekistan' for £1245, and the 25-day Silk Road' tour for £2100, which covers the Chinese part of the route described in this book, but then heads off into Pakistan.

• **Exodus Expeditions** (☎ 0181-675 5550), 9 Weir Rd , London, SW12 OLT, have a 17-day 'Samarkand and the Lost Cities' (£1650) tour which fairly comprehensively covers the Central Asian Silk Route cities, and a 'Silk Road Explorer' tour (£2100) which traces the route from Pakistan to Kashgar and thence to Beijing.

• **Atlantida Travel** (☎ 0171-240 2888), 55 Monmouth St, Covent Garden, London WC2H 9DG. Atlantida Travel specialise in small tailor made group tours but might be able to assist with individual travel arrangements too.

Rail enthusiasts' and specialist interest tours
• **Occidor Adventure Tours** (☎ 01243-582178, fax 01243-587239) 10 Broomcroft Rd, Bognor Regis, West Sussex PO22 7NJ
• **Enthusiasts Holidays** (☎ 0181-699 3654, fax 0181-291 6496, e-mail: vicallen@polxpres.itsnet.co.uk), 146 Forest Hill Rd, London SE23 3QR

Foreign Embassies in London
• **Russia** (☎ 0171-229 8027), 5 Kensington Palace Gardens, W8 4QS. Getting a visa here is not difficult but does involve some planning, as the office is open only from 10am to 12.30pm on Monday, Tuesday, Thursday and Friday.

If you want to stand even a moderate chance of getting in you will need to arrive early – by 8.30 am at least – and queue on the pavement. Many travel agents offer visa services, and there are specialist visa agencies who will do this for you (see p23).

Note that your first visit is simply to drop off your passport; you then have to return to go through the process all over again to get it back. You will need to bring your tour booking details, hotel vouchers, or letter of invitation (eg from the Travellers Guest House Moscow), to prove that you aren't simply going to wander around the country unattended. Three passport photos, and a completed application form are also required. Your visa will state the exact dates that you are allowed to be in the country (whereas most countries will simply give you a month, two months etc). The visa costs £10 and takes 10 working days to process if you deliver it by hand, and three weeks if it is sent by post.

• **Uzbekistan** (☎ 0171-229 7679). Although visas are issued by the embassy, make a mention of wanting a tourist visa and they'll refer you to the Uzbektourism Office (☎ 0171-935 1899;13 Marylebone Lane, London W1H 9LG), who in turn will tell you that you have to book a tour, or at least book accommodation. Should you get past this stage of the conversation you will be told that the visa costs US$40 for one week, US$50 for two weeks, and US$60 for one month (payable in sterling at the current exchange rate). It normally takes seven to ten days to get the visa, which should be valid for entry to Uzbekistan up to three months from the date of issue.

• **Kazakhstan** (☎ 0171-244 6572), 114A Cromwell Rd , South Kensington, SW7 4ES. As with Uzbekistan, you will be told that they only issue visas when the passport is presented along with proof of a tour or with an invitation from Kazakhstan, and hence they are more used to dealing with tour operators who obtain visas on behalf of their customers. The cost of the visas, however, is £19 for one week, £32 for a month, £44 for two months and £63 for three months. The visa takes seven days to be issued, and they require proof of your tour/hotel bookings, along with one passport photo and, of course, your passport.

Booking direct through Uzbek travel companies

Several small, privately-owned travel companies have been started recently in Uzbekistan, giving travellers the chance to book accommodation and transport directly and hopefully get good deals by doing so. These agencies are probably the only people capable of organising legitimate homestays, so in this respect too, it makes sense to use them. A warning however: none of the agencies listed here is bonded in any way, and they are only just getting started, so their idea of reliability and yours may be rather different. On the other hand they are keen to make a name for themselves, so the incentive is there to give you a good service:

• **Company Salom** (☎ +7-3712 410140, fax +7-3712 568722, e-mail: bcctash @tacis.silk.glas.apc.org), TACIS Business Communication Centre, PO Box 515, Navoi 18, 1st Floor, Tashkent, Uzbekistan, 700011. The owner of this company, Raisa Gareyeva, was formerly an Intourist guide based in Bukhara, and she still has an office there. The company offers homestays, hotels, tours and visa support.

• **Orient Star** (☎ +7-3662-331914, fax +7-3662-311423), Mirzo Ulughbek 39/9, Samarkand, Uzbekistan 703000. During the research for the update of this book we met two French women who had arranged their trip through Orient Star, and it has to be said that it wasn't going perfectly, but on the other hand they'd stayed in some good places, and were having more fun than if they'd taken a tour.

• **Optimist Travel** (☎ +7-3662-352942, fax +7-3662-310589, e-mail Optimist @Sam.silk.glas.apc.org), 237 Dagbitskaia Str, Samarkand, Uzbekistan, 703020. Iskander Saidaliev, who set up this company, offers homestays in pleasant private houses in Samarkand and the other major cities.

• **People's Republic of China** (☎ 0891-880808 visa information line), 31 Portland Place, London W1N 3AG; and Denison House, Denison Rd , Victoria Park, Manchester, M14 5RX. Getting a Chinese visa is straight-forward, and takes three to five days if you apply in person. Tourists are normally given a one month single entry visa, valid for three months from the date of issue. It is quite possible, however, to apply for a double entry visa, and up to two months duration. The single entry visa costs £25, (or £35 if applying by post), and on application the following must be pre-sented: a completed application form, two passport photos, and passport which is valid for at least six months from the date of application.

Visa agencies
Two agencies which can help with advice and obtaining visas are:
• **Travcour (UK)** (☎ 0171-223 7662) Tempo House, 15 Falcon Rd , Battersea, London SW11 2PJ
• **Overseas Business Travel** (☎ 0171-702 2468, fax 0171-488 1199), 8 Minories, London, EC3N 1BJ

MAKING A BOOKING IN CONTINENTAL EUROPE

From Belgium
• **Intourist Benelux** (☎ 02-502 4440, fax 02-502 7913), Galerie Ravenstein 2, 1000 Brussels
• **Boundless Adventures** (☎ 02-426 40 30, fax 02-426 03 60), Ave Verdilaan 23/15, 1080 Brussels - Ganshoren

From Bulgaria
• Sofintour Ltd (☎/fax 2-880628) Burl Stambolijsky, 24, Sofia

From Denmark
• **Kilroy Travels** (☎ 33-11 00 44, fax 33-32 32 69), Skindergade 28, DK-1159, Copenhagen K; they also have offices in Aarhus (☎ 86 20 11 44), Fredensgade 40, DK 8100, Aarhus C; Aalborg (☎ 99 35 11 00) Oesteraagade 23, DK 9000; Odense (☎ 66 17 77 80) Pantheonsgade 7, DK 5000; Lyngby (☎ 45 88 78 88) Lyngby Torv 6, DK 2800
• **Albatros** (☎ 33-32 24 88), Frederiksberggade 15, DK-1459, Copen-hagen K

From Finland
• **Kilroy Travels** (☎ 90-680 7811), Kaivokatu 10 D, Helsinki; also in Oulu (☎ 981-372 720) Pakkahuoneenkatu 8; Tampere (☎ 931-223 0995) Tuomiokirkokatu 36; and Turku (☎ 921-273 7500) Eerikinkatu 2
• **Sindbad Travel/Russian Youth Hostels** (Russia ☎ 812-329 8018, fax 812-329 8019, e-mail ryh@rhy.spb.su), PO Box 8, SF-53501, Lappeen-ranta; Sinbad Travel are associated with Russian Youth Hostels and will make hostel reservations, provide visa support and sell air/train tickets

• **OY Finnsov Tours Ltd** (☎ 90-694 2267/2011, fax 90-694 5534), Eerikinkatu 3, 00100 Helsinki, (Intourist's Finnish office)

From France
• **S.A.R.L. Intourist** (☎ 01-47 23 80 10, fax 01-47 23 01 00) 25 rue Marbeuf, 75008 Paris
• **Office du Tourisme de Chine** (☎ 01-42 96 95 48), 116 ave des Champs Elysées, 75008 Paris
• **CTS** 32 rue Vignon, 75009, Paris

From Germany
• **TSA Reisen** (☎ 07371-8522, fax 07371-12593, e-mail: 100140.3174 @compuserve.com or TSA-Reisen@t-online.de), Schulgasse 1, D88499 Riedlingen – worth contacting even if you don't live in Germany
• **Lernidee Reisen** (☎ 030-786 50 56; fax 030-786 55 96) Dudenstrasse 78, 10965 Berlin; specialises in Russia & the CIS, Mongolia and China
• **STA Travel:** STA has many branches in Germany some of which include: Hamburg (☎ 040-450 38400, fax 040-410 3665), Renzelstrasse 16, 20146 Hamburg; Bonn (☎ 0228-225579, fax 0228-213123), Nassestrasse 11, 53113 Bonn; Berlin (☎ 030-311 0950, fax 030-313 0948), Goethestrasse 73, 10625 Berlin; Frankfurt/Main (☎ 069-703035, fax 069-777014), Bockenheimer Landstrasse 133, 60325 Frankfurt/Main; Mannheim (☎ 0621-10074, fax 0621-26958) L14.11, 68161 Mannheim; Cologne (☎ 0221-442011, fax 0221-421254), Zuelpicher Strasse 178, 50937 Cologne; Heidelberg (☎ 06221-23538, fax 06221-167825), Haupstrasse 139, 69117 Heidelberg
• **SRS** (☎ 030-281-6741), Studenten Reiserservice GmbH, Marienstrasse 25, 1040 Berlin
• **Fremdenverkehrsamt der Volksrepublik China** (☎ 069-528465), Ilkens Strasse 6, D-6000 Frankfurt/Main.
• **CTS** (☎ 069-250515), Dusseldorfer Strasse 14, D-6000 Frankfurt/Main

From Israel
• **China National Tourist Office** (☎ 522 6272) 19 Frishman St, Tel Aviv, 61030

From the Netherlands
• **Global Travel** (☎ 020-696 75 85, fax 020-697 35 87) Anne Kooistrahof 15, 1106 WG, Amsterdam; can make train reservations in 51 countries – worth contacting even if you don't live in the Netherlands
• **Kontakt International** (☎ 020-623 47 71, fax 20-625 80 57, e-mail: kontakt@tip.nl) Prins Hendrikkade 104, 1011 AJ Amsterdam, specialise in tailor-made individual tours, and small groups
• **NBBS** (☎ 071-25 33 33), Schipholweg 101, PO Box 360, 2300 AJ Leiden; branches in Groningen (☎ 050-12 63 33), Amsterdam (☎ 020-20 50 71), Utrecht (☎ 030-31 45 20) and Rotterdam (☎ 010-414 9822)

From Norway
• **STA** (☎ 22 42 10 20, fax 22 33 21 02, e-mail: Kilroy@Kilroy.no., Nedre Slottsgate 23, 0157 Oslo 1
• **Intourist** (☎ 22 42 28 99/97, fax 22 42 62 01), Fr Nansens Plass 8, 0160 Oslo

From Sweden
• **STA** (☎ 08-234515), Box 7144, Kungsgatan 4, S103 87, Stockholm
• **Fram Resor AB** (☎ 08-215934, fax 08-214060), Box 64, Kingsgatan 56, 11132 Stockholm

MAKING A BOOKING IN NORTH AMERICA

From the USA
• **China National Tourist Office** (☎ 212-760-9700), 350 Fifth Ave, Suite 6413, New York, NY 10118; another branch at 333 W Broadway, Suite 201, Glendale, CA 91204 (☎ 818-545-7504)
• **General Tours** (☎ 800-221-2216), 53 Summer St, Keene NH 0343
• **Intourist/Rahim Tours** (☎ 561-585-5305, 561-582-1353, toll free ☎ 800-556-5305), 12 South Dixie Highway, Lake Worth, Florida 33460
• **Russian Travel Bureau Inc** (☎ 800-847-1800, fax 212-490-1650, e-mail russtvl@interserve.com, http://www.asternet.com/get/russntrvl) 225 East 44 Street, New York, NY 10017
• **Russian Youth Hostels** (☎ 310-379-4316; fax 310-379-8420, e-mail 71573.2010@compuserve.com.) 409 N Pacific Coast Highway #106, Suite 390, Redondo Beach, CA 90277; RYH organises visa support for foreign visitors who want to travel independently, and they set up the first youth hostel in St Petersburg
• **STA** (☎ 415-391-8407, fax 415-391-4105), 51 Grant Avenue, San Francisco CA 94108; STA has many branches including: Boston (297 Newbury St, Boston, MA 02115, ☎ 617-266-6014, fax 617-266-5579), Santa Monica (120 Broadway, Apt 108, Santa Monica, CA 90401, ☎ 310-394-5126, fax 310-394-4041), New York (10 Downing St [6th Avenue and Bleecker], New York, NY 10014, ☎ 212-627-3111, fax 212-627-3387), Washington DC (2401 Pennsylvania Ave G, Washington DC 20037, ☎ 202-887-0912, fax 202-887-0031), Chicago (429 South Dearborn St, Chicago, Il 60605, ☎ 312-786-9050, fax 312-786-9817), Philadelphia (3730 Walnut St, Philadelphia PA 19104, ☎ 215-382-2928, fax 215-382-4716), Seattle (4341 University Way, NE, Seattle, WA 98105, ☎ 206-633-5000, 206-633-5027) and Miami (3115 Commodore Plaza, Miami Fl 33133, ☎ 305-461-3444, fax 305-461-4772)

Foreign embassies in the USA There are **Russian Consulates** in Washington (☎ 202-939-8907, 1825 Phelps Place NW, Washington DC

20008), New York (☎ 212-348-0926, 9 E 91st St, NY 10128), San Francisco (☎ 415-928-6878, 2790 Green St, San Francisco, CA 94123) and Seattle (☎ 206-728-1910, 2323 Western Building, 201 6th Ave, Seattle, WA 98121).

There are **Chinese Consulates** in New York (☎ 212-330-7400, 520 12th Ave), Washington DC (☎ 202-328-5205), Houston (☎ 713-524-0780) and San Francisco (☎ 415-533-4885).

From Canada
• **Exotik Tours** (☎ 514-284-3324, fax 514-843-5493), Suite 806, 1117 Ste-Catherine St West, Montreal, Quebec H3B 1H9
• **Intourist** (☎ 514-849 6394), 1801 McGill College Ave, Suite 630, Montreal, Quebec H3A 2N4
• **CTS** (☎ 604-872 8787), 556 West Broadway, Vancouver, BC

MAKING A BOOKING IN AUSTRALASIA
From Australia
• **Passport Travel** (☎ 03-9867 3888, fax 03-9867 1055, e-mail bmc-cunn@werple.mira.net.au) Suite 11, 401 St Kilda Rd, Melbourne, Victoria, 3004; formerly Red Bear Tours, they can organise rail travel, visa invitations, group tours and individual travel arrangements; web site: http://www.travelcentre.com.au/
• **Iris Hotels Pty Ltd** (☎ 02-9580 6466; fax 02-9580 7256, e-mail iris-tour@mpx.com.au), PO Box 60, Hurstville, NSW 2220
• **Russia-Rail Internet Travel Service** (http://www.russia-rail.com/, e-mail russia-rail@russia-rail.com); can book rail tickets for anywhere in Russia, organise visas and provide timetable information
• **Sundowners Travel Centre** Melbourne (☎ 03-9690 2499), 151 Dorcas Street, South Melbourne 3205; Sydney (☎ 02-9281 4066), 108 Albion Street, Surry Hills 2010
• **Adventure World** North Sydney (☎ 02-9956 7766), 73 Walker St; Melbourne (☎ 03-9670 0125) 3rd Floor, 343 Little Collins St
• **STA** (☎ 02-9212 1255), 1st Floor, 732 Harris St, Ultimo, Sydney NSW 2007. There are dozens of branches around Australia including Adelaide (☎ 08-9223 2426) 235 Rundle St; Canberra (☎ 06-247 863) 13-15 Garema Place
• **China Travel Service** (☎ 02-9211 2633) 757-759 George St, Sydney NSW 2000
• **China National Tourist Office** (☎ 02-299 4057) 19th floor, 44 Market St, Sydney NSW 2000
• **Russian Travel Bureau** Sydney (☎ (02-9262 1144) Level 5, 75 King St; Melbourne (☎ 03-9600 0299) 3rd floor, 343 Little Collins St; Brisbane (☎ 07-6229 9716) 7th floor, 131 Elizabeth St; Perth (☎ 09-322 6812) 1st floor, 181 St George's Terrace

- **Gateway Travel** (☎ 02-9745 333) 48 The Boulevarde, Strathfield 2135
- **Safeway Travel** (☎ 03-9534 4866) 288 Carlisle St, Balaclava
- **Access Travel** (☎ 02-9241 1128) 5th floor, 58 Pitt St, Sydney
- **Classic Oriental Tours** (☎ 02-9261 3988) Level 4, 491 Kent St, Sydney

From New Zealand
- **Adventure World** (☎ 524 5118), 101 Great South Road, Remuera, PO Box 74008, Auckland
- **STA** (☎ 309 9995), 10, High St, Auckland. STA also has branches at 223 High St, Christchurch (☎ 799 098) and 207 Cuba St, Wellington (☎ 850 561)
- **Suntravel** (☎ 09-525 3074) PO Box 12-424, 407 Great South Rd, Penrose, Auckland. Specialises in China, Russia and Mongolia.
- **Eurolynx** (☎ 09-379 9717), 3rd floor, 20 Fort St, Auckland, is Sundowner's NZ agent.

MAKING A BOOKING IN ASIA

From Hong Kong
- **China International Travel Service** (☎ 2732 5888), Rm 1213-15, 13/F, Tower A, New Mandarin Plaza, 14 Science Museum Rd, Kowloon
- **Monkey Business** (☎ 2723 1376, fax 2723 6653, e-mail: 100267.2570 @compuserve.com web-site: http://www.hk.super.net/~shrine/monkey .htm), Block E, 4th Floor, Flat 6, Chungking Mansions, 36-44 Nathan Rd, Kowloon; not immediately interested in the Almaty to Urumqi route, but MB can give you all sorts of helpful hints, especially if you are considering a trip on the Trans Siberian at some point
- **Phoenix Services Agency** (☎ 2722 7378; fax 2369 8884), Room A, 7th floor, Milton Mansion, 96 Nathan Rd, Kowloon
- **Time Travel Services** (☎ 2366 6222, fax 2739 5413, e-mail: timetrvl@hkstar.com), Block A, 16th Floor, Chungking Mansions, 40 Nathan Rd , Kowloon
- **Wallem Travel** (☎ 2876 8231, fax 2876 1220/1, e-mail: wtlhk@wallem.com.), Hopewell Centre, 46th floor, 183 Queen's Rd East, Wanchai

From Japan
- **CTS** (☎ 03-3273 5512), Nihombashi-Settsu Building, 2-2-4, Nihombashi, Chuo-ku, Tokyo
- **Intourist Japan Co Ltd** (☎ 03-3238 9118, fax 03-3238 9110), 5F Daihachi Tanaka Bldg, 5-1 Gobancho, Tokyo
- **Japan China Tourist Office** (☎ 03-3433 1461), 6F Hachidai Hamamatsu-cho Bldg, 1-27-13 Hamamatsu-cho, Minato-ku, Tokyo
- **STA** Tokyo: 4th Floor, Nukariya Bldg, 1-16-20 Minami Ikebukuro, Toshima-Ku, Tokyo 171 (☎ 03-5391 2922, fax 03-5391 2923); 1st Floor, Star Plaza Aoyama Bldg, 1-10-3 Shibuya, Shibuya-ku, Tokyo 102, (☎ 03-

5385 8380, fax 03-5485 8373); 2nd Floor, Toko Bldg, 1-5 Yotsuya, Shinjuku-ku, Tokyo 160, (☎ 03-5269 0751, fax 03-5269 0759). Osaka: 6th Floor, Honmachi Meidai Bldg, 2-5-5, Azuchi-machi, Chuo-ku, (☎ 06-262 7066, fax 06-262 7065)

From Singapore
• **China National Tourist Office** (☎ 221-8681), 1 Shenton Way, 17-05 Robina House, Singapore 0106

Before you leave

WHAT TO TAKE

If you are travelling on an upmarket tour it doesn't really matter how much luggage you take because there will almost certainly be someone at the other end to help you carry it. If you are not, then think carefully about what you will really need. Budget travellers' fashion standards aren't that high, so don't bother with all the spares or the fancy washing stuff. Don't use the excuse that your bag isn't full yet to start poking in all those bits and pieces that 'might come in handy' – you will probably want some space for souvenirs.

Clothes

It all rather depends on what time of year you will be travelling: be prepared for frighteningly high temperatures in midsummer but note that wearing shorts in the CIS is rather like carrying a large sign saying 'tourist'; they are not considered to be proper dress for visiting religious sites. Jeans tend to be very hot in the sun and take ages to dry when wet, so take light cotton trousers; chinos are ideal. You are unlikely to want to buy clothing in Russia unless you are participating in the 1970's revival but China is a bit better, although large Western sizes can be impossible to find. A solid pair of shoes (trainers, for example) is essential, and you might want to take a light pair of sandals or espadrilles for loafing around in, too. Unless you're a moody Gothic type, take loose, light-coloured (sun reflective) clothes.

In spring or autumn temperatures drop at night, and winter tends both to arrive and disappear with little or no warning, so take a warm sweater. Excellent down jackets are available in China (£20/US$30), so you won't need to bring one with you, unless you are travelling in winter, in which case you'll need all the thermal underwear and padded clothing you can lay your hands on. Although it is very rare to see rain along the desert routes you may well get wet in Moscow or from Xi'an onwards, so you might want to bring one of those ultra-light 'roll-uppable' waterproofs. If the British ambassador is an old school friend and you are likely to be invited to dinner, take formal wear, but you won't need it anywhere else.

Luggage

For travellers who will be carrying their own luggage, the basic choice is between rucksack and zip-up shoulder bag. Arguments for and against each of these go on and on. A rucksack is probably better, simply because it is stronger and easier to carry over any sort of distance. It is a good idea to bring a small shoulder bag for day trips, as you will need something for carrying camera, films, maps, guidebooks and so on. A moneybelt or similar safe document carrier (perhaps a leg pouch) is essential. Remember that these should be worn underneath the clothing, so the 'bum-bag' fashion accessories so trendy a couple of years ago will not be suitable. Moneybelts are uncomfortable in the heat but the inconvenience of wearing one is far outweighed by the trouble you will face if you lose everything. Check that the belt has pockets big enough to take passport, airline ticket and travellers' cheques without having to fold them up into postage-stamp sized wads. It is a good idea to put everything inside the belt into your plastic travellers' cheque envelope or something similar to protect them.

Medical supplies

Come prepared, as you will have serious trouble getting hold of the simplest pharmaceuticals on this trip. As I guideline, essential items would be: aspirin; suntan lotion (at least factor 6); insect repellent; something for an upset stomach (eg Imodium); a tube of antiseptic cream, a few plasters and an anti-AIDS kit containing sterile syringes and swabs for emergency medical treatment. Other items you might want to bring include: lipsalve; multivitamins; toilet paper (although it is available, it's often not up to Western standards); moisturising cream and water purification tablets (see p34). Those planning on staying any length of time in China may want to bring Lemsip, as everyone there has a permanent cold. Don't forget to stock up on your favourite brands of tampons and contraceptives, and bring adequate supplies of prescribed medications.

General items

Even if you don't look like Tom Cruise, sunglasses are essential (it is extremely bright in the desert) and you should also bring a hat. Other items you might want to bring include: a small jar of instant coffee and a mug – for the long train journeys (hot water is provided); a Swiss army knife (essential for opening bottled drinks); pens and writing paper; a diary; the addresses of the hordes of friends and relatives to whom you will be sending tacky postcards (don't bring your address book – you may lose it); a flashlight; a universal bathplug; a couple of metres of string (useful as a washing line if nothing else); a few clothes pegs; something to read (see p35); a glue stick (Chinese envelopes and stamps are not gummed); a padlock and length of chain (for securing your rucksack while you sleep – a bike lock would be OK – or you can buy mini combination locks with extendible steel cord in travel shops); a water bottle is a good idea if you will be purifying your own water; a watch or clock with alarm; a compass; Chinese and Russian phrasebooks are invaluable.

If you bring a walkman, bear in mind that everyone will want a go, so have a suitably gargantuan supply of batteries (although they are available, they are usually of poor quality). It would be cruel in the extreme to travel through Russia without a cassette of the Beatles. The Chinese really get down to Lenny Kravitz's first album.

Gifts and gimmicks

The quickest way to make friends on the train is to produce something which will arouse the curiosity of your fellow travellers (never display something which is either fragile or expensive). Generally anything Western will do but you might want to try some of the following: postcards of Britain or the Royal Family; photographs of you and your family, preferably with house, car, boyfriend or girlfriend in the background; Western sweets (candy) and chewing gum (remember that chocolate melts in the heat); foreign coins or stamps (the Chinese are passionate collectors of both; try to bring stamps with interesting pictures); foreign magazines with as many pictures of celebrities as possible; badges or stickers are good gifts for children. In fact, virtually anything will do but expensive gifts just embarrass people, so don't spend too much money.

Current shortages will dictate the demand for black market goods, but most items are fairly commonplace in the CIS now, and you will be amazed by how much is available in China. Western 'brand name' goods (Marlboro cigarettes, coffee, perfume, spirits etc) will make excellent gifts if you really want to make a good impression with hosts, but the chances of making any money through speculation are minimal.

Fame

When we were researching this book, we took along a Sunday newspaper colour supplement to show people on the way, and were slightly surprised whose photographs people recognised: the Russians invariably picked out Mrs Thatcher, gesticulating enthusiastically and grinning (the Chinese didn't know her at all). They also recognised the Beatles about 90% of the time ('Bee-tuhls', they nodded, reaching for the walkman. Chinese, again, weren't interested). In Xinjiang Province, China, for some reason, the entire bus was on personal terms with Yassir Arafat – or so it seemed. More surprising, perhaps, Madonna was not picked out once and neither was John Major. The Queen was recognised on only one occasion, despite the fact that in the picture she was wearing a crown. Only one photograph scored a 100% success rate: the Russians call him 'Shvarts-ngr'. The Chinese simply say 'Arnie'.

Money

Times have changed considerably since we initially researched this guide, and the money situation is now much easier all along the route. Travellers' cheques can be changed in almost all the cities listed, and in some of them you can get cash advances with a credit card, too. Despite this, it is still necessary to carry a reasonable amount of hard currency with you, just in case there's a problem. Make sure, too, that you aren't relying on a credit card payment for any crucial part of your trip, as you will be completely stuck if, for whatever reason, your card is not accepted. Try to ensure that your travellers' cheques are a well known brand (American Express is the best known in Central Asia and China, though others are also acceptable), and preferably in US$ denominations. As for hard currency, you can't go far wrong with US dollars, although many travellers get caught out by the requirement throughout the CIS and China that dollar bills must be post 1990, and must be in mint condition.

Make sure that you have a small stash of low denomination notes, and that they are reasonably accessible, as it's quite possible that bribery may help in some places, and a few dollar bills can look like a lot of money to someone who's never seen them before. Finally, it's only common sense to keep most of your money in a money belt (or similar) worn under your clothing, while you keep a small amount of spending money to hand. An 'emergency' reserve of local and foreign currency should be kept separately from both of these (along with the numbers of your travellers cheques, of course).

In the past the black market in all these countries was worth using but this no longer applies except in Uzbekistan. Now you are better off changing money at official exchange desks. Any gain you might make on the black market is far outweighed by the risk incurred. If you do decide to use the black market anywhere along this route, however, be extremely careful as numerous travellers get ripped off. When changing money on the street only ever deal with one person at a time and never let a crowd develop around you. Take, count and pocket the other guy's money before even letting him see yours; don't count it out in front of him. If he

---

Post 1990 greenbacks

Throughout the countries dealt with in this guide, US dollars are the most widely recognised currency, and you will always find someone willing to accept them, either for services or for exchange. You will also find, however, that an Asia-wide paranoia exists about being fobbed off with fake bills, or bills which will not be accepted by the banks. Thus you can shout, scream or beg, but few if any street wise Russians, Uzbeks, Kazakhs or Chinese will accept your dollars if they are pre 1990 or if they are damaged in any way. This includes any writing on the note, torn corners or battered edges. To save yourself trouble when you arrive, insist that your bank at home gives you new notes.

suddenly decides he no longer wants to make the deal, demand your money back first and count it fully before returning his. Wiring money to Russia or the Independent States is mind-bogglingly difficult and will take at least a week. It's not much easier to China either, so make sure that you take enough and be very careful with it.

Photography

Most people will want to travel with a camera. Film is available in China and the CIS but you would be well advised to bring your own, especially if you take slides or use unusual film (ie high ASA). If you do buy it locally check that it's in date. It is a good idea to use a lead-lined film pouch for all X-ray machines, even if you are told that they are harmless. Beware of Chinese railway stations, where you may have to put all luggage through the machine before they'll let you onto the platform. Wait until you get home before having your film processed, although services in the large Chinese cities are generally pretty safe. Taking snaps of military installations or other 'sensitive' areas is not recommended; if you are unsure, don't. It's perfectly OK to shoot film from the train, but the windows are usually so grotty that you will have trouble, so look for a broken window or a door that opens. Finally, do ask your victim before you start filming: how would you like it if some dumb tourist started following you or your children around with a zeppelin-sized lens?

VACCINATIONS AND HEALTH SAFEGUARDS

Vaccinations

No vaccinations are listed as official requirements for Western visitors on this trip but you should give serious thought to some of the following. If you are unsure check with either Trailfinders (☎ 0171-938 3999), 194 Kensington High St, London W8 7RG, or the British Airways Travel Clinic (☎ 0171-439 9584), 156 Regent St, W1. Both offer sound advice on travellers' health problems and run on-the-spot vaccination services. It is worth paying them a visit well before you travel, as some injections may have to be given separately so popping in the day before you leave will be too late.

• **Diphtheria** There have been several outbreaks of diphtheria in the CIS over the past few years. Check with your doctor that you were given the initial vaccine as a child and a booster within the last ten years. The WHO recommends a combined booster dose of tetanus-diphtheria toxoid. If you've never had the diphtheria vaccine in any form you'll need two jabs one month apart, followed by a booster after six months.

• **Tetanus** Tetanus vaccine needs renewal every 10 years. If you cut yourself and you haven't had one, you may have serious trouble trying to get the right treatment abroad, so check.

• **Hepatitis A** The most commonly contracted serious travellers' ailment, this is spread via food, water and infected eating utensils; though it probably won't kill you, it can lay you out for anything up to a couple of months. Gamma globulin, given just before departure, affords protection for up to six months. Havrix Monodose lasts twice that time, and a second shot, given a year after the first, extends protection for up to 10 years.

• **Polio** The vaccine lasts 10 years, and is administered orally, usually in a sugar cube; check whether you are up-to-date.

• **Typhoid** A new vaccine, Typhim Vi, gives protection for three years.

• **Rabies** Probably not worth it unless you are the sort who actively hunts down and pets stray animals. The vaccine consists of two (or in some cases three) shots a month apart and means that if you get bitten you won't have to go through the ordeal that others will be enduring. Medical treatment will be necessary but this vaccine buys you time.

• **Malaria** For the route in this guide anti-malarial treatment is not required but if you plan on going any further south in either China or the CIS you will almost certainly need it.

Remember before you travel that it is worth carrying a small medical kit including sterile syringe needles and swabs. It's a good idea to know you own blood group, too.

Potential health problems
The only two potentially serious ailments with which you are likely to come into contact are sunburn and diarrhoea.

Prevention is the key to sunburn. The desert sun is incredibly hot; always wear sunglasses and a hat and get into the shade long before you think you may be burning. If you are badly burned and feel nauseous or dizzy, consult a doctor immediately as you may have sunstroke. Drink plenty of fluids.

As for diarrhoea, the best thing to do is simply to wait, as it is far better to let your body sort itself out than it is to mess around trying to 'cure' it; most people will get an upset stomach at some point, if only as a reaction to the spicy food. Don't panic, drink plenty of water, and if it does not start to clear up in a couple of days, then Imodium is usually effective. Don't take too many, or you'll regret it later.

Unless you speak either Chinese or Russian the best way to find a doctor fast is via the tourist agencies (Intourist, Uzbektourism or CITS), or the large hotels used by foreigners. Simple treatment should be free.

Drinking water
Water in Russia, the CIS and China is not always safe, so you should stick to drinks made with boiled water (eg tea or coffee) or bottled drinks.

Avoid ice cubes, salads and unpeeled fruit (all of which may have come into contact with contaminated water). Don't drink water from any tap or even use it to clean your teeth. Water may be purified by boiling or by adding five drops of 2% Tincture of Iodine to each litre of water. Allow to stand for 20 minutes before drinking. If you don't like the strong chemical taste, bring along fruit juice powders to disguise it. Iodine-based purification tablets such as Potable Aqua or Coghlan's are an alternative. Note that chlorine-based purification tablets are ineffective against the bugs that cause amoebic dysentery and giardia.

In China, provided water comes from one of the thermos flasks in a hotel it will have been boiled. Don't worry if you are using someone else's mug at a tea-shop – just rinse it out with boiling water.

Travel insurance
You would be foolish not to take out a combined medical and travel insurance policy (available at any travel agent) before you leave.

BACKGROUND READING

A number of books have been written by or about Silk Road travellers but most deal with either the Chinese side or the Russian one, not both.

CIS
• *A Ride to Khiva* – Fred Burnaby. Our Fred, strongest man in the British army, speaker of numerous languages and all-round bon-oeuf, sets off for Central Asia. Along the way he encounters frostbite, Russian bureaucracy and 'insubordinate natives' before actually arriving in Khiva in 1877. Sadly now out of print.

• *The Great Game* – Peter Hopkirk. A fascinating account of the covert operations carried out by Russian and British spies in Central Asia during the last century. Intrigue, espionage, massacre and more. And it's all true.

• *Apples in the Snow* – Geoffrey Moorehouse. Veteran travel-journo Moorehouse explores Soviet Central Asia in the days when it was still Soviet Central Asia (just -1989). A well-researched, thoughtful and thought-provoking book.

• *Journey to Khiva* – Nikolai Muravyov. This Russian envoy very nearly lost his head, literally, whilst trying to nurture his country's foreign relations with the city in 1819. Contains reams of information about Khiva, including some particularly gruesome details concerning torture and execution. Now out of print.

• *Journey to Khiva* – Philip Glazebrook. The best CIS book for this trip. Glazebrook visits Central Asia and ponders the Great Game, the Uzbeks, the Russians, life and other distractions.

• *The Lost Heart of Asia* – Colin Thubron. Thubron is a talented writer but this book, in which he follows much of the Silk Route through Central Asia, is depressing. Beautifully written and the history is impeccable.

• *Central Asia: A Traveller's Companion* – Kathleen Hopkirk. Peter Hopkirk's obsession with Central Asia was obviously contagious: his wife caught it, too. She writes quite as well as he does, relating the kind of fascinating anecdotes that travel guides would include – if they only had the space; history made interesting.

China
• *The Gobi Desert* – Mildred Cable and Francesca French. These venerable female missionaries travel throughout Xinjiang province in the early 20th century. Another book by them on the same subject is *Through the Jade Gate* (but *The Gobi Desert* is better). Both books are overtly religious at times but give an excellent insight into the area. They are out of print, but can be found quite easily if you look around.

• *Journey to Turkestan* – Eric Teichman. The Foreign Office sends this diplomat the length of China by car in 1935. Another classic.

• *Riding the Iron Rooster* – Paul Theroux. *The Daily Telegraph* is right – 'Theroux cannot write badly'. Accounts of his various travels by train in China – a 'must read' even if most of the action does take place off the Silk Road.

• *Foreign Devils on the Silk Road* – Peter Hopkirk. Essential reading for anyone interested in China, the Silk Route, archaeology or just plain adventure. This is the story of the Western explorers who prised open the history of the 'Lost Cities' of the Taklamakan Desert, collecting crates of antiquities as they went – usually at immense personal risk. If you are taking only one book to China make it this one.

• *From Heaven Lake* – Vikram Seth. In 1981 Indian Chinese student Seth hitched home along the northern arm of the Silk Route, and then south through Tibet. A classic travel account by the much-lauded author of *A Suitable Boy*.

• *Night Train to Turkestan* – Stuart Stevens. The author sets out to explore the southern route. Although he doesn't actually make it in the end, he has an interesting trip and the problems he faces are typical of China.

• *An English Lady in Chinese Turkestan* – Lady Macartney. The wife of British diplomat Sir George describes life in the consulate at Kashgar at the turn of the century. Fascinating.

• **Forbidden Journey** (Ella Maillart) and **News from Tartary** (Peter Fleming). This couple set out from Peking for Kashgar in 1935. Both books are amusing accounts of the same journey and are considered 'classics' by travel aficionados. Although they travel by the southern route, it is worth picking up one of the two. Both travellers would much rather have done the trip alone, and this shows in their writing.

• **Buried Treasures of Chinese Turkestan** – Albert von Le Coq. German archaeologist and explorer von Le Coq, travelling across Xinjiang in the early 20th century, took along a case of Veuve Cliquot for special occasions. This account of his expeditions is wonderfully understated and makes excellent reading.

• **Wild Swans** – Jung Chang. The story of China in the twentieth century, told through the real experiences of three generations of women. This first hand account of the violence and turmoil that has been experienced in little more than a single lifetime is compulsive reading, and adds immeasurably to the visitor's understanding of China.

• **Behind the Wall** – Colin Thubron. Colin Thubron visited China in the mid 1980's, and his account of the trip is insightful and thought provoking. Ten years on, his portrait of everyday China is amazingly accurate. A great book.

• **In Xanadu** – William Dalrymple. During a summer break from university, William Dalrymple set out to retrace Marco Polo's journey from Jerusalem to the fabled palace of Kubilai Khan. The account of his adventures en route and the constant comparisons with Marco Polo's original descriptions make this a fascinating and thoroughly enjoyable book.

Other books and guides

If you can spare more time travelling you will probably want to explore further. Lonely Planet's *Central Asia – a travel survival kit* and *China – a travel survival kit* are recommended. Cadogan Guides' *Central Asia* (2nd edition) by Giles Whittell, also has excellent information about this section of the route, and Bradley Mayhew's *Uzbekistan* (Odyssey) is the most comprehensive guide to that country. The *Blue Guide to China* (Frances Wood) contains less practical advice but the history sections are excellent – nine pages, for example, on the Mogao caves at Dunhuang alone. For a straightforward history of the Silk Route go for Francke and Brownestone's rather textbookish *The Silk Route. A History*. The classic volume, of course, is Marco Polo (*The Travels*, translated by RE Latham in the Penguin Classics series). It's widely available, quite fun and it is the original but it's not the most easily accessible of the books here.

The best source of information on trains in Central Asia is *Soviet Locomotive Types – The Union Legacy* by AJ Heywood and IDC Button.

PART 2: THE CIS

Facts about the region

GEOGRAPHICAL BACKGROUND

The Commonwealth of Independent States is simply the grouping of the sovereign states which constituted the former USSR. There are 12 of these altogether (the Russian Federation, Kazakhstan, Ukraine, Turkmenistan, Uzbekistan, Belarus, Kirghizstan, Tajikistan, Azerbaijan, Moldova, Georgia and Armenia), comprising all of the former USSR's republics apart from the Baltic states.

Russia, more correctly known as the 'Russian Federation of States', covers 17 million square km, over two-thirds of the CIS. Kazakhstan is the next largest after Russia, measuring nearly three million square km (one third the size of the USA). Its borders are formed to the west by the Caspian Sea and Russia, to the south by Turkmenistan, Uzbekistan and Kirghizstan, to the east by China, and again by Russia to the north. Uzbekistan is only a sixth the size of Kazakhstan, at just under 450,000 square km (still twice the size of the UK). It lies in the centre of former Soviet Central Asia, and is bordered by Kazakhstan and the Aral Sea to the north and west, Kirghizstan and Tajikistan to the east, and Afghanistan and Turkmenistan to the south.

Climate

The geographical layout of the CIS ensures that there is a wide range of climates across its borders. Basically the commonwealth consists of a vast, flat plain stretching up across Central Asia and into Siberia, right up to the Arctic, shielded to the west by the Ural mountains; thus cold Arctic air can sweep southwards unhindered in the winter, whilst at the same time the Himalaya and Pamir ranges to the south-east stop warm air from shifting northwards. In the summer the plains heat up rapidly.

The Russian Federation alone experiences massive climatic variations: in the northern areas and Siberia it is severely cold, with long arctic winters and short, hot summers. In Verkhoyansk the average January temperature is -47°C (-52°F) – pretty cold until we compare it with Oymyakon, which has an all-time low of -68°C (-90°F). In the south, though, the temperature is more moderate: Moscow averages -10°C (14°F) in the winter and 20°C (68°F) in the summer. The southern states also experience these wide variations, thus in Uzbekistan summers are long and hot (average July temperature is 32°C), whilst winters are dry and cold (temperatures have been reported as low as -32°C). Likewise in Kazakhstan temperatures range from high and dry in summer to cold and dry in winter. Both Kazakhstan and Uzbekistan incorporate large stretches of desert which receive very little, if any, rain annually.

Transport and communications

The mainstay of the CIS is the rail network, which covers some 450,000km, accounting for two thirds of all freight and over one third of all inter-city passenger traffic. Of this, 87,000km lie inside the Russian Federation. Rail is particularly important here because extreme weather conditions and the lack of private vehicles across the country mean that the road system is poorly developed. Inland waterways in the former USSR constitute the most extensive system in the world, and many rivers like the Volga and the Don are easily big enough to take ocean-going ships; the problem is, of course, that the severe winters cause the entire system to freeze up, rendering any sort of transport impossible for long periods of the year.

Completed in 1992, the Almaty to Urumqi line is the main link in the Trans-Asian line, part of a rail route that appears destined to become the main communication line in the CIS after the Trans-Siberian railway. The Trans-Asian line is planned to extend from Tashkent to Ashkabad and Krasnovodsk, then across the Caspian Sea via Baku, Tiblisi and Erzerum to Istanbul. Construction is currently more or less stalled but agreement has been reached between the Central Asian states on the completion of this railway. Agreement has also been reached between Uzbekistan and Iran over another new line between Tedzhen (east of Ashkabad) and Mashad in Iran which would link the Trans-Asian and Iranian railways – opening a route for Central Asian goods to the Persian Gulf. Thus it seems that Kazakhstan and Uzbekistan can both look forward to being the bridges between European and Asian cultures and economies, just as they were during the great days of the Silk Road.

The economy

• **Russia**   The Russian Federation is extraordinarily rich in natural reserves: huge deposits across the country including coal, oil, natural gas and uranium provide collateral for the massive foreign loans that have taken place since 1991. But why is financial assistance needed at all?

The breakup of the USSR created numerous problems: gross mismanagement under communism had meant that state industries (and all industries were state industries) survived on government subsidies rather than their own merits. Sooner or later the system had to break down which it did in the late 1980s. With the fall of communism its dismantling was badly handled: financial hardship was inevitable but it need not have hit as hard as it did. In 1992 markets, previously state controlled, were freed for the first time. Prices soared and hyperinflation set in (in the first week of January alone prices went up by 2-300%). Meanwhile, debts from former Soviet Bloc countries were paid in rapidly-printed roubles, flooding the market with increasingly worthless currency. Privatisation of state industries, moreover, started in October, was hindered by indecisiveness: political wrangling over just how reforms should be organised meant that little was actually done at all. The 'shock therapy' was dragged out and, as a consequence, the economy collapsed. By 1993 inflation was up to 900%.

The situation began to stabilise in late 1993, however, and Western experts now consider free market reforms to have passed the point where they can be easily reversed – no matter who wins the elections. The idea of buying and selling has caught on and small businesses are thriving: hopefully for Russia the worst is now over.

• **Kazakhstan** Former communists still run the country but they have moved quickly to establish a market economy and attract foreign investors. Kazakhstan is rich in mineral resources, ranking first in the former USSR for reserves of non-ferrous metals. It also holds a leading place in the world's coal and iron reserves. More importantly, oil is abundant. Bismuth, cadmium and thallium, indispensable in electronics, nuclear engineering and rocketry, are found here in purity unequalled elsewhere in the world, suggesting that Kazakhstan has a bright future in this electronic age. The soil here is also rich in gold: it is estimated that there is over 60 million tonnes of it!

The abundance of these resources has meant that foreign investors have ploughed in considerable amounts of money – over US$500 million so far. Despite this and other substantial creditors (US$115 million from Russia annually for the use of the Baikonur space centre; US$400 million from the US to dismantle nuclear warheads and over US$1000 million in economic aid), things are still looking shaky. Conditions are tough on the street and there is a general impression that things were better in the communist days. The next few years should see economic reforms having more obviously beneficial effects in the market-place.

• **Uzbekistan** Uzbekistan is close on Kazakhstan's heels; in fact, efforts are being made to integrate the countries' two economies. Like Kazakhstan, Uzbekistan is rich in natural resources: gas, copper and zinc are common; a vast oilfield was located in the Ferghana Valley in 1992, and the country is home to the Muruntao gold mine – the largest open cast mine in the world – capable of producing 75 million tonnes of gold per year. No surprises, then, that foreign investors are keen for a slice of the pie: US$2000 million has been pledged already.

There are problems, however. Recent government policy means that all state and high-ranking employees must speak Uzbek. Unfortunately, most are ethnically Russian and so have left, leaving unqualified locals at the helm. Moreover, Uzbekistan's economy has traditionally revolved around agriculture (70% of the USSR's cotton came from here). In order to produce such huge harvests large areas of desert were reclaimed, irrigated with millions of gallons of water from the Amu and Syr Darya rivers. The rivers' exploitation has meant that the Aral Sea, once the fourth largest lake in the world, has lost much of its input and thus is rapidly disappearing. Some 27,000 square km have dried up already, the water level has fallen 14m and in places the shoreline has receded by 120km. This has created a new desert rich only in salt and the poisonous residue of the 6000kg of chemicals sprayed on the cotton fields annually. The local population has been quick to notice the effects of this: infant mortality is up 400%, and 83% of the children living on the old shores suffer from serious illnesses. It is to be hoped that the country's abundant natural resources will offset the nation's dependence on cotton so that the economy can pick up without gutting the land itself.

HISTORY

Russia's early history is convoluted and, unlike Chinese history, there are no accurate records. Because early development was tribal, regions developed independently, the first gathering of the Slavonic tribes as a recognisable and ethnically independent group occurring only in the 6th century AD. This is not to say that nothing is known prior to this; we now know that early communities grew up around trade routes in the first centuries AD as commercial explorers came in to exploit the amber, furs and timber of the great forests. In fact, archaeological finds on the Lena River north of Lake Baikal indicate that man had been living on the steppes for a million years before this.

A unifying force really began to act with the invasions of the Varangian tribes (Vikings). In 862AD the city of Novgorod fell to the chief of one tribe, Rurik of Jutland, who is often seen as the father of the Russian sovereignty. Under Varangian rule the Baltic-Black Sea trade routes established themselves, the central principality of Kiev becoming dominant. Development came rapidly thanks to two of Rurik's descendants: the Varangian prince, Sviatoslav, was responsible for some large-scale territorial expansion, paving the way for civil organisation by his son, Vladimir.

Vladimir and Russia's conversion

Vladimir (980-1015) lives on in popular tradition: he promulgated the first codes of law and established codes of seniority within the dynastic system of his clan. Perhaps more important, and certainly better publicised, was his conversion of the Russian peoples to Christianity after a deliberate search for a state religion. As one recent chronicler writes:

'Since Islam and the consumption of vodka were incompatible and Judaism did not make for a unified nation, he chose Christianity as the state religion, and had himself baptised at Constantinople in 988AD. At his order the mass conversion of the Russian people began, with whole towns being baptised simultaneously'.

Quite apart from the spiritual well-being of the locals, Christianity was a wise choice for Vladimir to have made, as it ensured the arrival of all the new Western ideas and technology. It didn't do much for Varangian unity, however, and power struggles between his heirs were responsible for their subsequent loss of control.

The Mongol invasion

In 1223 the Mongols arrived and began systematically massacring the population and destroying the towns. Having established control they imposed heavy taxes. Some cities took considerable time to recover (especially in the south, where the destruction was particularly thorough; Kiev, taken in 1240, was notably slow), whilst others seem to have been left more or less intact, or perhaps just to have rebuilt themselves faster. Moscow gradually became the dominant principality. The Mongols were given to internal feuding, however, and their power began to wane in the 14th century. Their ultimate decline may be partly thanks to the arrival of Timur (Tamerlane, 1336-1405). Born near Samarkand, he was soon to lead a number of very successful and utterly savage forays into the surrounding areas, expanding his territory rapidly. Following a series of disagreements with the Golden Horde (the Mongol clan in control of Russia at the time) in the 1390s he took vast tracts of land from them, and they never recovered from this. At the height of his power Timur ruled most of the land between Mongolia and the Mediterranean. However, his empire began to crumble upon his death; ruled by weak or quarrelsome descendants, it was never destined to last.

Ivan the Great is usually credited with the overthrow of the Mongols in the late 15th century but their power had long since waned unassisted. Ivan, about whom very little is actually known, was responsible for the absorption of surrounding areas by Moscow; Novgorod, for example, was finally annexed in 1478. His son, Vasily III, succeeded him in 1505 and immediately took up where Ivan had left off, strengthening the monarchy and recruiting new states (eg Smolensk, 1514). When he died in 1533 he left two possible heirs: the mentally retarded Yuri and the sickly Ivan, the latter only three years old.

Ivan the Terrible

The epithet 'Terrible' probably referred to Ivan IV's explosive temper (he beat his eldest son to death in a fit of rage in 1581) but it is equally appropriate to the quality of his reign. Having been proclaimed Tsar (after 'Caesar'; Ivan was the first to use this title) at the age of 16, he surrounded himself with mercenaries and yes-men. Finally, having done his level-best to splinter the empire that his father had left him, he died in 1584, leaving only the mentally-retarded Fyodor to succeed him. Clearly Fyodor was incapable of ruling, so power passed largely to a courtier, Boris Godunov, whose meteoric rise to prominence was partly due to the fact that he had married off his sister, Irina, to the idiot Fyodor so as to gain himself aristocratic credibility. He was proclaimed Tsar in 1598 when Fyodor died.

Godunov was a surprisingly good ruler, managing to repair much of the damage done by Ivan IV. Yet with the turn of the century all was far from well: 1601-3 saw great famine, with hundreds of thousands perishing, and in 1604 came another blow, as a pretender claiming to be Ivan's son, Dmitri, appeared from Poland, claiming his birthright. As he moved west he gained support from the peasants along the way, and when Godunov died in 1605 the 'False Dmitri' entered Moscow and was proclaimed Tsar. Dmitri was not cut out for the job, though, and after a number of provocative moves was assassinated in 1606. A leader of this plot, Vasily Shuysky, was then proclaimed Tsar, but the so-called 'Times of Troubles' were not over yet, for another False Dmitri was on his way over from Poland. Meanwhile, the Polish king seized the opportunity created by the turmoil in Moscow to besiege Smolensk in 1609. There followed a complex struggle for power which was resolved only with the expulsion of the Polish and the election of a compromise candidate for Tsar, the 16-year-old Mikhail Fyodorovich, son of Fyodor Romanov and the founder of the last Russian dynasty, which was to rule for nearly 300 years.

Peter the Great and the Westernisation of Russia

Mikhail and his heir Alexis managed to put the country back on its feet and although there was more trouble following Alexis' death in 1676, this eventually led to the accession of Peter I ('the Great'). His was one of the truly formative reigns in the country's history. He travelled widely throughout Europe, returning home convinced that Russia was backward. He ordered the modernisation of the country, with the construction of a new capital city, St Petersburg, and recruited foreign experts to teach technology to his people. Yet his rule was not without its little failures. One of these was the 'Soul Tax' which was intended to eradicate tax-evasion but meant that ultimately all peasants became the landowners' serfs. Thus while Russia was lurching ahead into the 18th century, its peasants were left behind in the 17th.

The years after his death in 1725 saw a number of mediocre rulers come and go: he was succeeded by his second wife, Catherine, who lasted only two years, and then Peter II, Anna, Elizabeth and Peter III, none of whom really achieved much – it is a tribute to Peter I's reforms that the country kept itself going throughout this period. The third Peter was a particularly ineffective ruler who was overthrown by his German wife, Catherine, in 1762. Catherine the Great was almost certainly the best-educated Russian sovereign to date, winning her soubriquet because of her successful expansionist policies. During her reign Russia became a world power, gaining a large chunk of Eastern Poland, taking control of the northern coast of the Black Sea and annexing the Crimea. At home, the arts flourished; in St Petersburg, she commissioned the Hermitage and many other buildings in the opulent Classical style. Although liberal-minded, however, she stopped short of freeing the peasants. Catherine was notorious for her colourful love-life but rumours of her bizarre equestrian skills are exaggerated: she died, in 1796, of a stroke while seated on her privy. She was succeeded by her unbalanced son, Paul I (1796-1801). Terrified of revolution, he stamped down hard on liberal ideas and imposed tight censorship. Having thus incensed the educated and wealthy classes, he was assassinated. His son, Alexander I, was thought to have had a hand in the plot.

From Napoleon to the Decembrists

Alexander began his reign by reversing of most of his father's policies. He quickly restored normal relations with Europe, thus avoiding hostilities, and took steps towards liberating the serfs, although he never quite achieved this. Napoleon's eastward advance through Europe drove him into an alliance with the English and the Austrians but despite this he suffered a number of defeats at the hands of the French. The Treaty of Tilsit (1807), signed by Napoleon and Alexander, did very little to hold them back, and Napoleon marched into Moscow on 14 September 1812, only to march out, defeated, a month later. Alexander then pursued the beaten army west, occupying Paris in March 1814. Military triumphs were not enough to satisfy the peasants at home, however, and on Alexander's death in 1825 the first Russian Revolution, led by the 'Decembrists', broke out. In fact this was really rather a small-scale affair: a brief uprising in St Petersburg led by a number of secret societies managed to persuade a group of soldiers that Nicholas should not be the new Tsar. The movement was suppressed quickly and easily; its chief importance seems to have been as a source of inspiration to the founders of the later revolution. Perpetrators were executed or exiled to Siberia.

Nicholas I: defeat in the Crimea

Nicholas ascended the throne in 1825 only after it had been refused by his older brother, Constantine. His fear of revolution led him to order the tightening of the censorship laws and although he instituted a committee which was to be responsible for public reforms, he never actually approved any of their suggestions and so nothing was done. His reign was an unhappy, stagnant one for Russia, culminating in the disastrous Crimean War (1853-6). This war was caused mainly by bad diplomacy and, although Russia gained some credibility at the famous siege of Sebastopol, it led to an embarrassing defeat at the hands of the British, the French and the Turkish. Alexander II was proclaimed Tsar in 1855, and subsequent reforms were largely due to him. He finally liberated the peasants in 1861, declaring that serfdom would be better abolished from above rather than waiting 'until the serfs liberate themselves from below'. Their condition did not improve much in real terms, however. Despite other reforms and a number of successful foreign deals, including the sale of Alaska to America in 1867 for two cents an acre in 1867 (it seemed like a good idea at the time), Alexander II was assassinated in 1881. His son, Alexander III, led a stifling, repressive regime which succeeded only in antagonising the numerous revolutionary societies further.

Nicholas II

The year 1894 saw Nicholas II, the last of the Tsars, inherit a country heading for revolution. He might have been able to do something about this had he not also inherited his father's belief in autocracy. Meanwhile the Social Democratic Party, which had been founded in 1889, came under the influence of the politically-minded Vladimir Ulyanov (Lenin). The Russo-Japanese War broke out in 1904 as a result of Russian misguidance and bad diplomacy again (some claim that the Russians were looking for a 'small victorious war' in order to raise popular morale and divert revolution). It ended, in 1905, with the Russians soundly beaten and ceding land to Japan. By now the situation in Russia was critical: in January a huge crowd of workers led by a popular priest staged a protest in St Petersburg. They were gunned down in the square in front of the Winter Palace for their trouble. By October the country was crippled by a series of national strikes, as a result of which Nicholas II promised the formation of a democratic parliament, or *duma*. The duma was largely ineffective at first because it came to conclusions which he did not like, and consequently it was re-convened three times before any real progress was made. The new premier, Pyotr Stolypin, seemed keen to make reforms but his enthusiasm died with his assassination in 1911. While the strikes and riots continued, the Tsar's mind was elsewhere: his son, Alexei, was suffering from haemophilia and the only treatment available seemed to be that offered by the religious charismatic, Rasputin, whose influence in the royal household grew steadily until **he** was assassinated in December 1916.

1917: Revolution

With the outbreak of WWI the situation really deteriorated. Financial problems coupled with vast Russian losses in Prussia and Poland led to serious food shortages. Finally, on 15 March 1917, under extreme pressure from all sides, the Tsar resigned. A provisional government was set up under Georgy Lvov who was shortly to be replaced by Alexander

Kerensky. At this point, leaders of the outlawed Bolshevik half of the National Democratic Party, notably Lenin in Switzerland and Trotsky in New York, condemned the provisional government as 'bourgeois'. They returned, Lenin assisted by the Germans, and demanded the immediate overthrow of the government. Through efficient management and sheer revolutionary zeal the Bolsheviks grew rapidly in number and were in a position to seize power by the winter of 1917. This they did in November, after sporadic fighting. The real civil war was not to start until May 1918 with the Bolsheviks' struggle against the anti-communist White Russians. Two months later the Tsar and his family were murdered by Bolshevik soldiers; shot and mutilated in the basement of a merchant's house in Siberia, the remains of their corpses were positively identified in 1993.

Although the White Russians were supported by Western aid, by 1920 the counter-revolution had been turned back. Some two million wealthy Russians fled their country during this time.

Stalin and the purges
Lenin was immobilised by a stroke in 1923, leaving the Communist Party without a leader. Against the wishes of many, Josef Stalin took his place and launched a series of Party purges, exiling or liquidating those whom he perceived as threatening to his position (Trotsky, for example, was sent to Almaty and then exiled from the USSR altogether). But while Stalin was a ruthless tyrant, he did manage to haul the Russian economy up via a series of Five Year Plans, their emphasis lying on heavy industry. His efforts were also successful in that they re-established Russia's credibility as a force to be reckoned with on the world stage. By 1929, however, he was paranoid again and initiated another series of purges of the Party ranks. Victims ran into tens of millions.

Great Patriotic War
Following Hitler's invasion of Austria and Czechoslovakia, Britain and France declared that they would assist Poland if he tried to step in there. Instead of joining them in their condemnation, Stalin signed a non-aggression pact with Germany, agreeing that when Poland was invaded it would be divided into two, the Eastern half going to Russia. When the invasion actually took place (prompting the declaration of war on 3 September 1939), large strips of Poland were handed over to Russia as agreed, and Soviet troops were immediately stationed there. When Finland refused to cede territory to the Soviets a year later, fighting began. Yet in December 1940 Hitler turned on his agreement and gave orders for the invasion of the USSR, which commenced in June 1941 (for the Allies, this was one of the key points of the war). Losses on both sides were appalling but the superlative Russian war effort, together with the stretching of German supply lines and western Lend-Lease aid combined to push them back, the massive Russian victory at Stalingrad marking the

turning-point in the Soviet war effort. By 1943 two-thirds of the stolen Russian land had been repossessed; in April 1945 Berlin was surrounded. It is estimated that 15-20 million Russians died in action.

East-West relations deteriorate

The aftermath of the war saw the emergence of the Soviet 'satellite' regimes, so that by 1948 Poland, Czechoslovakia, Hungary, Romania, Albania and Bulgaria were all under heavy Soviet influence (Yugoslavia had managed to escape that year). The following 'Cold War' between the Eastern Bloc and the West was a grey era of suspicion, intelligence and counter-intelligence manoeuvres which achieved very little apart from making both sides edgy and producing a number of B-rate spy movies. Stalin's death in 1953 was followed by the election of Nikita Khrushchev who was responsible, among other things, for the Virgin Lands campaign, which sought to cultivate new areas, notably the Kazakh and Siberian steppes. In 1956 he made a notorious 'Secret Speech' denouncing Stalin, which greatly pleased the West when they heard it. A number of developments did just the reverse shortly afterwards: rapid scientific advances, particularly in rocket design, shook the world. The USSR's first intercontinental ballistic missile was successfully fired in 1957, shortly followed by the launching of the world's first satellite, Sputnik 1. America was intrigued, and the Russians proved this by shooting down one of their U2 spy-planes over Siberia, resulting in the collapse of the 1960 Paris Summit. Berlin was partitioned in 1961, and the next year nearly saw the start of hostilities with the Soviet positioning of nuclear warheads in Cuba, just 150 miles off the coast of Florida. They were finally removed at the threat of retaliation from US president JF Kennedy.

The 1960s and 70s – Czechoslovakia and Afghanistan

The put-down received in the Cuban Missile Crisis, together with a dreadful harvest in 1963 and the generally acknowledged low Soviet standard of living, resulted in Khrushchev's removal from office in 1964 'in view of his advanced age and deterioration in the state of his health', and he was relieved by the Alexei Kosygin/Leonid Brezhnev administration. While there were still problems at home, the Soviet gate-crasher society was as active as ever: in 1968, following Dubcek's 'Prague Spring' in Czechoslovakia, Soviet forces moved in, and although East-West relations thawed considerably in the 1970s with the signing of the first of the SALT treaties, much of the good-will evaporated in 1979 with the invasion of Afghanistan.

Gorbachev and *perestroika*: the end of the Cold War

Brezhnev died in 1982, to be relieved by two short-lived premiers in succession. First came Andropov, ex-head of the KGB, who was already terminally ill when he accepted the post, and who died in 1984. He was shortly followed by Chernenko who managed to hold on only for 13 months. On 11 March 1985 Mikhail Gorbachev was elected General Secretary, the youngest, at 51, since Stalin. He immediately commenced a process of liberalisation, and *glasnost* (openness) and *perestroika* (restructuring) became the key words. Although clouded in 1986 by the Chernobyl nuclear accident, the reforms began to arrive: censorship laws were relaxed, leading to the airing of secret footage of Stalin and the general acceptance of his atrocious human rights record, and consequently criticism of the past. Political dissidents were released (the most famous being Andrei Sakharov in 1986) and 1987 saw the rehabilitation of the victims of Stalin's purges. At the 1988 Party Conference Gorbachev outlined the way ahead, with competitive elections for state and Party officials. Thus by 1989 there were numerous popular political groups decrying communism, particularly in the Baltic republics. The Communist Party was unwilling to accept his changes and as a consequence there was a conscious break, leading to the formation of the Congress of Peoples' Deputies, which elected Gorbachev as the first Soviet president.

But by this time the USSR was already splitting; economic hardship and conservative hardline criticism were constantly undermining Gorbachev's credibility. The Russians were derisive about his Nobel Peace Prize in 1990. Inflation and crime rates rocketed as food became scarce. Ethnic violence broke out in the Baltic republics and in March 1990 an elected body in Lithuania proclaimed its country's independence, shortly to be followed by the other republics (Uzbekistan in June and Kazakhstan in October). Gorbachev began a battle to keep the states in the Soviet Union but, worn out by criticism from the military, the hardline communists and other political leaders (notably Boris Yeltsin) it soon became clear that he was losing his footing.

The coup

On Sunday 18 August 1991 a coup d'état took place. Gorbachev was isolated at his Crimean villa and on the morning of the 19th it was announced that he was incapacitated. Vice President Yanaev took control and declared, with the other conspirators (all senior political and military figures), a state of emergency. Although the idea was to make the whole operation look constitutional, the public soon cottoned on to the plot and by 11am on the 19th, Yeltsin had pronounced the coup illegal and was rallying support in Moscow. He was backed up by other key figures, notably Eduard Shevardnardze and the Patriarch, Aleksii II, who demanded to hear Gorbachev's voice. On the night of the 20th a curfew was declared. It was not obeyed, and there was a limited amount of fighting in the city centre (three casualties). Yet the troops were unwilling to fire on civilians and by the morning of the 21st they had been withdrawn. The coup committee was put to flight.

Gorbachev's decline

The coup drove home the need for radical change and on 24 August Gorbachev resigned his post as General Secretary of the Communist Party, recommending that it be dissolved. Four days later it was. By the end of August, in a domino-like effect, all the states which today constitute the CIS had declared their independence. Gorbachev began a desperate struggle to keep them in some sort of Russian federation but he was fighting a losing battle. Meanwhile radical changes thrust themselves upon him: the KGB was abolished on 11 October; 1.2 million servicemen were axed in massive defence cuts; vast loans were promised by the World Bank and the USA. As the USSR headed into a downwards spiral it was sped on its way by food shortages, 1991's harvest being some 40 million tonnes lower than that 1990's. On 8 December after a meeting in Minsk Boris Yeltsin and Leonid Kravchuk (the Ukrainian president) declared that the USSR was defunct. Gorbachev dismissed this, labelling their statement 'dangerous'. Thirteen days later at a conference in Almaty the abolition of the USSR was announced; Gorbachev was not even there. The collapse of his plans for a centralised authority at the heart of the CIS left him no alternative but to resign, which he did on 24 December.

Yeltsin vs the Congress of Deputies

Yeltsin took control. In January 1992 markets were freed in Russia (and also in Kazakhstan and Uzbekistan) and prices leapt between 300 and 3000% overnight. Yeltsin planned a series of economic changes radical enough to push the Russian economy into 'shock therapy' and put it back on its feet. Unfortunately this was to prove more tricky than even he had expected: opposition from inside the Congress of People's Deputies meant that reforms seldom made it through parliament; Congress members were all too aware that by voting for reform they were, in effect, abolishing their own jobs. Economic conditions deteriorated as the reform process stagnated until Yeltsin, in desperation, dissolved parliament and called for fresh elections.

Congress, led by hardliners Alexander Rutskoi and Ruslan Khasbulatov, denounced this as unconstitutional – a coup d'état, no less – and called for civil disobedience from the public. Yeltsin countered by surrounding the White House (with the hardliners inside), and a siege ensued. This was eventually resolved on 4 October when pro-Yeltsin troops successfully stormed the building. Rutskoi and Khasbulatov were locked up, although both were released and pardoned in 1994.

Yeltsin, Chechenia and the future

The wheels are turning more smoothly today but continual opposition has kept the brakes on the reform process. One unwelcome distraction has been the irksome behaviour of the breakaway republic of Chechenia. Run by ex-Soviet general Dudayev, Chechenia declared independence, to

Russia's dismay, in 1991. Russia then stirred trouble continually within the republic until 1994 when a Russian-organised Provisional Chechen Council caused enough trouble to merit a real response. Under the guise that this trouble might spread, Yeltsin had the republic surrounded by the military.

Escalation was inevitable. In December 1994 the troops went in and there followed a protracted, bloody conflict. This reached a peak in June 1995 when Chechen soldiers, hopelessly outnumbered, attempted to spread the fighting beyond Chechen borders by taking 1000 Russian civilians hostage in a hospital in a small Russian town. A ceasefire was signed in late June and more agreements are made continually but occasional shots are still exchanged.

Russia's future is anyone's guess. One thing that most in the West agree, though, is that everything is probably all right while Yeltsin is in control. However, electoral success by former communist chiefs (state elections in 1995 gave the communists the majority in the duma, with 157 out of 450 seats) makes everyone uncomfortable. Moreover, Yeltsin's continuing ill health and problems with alcohol mean that his behaviour can be unpredictable – even if he does retain control. Most Russians see free market reforms as tough and often a mistake; Westerners say that things will get better – but then they don't have to live with them.

THE PEOPLE

The Soviet Union used to be the third most populous country in the world (after China and India) with a population of 286 million. Naturally, since its fragmentation each constituent country is considerably smaller. The Russian Federation is currently home to some 148 million people: about 21 times the population of the UK. Uzbekistan's population is 21 million and Kazakhstan's is 17 million. Before independence, whilst individual identities and ethnic rights in each of the states were fiercely protected, there was only a certain amount that they could do; certainly, the first language in each was Russian, and large numbers of individuals were transported in from other areas around the USSR (notably during Khrushchev's Virgin Lands campaign). Since independence, however, the republics constituting the CIS have seen an upsurge of nationalism which has usually tied in with the emigration, sometimes under pressure, of many recent immigrants. Thus in Kazakhstan the native language is now Kazakh, and in Uzbekistan it is Uzbek. Russian remains the most widely spoken language, however.

Government
• **Russia** The country is now governed by a European-style two-tier parliament very similar to that of France, with a 450-seat State Duma and a Federal Council made up of 178 delegates, two from each member of the

Federation. Despite the theory, Russia is far from democratic. The real power of the country is actually vested in a few hundred chief executives of huge corporations who picked up enormous wealth through the corrupt privatisation of the state enterprises originally under communism. These people now monopolise the media, gas and oil, military, production and banking sectors, in effect controlling the entire Russian state.

• **Kazakhstan** The country is run by the Supreme Kenges, headed by President Nursultan Nazarbayev, a former communist. Currently there is a big rift in the government, the result of cultural differences: a new constitution was passed in January 1993 stating that the Kazakh president had to be a Kazakh speaker, and misgivings were expressed over the fact that 37% of the population are ethnic Russians. This ethnic blend demands careful management if there is not to be trouble – already there are periodic calls by ethnic Russians to let the northern half of Kazakhstan secede and become a kind of Russian Kazakhstan. Ethnic intolerance creates problems for any government, and Kazakhstan is no exception: 1994's elections here saw the clear victory for the People's Unity of Kazakhstan Party (SNEK: the former communists). Their main opponents, however, the Russian-backed LAD party, cried foul play. Accusations reached such a pitch that Nazarbayev eventually dissolved parliament but with the ingenious twist that all members should retain their seats until new elections had been organised. This offers some cause for concern but not for him: he's been voted in until the year 2000.

• **Uzbekistan** In Uzbekistan the story is similar: the country is ruled by the 250-seat Supreme Assembly (Oliy Majilis), to which delegates are directly elected. Currently occupying 205 of these 250 seats is the Peoples' Democratic Party – essentially the old Communist Party by another name. PDP tends to win rather convincingly in elections perhaps for the simple reason that, despite all sorts of guarantees in the constitution, political opposition is not really tolerated. The PDP's two main opposition parties, for example, ERK and BIRLIK, have been banned since the introduction of the multi-party system in 1992 – which should give the shrewd-minded an idea of which party to join if they want to get ahead in politics. As with Kazakhstan, though, the president has nothing to worry about: Islam Karimov has been in power since the demise of communism. He was recently voted in again – until at least the year 2000.

Uzbekistan is not noted as an especially liberal country: state censorship is still common and there have been questions raised concerning human rights.

Education and social welfare
Throughout the former USSR education is compulsory until the age of 17 with the result that there is an almost 100% literacy rate (according to

official figures: in fact this is probably only the case in the big Russian cities). Some republics, Kazakhstan and Uzbekistan, for example, have recently changed their primary language, and thus ethnic Russians in these areas are disadvantaged (when this act went through in Kazakhstan, virtually all ethnic Russians in senior posts were summarily dismissed).

University places are determined by entrance examination and competition is fierce: funding is scarce and numbers of students in higher education have been falling for some time now. Health care is also provided free and although periodic outbreaks of diphtheria and anthrax have focused Western media attention on the substandard service provided in the CIS, these outbreaks are probably the result of substandard inoculation programmes operated under the former regime.

Religion

A ruling made immediately following the foundation of the USSR declared, 'To all young working Muslims of Russia and the East. Henceforth your beliefs and customs, your natural and cultural institutions are proclaimed to be free and inviolable'. In reality, there were deliberate campaigns against religion at various points throughout this century. In 1929 Soviets were permitted to form 'religious societies' but public ceremonies or rituals were forbidden. This was gradually modified under Stalin until citizens were permitted to hold religious beliefs but not to spread them.

With the Great Patriotic War religion made a dramatic comeback, nurtured partly by Stalin to help whip up nationalistic fervour; this was not to last, and it was again swept under the carpet after the war. Both Khrushchev and Brezhnev conducted anti-religious campaigns which seem to have been successful, reducing numbers of churches drastically; in fact they probably had limited effects on the numbers of believers themselves. The Gorbachev attitude to religion was, predictably, more relaxed. The re-opening of churches and mosques began in 1984 and smaller sects were no longer persecuted.

At present, the main religion in the CIS is Christianity (numerous denominations, with the majority adhering to Russian Orthodox beliefs). Islam (Sunni) in the south was never efficiently repressed, although numerous mosques were closed down. It is currently making a big comeback, leading to concern from ethnic Russians about the risk of fundamentalist Islam. It's not hard to see why: in 1990 there were 63 functioning mosques in Kazakhstan; in 1996 there are over 4000.

Many Jews left in the early 1990s; about one million remain. Buddhism is a minority religion in the CIS with just a few hundred thousand adherents, mainly in Siberia. Western sects such as Jehovah's Witnesses, Baptists and Seventh-Day Adventists appear to be flourishing in the aftermath of glasnost.

Practical information for the visitor

DOCUMENTS, TICKETS AND VOUCHERS

Don't forget your passport, of course, not that you'll be allowed onto the plane without it. While the Uzbek visa is normally in the form of a whole page stamp, and the Kazakh visa is glued into the passport, make sure that you've also got the Russian one, which comes on a separate sheet of paper. Unless you are travelling totally independently, you will need your hotel and travel vouchers (for Uzbekistan at least), and it's worth carrying your letter of invitation too. Student identification can be extremely useful in Moscow, though it is less so thereafter, and an ISIC card or similar is worth bringing. Bring inoculation certificates, and at least four passport sized photos for visa extensions.

Customs declaration forms

At CIS and Chinese borders you will be required to fill in customs declarations specifying the amount of money and travellers' cheques you are carrying, your purpose in the country, and asking you to list any valuables that you may have with you (walkman, camera etc). You may have to present your copy of this form as you leave. In the former USSR the form used to be thoroughly checked on departure and if you could not produce all of the items originally listed (or bank receipts to account for money no longer in your possession) fines were occasionally imposed. Nobody seems to be too bothered any more but there could still be problems if you give away or sell all the valuables you listed on the form. Likewise it's worth being honest with your declaration, as the Kazakh authorities, in particular, tend to count your cash, just to check, and could conceivably levy a fine for a false statement.

Customs allowances

Visitors may bring up to one litre of spirits and 200 cigarettes into Russia, although the rules are not strongly enforced, because both are available at much cheaper prices in Russia. There are currently no border checks on trains travelling between CIS countries but this may change. Check with the Uzbek and Kazakh embassies before you go, as new rules are being introduced which may make bringing alcohol into the country illegal.

HOTELS

Hotels in the CIS are usually large rectangular concrete affairs that do not compare well with their Western counterparts. When you check in you will have to fill in a form and surrender your passport so that the visa can be checked (this is sometimes the point where those without visas for that town start counting US$1 bills on the top of the counter). Most hotels give you your passport back once they've checked it but some like to keep it until you check out; in which case try to get a receipt, and remember above all things to reclaim the passport before you leave. Should you need it to change money, the hotel staff are usually amenable to persuasion. Once you have checked in, you will be given a slip of paper or a key; if it is the former you will have to pick up and hand back your room key to the *dezhurnaya* (the floor attendant resident on your level) each time you come and go.

Intourist hotels appear to have predated the current 70's fashion revival by some twenty years. The decor in some hotels, it is true, is much better, but then they are also much more expensive. Bedding is often a duvet which you have to assemble yourself, fitting the blankets into the

---

Shakedowns

In the CIS, interest from anyone in a uniform usually means trouble. Peter Holdforth (UK) was on the Urgench-Tashkent train: 'The policeman pushed his way into my compartment, so drunk that he was having difficulty standing upright. 'Most travellers bring me $100' he said, 'but you will give me $200 – or I will make trouble for you'. I refused to hand him my passport, whereupon he produced a pair of handcuffs and tried to put them on me. When I folded my arms and refused to co-operate, he lost what little control he had left and started to scream incoherently. He then upped his demand to $1000. Eventually, however, he needed to go to the toilet and lurched off'.

It is difficult to advise what to do in a situation like this: you have to play it by ear. Peter eventually got away with it by being belligerent and refusing to co-operate but this is not always the best way: generally the trick is to be polite. Being ripped off may be inevitable, but by bargaining coolly you can minimise the damage. To defuse situations like this, carry plenty of cheap, interesting items at the top of your shoulder bag: photographs and postcards of home, family and friends; a couple of packets of cigarettes; magazines; Western coins etc. When officials start rifling through your bag, they'll find these first. Be sure to explain at great length who is in each photograph and exactly what they're doing. Be very friendly. Offer the guard a cigarette; tell him to keep the pack – anything to make pretend that this is a friendly chat. You never know, it may well turn into one.

If money is definitely going to change hands, keep cool. Police asking for US$100 are not really expecting it. Bargain with them: with patience and a little charisma you'll get them down to US$10. If you can't pay in local currency, pay in US$1 bills – it looks like more. Or try a travellers' cheque (they'll have no idea what to do with it and cheques are replaceable). Don't be intimidated but always be respectful.

Finally, try to make sure that your negotiations take place in public: officials don't want to be seen to be taking bribes and your fellow travellers, if you're on good terms with them – may well help out. Get a local friend to accompany you to likely shakedown spots like railway and bus stations.

cover, leaving the huge diamond-shaped hole pointing upwards. Most rooms contain televisions and internal telephones; it is very rare to find IDD from hotel rooms. The en suite bathrooms tend to waver between 'leaky' and 'no water at all'. Electricity supplies can be unreliable on occasion. There have been reports of theft from hotel rooms by staff, almost always small items like cigarettes or fancy toiletries, so don't leave your belongings lying around. Readers of Philip Glazebrook's *Journey to Khiva* will understand immediately why it is unwise to leave your hotel room door open even when you are inside.

PRIVATE ACCOMMODATION

Over the last few years a few privately owned guesthouses have opened up in the cities along this route, and the possibility of staying in local people's homes has also emerged. The advantages of staying in such places are numerous: the food you receive will probably be better than hotel fare, you will get to live with a family and make new friends and you'll get a good insight into what things are really like for the locals. You will also end up paying far less, and your money will go to a family which probably needs it more than Intourist does. In addition, if you get on with them well, your hosts may help you get tickets, show you around their town, and so on.

Although, in the past, travellers have reported being able to find homestays by simply chatting to people, and being invited home by their new 'friends', there are obvious problems with this. How, for example, do you know whether your prospective hosts are honest – there are stories of travellers getting robbed and being left with nothing. In Uzbekistan also you may have a problem if you are stopped by the police; you should be able to prove where you have stayed so far, and where you are due to stay (ie in approved hotels) and you run the risk of getting both yourself and 'your' family in trouble (homestays are likely to be regarded as legal by the police if they are organised through a licensed travel service, but may be seen as illegal if they are not). On a more mundane level, do you really want to go through the hassle of trying to 'suggest' to locals that you need somewhere to stay? If the opportunity presents itself, great, but there has to be a better way.

Taken in context with the need, when applying for CIS visas, to show where you intend to stay, the best way to approach the problem of getting good local accommodation is to go through a local travel service. They will of course charge a commission, but on the other hand they will also be able to guarantee you a night's accommodation with a family who are used to dealing with foreigners and who know that you are coming. Remember that even if you are staying with families along the way, the travel service should be able to provide you with vouchers to prove it so that, should you be stopped by the police, you can produce evidence of your itinerary.

Remember if you do stay with a local family, whether it was pre-arranged, or on the spur of the moment, that it is someone's home; don't treat anyone as a hotelier or you are sure to offend. Western gifts may be appreciated as payment but don't take advantage of this, and always leave more than the hospitality you received was worth.

TOURIST OFFICES

Intourist's monopoly over the CIS is now over, its place having been taken by smaller, state tourism companies, which in turn are trying to maintain their own monopolies. Uzbektourism operates in almost exactly the same way as its former self, corralling package tourists into overpriced, substandard hotels, in which the staff have little interest in doing anything other than holding on to their cushy state jobs. Uzbektourism is, however, now being challenged both by the arrival of new top class joint venture hotels and also by some small privately owned travel agencies which are much more flexible and are less greedy. Kazakhstan's new tourism company is in its early stages, and you are unlikely to come across it.

Whatever the local state tourism company is called, the system throughout the CIS still operates in much the same way as it did, and in every CIS city mentioned in this book you will find at least one large central hotel which used to be the Intourist hotel, and in many cases is still known as just that by the taxi drivers. Although you may not want to stay in this hotel, this is often the place to make for if you are after tours, transport, interpreters and other facilities. It might be more advantageous to engage guides independently, as they are likely to be happy to work privately, and without you having to pay a commission to the hotel.

The 'Intourist' hotel is also the best place to go if you have any problems; the service may be terrible, but at least you will be able to get hold of someone who can speak your language.

LOCAL TRANSPORT

Hotel transfers

Pre-arranged trips almost always start off with a 'transfer' from the airport to the hotel. The price for this is usually high but most are happy to pay it because after a tiring flight the last thing anyone wants to do is to attempt to figure out a foreign country's public transport system. Getting from airport to hotel is rarely very difficult unless you are arriving either very early or very late. Try to pick up a cab at the airport when you arrive and prices will rocket as soon as it becomes obvious that you do not really know what you are doing. Find out what time you will be arriving, and if it is during the day and you are feeling adventurous, go for public transport. If not, order a transfer.

Trains

It can be infuriatingly difficult to get hold of tickets in the CIS for each leg of the journey. You will find that ticket office workers tend to specialise in doing very little, especially when there is a huge queue waiting; they would much rather tell you that the train is full than have to go to the trouble of selling you a ticket. This means that when the train is 'full' there is usually some more space.

There are various options you could try. Some have reported that just getting on the train and bargaining with the carriage attendants can work, but it's best is to play by the rules, as you really don't need to be accused of fare dodging at a time when your worldly wealth will be a conversation point anyway. If you're having no luck getting a ticket for yourself, try to get a friend to help (someone from the reception desk of your hotel can normally be persuaded to accompany you, either just out of kindness or for a small fee). Alternatively there will probably be a booking service in the local tourist hotel, and as a last resort you can pay a guide/interpreter for half an hour's work in accompanying you to the railway station.

Rail travel in the CIS

Life on board revolves around the samovar, the hot water heater at the end of each carriage, and it is from here that your companions will be recharging their jam-jars of steaming tea throughout the trip. Food is easily available both from platform vendors (beware of hot dishes left to cool since these may not be safe) and the restaurant car. In Russia these serve soups followed by great hunks of beef topped with fried eggs but in Central Asia you can expect rice dishes. A number of travellers have complained of stomach upsets after dining car meals so, here again, it is wise to be careful. Bread and eggs, or fruit and salad washed in water from the samovar will always be safe.

Be careful with your belongings as compartment doors don't lock securely; either use the bottom bunk and deposit your gear in the steel box beneath it or chain your bags in the space provided above the door. Don't leave your camera or walkman lying around and wear your moneybelt at all times. Shortly after boarding an overnight train, the carriage attendant will come round demanding a small amount of money (typically US$0.50-US$2), for bedding, which should include sheets, blankets etc. Hand the bedding back (folded) to the carriage attendant just before you arrive at your destination.

Music is piped through the train but is usually quite atrocious: look for the volume knobs in the corridors and pray that your cabin mates won't object to your turning off the noise. Ask the carriage attendant and you may be allowed to put on a tape of your own; the Beatles ensures instant popularity.

Rail travel throughout Central Asia is rarely simple but it is by far the most interesting way to go. Those not taking tours, however, should note that conditions can be basic. The number one complaint is the state of the toilets: generally so utterly repulsive that even the cockroaches steer clear. You have been warned!

Taxis

There are taxis and there are taxis. An official taxi has a meter, a green light to indicate when it is free and 'такси' written on it. Unofficially, the majority of the cars in the CIS will stop for you if you stand in the street waving. Unless you chance upon a particularly morally upright driver who will use the meter, you will need to bargain, or end up paying the price that the taxi driver thinks is fitting – which can be many times the proper fare. The problem is, of course, that if you don't speak Russian (or Uzbek, or whatever) you are clearly a tourist and thus utterly wealthy. Taxi drivers will normally expect local currency, although US$ are usually acceptable, and you could try bargaining with dollars to try to get the fare down.

Alternatively, if you have made some friends on the train, make a point of asking their advice, and then stand back and let them do the bargaining for you; at all events, fix a price before you start your journey, in order to avoid an unpleasant argument at the other end. The only non-Russian speaking travellers we found to have got around this used to leap into the cab, present the driver with a piece of paper with their destination written on it, and then say absolutely nothing throughout the journey. When they arrived they got out, paid the driver what they thought was a reasonable fare and walked away in silence.

Metro

In Moscow the metro is easily the best way to get around. The turnstiles work on plastic tokens, which cost the equivalent of US$0.03, although the prices seem to go up on a fairly regular basis. To get in, post the token into the turnstile and walk through; you do not need to reclaim it as there are no ticket inspectors. If you like you can spend all day in the palatial system for one token, but as soon as you leave one of the stations you will have to pay again to get back in. The Tashkent metro works on a similar system.

Bus

Buses and trolley-buses generally provide good coverage of local areas but can be difficult to use. Tickets can be bought in any number of ways from paying the conductor as you get on or off, to using ticket machines. In the latter case you will be expected to punch your own ticket using the hole-punches stuck on the wall of the bus. If people are giving you their tickets for no apparent reason, see if you are standing next to the punch. It is not uncommon to see money being passed right from the back of a bus to the front and then the ticket returning along the same way. Usually there is a set fare for any distance. Minibus route taxis also operate in most cities, and can be the best way of travelling short distances. Long-distance services operate between the towns in this guide with the exception of the Moscow-Khiva link.

Internal flights

Internal flights between any of the cities in this guide are a useful time-saving option. Unless you have made any bookings before starting your trip, you may find it easiest to book seats through with Intourist, or the local equivalent. In Tashkent and Almaty, however, there are airline offices where you can book your flights yourself.

ELECTRICITY

Generally 220V/50 cycles AC, and you will need a continental-type two pin plug to use it. Enquire first, as in some places the voltage is 127V.

TIME

The CIS spans 11 time zones but it is important to note that transport timetables throughout the CIS still run on Moscow Time, which is three hours ahead of Greenwich Mean Time (GMT+3). The more western of the Central Asian cities in this guide (ie the Uzbek cities of Urgench, Khiva, Samarkand and Bukhara are five hours ahead of Greenwich Mean Time (GMT+5), while Tashkent and Almaty are six hours ahead (GMT+6). As soon as you cross border into China you move onto Beijing Time, which is eight hours ahead (GMT+8). See the Route Guide for details of time zone changes.

MONEY

Currencies

Since the formation of the CIS, the countries of the commonwealth have all adopted separate currencies. It's worth chatting up your fellow travellers (locals that is) while you are still on the train, to ascertain the exchange rates. If possible, try to change enough money with them to allow you to get to the nearest hotel or bank, before getting off the train in a new country.

Russia The basic unit of currency is the rouble, which is theoretically divided into 100 kopecks (now virtually worthless). Roubles come in notes of 1, 3, 5, 10, 100, 200, 500, 1000, 5000, 10,000, 50,000 and in coins of 1, 5, 10, 20 and 50. In early 1997, the exchange rate was around R5800 to US$1. It's currently not worth using the black market in Russia: the rate tends not to be much better and you're liable to be ripped off.

Uzbekistan The Uzbek unit of currency is the sum, and it comes in 1, 3, 5, 10, 25, 50, 100 and 500 sum notes. At the time of writing, the black market was definitely worth using, with the official exchange rate at 35 sum: US$1, and the black market rate being 50 sum: US$1.

Kazakhstan The new currency in Kazakhstan is the tenge, which comes in 1, 3, 5, 10, 20, 50, 100, 200, 500 and 1000 tenge notes.

The black market rates and the official rates were pretty similar when we visited, making black market speculation rather pointless.

Inflation

Inflation in the CIS can make it difficult to keep pace with foreign exchange rates. With Russian currency, for example, for £1 you could get R1 in 1989, R50 in 1991, R1700 in late 1993 and R5800 by 1997. Since any prices quoted in roubles/sum/tenge in this guide would be way out of date by the time you read them, we've converted them into US$ but they must be paid in local currency.

Tipping

Whereas tipping was frowned upon until recently, the arrival of foreign ventures in the CIS ensures that it is catching on. A great number of the people you will be dealing with are likely to give themselves tips by not having the right change anyway; it is probably best not to bother. If you really get on well with a guide, or if someone helps you out then give them a present instead (see p30).

POST AND TELEPHONES

Postal services

Postcards from Central Asia take ages to get through but they generally get there in the end. Intourist is as good a place as any to get writing paper, postcards and stamps, and they will be able to tell you the current fee. A number of people have suggested that mail is more likely to get through if postcards are in envelopes. Before you write your card, buy the correct number of stamps, for if only small denominational stamps are available you may have to use 15 or so, covering your message. The best way to address a letter abroad is:

> Country in Cyrillic: Австралия (Australia),
> Великобритания (Britain),
> Канада (Canada),
> Новая Зиландия (New Zealand),
> США (USA)
>
> Address as normal, in Roman
> Name of recipient

Some mail may not get through unless you include the sender's (ie your) address, and envelopes have a special 'sender's address' box.

Mail can be received poste restante in the CIS, but the service is very dodgy, though reputedly less so in Tashkent than the other cities in this guide.

Telephones

These are fairly reliable in Moscow but the further south you go the less likely they are to be working. Old payphones work on kopeck coins which are no longer available, so you will have to ask for special tokens to use them. For international calls, the easiest place by far will be at the nearest big hotel: many of the larger hotels now have international credit card phone boxes, or try the hotel's business centre if it has one. It's cheaper, though, to go to the telecom office, although you may have to wait some time for your call to be placed.

NATIONAL HOLIDAYS

It is wise not to bank on many services being available either the day before or after one of these holidays.

Russia
• 01 January: New Year's Day
• 06 January: Russian Orthodox Christmas Day.
• 08 March: International Women's Day
• 01 May: International Working People's Solidarity Day
• 09 May: Victory Day. The end of the Great Patriotic War (1941-45).
• 07 June: Independence Day
• 22 August: Holiday in honour of the defeat of the 1993 coup
• 07/08 November: Day Of Reconciliation (formerly known as the
          Anniversary of the Great October Socialist Revolution)

Uzbekistan
• 08 March: International Women's Day
• 21/22 March: Moslem New Year (*Navroos*)
• 01 May: International Working People's Solidarity Day
• 09 May: Victory Day
• 01 September: Uzbekistan Independence Day
• 08 December: Uzbekistan Constitution Day
• 31 December/01 January: Christian New Year

Kazakhstan
• 28 January: Kazakhstan Constitution Day
• 08 March: International Women's Day
• 21/2 March: Islamic New Year (*Navroos*)
• 01 May: International Working People's Solidarity Day
• 09 May: Victory Day
• 25 October: Republic Day
• 16 December: Kazakhstan Independence Day

FOOD

If you have come to the CIS looking for a true gourmet experience you will be disappointed, but then you will also be surprised if you have come looking for food queues and empty restaurants. Unfortunately, getting a good meal is not as easy as it might seem: waiters are unwilling to serve you, cooks appear to be unwilling to cook for you, the menu is invariably constructed in a complex military code and about 90% of the dishes advertised in it will not be available anyway. Don't give up; don't be embarrassed if you are left sitting at your table (provided you are allowed to sit at a table at all) for prolonged periods while the staff clearly avoid you. Small bribes may work, but once the staff realise that you've got hard currency, they may demand it.

The problem is not nearly as acute in the south, but there are so few public restaurants here that just finding one of them is enough of a hassle in itself. If you do find a suitable place which is open, eat there without delay, as anything could have happened to it by the time you get back. Most people survive on the kebab stalls around the local markets. There is a very good chance that you will have had enough of CIS food by the time you actually leave.

Russia

The typical Russian meal will start with *zakuski* (hors d'oeuvres) which invariably include a tomato salad, other cold vegetables and slices of cold meat. At this point the wealthy eat caviare, and the foolish drink loads of vodka. Zakuski may be followed by soup, usually watery and rather tasteless. Bread comes in two varieties: either brown with a distinctive, slightly bitter taste, or white with a lack of taste altogether but with an intriguing physical structure that ensures that literally no crumbs are released when you break it. The choice of main course is limited, but the most famous Russian creations are Chicken Kiev and Beef Stroganov. In the absence of these you can expect some kind of meat – it is usually called 'bifstek' or 'cutlet', may be covered in breadcrumbs (how did they make them?), and there's a fair chance that it will be accompanied by some comprehensively overcooked cabbage. If you are lucky there may also be potatoes, sliced, as if to resemble chips.

Uzbekistan and Kazakhstan

As you head south on the train you will notice a change in food style. Most local people tend to bring their own food and buy more as they go along rather than use the restaurant car, and this is easy enough to arrange. Thus expect picnic lunches in your carriage every day. Usual constituents include bread, huge chunks of cheese, sausage (*kalbassah*), green salads, heaps of tomatoes and cucumbers and fruit (try to wash anything you buy from station stalls in water from the samovar). Vodka is a common aperitif. As you get further south, progressively less Russian' food starts appearing: the bread soon becomes huge unleavened discs (*non*), samosas (*sam-sar*), filled with meat and vegetables are hawked; huge numbers of melons are consumed, along with other seasonal fruits. Keep an eye out for the more unusual foods for sale: snake fish (*solnaya riba*) might make an appearance and is definitely something to look out for. These fish are opened up and smoked until thoroughly dry; they look like leather and taste like rough smoked salmon – wonderful. One to avoid like the plague is *salo*, which may be offered to you by English speakers as 'pig'. If you are foolish enough to accept some of this Ukrainian speciality then you deserve all that's coming to you: 'pig' consists of huge gelatinous lumps of congealed pork fat occasionally preserved with salt. It looks like sweaty white cheese and even the Chinese think twice before trying it. Beware!

The southern states' specialities, of course, do not feature pork. At the top of the list of regional favourites will always be *pilov*, which seems to be a catch-all phrase for any number of combinations of rice and mutton. It's said to have been invented by Alexander the Great, who needed a nourishing meal for his men which was light enough for them to carry. Some believe that only men are capable of making it properly. As popular as pilov, though, is the ever-present *shashlik* (mutton kebab), grilled in the open air and sold by the skewer in markets everywhere. This is the easiest food to eat in Uzbekistan, but take it from one who knows – shashlik for every meal for more than a day or two is guaranteed to upset your internal economy. Often there will be bread and onions at the stall; the liquid poured over the kebabs is vinegar. Other popular dishes that crop up all over the place are *bilini* (small meat-filled pancakes which are often eaten for breakfast), *shoorpa* (soup), *tushsvera* (meat dumplings served as starters) and *dim lama* (a meat and potato main dish).

DRINKS

Non alcoholic

In Russia tea predominates, invariably served black. Coffee is fairly common too but is usually quite revolting. You can stock up on tea, coffee, whitener (eg Coffeemate) and other beverages for the journey in Moscow but these may be tricky to find elsewhere. Mineral water is common and is safe, though check the seal if you are worried. Western soft drinks are available from black market vendors and hotel beriozka shops but are almost always warm. In the far south green tea is the drink, and while native Russians may sweeten their tea with jam, in the south it comes straight. To get served at a tea shop it may be necessary to clear someone else's table, taking the pot to be refilled and rinsing out the cups yourself. These tea shops are the best places for a rest, usually half full of the town's elders sitting, chatting and playing backgammon. Very mellow.

Alcoholic

Fred Burnaby, in *A Ride to Khiva*, notes that 'to get drunk lowers a man in the opinion of the public in our country. It is rather a feather in his cap in Russia'. The national drink, of course, is vodka. Extreme caution is advised when drinking with locals, as they take a peculiar pride in demonstrating that they can drink well beyond the point when you pass out. Vodka should be drunk in small shots, straight, and followed immediately by food (tomato or cucumber is ideal). Beer (*piva*) is also popular and may be brewed locally; return the bottles to the vendor to get your deposit back. Wine is almost always sickly sweet but Russian 'champagne' is much better and is also very cheap. A less alcoholic drink is *kvas*, sold by street vendors from huge tanks on wheels. Believe it or not it is made from bread; people either love it or hate it. Finally, in Kazakhstan and Uzbekistan even the most staunch non-drinker ought to try *koumiss*, the traditional drink of fermented mare's milk which Marco Polo recommended. It is available in most markets – look for the milk churns.

WHAT TO DO IN THE EVENING

Go to bed. Apart from in Moscow, and to some extent Tashkent and Almaty, don't expect anything to be going on unless there is some sort of a tourist show. Restaurants and bars tend to close very early in the south, so if you want a drink later on it will have to be from the hotel bar, if that's open. It is worth going to the cinema, though: moviegoing is very popular throughout the CIS and there are numerous cinemas. Many, however, appear to be showing only Stallone or Schwartzeneggar films. These films are dubbed but luckily for foreigners the word 'Aaaarrgh' is the

The Russians also cry

Forget Marx: religion isn't the opium of the people. Television is. Witness the effects of *The Rich Also Cry*. Despite being a soap opera, 13 years out-of-date and in Mexican, this 249-show epic really hit the spot. For its entire run, shops and restaurants throughout the CIS closed when it was on; work in the Kremlin ground to a halt; there were even reports of the shelling along the front line of the bloody Georgian-Abhakzian conflict stopping. They took it seriously? You bet: one woman stabbed her husband to death after he made a rude remark about the heroine. 200 million viewers tuned in – over 70% of the entire CIS.

Currently hoping to duplicate this effect is a small production office in London, where they have been working on a British Foreign Office funded programme called *Crossroads*. This soap, created by one of the inventors of *East Enders*, is designed to ensnare viewers in tales of a soapworthy nature whilst actually mercilessly spreading capitalist propaganda. In one edition, for example, an old woman is chastised by her son for hiding all her savings away rather than keeping them in the bank. Topical? Absolutely. The action takes place in Almaty. But Russians should not feel left out: the Foreign Office is also sponsoring a radio soap set in Moscow with exactly the same aim. What **would** Lenin have said?

same in Russian, so none of the original contexts are lost. Between September and May the Bolshoi performs in Moscow. Tickets are available from Intourist at around US$50. It's cheaper to get a Russian friend to buy a ticket for you or you could go a couple of hours early and haggle with the touts on the steps outside the theatre. Make sure that the ticket you buy is a valid one and for a performance of the Bolshoi company, since many companies dance at the Bolshoi Theatre.

SHOPPING

It is probably not wise to bank on buying too much in the CIS. If you do track something down, actually buying it can be something of a challenge: first find out the price by asking an assistant, then go the cash desk to pay and then take the receipt back to the counter to pick up the item. This is not to say, though, that there is nothing worth buying at all: on the contrary, there are numerous shops selling all kinds of pricey luxuries.

Beriozkas and 'Western' stores

A beriozka is a retail outlet normally located in a hotel (usually the former Intourist hotel). Because the items on sale are sold almost entirely to tourists, prices are about the same as they would be in the West, and it is possible to buy Western-made consumer goods here, from biros to soft drinks and newspapers. Beriozkas also sell Russian goods including souvenirs, guidebooks, maps and food; expect to find vodka and caviare either here or on the black market. Joint venture stores are opening gradually across Moscow (an example being the Irish Centre on New Arbat St) and these offer Western household items at standard Western prices, which means that only the wealthy Russians can afford them.

Street markets

Probably better value, though less legal, is the black market trade in virtually anything imaginable: kiosks throughout Moscow are crammed with Western cigarettes, alcohol and confectionery. These should be paid for with loads of roubles, although you might be asked for hard currency. In a beriozka or an upmarket store you are unlikely to get ripped off, but prices will be high. On the black market, you take your chances. Note that maps and postcards will also be available outside beriozkas. Check the dates on street maps, as names have been changing recently and it is easy to buy something which is out-of-date. Bargaining is certainly in order.

Shopping in Kazakhstan and Uzbekistan

Although you may be asked for Western currency in the south there are so few tourists that no-one really expects it, and many people you meet

---

(Opposite) 'I **inhale**, you know'. A young lady in Dunhuang with plenty to smile about.

may be interested to see what a US$1 bill, for example, looks like. Prices are in local currency and it is generally easy to buy black market merchandise simply because local people just can't afford it. Thus vodka, both Western and Russian, is openly sold on the fringes of markets along with other rarities including Coke, Diet Coke, chewing-gum and Western cigarettes. Prices are still reasonably cheap for some products (imported vodka may work out at £4-5/US$6-7.50 per litre). Otherwise haggling is the order of the day in the markets but generally if an item is stuck behind glass and wearing a price-tag don't bother arguing.

Opening hours

Large stores are open from 09.00 to 20.00 and closed on Sundays. Smaller shops, kiosks and markets can be open virtually any time, and often may open very early and then close early, too. The best time to shop in Uzbekistan and Kazakhstan is probably mid-morning, when the early rush is finished yet everything is still open and it is reasonably cool.

THINGS TO BUY

Handicrafts

In Russia *matrioshka* dolls (sets of hollow wooden dolls which fit inside one another) reign supreme as **the** souvenir and consequently they are to be found everywhere at varying prices. Perhaps more interesting than the usual matrioshka family would be the sets of political leaders, which will display their age as new premiers come and go. Other favourite souvenirs include lacquer boxes and ornaments, balalaikas and headscarves. Everyone ought to buy some real Russian vodka, of course. Many souvenir stalls are cashing in heavily on the decline (or not?) of communism, with all sorts of memorabilia for sale: Red Army or Navy uniforms are common, as are cap badges, badges of rank and medals. It would probably be best to conceal medals when you are leaving the country as they may be classified as 'cultural relics' and confiscated at customs. Cheaper and potentially more valuable souvenirs are postcards or miscellaneous memorabilia of communist heroes; these used to be incredibly common but are now increasingly rare.

In Uzbekistan and Kazakhstan there is not much of a tourist market but local handicrafts can be good souvenirs. Woven cloth like carpets or wall hangings can be excellent. Antique wall hangings from Shakrisabz (see p151) in particular can be surprisingly valuable. Be careful when buying 'antiques', partly because they are likely to be less valuable than the shop-keeper says, and partly because if they are genuine antiques it is illegal to export them.

(Opposite) A quiet corner at the Sunday Market in Kashgar, Xinjiang province. About 50,000 of the region's inhabitants descend on the town once a week to buy, sell, or just gossip.

Other items

You are unlikely to find books in English outside Moscow, although there may be some (particularly guidebooks) on sale at hotels. English language copies of *Pravda* and a few Western newspapers may be available in Moscow. There is a thriving market in bootleg cassettes; it seems that techno music has arrived, although some 'real' music is available. The Beatles and Pink Floyd are popular, and small-time vendors sell cheap recordings (around £1/US$1.60), ideal for those whose consciences are not bothered at the prospect of cheating money from those paupers in the Western music industry. Listen to tapes before you buy as quality varies. It is probably best not to shop for clothes in the CIS, although many visitors may want to buy furry 'Moscow hats'. The ethnic stuff you see in the south (boots, thick jackets etc) is mostly available in Xinjiang, China.

SPECULATION

Everyone you meet in the CIS would like your hard currency. Some may offer to buy it, and in Uzbekistan you are likely to get much better rates on the black market than you would in banks. In Russia and Kazakhstan, however, you may find that the black market rate is little, if any, better than the official rate. If you are going to use the black market, be careful.

The situation is slightly different with Western items, for it is no longer possible to rock up with a couple of pairs of Levis and a Bart Simpson T shirt and use them to pay for your holiday. The fact that there is less money around means that very few people can afford to pay a reasonable price for something Western. You would doubtless get a better deal bringing in Western stuff and exchanging it for souvenirs in the markets. An excellent way of cementing friendships is by giving small tokens to people who have been helpful to you – classy toiletries go down well with Soviet women, and everyone loves instant coffee and sweets.

CRIME

Russia and the CIS have seen a massive upsurge in crime in the last few years. Protection rackets seem to be at the head of this and Western news programmes periodically carry reports of profiteering and organised crime syndicates. You are unlikely to see any of this. The CIS is a safe place to visit but as with all other countries it is worth taking simple precautions: for a start, leave all your valuables at home. Don't wave your walkman or flashy camera around, and when leaving your hotel room in the morning make sure that no small trinkets are left out; try not to wander about after dark, and take very good care of your money. Remember that digging cash out of your moneybelt in public demonstrates to observers that you are a walking bank. Be careful in hard currency bars and restaurants, where pickpockets will know that you have money.

PART 3: CHINA

Facts about the country

GEOGRAPHICAL BACKGROUND

The People's Republic of China is the third largest country in the world today after Russia and Canada. Incorporating 9.6 million square km of land it stretches 5500km from north to south and 5200km from east to west, making it approximately the same size as Europe. Its borders reach across some 20,000km – with Russia and Mongolia to the north, Korea, the Yellow and East China Seas to the east, Vietnam, Myanmar (Burma), India, Bhutan and Nepal to the south, and Pakistan, Afghanistan, Tajikistan, Kirghistan and Kazakhstan to the west.

Despite its vast size, however, only around 10% of its land is agriculturally viable and a recent census indicated that over 50% of the 1.2 billion population lives in urban areas. This figure increases annually as poorer workers seek better pay and living conditions in the cities. Great Britain would fit into China some 102 times and each female in the country would have to produce 39 children in order to populate the land to its current level should this actually happen.

Climate

The sheer size of the PRC ensures that there will always be extreme climatic variations here. Highland plateaux in Sichuan province or Tibet, for example, are frost-free for only two months per year, whilst in the far south temperatures rarely drop below 16°C (62°F). The eastern half of the country is particularly wet because the natural elevation of the land tends to draw in moist air from the Pacific; in the Pearl Valley, for example, the average rainfall per year is over 2000mm. In the far west of the country, however, Xinjiang province is lucky to see 100mm, and the deserts here receive considerably less than this. The greater part of the country has a temperate climate with rain falling mostly in the summer (May-October) and dry winters caused by the high pressure system which circulates over Siberia and Mongolia.

Transport and communications

There are 1,100,000km of roads in China, and the major percentage of freight travels across the country by truck (those who take the bus from Urumqi to Kashgar will witness this movement). Yet despite the estimated 4.4 million lorries in use, only 0.2% of all passenger vehicles in the

PRC are actually owned by private individuals; the rest all go by bicycle. Railways are the major long-distance people carriers and there are some 53,000 km of track, of which about one fifth is electrified. The Beijing-Lanzhou line connects with the Trans-Siberian railway, and it seems likely that the Almaty to Urumqi link will become the major route for freight heading west as the Central Asian situation improves. Air travel is popular amongst the wealthier Chinese but is rarely used for cargo, being too expensive. The inland waterway system is extensive, carrying some eight million tons of freight per year (about half of the total taken by rail).

The economy

After years of exploitation by Chinese and foreigners alike, the Chinese economy is well on the road to recovery. Since the Revolution, economic planning has taken the form of Soviet-style five and ten year plans which, despite a couple of setbacks (Great Leap Forward and Proletarian Cultural Revolution – see p74) have been very effective in putting the country back on its feet. Mao Zedong, much denigrated in the West, is to be thanked for this. Since his death, further steps have been taken to put China on a par with the West: in 1978 an 'Open Door' policy was announced, decentralising the economic system and enabling foreign investors to put money into China for the first time since the British had done their best to create a race of drug addicts in the 19th century (see p72).

The result was rapid economic growth. In 1985 further measures were announced, offering more reductions in the state monopoly and a continuing trend towards private enterprise, with wages varying according to performance and prices fluctuating according to demand. In 1993, the yuan was floated. Growth rates are impressive: there was a 31% increase in exports in 1994 alone. 1996 saw the start of the 9th Five Year plan, together with a new measure: the 15-year 'Long-term Target for 2010': basically a measure to ensure that progress continues at its current rate.

But it's not all good news. Rapid boom carries with it the risk of rapid bust: the Chinese economy has grown so fast that there are periods when the economy 'overheats'. To quell this risk, draconian measures are imposed from time to time (1993-5, for example) to control inflation.

HISTORY

Prehistory

It is often difficult to separate fact from myth in Oriental history but we can be sure that China has been populated since at least 500,000 BC. (Some evidence suggests human activity dating right back to 2,000,000 BC). The discovery of Peking Man at the Zhoukoudian site south-west of Beijing in 1921 highlights this and despite the fact that what remained of Peking Man himself (a part of his skull only) was unfortunately 'lost' during the Japanese invasion, scientists believe that he was a hunter, cooking meat and also eating nuts and berries. Certainly, by 50,000 BC he was widespread throughout China; gathering rather than hunting was now the preferred method of collecting food.

The Neolithic era dawned here between the 7th and the 5th millennia BC, well ahead of other parts of Eastern Asia and at least 5000 years before Japan. Artifacts are fairly common, the Banpo site near Xi'an being a good source (see p232), hence we have a fairly accurate idea of what sort of pottery and tools were being used. Agriculture arrived between 6000 and 2500 BC and around this time scientists have identified two types of farming: the green vegetable cultivation of the north, and the rice domination of the south. By 3000 BC pigs, dogs, cattle and water-buffalo were domesticated. Bronze casting had made its appearance by 2000 BC.

The first dynasties

Chinese legend tells that the first dynasty, the Xia (2200-1800 BC), was founded by Yu, who appeared after a great flood. Historians aren't convinced, generally agreeing that the first dynasty was the Shang (traditionally 1700/1600 BC to 1200/1100 BC), whose capital was eventually settled at Anyang. They were a superstitious people who divined by the use of oracle bones. Tomb excavations have revealed evidence of human sacrifice at funerals.

The Shang were overthrown by the Zhou around 1100 BC. During the early period ('Western Zhou') their capital was at Hao near modern Xi'an, while later on ('Eastern Zhou') it was moved to Luoyi, near Luoyang. The Zhou culture was not dissimilar to that of the Shang but its historical conditions were: subject to barbarian attack from the north, the capital was moved, and so began the 'Spring and Autumn' and the 'Warring States' periods. In both, Zhou power was dissipated to leave numerous separate states, each fighting for its own supremacy. During this period iron casting (c500 BC, 1500 years before Europe), mounted cavalry, the crossbow and Confucius (551-479 BC), all made their appearances, although the feuding continued until the foundation of the first 'imperial' dynasty, the Qin (221 BC). During this reign many of the traits we find in later dynasties were laid down: standardisation of weights and measures, universal script for official documents, organised judicial system etc. Stretches of earthen ramparts were linked, forming what was to become the Great Wall.

The great Han dynasty

The Qin dynasty lasted only 15 years, however, and after inter-factional fighting Liu Bang emerged in 206 BC to adopt the title, 'Han', and so start one of the great dynasties. Characterised by territorial expansion, intelligent emperors, Confucianism and progress generally, this period was a golden age in Chinese history. In the middle of the dynasty, however, high-ranking official Wang Mang seized power to create the Xin ('New') dynasty, although this lasted for just 14 years before Han power was restored. The Han dynasty is split into sections before and after the Xin, these being, respectively, the Western and Eastern periods, depending on the location of the capital (Chang'an and Luoyang). With the fall of the Han in 220 AD China was once again split up, this time for four centuries, during the so-called Three Kingdoms, Northern and Southern, and Jin dynasties. This period is noted for its regional feuding and for the occasional invasions of barbarians from the north. Buddhism, introduced during the Han dynasty, began to flourish, and literature and science made great leaps, too, for despite the fighting large areas of China did experience prolonged periods of peace.

Reunification; the Sui and Tang dynasties

China was finally reunited by Yian Jian ('Wendi'), a good ruler despite the fact that he was notably subject to fits of rage and, on occasion, would personally beat government officials to death. Under his reign civil service, tax collection and the legal system were revamped, and he constantly strove to increase the size of his empire. However his (Sui) dynasty lasted only for a brief period before collapsing in 618 AD to be followed by the great Tang dynasty (618-907 AD). The Tang is now looked upon as a great era: its two capitals, Luoyang and Chang'an, attracted trade and traders, ensuring a constant influx of new ideas. The empire expanded right up to modern Afghanistan and Central Asia and culture flourished along with all aspects of science. Buddhism was still

Chinese dynasties

Xia		2200-1800 BC
Shang		c1700-1200 BC
Zhou	Western Zhou	c1200-771 BC
	Eastern Zhou – Spring & Autumn Period	771-c475 BC
	– Warring States Period	c475-221 BC
Qi		221-206 BC
Han (Western)		206 BC – 9 AD
Xin		9-23 AD
Han (Eastern)		23-220 AD
Three Kingdoms, Northern & Southern, Jin Dynasties		220-581 AD
Sui		581-618 AD
Tang		618-907 AD
Five Dynasties and Ten Kingdoms		907-960 AD
Song	(Northern)	960-1126 AD
	(Southern)	1127-1279 AD
Yuan		1279-1368 AD
Ming		1368-1644 AD
Qing		1644-1911 AD

the overriding influence and it was during the Tang that Xuan Zang (602-664 AD, see p192) made his pilgrimage to India. Unfortunately by the mid 8th century the dynasty was in a decline. It fell in 907 AD, leaving China fragmented again.

Five Dynasties and Ten Kingdoms; the Song dynasty

The following period of disorientation, known as the Five Dynasties and Ten Kingdoms period, officially lasted for 50 years but was actually longer than this, for feuding began well before the end of the Tang and really ended later, with the final submission of the south to the Song dynasty in 975 AD.

Song was founded by a military leader of one of the Five Dynasties who managed to unite the majority of the warlord-run states. It featured rapid military, economic and technical growth, and some see it as the formative period for the later imperial era; education, taxation and civil service examinations were restructured. Yet the seat of power moved south in 1127 at the threat of more barbarian invasions from the north, and thus we find the Northern and Southern Song periods. The north, meanwhile, from 1127 onwards, was ruled by invaders who set up, respectively, the Liao, Western Xia and Jin dynasties.

The Mongol invasion and the Yuan dynasty

The Mongol arrival swept the country clean of its divisions but this was a gradual process; Genghis Khan started it with the unification of the northern tribes in 1206, and the conquest and reunification of China was only completed under his grandson, Kubilai Khan, 75 years later to form the Yuan dynasty. Although different areas were disputed among the Mongol princes, China under Kubilai was the largest single country the world had ever seen. It is this China that Marco Polo writes about, for the Pax Mongolica meant that the East was under one rule, hence travel was reasonably easy. The Mongol capital was at Beijing, and the population in 1340 was 60-80 million. The Silk Route flourished during this period as international trade boomed; the despatch postal service was introduced, facilitating fast communications throughout the empire. Gunpowder was invented and astronomy took great steps forward; at this time China's technical level was on a par with, if not ahead of, that of the West.

The fall of the Yuan; the Ming dynasty

Unfortunately the Mongols were given to feuding among themselves and the dynasty collapsed in 1368. It was immediately replaced by the Ming, founded by one-time peasant Zhu Yuanzhang, with its capital at Nanjing. Steps were taken to improve the lot of the farmers, and the old Confucian ethic which constituted the basis of civil service recruitment (thus holding considerable sway in the practice of government) was resurrected.

Most of the traces of the Great Wall that we see today date from this peri-od. Although China was still developing, its rate of progress was slowing and it was certainly not keeping up with that of the West now. The main themes of the Ming dynasty, particularly in its later years, were stagna-tion and isolation. The end came with popular rebellions in the north-west in 1644; seeing chaos prevailing, the Manchurian chieftain, Dorgon (1612-1650), marched straight into Beijing (supposedly he was invited to cross the Wall by a Chinese general) in June 1644 to form the Qing dynasty (1644-1912).

Qing and the opium problem

This period really illustrates China's decline as a result of Western inter-ference. Although the early part of the dynasty was a period of great pros-perity, this was mainly thanks to the efficiency of three particularly strong emperors from 1661 to 1799. After the death of Qianlong in 1799 gov-ernment corruption increased and foreign opium began coming in, heralding the collapse of the economy – already weakened by lengthy military excursions. A ban on opium imports in 1896 did nothing to stem the flow, for the East India Company simply sold it to independent traders who smuggled it in. As addiction became widespread demand rocketed and from an average of 4000 chests per year before 1829, the nation's intake leapt to 19,000 in 1830 alone. Attempts to suppress opium imports by force (the burnings in Canton in 1819, for example) led to the Opium Wars with Great Britain, each of which ended with ignominious defeat for the Chinese and huge indemnities for them to pay.

Internal confusion – the Taiping and Boxer rebellions

Opium and foreign traders weren't the only problems: the economy was in tatters following a series of natural disasters, and silver was pouring out of state coffers into the pockets of foreign governments. There was also a series of popular uprisings, the most famous of which were the Taiping Rebellion and the Boxer Movement. Taiping was led by one Hong Xiu Quan who believed he was Jesus' younger brother and man-aged to gain enough support in the south to occupy Hankou and Nanjing in 1853, the latter of which was to become the capital of his 'Heavenly City of Great Peace'. His rebellion was suppressed only in 1864, with Western assistance.

The Boxer Rebellion was more serious both for the Europeans and the Chinese. This uprising originated in the north around 1900 as a protest against Manchurian rule and foreign exploitation. Although they had no weapons but their 'harmonious fists', the Boxers believed themselves impervious to Western bullets. Encouraged by the cruel Empress Dowager CiXi they laid siege to the foreign legation in Beijing, having first killed a number of foreign missionaries. The Westerners managed to hold out until reinforcements arrived on 4 October 1900, whereupon they occupied the city and wreaked havoc wherever they found anti-foreign feeling. CiXi, for her part, fled to Xi'an. Western governments imposed the Peace Protocol in 1901 involving yet another indemnity from China, this time so big that even foreigners recognised that it was too high and offered to spend it on the education of Chinese students abroad.

Acceleration towards revolution

Meanwhile China was being divided up between the Western powers, including some callous acts on behalf of the Russians who, fearing uprisings in territory ceded to them in 1860, started slaughtering the local Chinese and then seized Manchuria. (This, incidencitally, was to become one of the causes of the 1904-5 Russo-Japanese war). The Qing dynasty was falling apart. CiXi, having herself usurped the throne, had juggled with the line of accession so that her five-year old nephew, Guangxu, became the heir whilst she kept control. Even when he succeeded her in 1875 she kept the real power and eventually had him imprisoned in the Summer Palace in Beijing. She died in 1908, and Pu Yi was proclaimed emperor at the tender age of two.

In 1905 the force for change inside the country found vent in the formation of the Tongmenhui, the Chinese Revolutionary Party, by Dr Sun Yat Sen (1866-1925). This party later formed the foundation of the Kuomintang, the Nationalist Party. There was a brief coup, and on 12 February 1912 General Yuan Shi Kai proclaimed the abdication of Pu Yi (still only six years old), Sun Yat Sen having handed to him, under pressure, his presidency of the 'republic'. The Kuomintang was not the only people's party, however. The Chinese Communist Party, fuelled by the USSR, held its first congress meeting on 1 July 1921. In 1922, at Stalin's insistence, it joined forces with the Kuomintang. The alliance was short-lived, for undermining their unity was a disagreement concerning the exact nature of the revolution itself. Supposedly a telegram from Stalin to the CCP ordering them to seize power from the Kuomintang was intercepted by the Kuomintang leader, Chiang Kai Shek, in 1927. Ruthless persecutions of Communists followed and China, already fragmented and controlled by warlords, had a civil war on its hands.

Civil war and the Japanese invasion

The Communists were severely outnumbered by the Kuomintang at the outset of the ensuing war and barely managed to survive. They relied on guerrilla tactics and withdrawals, and eventually set up camps south of the Yangtse River in Jiangxi Province.

After heavy losses there they decided to retreat to a safe haven in Yan'an, Shaanxi Province, resulting in the 'Long March' of 1934-5. This is something of a misnomer as there was not one long march but rather a series of them. Mao Zedong, by now a recognised luminary in the CCP, led one group which covered 9600km at a rate of 27km per day. Only about one-tenth of the original marchers actually made it to Shaanxi. Of 100,000 starters only 8000 survived.

By this time, there were other things to worry about: Japan had marched into Manchuria and installed Pu Yi as puppet emperor of the state of Manchukuo, declaring its independence in 1932. In 1935 the CCP issued a statement appealing for a united front against Japan but Chiang Kai Shek did not respond. On 12 December 1936 he was seized by his own men in the so-called 'Xi'an Incident' (see p227) and CCP leaders flew in to persuade him to fight the Japanese instead of them. He agreed, although there is some debate as to how much effort he really put into fighting the Japanese. Military and economic aid was sent by the Allied Forces during the 1939-45 war together with troops under US General 'Vinegar Joe' Stillwell, who was not at all impressed with the Oriental war effort. At Chiang's request he was removed from office in 1944.

Communist victory and the Liberation

It didn't take long for the civil war to start again after the Japanese surrender but this time the Communists gained the upper hand. Mao Zedong was convinced that the real power lay in the hands of the rural peasants and by mobilising them he eventually won, forcing the Kuomintang to flee to Taiwan, taking with them as much of the state funds and antiquities as they could carry.

Mao, now officially leader of the CCP, proclaimed the foundation of the People's Republic of China on 1 October 1949 ('the Liberation') and immediately set about trying to repair its wrecked economy. With Soviet aid, he was extremely successful and by 1952 it was back to its pre-war levels. Mao's ambitions for China, however, led him to initiate the 'Great Leap Forward' in May 1958. This was an ambitious but ill-fated attempt to stimulate industry and the economy generally by organising workers into self-managing communes. Unfortunately, for a variety of reasons (perhaps Mao should have heeded Soviet warnings that the communes idea was Utopian) the Great Leap was a disaster. Its failure, together with a series of natural disasters and the withdrawal of Soviet aid, resulted in catastrophic famines. It has been estimated that 16.5 million Chinese died in the three years around 1960, and some statisticians claim that China's population actually decreased during this period.

Cultural Revolution

Mao became disillusioned. His failures at home, together with the new policy of coexistence between the USSR and the USA convinced him that something was wrong. As he saw it, communism had been corrupted, and something had to be done to restore the revolutionary spirit. As he said, 'You learn to swim by swimming. You learn to make revolution by making revolution'. Thus he launched the Great Proletarian Cultural Revolution (1966-9) to set the country back on its feet.

The revolution was a catastrophe. Its first step involved the removal of the 'Capitalist Railroaders' from the CCP. This was shortly followed by the removal of anything which could be seen as authoritarian or in any way representative of the old order, because it was here that the bourgeois influences were supposedly manifested. Temples and cultural relics were destroyed as Mao stirred up the country's youth: 'To rebel is justified', he declared, 'bombard the headquarters'. Schools and universities were closed, their teachers publicly humiliated and sent for 're-education' (usually manual labour in the country). The students formed the Red Guards and travelled (for free) the length of the country, leaving trails of destruction wherever they went and advocating 'Mao Thought'. As their slogan went, 'Everything that does not reflect the thought of Chairman Mao must be burned'. China was turned upside-down.

Mao's decline and the rise of Zhou Enlai

Whether Mao really believed in what he was doing or whether he was simply trying to consolidate his own political power is debatable. By 1968, however, the tide was beginning to turn and a new line of tolerance and moderation came in, most closely associated with Zhou Enlai, who had somehow escaped the party purges. The violence ended only in 1972-73 though, and by this time premiers Liu Shaoqi and Lin Bao had disappeared (the latter in a plane crash after an alleged coup attempt). Power gradually turned to Zhou, who helped to thaw relations with the West, inviting President Nixon to visit in 1972. Universities and schools reopened and the obsession with Maoism began to fade. China (rather than Taiwan) was accepted for the first time into the United Nations Assembly.

With Zhou Enlai's death in 1976 a public protest known as the Tiananmen Incident once again threatened public security. In early April Tiananmen Square began to fill up with wreaths and flowers for Zhou; Mao (correctly) considered this to be partly a statement of support for the emerging conservative leader Deng Xiaopeng, who had been discredited during the Cultural Revolution but rehabilitated in 1973. When the military tried to remove wreaths from the square, violence broke out. Deng was removed from office and another premier chosen. His first step, following Mao's death later that year, was to depose the so-called Gang of Four (including his wife Chiang Ch'ing), responsible for much of the underhand dealing behind the Cultural Revolution. They were given a show trial and finally convicted in 1981. China badly needed scapegoats for the lost decade.

The Democracy Movement and the Tiananmen Massacre

With the failure of the next Five Year Plan Deng Xiaopeng was once again rehabilitated, and he began to assume much of the responsibility of government. Foreign trade shot up and in 1980 China joined the IMF and

World Bank. This process of opening up, however, was hindered by the widely televised Tiananmen Square Incident of 1989.

Pro-democracy rallies started in April, leading up to the rally on 4 May which attracted some 50,000 students. Warnings had been given to officials demanding 'genuine dialogue' beforehand but were dismissed as 'naive and impulsive'. The previous day had seen 1000 students commence a hunger strike in Tiananmen Square. Gorbachev arrived for a state visit on 15 May to find over 100,000 protesters there and the Chinese government was embarrassed, particularly when a huge rally with over a million participants took place two days later. Martial law was declared.

By the start of June the authorities' patience had worn thin, and on 3 June 10,000 unarmed soldiers marched to Tiananmen Square, to find their access blocked by throngs of people. Armed police used tear-gas to disperse the crowds, but to little effect. Just before midnight troops opened fire, and heavy artillery fire was reported on the outskirts of the city. At around 1.30am on 4 June soldiers started to fight their way to the centre of the square. A vote was held at 5 am, whereupon student leaders decided to disperse but as they did so they were fired upon; Western media reported that hundreds of unarmed civilians were shot in the back as they attempted to flee. Realistic estimates put the dead at 2000 to 5000 but the Chinese official estimate says 300, and some cadres seriously contended that there had been no casualties at all. Blame was put on 'counter-revolutionaries', and the 'brave' soldiers were praised. Footage supposedly showing vicious attacks on the military by civilians was aired.

Within a month, over 2500 civilians were arrested and charged. A number of executions followed. Foreign reactions were strong, and in parliament the governor of Hong Kong suggested that the British Government had a moral responsibility to allow the three million British passport-holding Hong Kong Chinese access to the UK in 1997. The USSR was non-committal but Gorbachev was later reported as saying that he did not believe student motives to have been 'evil'.

After Tiananmen

Martial Law was lifted in January 1990 and major efforts were made to restore China's lost image abroad. Particularly helpful in this direction was the Chinese support of the US military actions during the Gulf War (China is one of the seven permanent members of the UN Security Council) and their support of the UN peace plans for Cambodia. By the end of 1990 international contacts were more or less back to normal. Deng Xiaopeng retired but retained most of his influence until 1994, when he bowed out owing to increasing ill health. There is still concern over who will replace him as China's senior statesman when he dies (stock markets nearly crashed in 1994 when it was rumoured that he was dead). Western attention still focuses on the East, though: in 1992 George Bush highlighted three areas in which he was unhappy about China, these being its human rights record, its export of goods produced in labour camps and its sale of ballistic missiles to the Middle East. This does not seem to have had much effect: in 1995 the US assistant secretary of state for human rights declared that China's treatment of dissidents had actually worsened over the previous year. The West's concern with human rights in China means that relationships between the two fluctuate wildly: whilst everyone wants a slice of the Chinese markets, no-one wants to be seen to be endorsing their human rights policies. Current opinion about this matter can usually be gained by checking out how close the US is to removing China's 'Most Favoured Nation' status.

There are still periodic outbreaks of national unrest (particularly in Xinjiang) and despite assurances that Tiananmen has been put in the past there is evidence to show that trials of political dissidents continues (nine were given hard labour sentences in a single trial in 1994). Reforms are under way, though; there is no doubt that China in 1997 is a more liberal and democratic place than it was in 1987. Where, exactly, this will lead is anyone's guess.

THE PEOPLE

China is by far the most populous nation on earth, with 1.2 billion people; this number grows by about 13 million (the population of Chile) every year. Traditionally Han Chinese see themselves as the original Chinese race, tracing their lineage back to the successful Han dynasty (206 BC to 220 AD); they constitute about 95% of the population, while the other 5% belongs to any of over 50 ethnic groups. This means that some 60 million inhabitants are looked down upon as non-Chinese.

China's huge population has been a source of worry for some time now and a birth control programme has been operating since 1953, although it wavered rather during the Great Leap Forward and the Cultural Revolution. Originally two children per family was seen as the ideal with a limit of three, but now one is the limit. Larger families are heavily penalised and the pressures on young mothers to conform can be considerable. Ultimately the aim is to limit the population to 1.25 billion by the year 2000, although Western concern has been expressed that the 'one child' policy may lead to cases of infanticide (male children are seen as more desirable than female). In an effort to combat this, rural families are now permitted to have a second child after a certain period of time – provided that their first is a girl.

The country itself is divided into twenty-two provinces, five autonomous regions (plus Hong Kong from July 1997) and three municipalities. The latter are the large cities of Beijing, Shanghai and Tianjin, while the so-called 'autonomous regions' are those populated densely with ethnic minorities (Xinjiang, Inner Mongolia etc). They allow some extra concessions, one of which is the relaxation of birth control regulations for minorities; despite this, numbers remain static.

Government

Since 1982 the National People's Congress has been the highest body of state power. Members are elected every five years and sit annually, and from the NPC is elected the State Council, which consists of the president, vice presidents, secretary-general, heads of commissions and state councillors. Election to the NPC is from the People's Congresses spread across the country. These are held under direct control of the central government. China is the last major bastion of communism but despite events like the Tiananmen Massacre is moving slowly towards more democratic means.

China is most certainly a military force to be reckoned with. ('It seems quite useless to kill the Chinese. It is like killing flies in July': Sidney Smith, 1842). The Chinese army is estimated at three million (compared with the USA's two million) and it does maintain a nuclear arsenal. There are articles in the Western press from time to time when one of these is tried out at the Lop Nor testing site.

Education and social welfare

Well over 180 million Chinese people are illiterate today (no doubt the result of the periods of civil war and, later on, the Cultural Revolution). Since 1976, however, education has been high on the national agenda and now there is a near 100% school attendance rate. Schooling is free and compulsory for six years at the primary stage and three years at the secondary stage. Following the Cultural Revolution, all students went to work in industry for two years before they were eligible for further education. Their academic ability was then coupled with employers' assessments of motivation, both political and practical, to vie for university places. This all changed in 1977 and now university entry is based entirely on results in the entrance exams. Although there are over 1000 colleges, universities and institutes, competition is fierce; since 1985, moreover, further education is no longer free.

China's main health problem this century has probably been opium addiction, for which the British are largely to blame. Following the Liberation in 1949 a major operation was mobilised to purge the country of its drug dependence. This was fuelled by zeal and sheer manpower and was so effective that by 1955 it was claimed that literally no addicts remained. This was only one of a series of crusades against specific problems, however: another example of this type of action was the campaign against bilharzia, a debilitating disease often termed Snail Fever since the parasite responsible develops in snails before passing into the water supplies. Vast numbers of Chinese were mobilised to destroy the snails manually twice a year. It was a typically labour-intensive strategy but it worked, as did other campaigns against lice, mosquitoes, cockroaches and rats.

Traditional Chinese therapies have long been considered archaic by the West but the more researchers investigate them the more they are impressed; this is the case particularly with acupuncture, which is still used in the East for its anaesthetic qualities during surgical operations. Western know-how has flooded in, however, and Chinese medicine now flourishes on a mixture of the two cultures' knowledge. Workers' medical care is usually financed by their employers.

Religion

Confucianism and Taoism are the sources of traditional beliefs in China and with Buddhism form the foundations of Chinese culture. **Taoism**, founded by Lao Tze in the 5th century, posits a sense of all-pervading unity behind objects and their ideal state. This is the Tao or 'Way'. Life should be lived in accordance with the Tao in order to promote oneness and harmony. Various ways of doing this are prescribed, including such diverse disciplines as yoga, meditation, philosophical dispute and magic. **Confucianism** was founded in the 5th century by Confucius himself, who wrote numerous discourses on the art of successful government. Although he was largely unrecognised in his own lifetime his writings were adopted by virtually all Chinese dynasties later as models for civil service training, recruitment and practice. See p201 for information on **Buddhism**.

Since the Liberation China has had an ambivalent attitude towards religion. Despite Mao's 1954 guarantee of the individual's rights to freedom of belief there is considerable evidence of suppression over the last 40 years. The Cultural Revolution stopped all overt religious activity and was responsible for the wholesale destruction of religious centres and symbols. Thus it appears that institutional religion may have suffered fairly severely, although whether this reflects in individuals' beliefs is a matter for debate. Following the trial of the Gang of Four in 1976 religious practices became more open.

Amongst the ethnic minorities, **Islam** is strong with an estimated 12 million adherents. There are about 50 million **Christians** and the evangelical sects are reported to be making new recruits. Whatever the religion, however, virtually all Chinese perform solemn ceremonies of ancestral reverence.

Practical information for the visitor

DOCUMENTS

Those who have booked tours through China should remember to bring all vouchers and receipts necessary. Bring your inoculation certificates as the Chinese border officials often check the health documentation of those entering the country; in practice all that most foreigners can produce are vaccination certificates but they seem happy with these. In China any official-looking document can be helpful in establishing the fact that you are an individual with some serious kudos back home. Identity cards of any sort can be useful as a deposit (eg for bike hire); anything with your photo on it will do (video cards, old library cards, expired passports etc). Don't forget your ticket home, or onwards, from Beijing, or your travel insurance policy and a separate record of your travellers' cheque and credit card numbers. Give a friend or relative copies of all before you leave and then if anything goes wrong they can sort it out for you.

A useful document is a Chinese student/teacher's card, as this will entitle you to get into all tourist sites at a fraction of the normal foreigners' price. Obviously you are entitled to one only if you are actually studying or teaching in China, but there are several places in larger cities which offer to 'procure' fake cards at a price. Many people seem to think that this is worth a try, and will insist that you are foolish not to get hold of one. It is obviously illegal, however, and reportedly some travellers were caught recently in Xi'an, because the local university, unbeknownst to the forgers, had changed the style of its ID cards. A US$100 fine was apparently levied on the offenders

Customs declaration form

In China, as in the CIS (see p52), you are required to fill in a customs declaration form on entry into the country, and technically you must produce the same form on exit. If challenged, you should be able to prove that you still have all your valuables and can account for the money that you brought into the country by showing exchange certificates. In actual fact, with the increasing number of foreign tourists entering the country, and the ease with which money can be drawn on credit cards, it would be very difficult to enforce these rules. There is no guarantee, however, that you won't bump into the one conscientious customs official, so it's best to play safe: keep your currency exchange slips, and if you lose an expensive item like a camera, get a report from the local police. There used to be a rule that you could change back into your own currency only half the

Chinese money for which you have exchange slips. Even if this rule is brought back it shouldn't be a problem (as a tourist you are unlikely to change wads of money in to yuan shortly before trying to leave the country) but it's another good reason to keep your exchange certificates, as two or three of these should prove that you've been playing by the rules.

HOTELS

Check-in requires a passport but they don't keep it, only the slip of paper with personal details they will have given you to complete. As in the CIS you will often not be given a key but a piece of paper which you must present to the floor attendant in order to get into your room.

If you are staying 'upmarket', expect hotels to be of a similar standard to those in the West. Budget travellers don't get it so easy although rooms are generally hygienic if basic. Most budget hotels have dormitories which can hold anything from two to twenty or thirty beds. They are suitably cheap (£2-3/US$3-5) and can be very pleasant, though some people are unhappy about leaving their possessions in a room full of strangers when they go out. If you check into a three- or four-bed room do not be surprised when someone else rocks up at 2am. Equally, if a bed in a three- or four-bed room seems unduly expensive, make it clear that you want only the one bed rather than the whole room to yourself.

Hotel rooms come equipped with wash bowls, spittoons, televisions (sometimes) and plastic slip-on sandals in which you are supposed to potter off to the showers. If it is cold expect high quality eiderdowns. Every room has its own thermos flask which is periodically refilled by the Thermos Lady, and even if the water inside is only tepid it should be safe to drink as it will have been thoroughly boiled recently. If you are unsure, or very thirsty, the hot water still is usually to be found in the communal washroom.

In budget hotels washing facilities are limited: the showers, as often as not, are in a separate block around the back of the building and it may be necessary to take along your room card or a shower token in order to get in. On each floor there will be a washroom with a line of sinks along the wall; it is from here that the ringing noise of hawking and gobbing emanates throughout the morning as the locals brush their teeth and clear their sinuses. Toilets are usually simple holes in the ground with minute partitions between them, occasionally none at all. Toilet paper is available from hotels and department stores but is not provided in toilets, so make sure you have some with you.

CITS, CTS, CYTS

CITS (China International Travel Service) is the organisation which most foreign tourists deal with when they are in China. In fact, however, CTS

(China Travel Service), CYTS (China Youth Travel Service) and FITS (Foreign Individual Travel Service) perform much the same functions and although originally set up to cater for Hong Kong and Taiwan Chinese they will deal with foreigners, too. Tours may be booked from abroad with either CITS or CTS, and 'in house' travel agents' tours may well be run through them when you actually get to China. CITS services are generally expensive and, like Intourist, the company is struggling with its own somewhat dodgy reputation. Like Intourist, they see themselves as a money making business, rather than a tourist information service. It is worth noting that just because CITS is the official tourist organisation this does not mean that their tours will go like clockwork. What you are guaranteed if you book with them, however, is that the difficult organisation will be done for you and that the trip will go as smoothly as is possible at the time. Generally speaking, if you are going with CITS or CTS it is better to join a tour group rather than to book alone, as groups get priority everywhere. Whatever happens, if something goes wrong don't create a scene midway through your tour – you are unlikely to accomplish anything and it will only spoil your holiday; wait until you get back and then try for a refund.

CITS can be useful for the independent traveller, too: in virtually every Chinese town which is open to foreigners there will be an office run by CITS. These offices should be staffed by foreign-language speakers who are qualified to advise and assist tourists, and services offered include tours, interpreters and ticket booking. There are actually some wonderfully helpful and knowledgeable people working here but you're just as likely to run into individuals who appear to be recent immigrants from the Planet Zanussi, having learnt just two words of Chinese: 'Mei Yo'.

Most offices would rather you showed up and booked a place on one of their tours instead of asking difficult questions about independent travel but a lot probably depends on how you approach the representative concerned. When you do encounter CITS be aware that a commission will be charged for booking tickets, and any other services; still, sometimes it's worth paying to save the hassle of going to fetch the ticket yourself. Most budget travellers avoid CITS but it is probably worth sticking your head around the door, if only because they occasionally give away free maps.

PUBLIC SECURITY BUREAU (PSB)

If you get into trouble in China CITS may well help, but will probably refer you to the Public Security Bureau. When something has been stolen try to get a signed official declaration to that effect, partly because customs may want proof that you haven't simply sold all your fancy Western gadgets, and partly because you will need a letter if you want to claim on your insurance when you get back. Visa extension is handled by the PSB and is usually a straightforward procedure which takes as little as ten minutes, although this can vary from city to city. Along this route, if you need to you should try to renew your visa in a provincial capital such as Urumqi, Lanzhou or Xi'an. The visa office in Beijing takes a ridiculously long time and is best avoided.

LOCAL TRANSPORT

Train

Getting around in China is considerably easier than it is in the CIS, if only because the transport systems are fairly used to dealing with foreigners. That is not to say that it is always easy. Foreigners' tickets (which used to be nearly twice the price of locals' tickets) have now been abolished, and there are standard fares. There are even special foreigners' ticket windows in some places (though not many).

To buy a ticket or to get anywhere in China it helps to have your destination written on a piece of paper in Chinese – ask a receptionist or friend in your hotel to do it for you, including date and time of travel, and class if you are buying a train ticket. When you get your ticket it should have the number of the train and the price paid printed on it. Unless you are travelling Hard Seat without a reservation, the ticket should have carriage and seat numbers printed on it too. Always keep your tickets, as you will need to produce them at your destination in order to leave the station.

Rail travel in China

Chinese trains are more user-friendly than those in the CIS, occasionally even running to some form of schedule.

Food is easy to come by: platform vendors hawk snacks and drinks, the restaurant car is reasonable (but expensive at about £1.50/US$2.20 per dish) and box meals are periodically brought through the train. These are usually as good as the dining car fare and under half the price. Standard procedure seems to be to heave the polystyrene container, plus all other rubbish, out of the window.

Chinese trains lag behind CIS ones in the hot water stakes: samovars are rare and often broken, and thus for many Chinese passengers the journey becomes a desperate struggle to find something with which to brew tea in the jam-jars they all carry for this purpose. When supplies run really low watering cans full of boiling water may be brought through the carriages.

The most entertaining way to get around is by Hard Seat (see p13). Much maligned by travellers, this offers all the hustle and bustle of a street market and guarantees monosyllabic conversations the whole way. Long journeys are tiring, though, as there is nowhere to sleep but on the floor, which is invariably carpeted with a thick layer of compost, phlegm and general debris. Tickets may be upgraded once on the train but don't bank on it.

Another delightful quirk is **CITS travel insurance**. If you are in Gansu province you are not allowed to use public buses unless you have this policy, which can be bought from CITS offices, and selected other places for Y30-35. Many people manage to get by without it but you can be sure that the one time that you really need to go somewhere you will be refused a ticket if you haven't got it. The insurance itself was introduced after a Japanese tourist was killed in a bus crash and his parents sued CITS. Gansu is currently the only province on this trip which demands it.

Taxis
Drivers are very unlikely to speak English so get a friend to write down your destination for you. Minibus taxis are available in some places and these are ideal for groups; rickshaws are also common. Before you get in, either negotiate a price or agree to use the meter. Generally speaking, taxi and rickshaw drivers are much keener to get you into their cabs than they are to listen to where you want to go, so make your destination clear or you could be in for a slow, expensive ride while the driver stops at random to ask pedestrians where they think you want to go.

Hitching rides on motorbikes (see Jiayuguan p209) is catching on, but it would be wise to be careful here.

Buses
Chinese public buses are fairly simple to figure out as their routes are marked on most city maps; the problem lies in getting on to the things. As the bus pulls in, its doors open to reveal 80% of China's entire population heaving under tens of thousands of tons of pressure per square inch inside. Despite the fact that half the passengers want to get off, everyone who wants to get on just does. The ensuing struggle can be violent and there is no sympathy for the weak, with grannies and small children often knocked to the floor. If you wait, British style, for the other passengers to get off before you get on, you probably won't make it. Equally, don't bother waiting for the next bus as it will be just as bad: elbow your way on. Chinese buses generally have one or more conductors who sit in the small recesses behind the doors; tell them where you want to go (yes, in Chinese...a note may help here) and try to make it clear that you would like to know where to get off. Those who can't reach the conductor pass their money to the person next to them who passes it on. As with buses in the CIS, if everyone is staring at you and passing you money you are probably right next to the conductor. Numerous foreigners are pick-pocketed on Chinese buses, so do be careful. If you are carrying a large piece of luggage (rucksack etc) it is probably better to take a cab.

Bicycles
By far the best way to get around town is by bike, although in some of the towns in this book, bike hire stalls are difficult to find. You will have

to leave a deposit to rent one (perhaps Y200, or try one of your ID cards) and they should not cost more than a couple of yuan per hour (£0.20/US$0.30). Before you accept a bicycle test it, or you could find yourself paying for its repairs – or yours – later on; ensure that brakes, pedals and wheels all work smoothly. Check that the saddle can't suddenly tip up, or you could be in for a painful ride. Finally, check the bell (no-one cares whether it works or not but you will blend in better if you ring it constantly). Never accept a bike without a lock.

When cycling around town bear in mind that it is an offence to leave a bicycle just lying around in China; there are bike parks scattered around each city and when you fancy a rest you will have to leave your machine in one or it will be confiscated. Generally, bike park attendants give you two metal disks with numbers on them: one stays on the bike and you keep the other so that you can reclaim it later. There will be a small fee (usually Y0.10).

Internal flights

CAAC is the Chinese airline, and it is possible to book internal flights all over China from their office in each town. It has a fairly bad record for cancellations and you should always try to book as far in advance as possible, though don't give up trying if you want to travel very soon, as sometimes it is possible to get seats right up to the last minute. CAAC usually runs a convenient bus service from their office to and from the airport, so it is well worth enquiring about this.

ELECTRICITY

Mains electricity supply throughout China is 220V, and two main plug types seem to be in use: North American style two and three pin plugs.

TIME

China operates entirely on Beijing Time (GMT+8). In reality however, Xinjiang province lags behind by two hours and watches and clocks here may be set either to Beijing time or local time, so it is important to check which you are using when dealing with travel tickets. All timetables work on Beijing time. Note that when you cross the border from Kazakhstan into China you must change your watch from GMT+6 to GMT+8.

MONEY

Despite what you may have heard from hardened travellers about the confusing 'tourist money' system in China, 'Foreign Exchange Currency' has been abolished and tourists and Chinese alike now use 'People's Money' or 'Renminbi' which is abbreviated to RMB. Most businesses and hotels are only allowed to take RMB (airlines may take US$, and top hotels often quote their prices in dollars but apart from this everyone uses Chinese currency).

The basic unit of currency is the *yuan* (commonly called the *kwai*). This is subdivided into 10 *jiao* (which have the nickname 'mao'), and one jiao is in turn divided into 10 *fen*. In practice fen are rarely used, because they are worth so little, although there are still some fen coins and notes in circulation, just to confuse tourists. The largest banknote is the Y100 note after which there are notes for Y50, Y10, Y5, Y2 and Y1, as well as a Y1 coin. There are notes and coins for 5 jiao, 2 jiao and 1 jiao. At the bottom of the scale there are 1 fen notes and 2 fen coins. The current exchange rate is approximately Y8.2 to US$1 and Y12 to £1.

As far as travellers are concerned, since travellers' cheques command a higher rate than the equivalent hard currency, the attractiveness of carrying a wedge of dollars has diminished. This also means that using the black market to exchange money is something of a pointless exercise – not only do you expose yourself to the risk of being robbed, but you don't get an official exchange certificate; you'd get a higher price for travellers' cheques anyway. The only real advantage of having hard currency is that if the local Bank of China is closed hotels will usually change hard currency for anyone, while they are willing to change travellers' cheques only for guests who are staying there. You're probably best off travelling with a small amount of money in hard currency and the rest in travellers' cheques. If you are going to carry hard currency, US dollars are a good bet because they are universally recognised; ensure that they are recent notes which are in pristine condition. American Express is the most commonly recognised brand of travellers' cheque, although other large names are also acceptable.

The best place to change money is the Bank of China (the location of which is marked on each Chinese city map in this book) although larger hotels have exchange counters. Withdrawals on credit card are usually easy to achieve in large cities – again try the main branch of the Bank of China. It's not a good idea to rely on your credit card for cash advances, however, since there are occasional problems with transactions.

Tipping
Official Chinese policy is against tipping and it is common to see signs in hotels reminding you of this. The influx of Western tourists is taking its toll though, and upmarket services often expect it, particularly in the larger cities. Chinese service can be a little on the brusque side; many visitors don't want to tip.

POST AND TELEPHONES
The postal service is generally reliable, though it is worth noting that international mail all departs from Beijing or Shanghai, so if you post

something from Kashgar it will have to go over a thousand miles east before going west. Stamps are sold in post offices and the bigger hotels but they are not gummed; there are pots of glue strategically positioned around post offices.

In 1996 the fee for an international post card was Y2.3. Officially, letters should be addressed with the name of the sender in the top left hand corner. Poste Restante services are generally pretty efficient, and you can usually expect to pay Y1 or Y2 per letter.

International phone calls are easier from China than they are from the CIS but the first place to try is usually the nearest expensive hotel rather than the post office. IDD is available from the major cities.

NATIONAL HOLIDAYS

January/February: two days for the Spring Festival (Chinese New Year)
08 March: Women's Day
01 May: Labour Day
01 October: National Day
Banks are closed on Sunday; museums are frequently closed on Monday.

PRESERVING YOUR SANITY

There are a number of Chinese behavioural quirks which tend to annoy Western visitors, so it would be as well to be ready for these. First, there is the matter of pricing: virtually everything you buy in China will be 'Tourist Price'. Tourist Price can be anything from a little bit more expensive than usual to four or five times the regular price (or more!). In addition, there is a national tendency to short-change visitors. It is best just to get used to the idea of this as there is seldom anything that you can do about it: restaurants, travel tickets, hotel rooms and tourist attractions all work on this inflated price scale and often there is little point in complaining because the whole issue is just accepted.

Next it is worth noting that despite national campaigns to stamp out the habit, the Chinese tend to spit a lot. Spittoons litter most hotel corridors, and the streets are positively slippery with other people's catarrh. As likely as not, when you wake up in a cheap hotel it will be to the sound of four or five individuals hawking in the bathroom, all apparently trying to eject their lungs through their mouths. You will shortly realise why spitting is generally frowned upon in the West – because it is unhygienic – and thus you should expect to have a streaming cold at some point during your stay (hence the Lemsip in 'What to bring').

Attitude
Generally the Chinese are charming, and it is easy to make friends just walking down the street but to the Western visitor some Chinese can

appear incredibly short (in manner I mean, although if you are tall by Western standards you will be very tall by Chinese ones). This is something to do with the Chinese outlook itself, so don't lose your temper as this won't get you anywhere at all.

The phrase budget travellers are most likely to remember from their time in China is almost certainly 'mei yo', which can mean virtually anything, as long as it is negative, from 'There are no rooms free at this hotel' to 'This train is full', or 'Go away – I can't be bothered with a foreigner'. 'Mei yo'-mongers are usually people working in the service industries (shop assistants, bus conductors, hotel receptionists and restaurant waiters). Occasionally the 'mei yo' response comes before you even open your mouth to ask a question, which may mean 'I don't speak any languages apart from Chinese'. Even if you do speak a little Chinese, the chances are that having said 'mei yo', the individual concerned will not listen to you, as he or she will be convinced that you are speaking a language that they do not understand.

This attitude is symptomatic of an outlook found peculiarly in China which appears on the surface to be a stifling of lateral thinking; thus even when you do find someone who will answer your questions the answers you get may well be utterly, obviously, incorrect – and it appears, on the face of it, that this is because the individual concerned can't be bothered to find out the correct ones. Hence many of the answers you receive are 'maybe's; it is very difficult to pin anything down and get a 100% correct, straightforward answer.

Buying a lighter

My musical Mao Zedong lighter was actually the second one I had seen; I was unable to buy the first one, apparently because it contained a flat battery. I went through the possible solutions with the (very charming) shopkeeper who spoke excellent English:

Q: 'Perhaps we could replace the battery?'

A: 'I don't have another battery'.

Q: 'Can you get one?'

A: 'No.'

Q: 'How much is the battery worth? Take the price of the battery off the price of the lighter, and sell me the lighter so that I can go and buy a battery myself.'

A: 'Eh?' Blank astonishment. 'Mei yo.'

Q: 'Sell me the lighter. I will buy it for the full price even though the battery is flat and it doesn't work.'

A: Shakes head vigorously. 'Mei yo.' Places lighter back inside display cabinet.

It's a crude illustration but it does, I think, demonstrate the point. Be prepared for, if not a lack of logic altogether, then a logic that you will be unable to understand. And be patient. Thomas de Quincey wrote of the Chinese character that 'obstinacy – obstinacy like that of mules – is one of its foremost features'. You may agree with him by the time you get back.

Staring

If you do not look Chinese then you can expect to be under public scrutiny from the moment you arrive. In Beijing, where foreigners are common, the problem is not so bad but get further from the mainstream and it becomes apparent. Whatever you do you will be stared at. Heaven help you if you have hairy legs and wear shorts, or any other non-Chinese trait which may be considered interesting. The novelty of a Western person does not seem to have worn off in China, which is a pity because the novelty of being the centre of attention of a group of silent, inquisitive locals soon wears off. Any attempt to indicate that you don't like being stared at will create amusement and generate a larger crowd. The best bet is probably to be overtly friendly: keep some interesting photographs close at hand and produce them (they will be passed around in a frenzy of excitement). Try shaking hands with the more forward, smile and say hello to everyone. Say anything in Chinese. You will still be the centre of attention, of course, but you will have made a lot of new friends. Never lose your temper and keep smiling.

FOOD

After the CIS Chinese food is likely to provoke a near-religious experience. This wears off eventually, though, and some travellers complain that after a few weeks they are getting sick of it. There is, in fact, a lot of variety, it's just that some dishes can be difficult to find, particularly in restaurants frequented by Western travellers. Alternatively, the hotel restaurant may be just the place to find a local speciality which is elusive elsewhere, as is the case with camel's hump in Jiayuguan (see p208). Virtually nothing is off-limits to Chinese chefs, so whether it's snake-meat, horsemeat or whatever, dig in!

The best way to find out what's good is just to ask; there is usually someone around who speaks a little English. All along the Silk Route in China the staple filler is wheat, invariably in the form of pasta, so you can expect noodles galore. Chinese noodles take a variety of shapes and forms, the most flamboyant being the stretch noodles (*ban mien*) which you can see being created throughout the country. They are made by pulling the dough into a long strip, shaking this up and down so that it stretches and then joining the two ends together and continuing; it's very impressive to watch. Aside from noodles, pasta is often made into the ravioli-like *jaotse*, which can be very extravagantly folded before being boiled and then either served fried, or in a soup. Fillings vary but the further west you get the more Islamic China becomes, so don't expect pork in Xinjiang.

Although rice predominates in the south there are numerous rice dishes to be had all along this route: basically you choose the meat or vegetables that you want to be fried with it. Chicken and pork are very popular in the east but lamb is dominant to the west. Be careful with any dishes which involve chilli, as the Chinese notion of 'delicately spiced' and the Western notion of it can be rather different. This is the case particularly with noodle soup, which is the speciality around Lanzhou, where beef is usually the filling, and with Sichuan/Mongolian hotpot. This latter dish consists of wooden skewers of various uncooked meats and vegetables left to boil in a vat of unsavoury-looking water and then painted with chilli sauce; it may be termed *malatang*. It is possible to buy skewers in stalls and to have them cooked for you, or you can find restaurants with little vats of boiling water on each table and cook your own.

Food in Xinjiang province

In the far west, apart from the noodles, the food bears a strong resemblance to that of Kazakhstan and Uzbekistan, which is good news for those who have not yet eaten themselves sick of shashlik. Bread is similar to the unleavened *non* of the CIS and samosas are also to be found here (*sam-sam*). It is interesting to watch these being made, as they are cooked inside the common hollow clay ovens: first the dough is splashed with water and then the raw samosa is slapped onto the inside of the oven where it sticks until it is cooked. A variation on this theme is *lujabee* which is simply spicy fried mince packed inside a bread roll. Generally, wherever you find a stall selling meat-filled samosas or jaotse there will be another close-by which specialises in using the off-cuts, and this will be a good place to try one of the local soups, which are extremely greasy and usually contain a huge lump of meat on the bone.

Snacks

Snacking is easy and cheap in China: try *baotse*, the wonderful steamed dumplings which contain either meat or vegetables or both. They are spongy, white and very filling. The Chinese are fond of sweet potatoes, too (the vast misshapen objects seen on barbecues in the streets; the flesh inside is yellow and tastes like a cross between a baked potato and a roasted sweet chestnut). Hard boiled eggs are sold all over the place, usually picked from their mini-charcoal stoves with chopsticks (a real test to see if you have mastered them!), often having been cooked in tea.

Chinese bread gets progressively more doughy as you head east; there is white bread for sale in railway stations but it tends to be rather spongy and cake-like. Check before you buy that it does not have a sweet filling inside.

There is plenty of fruit around, notably melons and grapes during the mid-late summer; Hami, just to the north-east of Dunhuang, is particularly renowned for its melons, and Turfan's grapes and raisins are supposed to be the best in China.

DRINKS

Non-alcoholic
The staple drink is tea (*cha*) which is always served very weak and with-out milk. Coffee and Western hot drinks are often available in shops or hotels and it is worth buying a small jar of something instant, as eventu-ally you will want something other than tea or hot water. Fizzy drinks and bottled water are available too, though local Chinese brands often aren't up to much. Always check the seals on bottles to ensure that the contents have not been diluted. Keep an eye out for the utterly excellent fresh yoghurt which is sold on street corners throughout the country.

Alcoholic
Chinese beer (*piju*) is excellent and should be quaffed as often as possi-ble. It is sold by the bottle and at train stops it is common to see small children rush into the carriage hunting for the empties; this doesn't stop the passengers simply tossing the bottles out of the window, though, along with the rest of their rubbish. Unlike the beer in the CIS, Chinese beer and soft drinks are often kept in fridges, which makes all the differ-ence on a hot day.

Chinese wine (*putao jiu*) tends to be very sweet, but there is dryer stuff around if you look hard. Watch out for the local clear spirits which are very strong and extremely cheap but rather rough for the Western palate.

RESTAURANTS

Traveller-type restaurants are easy to find throughout this trip and they tend to offer snappy service, English menus and reasonable food at OK prices; what you are paying for, of course, is the convenience factor.

Trying to get a meal in a restaurant where there is no English spoken at all can be tricky. The best thing to do if you don't speak Chinese or have a phrasebook is just to look around and point at someone else's meal to indicate what you want. Unfortunately it's not always as easy as this, though: in some restaurants you will be expected to pay for your meal before you eat and to collect a receipt which you then give to the waiter. The menu will be displayed on the wall but only in Chinese, and the per-son at the ticket desk won't be able to see what meal you are pointing at.

In smaller restaurants it's much simpler, if only because there may well be just the one set dish so that all you have to do is nod; likewise with street vendors. The best places to eat are often the day and night markets, where large numbers of vendors gather, thus offering a wider choice of dishes. Other advantages of eating in markets are that there are fewer (if any) tourists about, and that the food is authentic and very cheap. The disadvantage, of course, is that utensils can be unhygienic, so it's a good idea to rinse chopsticks and bowls with hot water or tea before using them. If you're given disposable chopsticks to use make sure they're unseparated (ie unused). Some travellers take their own chopsticks with them.

SHOPPING

China's shops are much better stocked than those in the CIS. In every town there is at least one large department store selling everything from toothbrushes to electrical goods, and these shops often stock some very high quality products. Making a purchase is also a lot simpler: more like shopping in the West. One good point about these large stores is that prices are fixed, remaining the same even for foreigners. In street markets prices may go up and down, so if you want to buy particular souvenirs it might be worth asking other travellers or Chinese friends how much the item should cost. Try to avoid buying too many souvenirs early on, as they usually turn up cheaper elsewhere.

Bargaining

If bargaining were an Olympic sport, China would probably win gold every year: there is something about the Chinese which enables them to appear utterly unshakeable, and they are often both capable and willing to suggest ridiculous prices for items whilst maintaining blank expressions. The key to bargaining lies in maintaining an aspect of quiet indifference; never reveal that you particularly want something, or all will be lost. While price tags in department stores are unquestionable, the same is sometimes not true of tourist shops, although you may be assured otherwise at first. Often tourist stalls come in groups so it is possible to bargain a price in one stall and then move on to the next one, which will invariably be selling the same stuff, and start the process that much closer to the 'real' price.

Never buy anything on the condition that it will be sent on after you by the shop owner, because if the item does not arrive when you get home you will find that there is nothing that you can do about it. Friendship Stores and major hotels generally prove exceptions to this rule but make a note of their addresses.

Friendship Stores

Originally these were the only shops which sold Western goods, and the fact that only FEC was accepted in them was part of the reason for the growth of the currency black market. These days Friendship Stores often represent mediocre value for money, although the products on sale in them are more or less guaranteed not to be counterfeits. Most of the items will actually be available elsewhere at lower prices, so shop around.

THINGS TO BUY

There are a number of standard souvenirs which tend to be on sale virtually everywhere: Chinese art is often snapped up by foreigners, both calligraphy and watercolours being popular. Most 'tourist' art tends to be cheap (well under £100/US$150), with prices going right down for mass produced hangings but it is possible to buy really high quality work in some places and to pay tens of thousands of RMB for it. Be careful when buying art unless you really know what you are looking for, and if you're buying calligraphy it's always a good idea to try to find out what the characters actually mean. I met a CITS guide who had to explain to one tourist that he had just spent a large sum of money on a sign which simply said 'Toilet'.

Other favourite souvenirs include glass scent bottles with paintings on the inside, *tienshenqiu* (hand exercising balls), carved jade and, in Xinjiang, ornamental knives. Instead of paying a wad of FEC for box sets of calligraphy brushes you would do much better to go to the local art shop and buy the same brushes without the box at a quarter of the price.

There are endless possibilities for those who want to buy something out of the ordinary: Mao memorabilia can make interesting gifts when you get home. Pictures of the man are common, or perhaps a musical Mao lighter is more your style (plays *The East is Red* when open). Also popular are badges, copies of the *Little Red Book*, posters and other miscellaneous items relating to him. Otherwise it might be worth buying things just for the 'Western' brand names: try a shell suit emblazoned with the legend 'Luckbird Enriched for Higher Concentration'.

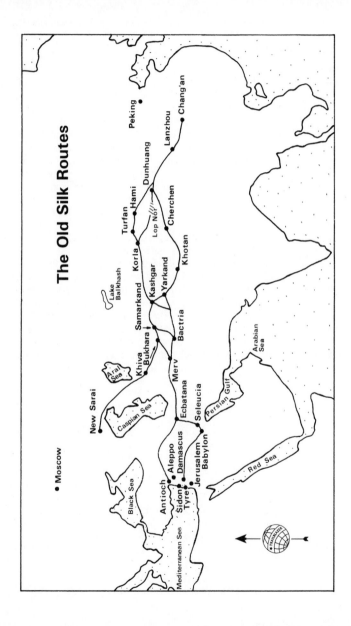

The Old Silk Routes

Moscow

New Sarai

Lake Balkhash

Aral Sea

Caspian Sea

Khiva

Bukhara

Samarkand

Merv

Kashgar

Yarkand

Bactria

Khotan

Korla

Turfan

Hami

Dunhuang

Lop Nor

Cherchen

Lanzhou

Chang'an

Peking

Ecbatana

Seleucia

Babylon

Jerusalem

Damascus

Sidon

Tyre

Aleppo

Antioch

Black Sea

Mediterranean Sea

Red Sea

Persian Gulf

Arabian Sea

PART 4: THE SILK ROUTE

A brief history

First a disclaimer: it is impossible to relate the history of **the** Silk Route. This is because there was no one route; those who envisioned some kind of intercontinental M1 stretching 5000 miles from east to west, then, will be disappointed. Ferdinand von Richtofen, the 19th century German explorer and geography boffin (and, incidentally, uncle of Manfred von Richtofen, the Red Baron) is perhaps to blame for this misconception, for it was he who first coined the term 'Seidestrasse', or Silk Road. The term is misleading once again in that it gives the impression that silk was the only commodity that travelled down the 'Road', when nothing could be further from the truth. While vast quantities of silk did pass from east to west, other products were carried along, too: porcelain, paper and oranges all headed westwards, while the Chinese were receiving horses, glass, gems, cucumbers and wine to name but a few. More significant was the east-west exchange of ideas, which included the diffusion of religions (Buddhism, Islam and Christianity) into the East, while the West was learning from the ancient civilisation that gave it paper, printing and gunpowder.

What we can say is that this exchange and expansion of trade and know-how did occur along a few set routes, each advocated, perhaps at different times, for different reasons. Silk, among other products, was carried from the Far East all the way to the West, and there were a number of common routes which it took. In this generic sense then Richtofen was correct when he referred to the Silk Road. The Road is generally seen as having run from the heart of China, Chang'an (modern-day Xi'an), to the West. How far west? A large proportion of the goods carried either east or west were sold along the way, but we know for sure that the Chinese and the Roman empires were actually trading with one another at least as early as the 1st century BC. Once Eastern products reached key distribution points in the Roman empire, they could easily have been carried throughout Europe; thus in conventional terms the Silk Road is seen as stretching as far west as the cities of Antioch and Tyre on the Mediterranean coast.

Origins
It is impossible to posit a date as to when the Silk Road was first used. Trading across Asia dates right back into prehistory and there's no reason

to believe that some products (spoils of war etc) might not have been carried immense distances from their original homes and then traded even further.

The traditional 'founder' of the Silk Road, however, is often cited as Zhang Qian. In the 2nd century BC, when China was considerably smaller than it is now, the areas to the west of Chang' an were largely uncharted and open to invasion by the barbarian nomadic tribes of the north. The villains in this case, as for the next 800 years, were the dreaded Xiong Nu tribesmen, then in the process of expanding their territory. The Chinese recognised the threat and thus were keen to ally themselves with other 'anti-Xiong Nu' tribes in the area. The chief candidate for an ally at this time was the Yueh Chih tribe, which had recently suffered a terrible defeat at the hands of the Xiong Nu: one chronicler reports that the head of their king had been cut off and used as a drinking vessel.

Zhang Qian's mission

In 138 BC the Han emperor Wu dispatched Zhang and 100 men with orders to form an alliance with the recently defeated Yueh Chih tribe. Unfortunately Zhang did not manage to sneak through the Gansu Corridor (see p99) undetected and was taken prisoner by the Xiong Nu. Ten years later, during which period he had married and become a father, he escaped. After many months of travelling he arrived safely in the Ferghana Valley (present-day Uzbekistan, Tajikistan and Kirghizstan), where he gathered a wealth of information before finally tracking down the Yueh Chih in Bactria (Balkh, in modern Afghanistan). By this time, however, the Yueh Chih had given up all thought of revenge against the Xiong Nu. Zhang returned home, managing to get himself captured again on the way and arriving back in Chang' an in 125 BC. Of his original 100 men only one made it back with him. Although disappointed at the lack of response from the Yueh Chih, Emperor Wu was delighted to receive so much military intelligence. He was particularly interested, moreover, in Zhang's reports of the hugely powerful horses to be found in the Ferghana Valley.

In 121 BC, having ejected the Xiong Nu from the Gansu Corridor, Wu dispatched Zhang Qian west once more, this time at the head of 300 men and carrying suitable goods with which to barter and trade for some of these 'heavenly horses'. Although the horses were not actually procured until China besieged the city of Kokand in 102 BC, the emperor was pleased with Zhang, bestowing on him the epithet 'Great Traveller'.

(**Opposite**) The portal of the Divan Begi Madrassah in Bukhara (p140) is made up of over 1.5 million ceramic tiles. Pity the poor guy who had to do the grouting. (**Overleaf**) Tillya Kari Mosque, Samarkand (p148). Over two kg of gold leaf was used on the ceiling alone.

Evidence of early trade

While Zhang Qian gets the credit for forging a route across China into Central Asia, there is much evidence to indicate that he was not the first Chinese to have 'discovered' the West: according to one legend, Emperor Mu of the Zhou dynasty made a similar journey some 900 years earlier, trading and receiving tributes from other tribes along the way. Certainly the idea of an emperor travelling along these dangerous routes seems unlikely but it is more than possible that he took the credit for someone else's journey. It at least indicates both knowledge of and interest in the lands that lay to the west.

Zhang's own chronicles prove that he did not forge the first link between China and the West since he reports his surprise at finding Chinese goods already for sale in Balkh. Archaeological evidence confirms this, as it is now clear that much of the early jade in the Chang'an region was actually quarried in Khotan and Yarkand at the far western end of modern China, around 2000 BC.

The discovery of silk

Archaeological evidence suggests that Western Asia was already trading with Central Asia by this time, for Iranian pottery dating back to 3000 BC has been found in the Ferghana Valley. Meanwhile, the Chinese made an important discovery: legend relates that in 2500 BC Emperor Huang Ti's wife, Si-Ling-Chi, was idly toying with a cocoon she had found under a mulberry tree when she accidentally dropped it into her cup of tea. Upon removing the cocoon, she found that she could pull off a long filament from it, and immediately realised the potential of silk (as a fabric rather than a hot beverage). However silk was discovered, we can be sure that it was in widespread use across China by 1500 BC.

The Romans

The Romans first encountered silk in 53 BC. Under Crassus their legions suffered a crushing defeat at the hands of the Parthians at Carrhae when they were taken by surprise as their retreating enemy suddenly wheeled round and launched a multitude of arrows at their disordered ranks (the original Parthian Shot). At the same time they unfurled huge silken banners. The effect was devastating, and while one supposes that the arrows made more of an impact than the banners, news of the fabric made it back to Rome. It caused a commotion amongst the hip and the wealthy and shortly silk started to flood in to the empire. It was so expensive, however, that officials soon began to object to the vast amounts of money being spent on this unnecessary luxury. The historian Pliny (AD61-113) was

---

(**Opposite**) The exquisite majolica tiling inside the Shir Dor Madrassah is typical of Samarkand.

particularly outspoken regarding the Romans' hedonistic tendencies, although he may have put his finger on the problem when he wrote of a fabric 'by which women shall be dressed and yet naked' (early silk was transparent). The senate did their best to ban men from wearing this revealing cloth in 14 AD. No-one complained about the women wearing it, though.

Silk
Having discovered the secret of sericulture, the Chinese were loth to give it away. Silk is produced by moths of the genus *Bombyx*, usually *Bombyx mori*, commonly known as the silkworm. The larvae of this moth gorge themselves on mulberry leaves and then surround themselves with cocoons made of one continuous thread, usually 600-900m long. Unfortunately for the moth, if it breaks the cocoon the thread will break too, so silkworms are killed before they get the chance to do this, usually with bursts of steam or hot air. The cocoons are unwound in a process known as 'reeling', and a number of filaments are wound together to make yarn by another process called 'throwing'.

It is impossible to know exactly when or how the secret got out first. It is clear from Roman chronicles that Westerners had no idea how the fabric was made: having only seen cotton they naturally assumed that silk was a plant, and Pliny actually described how it was harvested from the trees. The secret seems to have arrived in the West some time in the 5th century. One legend recounts that silkworm eggs and mulberry seeds were smuggled to Khotan by a Chinese princess who was unwilling both to marry a stranger and live without silk. This story links up to some extent with another legend which tells of the theft of eggs and seeds from Khotan by Western travellers, who concealed them inside a hollow walking stick. The secret alone was probably not enough to help them, however, for by this time the Chinese had been practising making silk for nearly 2000 years and thus theirs was considerably superior.

The routes themselves
While there was never one Silk Road, the incredibly harsh terrain between east and west limited the options open to travellers. Heading west from Chang'an, for example, goods had to go across the Lop and the Taklamakan Deserts. These two areas are particularly inhospitable and safe routes through them scarce. Likewise at the end of the Taklamakan, travellers were faced with the Pamir Mountains. Since there were only a few safe passes through this range, we find generations of traders following these same paths. The story is similar along the rest of the routes, as extremes of temperature and terrain limited the choices.

From Chang'an to Dunhuang
From Chang'an (Xi' an) the going was fairly easy along the 250-300 miles of the Imperial Highway as far as Lanzhou; in fact it was so easy that it was possible to drive carts along this way and in places it was even

Marco Polo

The most famous Silk Road traveller was by no means the first European to make the journey to the Far East; not only do we have records of missionaries making their way along the route, but Marco Polo was in fact taken along on his journey by his father and uncle, who had themselves returned from China. Brothers Niccolo and Maffeo Polo, two Venetian traders, headed east for the first time in 1260 but ended up, thanks to a Tartar feud, stranded in central Asia. Knowing that they could not get back west, they headed east until they arrived in Bukhara, where they stayed for three years. Here they were approached by one of Kubilai Khan's emissaries, who invited them back to Khanbalik (Beijing) as guests and ambassadors. From Bukhara they travelled through Samarkand to cross the Pamirs into Kashgar, and then headed along the northern route to Beijing. This stint of their journey took one year.

The Khan was delighted to meet the two Italians and was particularly intrigued with their religion. He sent them back to Italy as envoys to the Pope, from whom he demanded 100 men 'learned in the Christian religion, well versed in the seven arts and skilled to argue and demonstrate plainly to idolaters and those of other persuasions that the Christian religion is better than theirs'. Upon arriving home three years later (1269), the two intrepid travellers discovered that Niccolo's wife was dead, and that the Pope had recently died, too. They made arrangements to leave, along with Niccolo's fifteen year old son Marco, and waited for the papal election. Eventually they were given two Dominican friars to escort to the Khan, both of whom returned home at the first sign of trouble (it has been suggested that had more friars been sent, or had the two actually made the journey, China might be a Christian country today).

After a number of detours the Polos ended up in Kashmir, and from here they crossed the Karakorums into Kashgar, heading west by the southern route and eventually meeting up with the Khan at the summer palace at Shang-Tu. They stayed with him for seventeen years, during which time Marco was given a number of diplomatic jobs. In fact it seems that they were lucky to get away at all: 'Time and time again they asked the Khan to give them leave to depart, but he was so fond of them and so much enjoyed their company that nothing would induce him to give them leave'. The trio finally escaped by sea as escorts for a princess who was to be married to a prince in Persia. They made it back to Venice in 1295.

paved. Lanzhou was the standard setting for the crossing of the Yellow River. It also marked the eastern end of the Gansu, or Hexi, Corridor, a narrow strip of fertile land sandwiched between the Qilian Mountains to the south and a ridge of mountains lining the southern rim of the Gobi Desert to the north. Because there was no way out of this corridor except at each end, its strategic significance was immense, and China was always keen to keep it clear, since essentially it controlled all traffic to and from the West.

The hazards of desert travel

After passing through the narrow Jiayuguan Pass, traditionally the outer-most gate of the Chinese empire and the termination point of the Great

Wall, travellers came to Dunhuang. Chinese traders were unlikely to travel any further than this and so their wares would be sold off to some 'barbarian' who would take them on and then resell them; in this way the route was joined by a series of links, like a human chain. Dunhuang presented a serious problem, however: the Lop Desert, the remains of a huge inland sea, lay to the west and was immediately followed by the larger Taklamakan. These two deserts constitute the Tarim Basin, and while they hold few fears for the modern traveller, they are considerable obstacles for those on foot. As if the heat and lack of water were not enough, the Taklamakan particularly is liable to sudden sandstorms. Albert von Le Coq describes one in *Buried Treasures of Chinese Turkestan*:

'Quite suddenly the sky grows dark.. .a moment later the storm bursts with appalling violence upon the caravan. Enormous masses of sand, mixed with pebbles, are forcibly lifted up, whirled round, and dashed down on man and beast; the darkness increases and strange clashing noises mingle with the roar and howl of the storm... The whole happening is like hell let loose...'

Storms were a threat but to the ancient traveller there was another important danger here – ghosts: the deserts were the homes of supernatural beings who would distract weary travellers by wailing in order to lure them to their deaths. Marco Polo writes of them in the Lop Desert:

'When a man is riding by night through this desert...he hears spirits talking in such a way that they seem to be his companions. Sometimes, indeed, they even hail him by name. Often these voices make him stray from the path, so that he never finds it again. And in this way many travellers have been lost and have perished'

These beliefs were not just archaic, though: Cable and French were warned about demons here as late as 1942:

'This place is full of them, and many have heard their voices calling...They call out just as a man would shout if he wanted help, but those who turn away from the track to answer them never find anyone, and the next call is always a little farther away from the true path, for these voices will lead a man on, but they will never call him back to the right way'.

Western travellers were certainly not immune to the terrors of these two deserts: Sven Hedin, a veteran Swedish explorer, very nearly died of thirst here in 1895, and Hungarian/British archaeologist, Sir Marc Aurel Stein, wrote that the deserts of Arabia, in comparison with the Taklamakan, were 'tame'. These factors are all echoed in its name, which means literally 'If you go in, you won't come out'.

The southern route
Dunhuang presented a choice for Silk Road travellers: they could take either the southern or the northern route west. The north was generally held to be easier, yet because of the inhospitability of the south the chance of meeting bandits was lower. Those heading south would pass through

the Nang Kuan Gate and forge their way southeast towards the first major oasis, Cherchen (Shan-Shan), of which Marco Polo notes, 'It used to be a splendid and fruitful country, but it has been much devastated by the Tartars'. He also notes of this area, as do Cable and French nearly 700 years later, that inhabitants in the region lived in constant fear of marauding bandits and armies. Whenever they heard advance warning of an army passing through they would take their animals and hide out in the desert, and 'when they harvest their corn, they store it far from any habitation, in certain caves among these wastes, for fear of the armies; and from these stores they bring home what they need month by month'.

From Cherchen the route bore west until Khotan, a major stop not only because it was a large city on the route towards Europe but also because it lay at the foot of a major pass through the Karakoram mountains to India. Marco Polo notes that Khotan 'is amply stocked with the means of life... it has vineyards, estates and orchards in plenty. The people live by trade and industry; they are not at all warlike'. Moving on, the next large stop was Yarkand which, together with its northern neighbour Kashgar, provided the final rest stop for those passing east over the lofty Pamirs. These constitute a serious obstacle to any traveller and were known to the Chinese as the 'Onion Mountains' because the onions that grew there were held to be responsible for the nausea that was actually altitude sickness. It was at Kashgar, or occasionally at Yarkand, that the northern and the southern routes converged.

The northern route

There were two main choices for travellers passing along the north side of the Taklamakan: either they could head directly west, across the utterly barren Lop Desert, or they could skirt it to the north, cutting across a stretch of the Gobi to get into the foothills of the Tien Shan as soon as possible. Neither of these routes was without its dangers but the former gradually became redundant as its main oasis, Loulan, on the banks of the 'wandering lake' Lop Nor (see p291), slowly dried up. The remains of the city, one of the original 'Lost Cities of the Desert', were accidentally discovered by Sven Hedin in 1899 – a tale recounted in Peter Hopkirk's excellent 'Foreign Devils on the Silk Road'. Loulan seems to have been deserted during the 3rd century, and thus had lain empty for some 1600 years awaiting his arrival. From here, the route stretched east to Korla, where it met its northern cousin.

Those heading into the Tien Shan would probably have left the trail before Dunhuang, not passing through the famous Yumen Kuan (Jade Gate) so familiar to those heading across the Lop. Trekking north-west, the famous stops on this route were Turfan and Hami. Cable and French describe this part of the desert as a 'howling wilderness', and tell of the only water along the way:

'sometimes it ran from beneath boulders in a limpid stream, sometimes it lay in a sluggish pool, its surface covered with a repulsive scum; at other times it would burst through the soil.. .but whatever its immediate source, it was always brackish and thirst-creating. Its taste was sometimes that of magnesium sulphate, and sometimes more reminiscent of a copper salt, but it was always unsatisfying and always nauseating'.

Hami, famous for its luscious melons, was previously known as Cumul, which Cable and French identify as Marco Polo's 'Kamul'. Polo was intrigued with the place, particularly its custom of hospitality towards strangers:

'I give you my word that if a stranger comes to a house here to seek hospitality he receives a very warm welcome. The host bids his wife do everything that the guest wishes. Then he leaves the house and goes about his business and stays away two or three days. Meanwhile the guest stays with his wife in the house and does what he will with her, lying with her in one bed just as if she were his own wife; and they lead a gay life together. All the men of this city and province are thus cuckolded by their wives; but they are not in the least ashamed of it. And the women are beautiful and vivacious and always ready to oblige...'

From Hami the (presumably exhausted) travellers forged on to Turfan, the hottest city in China, a hugely fertile oasis noted for its grapes thanks to ingenious man-made irrigation systems. Situated in the second deepest natural depression in the world, it is 'a green island in a sandy wilderness... its fertility is amazing, and the effect on the traveller, when he steps from sterility and desiccation into the luxuriance of Turfan, is amazing'. 'There is' continue Cable and French, 'no more interesting oasis on the Asian highways'. Having left here, the route wound down to the south-west, where it linked up with the other 'northern' route at Korla. They then went on together through the major oasis towns of Kuqa and Aksu until Kashgar.

Into Central Asia

The trek across the mountains was invariably tough: shooting up above 25,000 feet, the Pamir range has been termed 'The Roof of the World'. On the other side conditions improved considerably, but because of this numerous routes were available for the travellers and thus it becomes more difficult to follow 'the' or even 'a' route. We can say, however, that most travellers headed either due west, perhaps via Bactria to Merv (present-day Mary, in Turkmenistan), or north-west towards New Sarai, directly to the north of the Caspian Sea. The route which really concerns us here is the former, as it passes through Kokand, Tashkent, Bukhara and Samarkand. These Central Asian states have changed hands numerous times, although this appears not to have stopped the latter two from achieving near-legendary status in the West. Bukhara was for a long time renowned as 'The Pillar of Islam', and although Marco Polo himself did not visit the city, his father and uncle spent three years there, so it was on good authority that he was able to write of it as 'a large and splendid city... the finest city in all Persia'. It was during their stay here that Niccolo and Maffeo Polo were accosted by an envoy from Kubilai Khan, who 'lived at the ends of the earth in an east-northeasterly direction', and who made them an offer they could not refuse: 'the Great Khan of the Tartars has never seen any Latin, and is exceedingly desirous to meet one. Therefore, if you will accompany me to him, I assure you that he will be very glad to see you and will treat you with great honour and great bounty...'. The toll of the years, together with the incredibly harsh 19th century regime here, which so terrified Great Game players (see p280), obviously did nothing to harm Bukhara's standing, as Lord Curzon declared it 'the most interesting city in the world'.

Samarkand needs little introduction: appearing in the works of Marlowe, Milton and Keats among others, the most famous literary reference probably comes from one J Elroy Flecker, who dreamed:

> For the lust of knowing what should not be known,
> We take the golden road to Samarkand'.

The glorious image of Samarkand no doubt stems partly from its physical beauty. Surely more important in the formation of its reputation, however, was its sheer inaccessibility, which nurtured the romantic myth of a bejewelled Eastern capital eternally beyond the Western grasp. Samarkand in literary references stands for more than itself as Geoffrey Moorhouse notes, so that 'Every journey through Central Asia is a quest for Samarkand'. Both Samarkand and Bukhara stand unrivalled, immortalised by literature and the imagination. As one Eastern proverb says: 'In other parts of the world light descends upon earth. From holy Samarkand and Bukhara it ascends'.

Across the Middle East

From Samarkand the road might head south to Bactria, totally destroyed now, but which Marco Polo describes as 'a splendid city of great size'. It was here that Alexander the Great 'took to wife the daughter of Darius'. Historians have put this wedding down to politics but it seems that more than this was involved, as chroniclers refer to Roxanne as the 'most beautiful woman in all Asia'. But whether via Bactria or not, most routes would end up passing through the caravan city of Merv. The Romans knew this city as 'Antiochena Marghiana', or 'Antioch in Marghiana' (a part of Persia). From here travellers were faced with the Iranian Plateau, which was generally skirted to the north so as to avoid the southern deserts.

The Persians were consummate traders. They were also extremely adept at forcing travellers to cross their land (rather than heading north to cross the Caspian Sea) so that they could extract tolls from them. The upshot of this was that conditions were tolerable for crossing Persia, with walled cities geared very much for travellers all along the way. On the western edge of the plateau was Ecbatana (now Hamadan), and from here the route south led traders to the Tigris and Euphrates rivers and to a number of great cities, notably Babylon, Seleucia and Baghdad. From this Asian crossroads the journey was either north and then west, or simply north-west across the Syrian Desert until reaching the trade cities of Aleppo, Tyre, Sidon or Antioch, all of which were key distribution points for eastern goods.

The decline of the Silk Route

Despite the variety of routes from east to west, international trade was ultimately at the mercy of the political situation. Thus we find certain periods when trade boomed as travel was safe, and times when it slumped. The Western Han period (206 BC-9 AD) was good for the route, for example, because in the East China was largely unified whilst the West was held by Rome at her zenith. Unfortunately things declined shortly afterwards. Likewise the early Tang dynasty (618-907) was a period of great prosperity for the routes because the Chinese 'system' was open-minded and took an active interest in foreign cultures and imports. The early 8th century, though, saw the big push of Islam towards the East, which created turmoil in Central Asia. Meanwhile the Tibetans disrupted trade routes within China.

Funnily enough it was Genghis Khan, usually portrayed as a master of destruction, who was responsible for the rejuvenation of the trade routes: by conquering vast tracts of land he unified the East once more and trade restarted. The period of Mongol peace was so beneficial for trade routes that Western travellers began making the entire journey east themselves; Francesco Di Balduccio Pegolotti even published *The Practice of Commerce*, a guidebook for traders on their way to China. It is worth noting that at this time the favoured route from east to west was what Franck and Brownstone call 'The Eurasian Steppe Route': instead of meddling with the Taklamakan and Lop deserts, travellers headed north into the Mongolian steppes. Here the climate was not so extreme and the land was flat enough to cross by cart. For a large part of the time, however, it was also packed full of aggressive nomads, and thus was extremely hazardous. The Mongol rule changed all this, facilitating relatively safe passage across Asia. With the decline of the dynasty in 1368, however, the last great age of the Silk Route was over, although there was a brief revival under Timur. Meanwhile Constantinople fell to the Ottoman Turks in 1453, thus signifying the collapse of order at the western end of the route. Within 75 years Portuguese merchant vessels had arrived in China anyway.

PART 5: CITY GUIDES AND PLANS

Moscow

Moscow has never been a part of the Silk Route, yet it is a key city on this journey because the trek south into Central Asia starts here. It is more than just a stepping-off point, however, and although the Silk Route capitals you will see later are more flamboyant, Moscow may be more evocative for the modern visitor. The city that launched a million spy thrillers is intriguing to explore, if only because it has been shrouded in mystery for so long. You can now wander freely into the Kremlin, breeze through Red Square, or explore the shadowy KGB headquarters around Lubyanskaya Square. It's an excellent place to daydream!

HISTORY

The oldest evidence of human settlement in the Moscow region comes from the Shchukino neolithic site on the Moskva river. Despite this, history books tell us that the city was founded by the Suzdal prince Yuri 'Longarm' Dolgoruki who invited a relative, Prince Sviatoslav, to attend a banquet in 'Moskov' in 1147.

The heart of the city, the Kremlin (either from the Greek word for citadel or the Russian *krem*, a particular type of conifer suitable for construction purposes), dates back to this time and we know that the first fortifications – ditches and ramparts with wooden walls – were erected in 1156. Moscow soon developed into a thriving trade centre.

The Mongols

The Mongol hordes rode in in the winter of 1238 and burned the city to the ground. It recovered rapidly, just in time for them to do it again when they returned a year later. During this period the whole of the area of Russia was under Mongol rule but Moscow soon established itself at the head of the anti-Mongol movement. In two huge pitched battles in 1378 and 1380 the Russians beat back the tribes, only for the city to be destroyed by fire once more when Khan Tokhtamysh passed through in 1382. He was put to flight when he tried it again in 1408.

By this time the Kremlin had been reinforced a number of times and all defences were now made of stone. Fortified monasteries were built around the outskirts of the town, which was itself to be ringed by a wall in the 16th century. Much of this building took place under Ivan the

Great, who christened his capital the 'Third Rome' following the sacking of Constantinople in 1453. He drafted in Italian architects to beautify the inside of the Kremlin, and many of the buildings you see inside the walls today are the product of this period.

Moscow's ability to rise from its own ashes is one of its most notable qualities. Unfortunately, so is its ability to get itself incinerated: in 1547 the city was obliterated by fire on two separate occasions. Just as repairs were nearing completion in 1571, a Crimean Tatar khan arrived with 100,000 men. The city was razed to the ground: only the Kremlin survived and this involved the sacrifice of all the Muscovites who hadn't made it inside the gates in time. Of the 200,000 population only 30,000 survived.

While these invasions were costly, they taught the Russians valuable lessons, so that when the Novodevichy Convent (see p119) was besieged by the Poles in 1610 it held out. Moscow was secure at the heart of the kingdom. Trade boomed and at the start of the 17th century things looked good for the capital.

The Times of Troubles

The opening years of the 17th century soon changed this, however. The Times of Troubles hit hard and thousands starved in the famines of 1601-3. During the first ten years, sovereignty of the state was under dispute thanks to the appearance of the two False Dmitris and their Polish supporters. With the ejection of the Poles in 1612, a large proportion of the city was destroyed once again but the Romanov dynasty came to power shortly afterwards and managed to restore order.

The eighteenth and nineteenth centuries

Although the lot of the peasants was harsh, Moscow thrived and when Peter the Great moved Russia's capital to the more modern St Petersburg in 1712, the real wealth and power stayed here. This was well understood by Napoleon at the turn of the 19th century who commented 'If I take Kiev, I will take Russia by the feet; if I capture St Petersburg, I will take it by the head; but if I occupy Moscow, I will pierce it through the heart'. Of course, by the time his army arrived, Moscow was deserted, and most of it burned to the ground shortly after this (whether by accident or as part of some Russian scheme is unclear).

Napoleon's catastrophic retreat in the winter of 1812 heralded a new era of construction and throughout the 19th century Moscow hummed with activity. Its central location put it at the hub of the newly-introduced railway system at the start of the 20th century. It was also at the heart of revolutionary activity and Lenin moved the state capital from Petrograd (the former St Petersburg – shortly to be renamed Leningrad) back here in 1918. With the civil war period Moscow suffered badly from severe food shortages but, as usual, recovery was swift.

The Great Patriotic War

Hitler was so confident that he would take Moscow that his troops were actually carrying the building materials with which to construct his headquarters here. The fact that the city withstood the Nazi siege played an important role in the Russian war effort, signalling their first real success. As a result of this, Moscow has awarded itself a number of accolades, including the title 'Hero City', the Order of the October Revolution, the Order of Lenin (twice) and the Gold Star medal.

Moscow today

The bizarre turn of events that led to the decline of the USSR, and then nearly to its re-establishment, really centred here. Current affairs fans will remember the dramatic scenes when the people took to the streets following the coup in 1989; two students were killed and there are usually still flowers on the bridge at the end of Arbat St where they fell. More recently, in 1993, the single most flouted image of Moscow was of the White House – under artillery fire from its own army.

Politically and economically Moscow is the country's heart, one of the reasons why it can be depressing to wander the streets here: you can bet that things are probably worse everywhere else. As with so many great cities the drab, grey exterior belies the wealth of interest within; it's just that if you catch Moscow in the wrong light it really is exceptionally drab. The problem here is two-fold: in the first instance a chronic housing shortage during the last three decades has resulted in the mass production of boxy apartments. In the second instance, the widespread poverty since the CIS was formed has meant that there is neither money for public work on the buildings nor for private renovations.

The last few years have not been kind to Moscow; it still appears that the majority of the population has yet to reap any of the benefits of changes sweeping the country. Wander through any subway and you'll find people selling useless family possessions: household goods, pictures, electrical fittings – it's a desperate combination of free market economy and crushing poverty. You can't help but wonder whether there is any more freedom now than there used to be: capitalism is one thing but having to hawk all your belongings to survive is quite another.

On the other hand, there are real differences: huge bill-boards advertise expensive goods and stalls all over the city sell both fake and real designer products. Remember that not so long ago it was impossible to buy a Coke here, and you can see how far Moscow has come.

You may well find yourself pleasantly surprised. Moscow is a city with a totally different 'feel' to it and the great thing about this one is that as long as you dress sensibly (no shorts) and keep your mouth shut, no-one will know that you are a foreigner. Sightseeing is so much more pleasant without crowds of salesmen.

ARRIVING IN MOSCOW

By air

Sheremetyevo International airport is 35km from the city centre. There is
a foreign exchange counter here, and since carrying roubles is now the
done thing, you'll need to change money here. To get into the city it's best
to take one of the airport buses which depart about every half hour (6am-
11pm), for either Planernaya (bus No 517) or Rechnoi Vokzal (bus No
551) metro stations. The fare is about US$2, with a small extra charge
(US$0.20) for luggage.

Taxi drivers will approach you as you leave the airport building. They
will charge anything from US$40 upwards (probably in US$, although
it's illegal) for a ride to the centre of town. A favourite trick is to show
official-looking 'rate cards' to tourists stating a 'standard fee' of US$60+;
bargaining is required here. It is wiser, if you think that you're going to
want a taxi, to arrange a transfer with your hotel before you arrive.

By rail

Moscow has nine mainline railway stations. If you are arriving from
Europe, you will stop at Belorusskaya, while most trains to Siberia use
Yaroslavl. Trains to and from the Central Asian Republics use Kazanskii
(metro: Komsomolskaya).

ORIENTATION AND SERVICES

Moscow's political and geographical heart is the Kremlin; hardly surprising, then, that this is the focus of most tourist programmes. Here you'll
find Red Square, the GUM department store and St Basil's Cathedral.

To the west along ulitsa Vozdishenka is Arbat St; north-east up
Theatre Prospekt is the KGB HQ in Lubyanska Square, and to the south
you'll find the Pushkin State Museum of Art. The immediate area is peppered with some of the city's best-known (and most expensive) hotels.

Intourist

The main office (☎ 292 2547, fax 292 2365) is located at ulitsa Mokhovaya 13, just to the south west of the National Hotel. The office has ticket booking services and tours, but the staff are often extremely busy (or
rather lazy), and better service for booking tours is sometimes available
by going to the booth in the lobby of the Intourist Hotel, round the corner. They offer the following standard tours: **Armoury Chamber and
Kremlin**: Mon, Tues, Wed, Fri, Sat, Sun (US$25, four hours); **City
Sightseeing**: daily (US$10); **Pushkin State Museum**: Thurs (US$15,
three hours). All prices are payable in roubles or by credit card.

Various other tours are available by special arrangement, including
trips to the **Sergiev Posad Monastery** and the old walled city of
Vladimir Suzdal. There is also the possibility of an impressive **KGB**

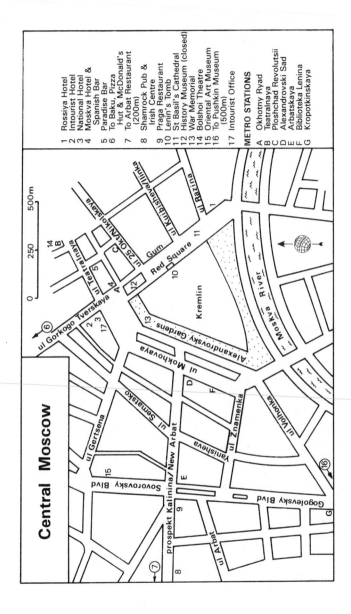

Central Moscow

1 Rossiya Hotel
2 Intourist Hotel
3 National Hotel
4 Moskva Hotel &
  Spanish Bar
5 Paradise Bar
6 To Baku, Pizza
  Hut & McDonald's
7 To Arbat Restaurant
  (200m)
8 Shamrock Pub &
  Irish Centre
9 Praga Restaurant
10 Lenin's Tomb
11 St Basil's Cathedral
12 History Museum (closed)
13 War Memorial
14 Bolshoi Theatre
15 Oriental Art Museum
16 To Pushkin Museum
   (500m)
17 Intourist Office

METRO STATIONS
A Okhotny Ryad
B Teatralnaya
C Ploschad Revolutsii
D Alexandrovski Sad
E Arbatskaya
F Biblioteka Lenina
G Kropotkinskaya

Map labels

500m
0   250   500m

ul Gorkogo Tverskaya
ul Gertsena
ul Semasko
ul Teatralnaya
ul 25 Oktyabrya
ul Kuibisheva
ul Razina
ul Mokhovaya
ul Znamenka
Yanisheva
ul Volhonka
prospekt Kalinina/ New Arbat
Suvorovsky Blvd
Gogolevsky Blvd
ul Arbat

Red Square
Gum
Kremlin
Alexandrovsky Gardens
Moskva River

Tour (must be arranged in advance; we were quoted US$60). This includes entry to one of the Lubyanka buildings, demonstrations of microdots, cryptography, miniature cameras and a question-and-answer session. You may be told that this tour is unavailable but keep trying: some have made it and reports are good.

The staff at either the main Intourist office or in the Hotel Intourist can help to book tickets for the ballet or opera (US$25-60).

Other tours
Tours of the Kremlin can be arranged on the spot; wander around the entrance or the Tomb of the Unknown Soldier and you'll be approached. These tours are roughly the same price as the official ones but you'll have your own personal guide, well worthwhile for two or more people. Local guides are also a great source of general information about the city.

Boat trips on the Moskva River are popular. They last about half an hour and you can pick one up easily at the piers in Gorky Park (metro: Oktyabrskaya), or near the Ukraine Hotel (metro: Kievskaya). Times are not fixed and if there is a commentary it will be in Russian.

Money
Travellers' cheques and credit cards are commonly accepted now and there are exchange booths all over the city with their rates clearly shown. It is illegal for any business to take US$ (although taxis will try); shops, restaurants and hotels will insist on roubles.

Post and telecommunications
Your hotel should have a postal and telephone service. If not, go to the telegraph office on ulitsa Tverskaya (Gorky St) where you can make international telephone calls. Poste Restante mail may be held here too but if your post is addressed to 'The Main Post Office' it will probably be at the small telegraph office opposite Chistoprudnii metro station.

Russian visa extensions
Transit visas are easily extended for up to five days (US$30 in roubles) in 24 hours. Contact the Immigration Office (OVIR) at ulitsa Pokrovka 42 (formerly ulitsa Chernishevskogo; metro: Kurskaya). Extending a tourist visa is more difficult. Contact the staff at TGH for advice.

Embassies
• **China** (☎ 143 1543) Leninskiye Gory, ulitsa Drukhby 6 (open Mon-Fri 9am-1pm). Take a passport photo (two if you are American) and get there early. 7-day service: US$70, 3-days: US$110, same-day: US$140.
• **Uzbekistan** (☎ 230 0076/1301/0054) Pogorelsky perevlok 12. Foreigners may be directed to **Uzbektourism** (☎ 238 5632), ulitsa Polyanka 41, 3rd floor, Room 53) who market grossly overpriced tours.
• **Kazakhstan** (☎ 208 9306/9852) Chistoprudnii Blvd 3A.

LOCAL TRANSPORT

By far the best way to get around is on the wonderfully ornate **metro** system, a tourist attraction in itself. One token (US$0.32 in roubles) takes you to any destination, no matter how far. Before you arrive at a station, its name will be announced (the Russian for 'station' is *stantsia*) and as the doors close the name of the next station will be announced too.

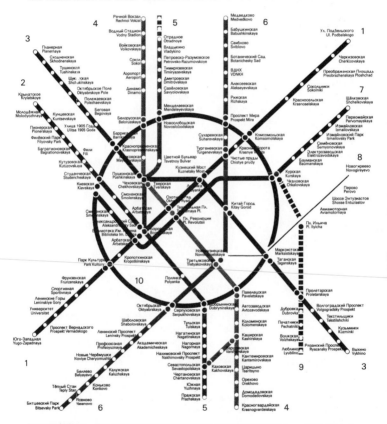

Moscow Metro – line names and colour codes 1 (Red) Sokolnicheskaya 2 (Light blue) Filovskaya 3 (Purple) Tagansko-Krasnopresnenskaya 4 (Light green) Zamoskvoretskaya 5 (Grey) Serpukhovsko-Timiryazevskaya 6 (Orange) Kaluzhsko-Rizhskaya 7 (Dark blue) Arbatsko-Pokrovskaya 8 (Yellow) Kalininskaya 9 (Dark green) Lyublinskaya (under construction) 10 (Brown) Circle

There are also trolley-buses, buses and trams but they are over-crowded and tricky for foreigners to use, so you might want to avoid them unless you're with someone who understands the system.

It's difficult to flag down a taxi anywhere in the country but it's always worth a try. Remember, however, that in Russia almost all cars are taxis if you catch the driver in the right mood (see p57). You should be charged in roubles but the driver may try asking for US$ anyway.

WHERE TO STAY

Budget accommodation

The hotel situation for shoestring travellers is improving. The best place to go for a bed if you haven't booked in advance is still the **Travellers Guest House** (☎ 971 4059, fax 280 7686), ulitsa Bolshoya Pereslav-skaya 50 on the 10th floor, where a bed in a three-bed room will cost you US$15 (US$40 in a two-bed room). The services here are excellent, including air and train ticketing (see p121) and up to date information on travel throughout the CIS. TGH can also arrange visa support for for-eigners applying from abroad (see p16). To get here, take the metro to Prospekt Mira and head north up the street. Take the third turning on the right (Banny per.) up to the T-junction and it's on your left. The walk takes 10-15 minutes.

Cheaper and more basic is the **Hotel Ipkir** (☎ 210 7148) where a sin-gle bed will cost you $7; there's a communal kitchen between every two rooms. It's 400m south of Dmitreyevskaya metro station at ulitsa Butirskaya 79, opposite a cluster of trees.

G & R International (☎ 374 7430, fax 374 7366, email grint@glas.apc .org) has rooms from $17 in the **Institute of Youth** hostel (Institut Molodyozh in Russian), ulitsa Yunosti 5/1. It's set in parklands and their office is in Block 6, Office 4. The closest metro station is Vykhino which is about 40 minutes out from the centre of Moscow. Then catch buses No 196 or 197 to the stop Institut Molodyozh. **Prakash Guest House** (☎ & fax 334 2595) runs a hostel with a bed from $10 a night at ulitsa Profsoyuznaya 83. The closest metro station is Belyaevo.

Mid-range accommodation

Bed & Breakfast now exists in Moscow. Private rooms or fully furnished apartments are available and additional meals if required. Guided tours, tickets for theatres, and translators can also be arranged. Costs start from $40 per day. A large number of homestays are advertised in the *Moscow Times*, and these include Rezon (☎ 369 6231), Vita Agency (☎ 265 4948) and Ya Servis (tel 231 0053, per Pyatnitsky 8).

Hotels with double rooms for $50-60 include **Hotel Kievskaya** (☎ 240 1234), ulitsa Kievskaya 2 (metro Kievskaya); **Hotel Sputnik** (☎ 938 7106, 938 7096), pro Leninski 38 (metro Leninski Prospekt); **Hotel**

Tsentralnaya (☎ 229 8589), ulitsa Tverskaya 10 (metro Tverskaya); and **Hotel Ural** ☎ 917 4258, 227 3289), ulitsa Pokrovka 40 (metro Krasnye Vorota).

The **Hotel Molodezhnaya** (☎ 977 33 55) is at Dmitryevskoe Shosse 27. A room in this vast blue creation (built for the 1980 Olympics) will cost you US$45. The decor is gaudy but the place is clean. It's a 10 minute walk north of Timiryazevskaya metro station; you can see it from the station exit.

The **Zolotoy Collus** (☎ 286 2703, nearest metro VDNK) doesn't get a lot of custom from tourists, but seems friendly. Singles and doubles are US$44. Although the sign is clearly visible from the metro station, the entrance to the building takes a bit of finding.

Upmarket hotels

Recently a number of foreign venture hotels have sprung up which offer Western style luxury and mod-cons; they're not centrally located, however. Among these new hotels is the **Hotel Aerostar** (☎ 213 9000), which is 7km from the city centre towards the airport, at prospekt Leningradski 37 (nearest metro: Dinamo). A single room here is US$282, and a double room is US$330. The **Renaissance Hotel** (☎ 931 9000) formerly the Olympic Penta Hotel, at prospekt Olympiskii 18 (metro prospekt Mira), falls into the same league with singles for US$349 and doubles for US$394. The **Sofitel Iris** (☎ 488 8000), formerly the Pulman Iris, is at Korovinskoye Shosse 10, and charges US$294 for singles or doubles.

If you have booked your trip with Intourist you're more likely to find yourself in one of the following. The **Hotel Intourist** (☎ 956 8400) is at ulitsa Tverskaya 3, and has the advantage of being about as close to Red Square as it's possible to get, while on the downside it is rather dowdy and charges US$130/155 for single/double rooms. At prospekt Teatralniy 7, (formerly prospekt Marxa), there's the **Hotel Moskva** (☎ 292 2994). Rooms here start at US$85 for a single and US$110 for a double. On the opposite side of Red Square, just behind St Basil's, at ulitsa Razin 6, is the ugly **Hotel Rossiya** (☎ 298 5000) – somewhat cheaper at US$60/80. It's outrageously drab, and is reported to be a big mafia hangout.

In the city centre, the top hotels include the luxurious **Hotel Savoy** (☎ 929 8500), at Rozhdestvenka 3, which has rooms starting at US$280 for a single room and US$360 for a double. The **Hotel Metropol** (☎ 927 60 00) is worth a visit even if you're not staying here just to see the Art Nouveau interior (scenes from *Dr Zhivago* were filmed here). It's at prospekt Teatralniy 1 and a room costs from US$372.

Finally, the **Hotel National** (☎ 258 7000) takes the 'silly price' award for their National Suite at US$1200. The US$255 single and US$294 double they charge seem pretty reasonable after that.

WHERE TO EAT

Getting a cheap meal in a Moscow restaurant can be a real challenge. Moscow is simply not a cheap city, and many authentically local restaurants are not particularly keen on taking foreigners. There are a couple of places which really are worth a try, but apart from these many foreign visitors either fork out the cash to eat at an expensive Western-style restaurant (or hotel restaurant), or else choose to resort to the multitude of new, Western-style bars and eateries that are springing up.

Cheap Western bars and restaurants

The situation for places to eat and drink is changing so fast in Moscow, that it's probably best to ask at your hotel for recommendations, or check out the *Moscow Times*, a free newsheet which you can pick up from the TGH or Pizza Hut, among other places.

The **Baku** takeaway at ulitsa Tverskaya 27 serves kebabs in under five minutes, and just up the street at number 12 is Moscow's first **Pizza Hut**. There's a takeaway service here (queue on the pavement or you can eat in). There's no longer a difference between communist and capitalist pizza, and the prices are about the same as in the West.

American-style sandwiches can be had at reasonable prices from **Combi's** (one at prospekt Mira – ideal for travellers at TGH – and another on ulitsa Tverskaya). Distinct New York flavour can be found at **Bagel's Cafe and American Bagel Shop**, at ulitsa Petrovka 24. **McDonald's** has lost some of its initial appeal (there were near-riots when the first one opened) but is still thriving. You can find branches at prospekt Mira, Pushkin Square, on ulitsa Tverskaya and on Arbat St. Big Macs are about US$1.70. There are cheap eateries springing up all along ulitsa Tverskaya, so it's probably worth having a wander around to see what's on offer.

Finally, one restaurant which was thoroughly recommended by English students studying in Moscow, was the **Georgian Restaurant**, 400m south of the Park Kultury metro station, near the river. Excellent local food will set you back about US$10 for a full meal.

Mid- and top-range restaurants

Again, easiest to get hold of is Western food, but try the **Baku** (see above; entrance around the corner from the takeaway), traditionally one of the 'real' Moscow eateries. The **Spanish Bar**, on ulitsa Tverskaya, just around the corner from the entrance to the Hotel Moskva, is hardly cheap, but has a good atmosphere and is clean, smart and well maintained. A meal and a couple of drinks here will cost US$20-40. Another place worth trying is **Praga**, or the **Arbat**, both on Arbat St.

Less ethnically European, try the **Hungry Duck**, **Rocky's** (both near Kuznetsky Most metro) and **Moosehead Canadian Bar** (Bol Polyanka

54/1, nearest metro: Serpukhovskaya), each of which will serve you cold draught beer for about US$5, and food for US$10-20. Or you can go Irish at **Rosie O'Grady's** (ulitsa Znamenka 9), the **Shamrock Pub** or **O'Connor's**, (both on New Arbat St), all of which serve good draught Guinness or Murphy's for US$5, and bar meals at around US$10. The restaurant at O'Connor's has a pleasant atmosphere; a meal here will set you back US$15-30.

Any of the five star hotels will, of course, have a number of top class restaurants serving both Western and local cuisine.

WHAT TO SEE

Red Square

This is what people usually imagine when they think of Moscow. Apart from the square itself there are three main attractions:

• **St Basil's Cathedral** Quintessentially Russian, the church which you see in every news broadcast from Moscow stands on the south-east corner of Red Square. It probably doesn't need too much introduction: suffice it to say that it was built at the order of Ivan the Terrible, who allegedly had the architect blinded when the work was complete. Legend holds that St Basil was a wandering mendicant who predicted that Ivan would murder his own son, and that his body lies buried beneath the church. Napoleon was unimpressed – 'Destroy this monstrosity', he is supposed to have shouted. Since the Revolution it has been a museum but it was recently reconsecrated.

• **Lenin's Mausoleum** Nobody's quite sure what to do with Lenin these days so it might be wise to pay him a visit in case he disappears (there are plans to move him to St Petersburg). His mausoleum is on the south-western side of the square, hunched against the Kremlin wall. It's a 1930 cubist creation in granite and red labradorite, which is a fancy way of saying that it looks as if it's made of lego. Behind the mausoleum are the graves of other communist heroes including Stalin, Frunze, Brezhnev, Gorky and Gagarin. The mausoleum is open 10am-1pm daily except Monday and Friday.

• **GUM Department Store** The largest department store in Russia has always been a trading centre but it was nationalised only in 1921. The building itself was built between 1888 and 1894, and was originally more like a mall containing individual stalls. It's called GUM (pronounced 'goom') because this is less of a mouthful than *Gosudarstvenny Universalny Magazin*. Post-1989 economic developments mean that the store is now crammed with designer goods that are beyond the means of most Russian shoppers. There is a food store in the right-hand entrance (on ulitsa Ilinka) that also sells cold drinks.

The Kremlin

Right at the heart of Moscow, the Kremlin has always been the city's nucleus. Adjacent to Red Square, there is so much to see here that you will probably need more than one visit.

Opening hours and tickets The Kremlin is open from 10am-5pm daily except Thursday. Entrance to the grounds is US$0.20 (in roubles) and ticket admission to each of the buildings inside costs US$6 (or $3 for students). A ticket to get into the **Armoury** costs US$14 (students pay US$7), and an access ticket for all the areas open to the public costs US$24 (students US$12). They are sold from the kiosk in the Kutafya Tower or you can buy tickets to the individual buildings as you enter them. Those wearing shorts probably won't be allowed in, and the Kremlin may be closed when there is a summit meeting in progress. Tours of the Armoury can be arranged by Intourist (see 108), or try the Kutafya Tower ticket kiosk. A brief cassette tour of the Patriarch's palace is available; it's not great but it's cheap, at US$3.

1   War Memorial
2   Kutafya Tower
3   Trinity Tower
4   Palace of
    Congress
5   Church of the
    Twelve Apostles
6   Church of the
    Deposition of the
    Virgin's Robe
7   Cathedral of the
    Assumption
8   Tsar Cannon
9   Bell Tower of
    Ivan III
10 Tsar Bell
11 Cathedral of the
    Archangel
12 Cathedral of the
    Annunciation
13 Faceted Palace
14 Saviour Cathedral
15 Terem Palace
16 Grand Kremlin
    Palace
17 Armoury
18 Poteshny Palace
19 Arsenal
20 Senate
21 Supreme Soviet
22 Spassky Tower
23 Ticket Kiosks
24 Patriarch's Palace

Moscow - The Kremlin

Kremlin walls and Alexandrovsky Gardens

The walled fortification marks Moscow's original site, although everything has been rebuilt a number of times and the present walls date only from the 15th century. The best way to get in is by walking from Red Square and passing through Trinity Gate but as you wander through Alexandrovsky Gardens there are a number of things worth noting: firstly there is the **Tomb of the Unknown Soldier** (inscription: 'Your name is unknown, your deed immortal') along with the 12 black polished marble cubes, each representing one of the 'Hero Cities' of the Great Patriotic War. Immediately past these is a grotto on the left made of the remains of buildings wrecked in 1812, and opposite this an obelisk which commemorates 300 years of the Romanov dynasty. The original inscriptions were replaced with those of Socialist heroes after the Revolution but there is talk of restoring them.

To pass through Trinity Gate, go through Kutafya (Big Woman) Tower. The only tower outside the Kremlin, this was originally part of the drawbridge (the present bridge was only built in the 16th century). Approaching the tower, note the clock above you, hanging in the place of the original icon which was destroyed after the Revolution. This is the tallest of the Kremlin towers, measuring over 80m, and the star on top is over 3m across. As you pass beneath it you can see the width of the walls, which vary between 3-6m and are over 2km around.

Cathedral Square

Right at the centre of the Kremlin, this is the very oldest part of Moscow. The most instantly recognisable building is the white **Bell Tower** of Ivan the Great (reigned 1532-43) which, at 81m, is the tallest building here despite Napoleon's attempts to blow it up in 1812. It houses the 70kg Uspensky Bell and this, along with the other 20 bells inside, pealed for the first time since the Revolution at Easter 1992.

Behind the tower is the **Tsar Bell**, the heaviest in the world at 200 tons, 72kg of which is gold (apparently it improves the tone). It cracked in 1755 when water was thrown on it before it had cooled properly, hence the $11^1/_2$ ton chunk beside it. Tour guides invariably joke that you can take this piece home with you as a souvenir if you want. Beside it is the **Tsar Cannon** (1586), the largest calibre firearm in the world. It has never been fired, possibly because the one ton cannonballs in front of it are too big to fit into the barrel.

• **Cathedral of the Assumption (1475-9)** Although designed by Italian architect, Aristotle Fioravanti, this building is typically Russian in style. All Tsars were crowned here, and the inside is suitably decked with 16-19th century frescoes (the centrepiece, 'Our Lady of Vladimir', is now in the Tretyakov Gallery – see p120). There are three thrones: the one to the right as you enter was Ivan the Terrible's, while the other two were for the patriarch and the tsarina. Note the huge chandelier, made from over 800lbs of silver recovered from Napoleon's troops on the retreat of 1812; he had used this cathedral as his stables.

The tabernacle immediately to the right of the door contains a piece of clothing allegedly worn by Jesus as well as the remains of Patriarch Germogen, tortured to death by the Poles in the 17th century.

• **Cathedral of the Archangel (1505-9)** Designed by another Italian, Alevisio Novi, this cathedral demonstrates a fusion of traditional Russian and Italian architecture: note the five domes and the seashell effect above the windows. It is the burial place of almost all tsars before Peter the Great, who moved the capital to St Petersburg. Napoleon used the building as a wine cellar.

• **Cathedral of the Annunciation (1484-9)** Opposite the Cathedral of the Archangel, this was built at the order of Ivan the Great. It was entirely a Russian affair and was solely for the personal use of the royal house – consequently all baptisms, marriages and private worship of its members took place here. The extra domes (there are nine) were added by Ivan the Terrible when he broke with Russian Orthodox doctrine by marrying more than three times. Artwork inside is the result of collaboration between Russia's two greatest icon painters, Theophanes the Greek and Andrei Rublev.

• **Other buildings in Cathedral Square** Also of note here are the single-domed **Church of the Deposition of the Virgin's Robe** (1484-5), built as a private chapel for the patriarch; above this, note the eleven domes of the **Upper Saviour's Cathedral**, part of the **Terem Palace** which was used by the tsars for the handling of state affairs. Immediately to the left of this is the **Faceted Palace** (15th century), where military and state receptions were held. Ivan the Terrible celebrated his victories here: one notable bash, in 1552, lasted for over three days.

Other Buildings in the Kremlin

The **Arsenal**, to the left of Trinity Gate as you go in, is easily recognised by the 875 French cannons, captured in 1812, piled up outside. Every now and again there is talk of converting it into a museum. Opposite is the yellow **Poteshny Palace**, now inhabited by the commandant of the Kremlin. As you look towards this from the gate, note the arches behind it, where foreign dignitaries stay: a flag above will indicate that someone is in residence. Diagonally opposite the arsenal is the only modern structure inside the Kremlin, the **Palace of Congress**. Constructed at Krushchev's command, it houses the largest stage in Russia (seating for 6000), and is used for forums. While digging the foundations in 1961, remains of the original wooden Kremlin walls were found. Also in this area are the **Supreme Soviet**: Yeltsin's office is on the right hand side of this building; the **Senate**, built at the order of Catherine the Great (1762-96) where both Lenin and Stalin lived; the **Patriarch's Palace**, and, adjoining it, the **Church of the Twelve Apostles** (now a museum of applied art). Take a guided tour of the **Armoury Museum** (or get in on your own) to see the vast hoards of foreign gifts and Russian valuables.

Arbat Street

Moscow's old 'Covent Garden' has toned itself down recently. Tourists used to flock here: to have their portraits or caricatures painted, to buy souvenirs, or to soak up the arty atmosphere – both Gogol and Pushkin lived in this area. It's lost some of the market now but you can still find the artists and coffee shops. If you decide to buy anything here, be prepared to bargain and perhaps to pay in hard currency. You could pick up anything from posters to puppies (there's a pet market in the underpass where the artists hang out), to old military uniforms and balalaikas. McDonald's (opened by Mrs Yeltsin in July 1993) is at the western end.

Novodevichy Convent

Founded in 1524 to commemorate Smolensk's liberation from Lithuania, Novodevichy has regularly functioned as a prison. This was particularly the case under Peter the Great, who banished most of the female members of his family here at one time or another. His sister, the princess regent Sophia, had an extremely tough time here after he accused her of plotting against him: he forced her to watch the execution of 300 of her 'conspirators', all of whom were hanged in a long line with their hands tied together as if in prayer, facing her. When she eventually retreated to her quarters Peter nailed the hands of her favourite courtier to her door. Sophia died in 1704, still confined in one of the towers.

The two most impressive buildings here are the **Bell Tower** and the **Smolensk Cathedral** (both 16th century). The carved iconostasis in the latter is particularly beautiful and is the work of more than 50 craftsmen. The fact that it survives today is purely thanks to the bravery of one nun, who managed to put out the fuses to the powder kegs when Napoleon tried to blow the place up in 1812. The convent grounds are tranquil and picturesque; you could easily spend a whole morning here (bring some food and have a picnic beside the lake). It's open 8am-5pm daily, but closed Tuesday and the first Monday of each month.

There are a couple of tourist stalls outside the main gate where you can buy a drink, or all the matrioshkas you forgot to get everywhere else. Just around the corner is the **cemetery** where you can visit the graves of, among others, Prokofiev, Eisenstein, Gogol, Chekhov and Khrushchev. Stalin, Khrushchev and the rest of the communist gang currently located in the walls of the Kremlin behind Lenin's mausoleum are supposed to be moved here at some point, too. The cemetery and the convent are a 10-15 minute walk west of Sportinava metro station. The massive building you can see in the distance from the cemetery gates is the university, which is usually included in most guided tours of the city because there is a good view from here (metro Universitet).

Museums

There are more than 150 museums in Moscow. Among the more well-known are:

• **Pushkin State Museum of Art** This huge gallery contains a celebrated modern collection including work by Rodin, Monet, Renoir, Manet, Degas, Van Gogh and others. Entry is US$6 ($3 for students). It's open 10am-7pm daily (not Monday) but don't arrive after 6pm. It's a 15 minute walk from Alexandrovsky Gardens at ulitsa Volkhonka 12 (nearest metro Kropotkinskaya).

• **Tretyakov Art Gallery** Also extremely large, this houses icons by Russian masters Rublev, Ivanov, Repin and Surikov. It's open 10am-8pm (not Monday) and is at 10 Lavrushinsky Perelok (five minutes' walk west of metro Novokuznetskaya).

• **Alexei Tolstoy's House** Tolstoy's house has no English labelling but there are interesting letters in English to or from Bernard Shaw, Thomas Edison and HG Wells. Entry is US$4 (students $2) and it's open 10am-6pm (not Monday). It is at 21 Lva Tolstovo, nearest metro Park Kultury. This is one of a number of writers' homes which have been preserved and opened to the public (others include Chekhov, Gorky and Dostoyevski).

WHAT TO BUY

It is hard to do anything in Moscow without finding matrioshkas for sale – if you don't buy a set, you stand the risk of being accused of being a subversive. Other popular buys include old Soviet artefacts (uniforms, badges etc), furry Moscow hats and local paintings. Beware especially of the latter because they may well be confiscated when you try to take them out through customs: there's a law against removing works of art from the country. If you must buy one, take a receipt and make it as official looking as possible.

To find the souvenirs, you won't have to look further than the subway outside the Hotel Intourist but you'd do better to make your way to Arbat St. A better market can be found at weekends at Ismailovsky Park (metro Ismailovsky Park). GUM is pretty useless for souvenirs but there's a good food store here. If you are looking for cheap vodka or caviare, beware of the small stalls around the streets: the labels will look authentic but the contents are sometimes not quite what you expect – safer to stick to the more expensive hotel gift shops and the Western supermarkets like the Irish Centre on New Arbat St (where you can pick up virtually everything that you forgot to pack). English language books can be found at Shakespeare & Co: 5/7 Novokuznetsky pereulok, between Novokuznetsky and Paveletskaya metro stations. It's somewhat difficult to find as it's in a basement flat, but it's opposite a small, beautiful Russian Orthodox church, which should be easier to spot.

MOVING ON

By rail

Since the first edition of this book, the number of trains running across the CIS has reduced drastically, and it may not be possible to get a direct train to **Urgench** (the logical place to head for after Moscow); instead you may have to go to Tashkent first, (or to Almaty if you're planning to skip Uzbekistan), and then backtrack to the west to see the Uzbek cities along the Silk Route. Things change, however, so it's worth trying for tickets to Urgench, as the service may be running by the time you travel. There were originally three trains daily (Nos 98, 24 and 12).

The **Tashkent/Almaty** train (No 86), however, departs Moscow daily at 11.44 from Kazanskii Station (metro Komsomolskaya). Unless you speak Russian, your best bet is to find someone to book the ticket for you. Most travellers make use of TGH's ticket booking facility, where tickets will cost US$127 to Tashkent, US$107 to Almaty, both of which include a commission. Intourist claim to be able to get you to Tashkent for US$106, but booking through them may prove more trouble than it's worth. If you want to try making the booking yourself, go to Intour Trans, near the Bolshoi Theatre, at 15 ulitsa Petrovka (second floor for reservations, third for bookings). Before getting onto the Tashkent train, note that it's a long way to Tashkent (72 hours, approximately). Buy some food.

TGH can also help to book international train tickets to other European cities, a sample of some prices being (all in US$): Prague $137, Warsaw $95, Berlin $185, Brussels $326, London $405, Helsinki $133. Tickets on the Trans Manchurian and Trans Mongolian trains can be arranged here too: The former will cost $242, and the latter $282.

By air

Russia is not the best place to buy international plane tickets, although prices are coming down now that the major airlines have opened ticketing offices in Moscow. These offices are mostly situated behind the Bolshoi Theatre, on ulitsa Petrovka; Aeroflot, generally the cheapest, has two offices here. The domestic flight centre is at No 15, while the international centre is at No 20.

The main international Aeroflot office is two minutes' walk from Oktyabrskaya metro station. Sample prices: London US$380, Berlin US$296 and New York US$434. Internal flights can still be tricky to arrange: Intourist can usually manage it for you. They are currently quoting Tashkent at US$176 (daily, with Uzbek Air) or US$286 (with Trans Aero), and Urgench US$145 (Mon, Wed and Fri).

Urgench

In order to visit Khiva you must get off the train at Urgench, a supreme-
ly uninteresting town 30km to the north.

ORIENTATION AND SERVICES

It's easy to find your way about Urgench. The two main hotels are a 15
minute walk north of the railway station, and the post office is right
beside them. The airport is 3km north of town. The best place to change
money is the Hotel Khorezm, although they will change only US$ and
will not touch travellers' cheques.

Uzbektourism organises trips to Khiva from the Hotel Khorezm but
these are usually for the large tour groups passing through; it's much
cheaper to take a bus or minibus yourself (see below).

The most interesting other prospect for a tour involves a little more
effort. A number of travellers have managed to hire a helicopter at
Urgench airport (pilot included, of course) to take them to see the remains
of the Aral Sea (see p278), 280km to the north. The six-hour trip has, in
the past, cost US$300-400 and included a photo stop at Kunya Urgench
and a lengthy pause to take pictures (à la National Geographic) of the
beached ships.

LOCAL TRANSPORT

There aren't many interesting places to go to in Urgench but there are
plenty of minibuses trying to take you to them. The bus station is just
north of the railway station but minibuses also tend to wait on the main
road near the station, and depart for Khiva (US$0.50) when they are full.

WHERE TO STAY

Accommodation is limited, expensive and not particularly inspiring in
Urgench. Although most tour groups stay here, there are a couple of nicer
(and cheaper) places to stay in Khiva itself (see p126).

Uzbektourism's **Hotel Khorezm** (☎ 65408), at ulitsa Al Biruni 2, is
quite pleasant, however, and singles/doubles with bathroom attached are
reasonable at US$35. This used to be the Hotel Intourist and taxi drivers
may still call it this. As the main package tour hotel it may well be packed
in peak season. Next to the Khorezm, and slightly closer to the railway
station is the new **Hotel Jeikhun** (☎ 66249). At US$20 for a single and

US$40 for a double, it's cheaper but the staff aren't very helpful if you don't speak Uzbek. If you're really on a shoestring, it is occasionally possible to stay the night in an old carriage at the **railway station**. Expect to pay all of US$0.50.

WHERE TO EAT

The **Hotel Khorezm** occasionally serves passable food but the 'live' music is excruciating. Still, you are more likely to get served here than at the Hotel Jeikhun. You can pick up snacks and more at the **bazaar**.

Probably the most interesting thing to do in Urgench is to visit Rosa the Incredible Warbling Waitress in the old **Hotel Khiva**. Rosa seems to have worked here since the beginning of time; if she finds out that you're a tourist, you're in for a serenading. She can arrange virtually any meal if you see her in advance. Even if she's not here, the food is fine and the staff friendly. The Khiva was the original Intourist hotel: it stands to the right of the big statue of Al Khorezmi on ulitsa Uzbekistanskaya. Make sure you get to the patio-style restaurant on the corner rather than the dingy sandwich bar inside.

WHAT TO SEE

There's a bazaar on ulitsa Uzbekistanskaya, but it's not wildly impressive. There is also a funfair and a theatre, neither particularly exciting in itself. The only really worthwhile visit is to Khiva.

MOVING ON

By rail

The train to Bukhara takes 10-14 hours. There's only one running these days, and it leaves at 04.00 daily. It costs US$11.

By bus or taxi

Minibuses to Khiva (30 minutes, US$0.50) leave from in front of the train station frequently. A taxi will cost you US$5-10 and save you the crush.

Buses to Bukhara are probably the easiest way of covering the next section of the route. From there trains to Samarkand and Tashkent are more frequent. The bus journey to Bukhara takes 7-10 hours and costs about US$15. If there is a timetable it's probably obsolete, so don't believe it.

By air

There are flights from Urgench to Moscow, Samarkand and Tashkent, but currently no flights to Bukhara. Bus No3 will take you the 3km to the airport from the main bus station.

Khiva

Hungarian traveller Arminius Vambery visited Khiva in 1863. One of his first recollections is of eight old men lying in a line on their backs having their eyes gouged out by a torturer, who wiped his knife clean on each victim's beard before moving on to the next. It's quite easy to imagine this when you get here; think 'Ali-Baba' or 'Aladdin' and you're on the right track.

Mosques, minarets and mausolea reign supreme in Khiva and as you wander through its maze of dusty, cobbled streets surrounded by towering Islamic architecture it's almost as though you have stumbled onto the set of an Indiana Jones epic. Brilliant.

HISTORY

Nobody seems quite sure exactly when Khiva was founded. One popular myth attributes its foundation to Noah's son Shem, who started building after a vivid dream of torches burning in the sand here (where did he find the people to inhabit the place?). The Greek historian, Herodotus (484-425BC), mentions the kingdom as Khorezm, noting its subservience to Darius' Achaemenid Dynasty. Yet at this time it is unlikely that Khiva existed at all in its present location, for the capital of the Khorezm kingdom was Kunya-Urgench, some 230km to the north-west. The kingdom was vast and particularly desirable because of its location along the Amu Darya river. Consequently it was invaded a number of times, most notably by Genghis Khan in 1221, against whose onslaught it held out for a whole 12 days, and Timur (Tamerlane), who stormed the city on no less than five separate occasions. Finally, exasperated, he ordered every building to be razed and crops to be planted amongst the rubble.

Khiva itself was probably founded in the 5th century and would have functioned as a rest-stop/fortress on the trade route from the Aral Sea southwards to Merv. It was already a noted intellectual centre by the 9th century however, having produced the great mathematician, astronomer and chess player Al Khorezmi, bane of all schoolchildren thereafter since it was he who produced the first treatise on algebra. But Khiva really came to prominence in 1593 when Kunya Urgench had been abandoned after the Amu Darya had changed its course. It soon earned notoriety for its trade in Persian slaves. Thus when the Persian king Nadir Shah (see p149) invaded in the early 18th century, he singled it out for special attention. Twenty years later the place was still almost totally deserted.

The arrival of the Russians

The Russians discovered this prosperous kingdom at around the same time as the Persians invaded and there are records of a number of Cossack-led plundering raids: on one occasion 1000 Khivan women were carried off, only to be recovered when the raiders were killed in an ambush shortly afterwards. The first real Russian push came in 1717: fuelled by reports of gold in the area and the certainty of treasure in India to the south-east, Peter the Great despatched a force of 3500 men under Prince Bekovitch Cherkassky. Bekovitch won the ensuing battle but was surprised to be welcomed into the city shortly afterwards by the khan. He was then persuaded that, since food could not be provided for such a large army in one place, his men would have to be split up. He fell for this and subsequently had the dubious pleasure of watching his entire army slaughtered. He was then flayed alive and his head was sent to the Emir of Bukhara as a trophy.

Another Russian catastrophe was narrowly averted in 1801 when Tsar Paul I, rapidly losing his sanity, sent a force of 22,000 Cossacks to take Khiva in mid-winter; luckily they were recalled after covering only 400 miles with the news that he was dead. The next attempt came in January 1840 with a bold campaign under General Perovsky but he was turned back by particularly severe weather; over 1000 men died on the retreat alone. Finally in 1873 it was General Kaufman who simultaneously mobilised 10,000 troops from Orenburg, Tashkent and Kranovodsk and took the walled city with hardly a struggle. In theory Khiva was taken in order to stop the slave trade there but in actual fact trading continued for another 50 years until 1917.

Khiva today

With a population of around 40,000, Khiva has not grown substantially under Russian rule. After a brief wander around you might be forgiven for thinking that nothing much has changed at all. Unfortunately this is not quite true: the reason that the monuments look so good is that they have all been restored with Russian patronage and, hand in hand with this restoration has gone the notion of Khiva as an 'outdoor museum'. Consequently you will find that the Ichan Qala, or *Shakhristan* (the inner, walled city) is largely deserted. While this makes for excellent photographs, it does seem a little harsh on the locals who have been kicked out. This 'museumisation' of the city is much debated: many believe that it should have been left in its crumbling state and that the atmosphere of the place has gone.

The inhabitants, whose main crop is cotton, have traditionally thrived along the banks of the Amu Darya. This is changing, however, also thanks to Russian interference (see p278).

ORIENTATION AND SERVICES

You are likely to be dropped off just by the West Gate. Basically the town is a square, with one main road heading north-south and the other heading east-west. Once inside, however, you are guaranteed to get lost but the Ichan Qala is not too big, so don't worry; keep an eye out for the Islam Khoja minaret as an orientation point. Maps are available and there's one just inside the main gate but they are all far from clear; ultimately your best bet is just to wander idly with a camera. Unfortunately children here have been spoiled by Western tourists, and they can get quite aggressive if you take their pictures and don't give them Western goodies.

WHERE TO STAY

Foreign tourists have traditionally been accommodated in Urgench but two hotels have recently opened inside Khiva itself, and these make much more interesting places to stay. Not only do these hotels have more atmosphere, but the chance to take photos inside the old city once the majority of tourists have departed, and in the late evening or early morning light, should not be missed. The **Hotel Khiva** in the Mohammed Amin Khan Madrassah now accepts foreigners (US$20 single, US$40 double). Although this is a reasonable deal, far better is the **Hotel Arkanchi** (☎ 52230) 100m to the south of the madrassah. Rooms here cost the same but meals are included, as are entrance fees to all the museums in Khiva. The Arkanchi is clean, friendly, and serves the best food you're likely to have had so far. Guides can be provided, too.

WHERE TO EAT

Even if you are not a resident, the **Hotel Arkanchi** is the place to make for in Khiva. Allow yourself plenty of time and preferably work up an appetite, too, as this may be some of the best food you come across in Uzbekistan. Apart from the Arkanchi, there really aren't any great places to eat in Khiva. You could try looking into the **Hotel Khiva** to see if they're serving food (they have done in the past). Alternatively, head for the **bazaar**, gorge yourself on shashlik and then retire to the chaikana by the East Gate to sit and drink tea. There are a couple of small shops which sell bottled water and soft drinks, but they invariably close in the early afternoon, so you should buy drinks whenever you see them.

WHAT TO SEE

Kunya Ark

Immediately to your left as you enter the Ichan Qala from the west is the former residence and court of the khan. Building started in the 17th century and work was pretty much continuous. The entrance to the Ark is particularly ornate as was noted by Russian envoy, Nikolai Muravyov, who was imprisoned for nearly two months before finally being allowed to enter in 1819. If you take the first right after entering, you will find the lovely Summer Mosque and, opposite this, the royal mint (now a tiny museum). Also to be found in here is the reception hall; look for the three entrance arches side by side. The left-hand entrance was for use by all the

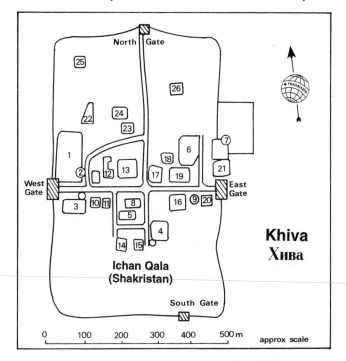

1 Kunya Ark	14 Mazarn Sherif Madrassah
2 Zindan	15 Russko Tuzemnaya Schkola
3 Mohammed Amin Khan Madrassah & Kalta Minar	16 Abdullah Khan Madrassah
4 Islam Khoja Madrassah & Minaret	17 Khodshash Magarram Madrassah
5 Pahalawan Makhmud Mausoleum	18 Mohammed Amin Inak Madrassah
6 Tashi Khauli	19 Kutlug Murad Inak Madrassah
7 Caravanserai & Bazaar	20 Al Mechet Mosque
8 Juma Mosque	21 Allah Kulli Madrassah
9 Chaikhana (tea shop)	22 Meched Ata-Murad
10 Matniyaz Divan Begi Madrassah	23 Isup Yasaul Bosh Madrassah
11 Kazi Kalyan Madrassah	24 Musa Tura Madrassah
12 Gorgovi Dom Palvan Khan	25 Kolodets Keivak
13 Mohm. Rakhim Khana Madrassah	26 Amir Tura Madrassah

non-officials and was built smaller than the others to make them stoop before the khan as they entered. In front of this hall is a raised circular brick pedestal which is where the khan's winter yurt (a circular felt tent used by nomadic steppe-peoples) was rigged. Muravyov describes the scene here nearly 200 years ago: 'on reaching the end of this corridor, we had to go down two steps into a fourth courtyard, larger than the other three, but surpassing them all in filth, and covered here and there with weeds. In the middle of this stood the khan's yurt.'

Zindan
Just outside the Kunya Ark in the large square is the jail, now converted into a grisly showpiece. Pictures inside depict favourite methods of execution: impalement, burial alive and tying people inside sacks with fierce wild animals were all favourites in their time. Muravyov comments that 'sometimes an impaled man will live for two days on the stake, only dying when the point comes through his shoulders or back'. These atrocities took place in the square outside.

Mohammed Amin Khan Madrassah and Minaret
A madrassah is an Islamic university. This one was built in 1852-5 and is easily recognised by its large arched entrance. It stands to the right of the West Gate as you go in and now houses the Hotel Khiva. While it is not particularly notable in itself, the stubby, multicoloured tower beside it is: this is Kalta Minar, the 'short minaret' which was commissioned, in 1852, to be the tallest minaret in Central Asia. There are two theories as to why it was never completed: one is that the Khan died; the other involves the Emir of Bukhara, who apparently contacted the architect and persuaded him to build an even bigger one in Bukhara when this one was finished. The Khan of Khiva, hearing of this treachery, ordered the architect to be executed and had him thrown from the top of his own minaret. Unfortunately the Kalta Minar stands only 29.4m/98ft tall (it was intended to be 79.5m/265 ft), and he was not killed immediately. The Khan then ordered the hapless architect to be hauled up to the top and thrown off repeatedly until he finally did die.

Islam Khoja Minaret
Khiva's tallest minaret stands 44.6m tall and is in immaculate condition. This is partly due to the fact that it was only built in 1908; still, it's a remarkable piece of work. Islam Khoja was actually the Grand Vizier of Asfandiyar Khan (ruled 1910-20), and was a benevolent, popular man. The Khan saw him as a political threat, however, and one night, after declaring a curfew in the town, summoned him to the palace alone. On the way, he was murdered by hired bandits. Asfandiyar then proceeded to

(**Opposite**) The Islam Khoja Minaret, the best orientation point in Khiva.

dispose of the evidence by having the bandits publicly executed the next morning. It's possible to climb to the top for an aerial view of the city; it doesn't smell too good inside, though.

Khivan justice
Englishman Fred Burnaby (see p34), on his visit in 1875 asked about the judicial system, and was told that men invariably owned up to their crimes for fear of Allah. "'But', I enquired, "are there never some wretches amongst you who will risk the wrath of Allah and, perjuring themselves, be released to commit other crimes?" – "No" was the answer, "the fear of God's vengeance is happily too great to admit of such wickedness" – "But supposing that there are witnesses who can prove that the man committed the crime, and he still denies it; what do you do then?" "Why, we beat him with rods, put salt in his mouth, and expose him to the burning rays of the sun until at last he confesses, and then is punished for his breach of the law."' Not much different from the Old Bailey, then.

Pahlawan Makhmud Mausoleum
Pahlawan ('hero') Makhmud was a furrier who helped the poor, wrote poetry, and was the strongest man in the kingdom. Since the 12th century he has been canonised as Khiva's protector. This mausoleum was constructed on the site of his fur-shop in 1810, but there has almost certainly been some kind of monument here since his death. Following Makhmud's burial, numerous wealthy traders and khans staked their claims to be buried near him, and hence there are a number of other tombs here. As you walk through the arch you will see a well to the right whose water is supposed to have miraculous properties. It is traditional to make a wish as you drink from it.

Inside the prayer hall directly ahead lie the tombs of three khans from the 17th century, and the hall to the left is Makhmud's; note the groups of devotees who will, no doubt, be posting money through the grille. The inscription above is from one of his poems and translates roughly as: 'it is easier to spend one hundred years in jail or to climb one hundred mountains than it is to persuade a fool of the truth'. Entrance is free but there are donation boxes and you will leave a more favourable impression if you give something. Remember to take off your shoes before going in.

East Gate (Palwan Darwaze)
Located in the oldest part of the city, this entrance was known as the Executioner's Gate. Its association with slavery is hard to miss as it contains small alcoves once used as cells, and the slave market is just inside to the right. The Khivan slave trade is described by Muravyov: 'A young Russian (up to 25 years of age) fetches from fifty to eighty tillas. The Persian slaves are much cheaper. Of the latter there may be 30,000 in

(**Opposite**) Children in Khiva make willing photo subjects but often demand payment for their posing. Don't encourage them.

Khiva, but there are not more than 300 Russian slaves there. The Persians...come into the market in batches of five, ten, and even thirty at a time. Their captors do not trouble themselves about them on the road, and, if they get exhausted, leave them without compunction to die on the steppe. On arrival at Khiva their owner sets himself down with them in the market, and purchasers surround him, inspecting and examining the poor wretches, and haggling about their price as if they were horses...masters have the power of putting their slaves to death, but seldom avail themselves of this right from economic considerations. They therefore punish their slaves, as a rule, by putting out an eye, or cutting off an ear...'. If this gate was not a very happy sight for slaves on arrival, it could be a considerably more unpleasant one for them later on: when a slave was suspected of trying to escape he was nailed to it by his ears and left there for a couple of days. The majority, already weak, battered and undernourished, died blistering deaths in the heat. When the Russians arrived in 1873 they counted 29,300 slaves still in bondage and over 6500 who had managed to buy their freedom.

Camel

There seems to be only one camel in Khiva, and, of course, it is there for tourists. Consequently it spends most of its time doing nothing apart from drooling and releasing great gastric belches which blister the majolica tilework and make the muezzin run for cover. It's not worth riding but is good news for 'authentic' oasis photographs (because all oases ought to have camels). It's usually to be found nearly opposite the Kalta Minar.

Tash Khauli

Tash Khauli literally means 'Palace of Stone'. It was built as a replacement for the aging Kunya Ark between 1830-8 under Allah Kuli Khan (1826-41). Inside you will find a number of courtyards, each decorated with beautifully crafted majolica tiling. Do bear in mind that every one of these tiles was made, glazed and fired individually, and only then were they assembled, rather like a jig-saw. They say that each tile is unique but with complex geometrical patterns like these it is difficult to tell. Certainly, assembling the jig-saw would have been nearly impossible without the help of the small numbers painted in the corner of each tile. Unfortunately the architect was never able to see the results of his work: having been given two years in which to build the palace, he was beheaded the day after that limit was up. While this may have satisfied the Khan's impatience to some degree, it didn't accelerate the building process: Tash Khauli was another six years in the making.

The first courtyard you enter is actually the only one open to the public at the moment. The quarters to the right were for the emir's harem, whose inhabitants wandered about with their faces uncovered inside the courtyard, knowing that any non-court official caught looking at them would be executed. The women were never permitted to leave. Note the swastikas at the feet of the pillars on the left, symbols of Zoroastrianism.

Caravanserai and bazaar
Directly opposite the entrance to the Tash Khauli is the old *caravanserai* (a caravanserai was a hostel catering for travellers providing food, shelter and fresh horses). The long covered corridor, rather like a cloister, which you have to pass through to get there is called the *Tim*. The caravanserai is now a covered market and the writing around the side is political rhetoric. Just beyond the market you step outside again to find the bazaar. This is open every day; Sunday is best.

Juma Mosque
This mosque's most notable features are its pillars: there are over 200 of them, of which the oldest (some have been replaced) date right back to the 10th century. It is extremely airy inside and if you're too hot this is a good place to sit and cool down. The carriage here was part of a gift to the Khan from Tsar Nicholas.

Khiva's museums
Khiva is peppered with madrassahs and other miscellaneous buildings which, no longer strictly in use, have been converted into museums of sorts. Generally they aren't worth visiting because the exhibits, not particularly noteworthy, are all rather decrepit, there is no English labelling, and it's very dark inside. You will always be charged a small entry fee at the door by some old lady who looks as though she's sound asleep until you try to creep past without being noticed. Frankly, the best thing about the museums is that they are usually extremely quiet; so if you're overheating, pop into one and rest your face against the cool walls.

WHAT TO BUY

The only places where you will find things to buy in abundance are the Tim and the bazaar, although neither of these specialises in tourist paraphernalia.

MOVING ON

There are frequent buses back to Urgench (see p123).

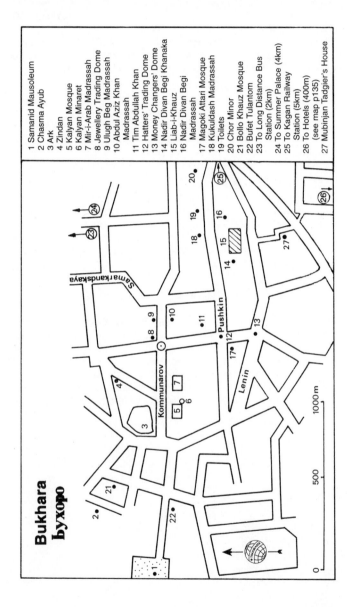

Bukhara
Бухоро

1 Samanid Mausoleum
2 Chasma Ayub
3 Ark
4 Zindan
5 Kalyan Mosque
6 Kalyan Minaret
7 Mir-i-Arab Madrassah
8 Jewellery Trading Dome
9 Ulugh Beg Madrassah
10 Abdul Aziz Khan
   Madrassah
11 Tim Abdullah Khan
12 Hatters' Trading Dome
13 Money Changers' Dome
14 Nadir Divan Begi Khanaka
15 Liab-i-Khauz
16 Nadir Divan Begi
   Madrassah
17 Magoki Attari Mosque
18 Kukuldash Madrassah
19 Toilets
20 Chor Minor
21 Bollo Khauz Mosque
22 Bufet Tulantom
23 To Long Distance Bus
   Station (2km)
24 To Summer Palace (4km)
25 To Kagan Railway
   Station (5km)
26 To Hotels (400m)
   (see map p135)
27 Mubinjan Tadgier's House

Bukhara

When Lord Curzon visited Bukhara (equipped with his inflatable 'india-rubber' bath) he commented that it was 'the most interesting city in the world'. This is debatable but it is certainly more engrossing than, say, Samarkand, because there is so much to see here. The whole of the old town is a web of fascinating little alleys and back streets where one can easily imagine life as it was a hundred years ago.

Bukhara has always been considered the most violent of the Central Asian states. Its emirs' tyrannical ways were notorious and following the gruesome deaths of two English army officers here in 1842, its name was familiar even in the West. Hand in hand with this notoriety has gone its reputation as a key centre of Islamic scholarship and as a consequence it is liberally endowed with mosques and madrassahs. (Bukhara is home to the tallest minaret and the second largest mosque in Central Asia).

HISTORY

According to the Persian poet, Abdul Hassim Firdausi, Bukhara was founded by an Iranian prince, Siyawush, who lies buried here. The story tells of Siyawush's sticky end: when he refused to respond to his step-mother's amorous overtures she suggested that her husband, the king, should have him beheaded. Hearing this, Siyawush fled to Turan where King Afrasiab (the founder of Samarkand's original site in another myth – see p143) betrayed him. Siyawush's stepmother, you will be glad to hear, was later put to death by Rustam, whose huge six-stranded whip used to hang over the main entrance to the citadel, or 'Ark'.

Actually, the first agricultural settlements located around modern Bukhara date from the 8th century BC but nothing survived the constant fighting. Thus the first real archaeological evidence dates from the 1st or 2nd century BC. The fact that when Alexander the Great took Bukhara by siege in 328 BC it was already heavily fortified (not heavily enough, obviously) seems to have been largely ignored by early historians. This accounts for a 6th century Arabic writer referring to it as Numijkat and telling of its foundation in the 1st century AD. Certainly by the 7th century, construction of the Ark on its present site was underway, and by the 8th the living quarters around the fort were surrounded by a 25km long protective wall. Whatever this achieved, it certainly didn't keep out the Arabs, who invaded in the 8th century, only to relinquish control to the Samanids in the 9th.

The first flourishing

Under Samanid rule Bukhara, now capital of the area, flourished both industrially and intellectually. Most prominent of the scholars who studied here was Abu Ali Abn Sina (980-1037), better known to the West as 'Avicenna', whose 'Canon' of medicine was the authoritative medical textbook throughout Europe until the 17th century. Ultimately he departed from Bukhara somewhat under a cloud, having been accused by his enemies of incinerating the city's extensive library. The golden age was not to last for long: Bukhara was invaded numerous times before being obliterated by Genghis Khan in 1220. After his men had stolen everything of value he ordered the city to be razed to the ground; residents who did not remove themselves fast enough before the incineration were executed on the spot.

Although the Timurids brought wealth and prosperity in the 14th and 15th centuries, their capital was actually at Samarkand and the dynasty was short-lived. Yet by 1500, under the Sheibanids and then the Janids, Bukhara made a comeback. It is estimated that 30,000 students flocked in to study at the 360 mosques and 80 madrassahs.

The expansion of the Russian empire soon put paid to Bukharan autonomy, however, and the state was absorbed in 1868. On 2 September 1920 the Soviets, under Mikhail Frunze, stormed the old town and the Ark, sending the emir, Said Ali Khan, into exile in Afghanistan.

Modern Bukhara

At Russian insistence all pictures depicting torture or death (so common under the cruel emirs) have been removed from the museums. The Ark, 80% of which was destroyed by Frunze, is now restored. The Registan, where so many atrocities took place, is empty apart from the passengers queueing at the bus stop. Bukhara's population of 300,000 makes it the fifth largest city in Uzbekistan and the discovery of natural gas resources nearby in 1953 has certainly contributed to this.

Note that in 1997 Bukhara celebrates its 2500th anniversary (by whose mathematics?), so expect crowds and festivities.

ORIENTATION AND SERVICES

The railway station (Kagan) is a 10-20 minute drive from the centre of town. From here, virtually all minibuses will take you to the centre (the standard fare is about US$0.50). The only part of Bukhara worth exploring is the old town, which is to the north of the main city. The telegraph office (open 8am-6pm daily) is near the Hotel Bukhoro.

Tourist information and tours

Uzbektourism, in the Hotel Bukhoro, offers the following tours: **City Tour** (3hrs; US$28), **Ark** (2hrs; US$17), **Kizylkum Desert** (4hrs,

US$32), **Afshona** – the birthplace of Avicenna (4hrs, US$33) and **Golden Embroidery Factory** (1hr, US$9). You will probably be able to pick a guide cheaper at the Ark or, if you're staying at Mubinjan Tadgier's house, ask Mubinjan to put you in touch with Zinnat Ashurova – who has been recommended by several readers.

Money
The Hotel Bukhoro may or may not change travellers cheques: they wouldn't for us but clearly can if they feel like it. Otherwise go to the National Bank for Foreign Economic Activities, which is a five-minute walk from the hotel – although they take a 5% commission and may be baffled by anything that doesn't have American Express written on it. They are open 0800-1700 Mon-Fri, closed 1230-1330.

LOCAL TRANSPORT

Most minibuses from the station go to the city centre. You could take bus No1, getting off just to the east of the central *khauz* (pond) and it's then a 10 minute walk (south) to the four hotels below. From the centre of the old town you are only likely to need transport to the railway station (bus No 1 from just east of the Liab-i-Khauz) but if you decide to wander around 'new' Bukhara there are extensive bus, minibus and trolley-bus services. Bus No 7 takes you to the main bus station. If you have arrived by plane, bus No 10 will take you the 3km into the town centre. Taxis are easy to find and are a good alternative if you find the buses too crowded.

WHERE TO STAY

The main hotels are located close to one another and there doesn't seem to be much difference between them. If you've booked in advance with Uzbektourism you'll probably end up in the **Hotel Bukhoro** (☎ 705 016)

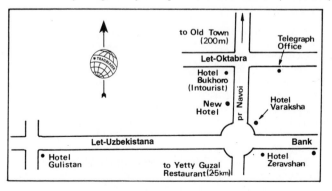

currently the most upmarket place in town, at US$43 for a double. A new Indian-Uzbek **joint venture hotel** is under construction about 200m from the Hotel Bukhoro, and will undoubtedly take over the top spot when it opens. Work appeared to have stopped when we visited, however, so this may be some time yet.

Nearby, the **Hotel Zeravshan** (☎ 37341) is pretty run-down and there tends to be no hot water. Rooms are cheap, though, at US$10 per person. Friendlier than the Zeravshan but further away is **Hotel Gulistan** (no phone), at US$13 per person. **Hotel Varaksha** (☎ 38494) seems OK, too. Tours can be organised here and some of the staff speak very good English. Rooms are US$15 per person.

Best of all, however, are two guesthouses near the centre of the old town. Just 300m from the Liab-i-Khauz, **Mubinjan Tadgier's house** (☎ 42005), at 4 Ishoni Pir Street, is a great place to stay. It's US$10 per person (in the off season the price also includes breakfast). The building is a traditional Uzbek merchant's house and the rooms, arranged around a shady courtyard are wonderful: white-washed walls and huge wooden beams make them airy and cool, and the traditional sleeping mats on the floor give a surprisingly good night's sleep. The only drawback is that apart from a wash basin there are no washing facilities; the public bath houses are, however, only a short distance away. Apart from this, the house is certainly a place you won't forget, Mubinjan and his family are tremendously hospitable, and the food is great. To get here, walk southwards from the south-west corner of the *khauz* (pond). About 200m down the lane there's a metal garage door with sporting pictures on it. Turn right immediately and knock on the next door. If you get lost, ask anyone for Mubinjan: everyone seems to know him. Similarly priced, the **Bed and Breakfast Hotel** (☎ 33890/35593) at Molodejnaja 13, has been highly recommended and is another place you could try.

WHERE TO EAT

The **Hotel Bukhoro** is generally regarded as having the best hotel food in town and can actually be quite good; expect to pay about US$4 for a good evening meal.

If you want an upmarket meal and don't mind travelling for it, try the **Yetty Guzal** (☎ 22966), about 2km down Pr Navoi from the Hotel Zeravshan (look for the big sign, left). Any trolley-bus going this way will take you but a taxi is easier. This place seems to be patronised by the upper classes in Bukhara but be warned that they don't speak any English here and the menu seems to have nothing to do with the food. Still, it's clean, and the food is good.

For cheaper food try either the **market** (near the Samanid mausoleum) where you can gorge yourself on anything from pistachio nuts to whole fried chickens, or the two **cafés** beside the khauz in the centre of town. The food is basic but very cheap (noodles, shashlik etc) and you couldn't ask for a better setting, although they tend to close by about 6.30 pm. Try the fruit juice at the supermarket by the khauz, too.

WHAT TO SEE

Before attempting any sightseeing, spend at least a day just wandering around but be prepared to get thoroughly lost. As Geoffrey Moorhouse notes, '...because these alleys twisted and doglegged erratically, it was very easy to lose all sense of direction and return to a starting point without the slightest inkling that one had gone astray. It was like trying to find a way through some gigantic maze made of baked mud' (*Apples in the Snow*).

Watch out for children begging in the backstreets – handing out Western goodies doesn't really help them or future visitors at all.

The Ark and Registan

Although the buildings you see today are either recently restored or date back only to the 16th century, there has been a large fortress here ever since the first century. The West Gate was one of many entrances but only this one, leading to the main square, or Registan, has been restored.

The Ark was the fortified residence of the emirs of Bukhara, who were notorious for their cruelty and corrupt ways. Hanging above the archway until 1920 was a huge six-tailed leather whip signifying justice. One emir, Nasrullah, commissioned a great clock to be mounted there too. Italian watchmaker Giovanni Orlando built it, only to be promptly executed over some triviality. The whip is in the museum inside the fortress but the clock has disappeared. As you walk through the entrance note the prison cells on the left, strategically situated under the stables so that when the yard was washed down all the effluent would flow into them.

The Ark was more than just a home for the emir: it was also his barracks, mint, shrine (there is a mosque inside) and prison. About 3000 people lived inside its walls. Each building has now been converted into a museum and although there is no English labelling, it's fairly easy to work out what's what. There is an especially valuable 10th-century Koran in the Friday Mosque. If you wander up directly above the West Gate itself you can see the curved stable floor which drains into the cells below. You can also see the spot where the emir would sit to watch floggings and executions in the Registan below – the square where Stoddart and Connolly were beheaded 150 years ago (see The Great Game, p280). their remains are probably still buried here somewhere to this day.

When the emir went to worship in the **Bollo Khauz Mosque** (1712) opposite the Registan, the whole square was carpeted. The small minaret here has leaned since an earthquake in 1976. The pond (*khauz*) is one of only two remaining in Bukhara today (there used to be more than 80 but they were so polluted that the Russians drained them).

The Ark itself is open all day, but the museums open from 9am to 5pm and are closed on Wednesday. There's a small entry charge plus camera and video-camera fees. Outside, high over the square, is an old water tower which was converted into a cafe. This is closed now, but if you can get up to the top you'll get a terrific view of the city.

Samanid Mausoleum

Not far from Bollo Khauz, this is generally considered to be one of the greatest pieces of Central Asian architecture in the world. Built at the order of Ismail Samani (reigned 892-907) for his father, it ended up as the family vault. It is one of the oldest surviving buildings in Bukhara thanks to the fact that Genghis Khan didn't find it (it was either buried or concealed by trees, depending on whom you believe). Despite all the superlatives it is small and deceptively simple, which is a pleasant surprise when most other buildings are huge, flamboyant creations. The two squares above each doorway are supposedly aerial plans of the building. Note also the crypt inside with a hole at each end: after it was discovered in the 1920s, resident mullahs spread it around that the mausoleum was an oracle. Locals placed their question, wrapped in a wad of banknotes, in one hole, and picked up the oracle's 'advice' from the other the next day.

Chashma Ayub

Very close to the mausoleum is Chashma Ayub, an ancient spring created, according to local legend, by the Biblical character, Job, during a drought. The building housing it has been remodelled a number of times over the years, notably in the 12th, 14th, and 16th centuries, resulting in a mismash of architectural styles. (The 12th-century conical cupola is considered particularly unusual). The spring itself has long been supposed to be curative and analysis shows that its water is potassium-rich. Chashma Ayub is right next to the bazaar and food market, behind which can be seen the crumbling remains of the original city walls.

Zindan

The most sinister relic of the days before Russian rule lies at the north-eastern corner of the Ark. Zindan, meaning 'alive' in Tajik, was the city jail. Inside are three cells, two of which were for debtors who were compelled to work for the jailers in order to redeem their debts. They were not fed, relying entirely on the charity of friends and relatives.

The third cell, for more serious offenders, is simply a hole in the ground known as the 'Bug Pit' because the guards used to sweep vermin and insects on top of the prisoners. One recent commentary suggests that tarantulas, specially bred for their size and venomous bite, were released in here but this seems unlikely. This is the cell where Charles Stoddart spent six months of his life, later to be joined by Arthur Connolly for a final three months before they were both beheaded in 1842.

Kalyan Minaret Ensemble (Poi Kalyan)

Probably the most impressive sight in Bukhara, the **Kalyan Minaret**, built in 1127, stands 46.5m tall; Genghis Khan was so impressed that he left it standing in 1220. The tallest minaret in Central Asia, its foundations go down 13m; and it's said that its strength comes from special mortar in which blood and camel's milk were used instead of water. Note the intricate bands of decorative brickwork, 14 in all. It's had a number of uses, including the calling of the righteous to prayer (pity the poor muezzin who had to climb the 105 steps five times every day), a lighthouse, and a launching pad for criminals tied up in sacks. Hardly surprising, then, that it came to be known as the Tower of Death (the last execution here was in 1884).

It is flanked by the **Kalyan Mosque** to the west and the **Mir-i-Arab Madrassah** to the east. The mosque was completed in 1514 and covers exactly one hectare. It can easily accommodate more than 10,000 people at a time, making it the second largest in Central Asia – after the Bibi Khanum in Samarkand. Note the stork's nest on the dome. The madrassah, meanwhile, is one of the few in Bukhara still in use. It was built by Ubaidullah Khan with the money he received from the sale of 3000 Persian slaves. The name 'Mir-i-Arab' means Prince of Arabs, the soubriquet of Abdullah, Sheikh of Yemen, who lies buried here.

> Local legend holds that the only person ever to have survived a 'fall' from the Kalyan Minaret was a young woman who had recently married a wealthy businessman. Just before the executioner was to push her from the top, she asked that, as a last request, she might be allowed to wear the dresses her husband had bought her. Not knowing which outfits to bring, the servant sent to her house brought her whole wardrobe – 40 dresses in all. Calmly she put on all 40, one on top of the other, and then allowed herself to be thrown from the top. The padding cushioned her fall, however, and she survived, whereupon the emir was so impressed that he spared her life. It is now a tradition that every man must give his wife 40 new dresses on her wedding day – just in case.

Ulugh Beg and Abdul Aziz Khan Madrassahs

Ulugh Beg's Madrassah, completed in 1417, is considered a fine example of really good Central Asian architecture. One wonders why he should have built a madrassah here in Bukhara before he built one in Samarkand, since that was where he lived. It is also famous for its inscription, 'The desire for sciences is the duty of both men and women' – a statement sure to cause offence to misogynistic Muslims. This helps to explain why he came to such an unfortunate end (see p150).

The Abdul Aziz Khan Madrassah opposite is a copy made 250 years later (1652) but never finished; note the beams still protruding from the walls. This building reveals the architect's poor sense of balance and proportion and his attempted rejection of the Islamic prohibition of animate images. If you can get inside, look for the man-made optical illusion to the right of the entrance: in the right light, the silhouette of a man is clearly visible but this fades away as the light changes.

Liab-i-Khauz and surroundings

Bukhara's water supply originally consisted of a series of tanks scattered around the city. Since the water in these was used for washing, laundry, horse-watering and drinking, it all got a bit soupy, and most of the population spent their time dying horrible scabby deaths from various plagues. It is still possible to find some of the empty pools around the town, but the Liab-i-Khauz, right in the centre, is still maintained. It was commissioned by Nadir Divan Begi in 1620, is five metres deep, and now, surrounded by ancient mulberry trees (planted in 1475), it provides a lovely shady haven; there is no better place in Central Asia to drink tea, contemplate life, or just sit. Helping to create the mellow atmosphere are three major buildings flanking the khauz.

The most colourful of these is the **Divan Begi Madrassah** (see photo opposite p96) to the east, with its remarkable portal: the mosaic covering the arch, featuring two large birds beneath a personified sun, consists of over 11 million ceramic tiles. This madrassah, also built by Nadir Divan Begi, was supposed to be a caravanserai. Shortly before it was finished, however, Khan Imamkuli rode by and commented that it was a beautiful madrassah. Not wishing to imply that the Khan had been mistaken, Nadir had it restructured.

Directly opposite the madrassah on the western side of the khauz is the **Nadir Divan Begi Khanaka** (1620), which was designed as an inn for Muslim dervishes. It is now an arts and crafts gallery and gift shop.

Nasreddin

The statue immediately to the east of the khauz represents Islamic comic hero, Hoca Nasreddin. A traditional story tells of his solving a local dispute: one afternoon, three men were standing beneath the Kalyan Minaret arguing heatedly. They could not agree as to how it had been constructed; the first thought it had been built upwards with bricks, rather like a house. The second thought that this was impossible: obviously it had been carved downwards out of a huge chunk of stone. The third, meanwhile, disagreed again: the only way to make something of this size, he argued, was to assemble it on the ground and then to haul it upright later.

Nasreddin happened to be listening from behind the minaret. 'Gentlemen, you are all wrong' he said, emerging with a grin. 'It took only two very simple steps. First they dug a huge well. And then they simply turned it inside-out.'

On the north side is the **Kukeldash Madrassah** (1568-9), once the key religious school in Bukhara and the largest in Central Asia. With the arrival of the Russians it was closed down and now houses the city's archives.

Magoki Attari Mosque
Of all the mosques in Bukhara, this is probably the most intriguing because its origins are shrouded in mystery. It was renovated in the 12th century, although the main facade is 10th century work. The reason that it sits so low in the ground is not that it was built underground but rather that, over the years, the dust has accumulated everywhere else: Bukhara is slowly being buried.

Nobody really knows much about this mosque; archaeologists have found evidence of previous worship beneath the building and some reports state that this area was already considered sacred by the Sogdians as early as 500BC. This is possible but is difficult to prove. Remains have been found of Buddhism and Zoroastrianism. Go into the main entrance and turn 180° sharp right or left to see the extent of the excavations.

Chor Minor
This building, constructed in 1807 as the entrance of a madrassah, is particularly worth a visit, if only because of its originality. An old proverb relates that he who manages to climb the steps of the building and then make it back down without being bitten by the snakes inside is 'sinless'. In fact, the chances of actually meeting a snake inside are remote. It's very photogenic and for some reason pictures always seem to make it look much bigger than it is.

Summer Palace (Sitori Makhi-Khosa)
Opinions vary: local people tend to rave about this as the most beautiful building in Bukhara, while visitors generally consider it little more than an exercise in kitsch. Built at the turn of this century, it reflects the emirs' attempts to keep up to date with modern European styles. It is now a museum and guides here show you the pool and tell you that the last khan (Said Ali, exiled to Afghanistan in 1920) would sit in the small pavilion (still standing) watching his harem frolic in the water. This is rubbish, since the pool is within full view of common land and if there was frollicking to be done it would have been done out of sight. The palace is open 9am-4.30pm daily.

Excursion to Chor-Bakr
A 20-minute drive from Bukhara, this necropolis is not really on the tourist main line but it should be. It's the resting place of Abu Bakr Said, a 'descendant' of Mohammed, and has become something of a pilgrimage destination. 'Chor' means beauty or purity, while 'Bakr' is the name of one of the wealthy families whose burial vaults lie here. With the

arrival of the communists, however, the families left and have never returned, apart from one clan who carried out a secret burial here one night in 1921.

You will find the tomb of Al Bakr Said if you look carefully; the tree beside it is decked with ribbons and faded pieces of string indicating supplications to the saint. Orthodox mullahs look upon this with disdain.

The mosque here has been under restoration since 1987 but it looks like they left it too late – there are massive cracks in the side. The site is fairly overgrown and there are snakes here, so either wear sensible shoes or don't go ploughing through the undergrowth.

To get here you will need to take a taxi; get the driver to wait for you, otherwise you'll be stuck. Best time to go is in the early morning or evening, when the ruins look particularly romantic.

WHAT TO BUY

Bukhara is famous for its rugs but you won't find many around today. There are other local crafts here, though: inside old madrassahs you may find arts and crafts stores where you can watch the craftsmen at work. Particular favourites are brass or copper plates and wooden boxes; some of the embroidery is very fine, too. Try the Nadir Divan Khanaka for a browse. Be extremely careful when buying 'antiques'. There is a good quality jewellery and souvenir shop in the Tak-i-Zargaran trading dome but it is fairly expensive. The Hotel Bukhoro sells postcards, maps and other tourist supplies.

MOVING ON

By rail
There are two trains daily to Tashkent (via Samarkand), Nos 53 and 61 departing at 16.00 and 20.15. Samarkand is seven hours away. The two trains to Urgench are Nos 54 and 918, leaving at 05.25 and 16.00.

By bus
From the main bus station there are long-distance buses to several destinations. For Samarkand (273km, $6^1/_2$ hrs, US$5) there are buses at 07.10, 09.30, 10.30, 11.30 and 13.20. Buses for Tashkent (555km, 12hrs, US$10) leave at 06.00, 08.30, 16.00 and 18.00. There's a bus to Urgench (450km, 9hrs, US$8) at 14.40.

By air
Flights operate regularly from Bukhara to Tashkent and Moscow. There are flights to Urgench and Samarkand but these tend to be irregular: check in advance.

Samarkand

Of all Central Asian cities, Samarkand is the one which most fires the imagination. Alexander the Great was moved by its beauty, Marco Polo admired it and Tamerlane made it the capital of his empire. European poets dreamed of it and sighed, and for the West it became a symbol of all that was forbidden and mysterious about the East. Things have changed; not much has survived. What there is, though, is astonishing both in scale and intricacy. Two days here is enough to see the main sights, although each monument probably merits as long on its own.

HISTORY

Samarkand officially celebrated its 2500th birthday in 1970 although it is probably much older than this. Reliable evidence is scarce but archaeologists have unearthed traces of a large human settlement dating way back beyond the 6th century BC.

The Greek historian, Strabo, writes of this city as Marakanda, the capital of Sogdiana in the Persian Achaemendi kingdom and records the arrival of Alexander the Great in 329/8 BC (who commented that it was 'even more beautiful' than he had imagined). It was here, in a famous drunken brawl, that Alexander killed Cleitus, one of his own generals, with a spear. Plagued with guilt afterwards he was reconciled to this act only by his friends' insistence that his drunken outburst was punishment by Dionysius (the god of wine) for not having made the correct sacrifices earlier.

Ten centuries of invasions

Alexander's Macedonian empire crumbled shortly after his death and, in the following centuries, Samarkand was invaded by the Seleucids, the Graeco-Bactrians, the Kushans and the Turks. The Arabs brought Islam with them in the 8th century, to leave the Samanids, in the 9th, as rulers of the first independent Islamic state in Central Asia. These power struggles and invasions continued until the arrival of Genghis Khan in March 1220. He wrecked the city so comprehensively that the original site of Afrasiab was abandoned altogether and the whole town was shifted to a patch of wasteland immediately to the south. Sources indicate that over 300,000 of the 400,000 inhabitants were killed or forced to flee. It recovered fast, though: by the time Marco Polo arrived fifty years later however, he noted that Samarkand, on its new site, was 'a very large and splendid city'.

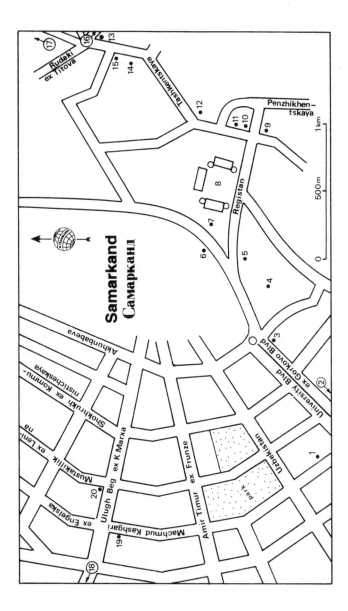

Timur, having been born in nearby Shakrisabz (in 1336), decided that Samarkand was to be the heart of his empire, the 'centre of the universe'. Artists and architects were recruited from all over Asia to develop it, and they didn't mess around: it was all done in some style. Timur's grandson, Ulugh Beg, a noted intellectual, brought the capital to the cutting edge of art and science: Omar Khayam (author of *The Rubaiyat*), Al-Biruni (who suggested that the earth might revolve around its own axis) and Avicenna (see p134) all lived here. Samarkand had reached its zenith.

By the 16th century the ruling Sheibanids had moved their capital to Bukhara, leaving Samarkand in decline until 1868, when the Russians arrived. On 15 May 1888 the first train pulled in, shunting it back onto the map. Restoration of monuments began under Lenin in 1921, and the city was declared capital of the Uzbek Socialist Republic in 1925, only to be replaced by Tashkent in 1930.

Samarkand today

You can't fail to notice the Russian influence. From being a relatively backward Islamic city in the last century, Samarkand has come a long way. According to the official figures, the surrounding region currently produces 500,000 tonnes of cotton per year, which is more than the entire state of Uzbekistan produced before the Revolution. While such figures may be suspect (Uzbekistan is notorious for its fraudulent crop statistics), they do ring true: Uzbek soil is virtually all farmed hyperintensively. Consequently the land, once rich, needs increasing doses of fertilisers in order to produce the required yield. Natural water supplies have been wrecked by artificial irrigation schemes and the earth is polluted with chemicals. One wonders how long farming of any sort can continue.

The corollary of this Russian input, however, is that Samarkand has been dragged into the 20th century. Main roads converging on Registan Square, one of the greatest Islamic architectural ensembles in the world, have converted it into a roundabout. Independence seems to have changed little around here. The inhabitants are fairly pessimistic about the future and are only too aware that withdrawal from the USSR has knocked Uzbekistan's status: from being a part of the world's greatest superpower it is now simply another backward country.

KEY

1 Hotel Zeravshan	9 Taxis to Shakrisabz	16 Shaki Zinda (400m)
2 To Hotel Wajan	10 Museum of Culture	17 Observatory (3km)
3 Hotel Samarkand	11 Café	18 To Railway Station
4 Gur Emir Mausoleum	12 Café	Hotels Sayor/Turist
5 Café	13 Shark Restaurant	(see map p147)
6 Afrosiab Hotel	14 Bibi Khanum	19 War Memorial
7 Marco Polo Stone	Mosque	20 Hotel Leningrad
8 Registan Square	15 Bazaar	

ORIENTATION AND SERVICES

Basically, for the old town, head east. For the new, go west. Samarkand is not a difficult city to find your way around in, and most hotels and sights are within walking distance of the centre of town, Registan Square. Be slightly wary of the maps on sale from street vendors; there is a considerable amount of building going on in Samarkand, and this combined with the renaming of streets after independence has meant that many city maps are now way out of date.

Uzbektourism is at the Hotel Samarkand. They offer the following tours: **city tour** (3hrs, US$25) – 'a total waste of time' was one report, **Penzhikent** (full day, US$180), **Shakrisabz** (full day, US$100), **Ismail Buchari** (3hrs, US$50). All prices are for a car. If there is already a bus tour going, however, you may be able to join at the last minute and this could be worthwhile (ie US$10 for the town tour or a trip to Penzhikent). The closer to the departure time you ask, the cheaper the seat seems to be.

Two other travel organisations also arranging tours are: **Orient Star**, Mirzo Ulughbek 39/9 (☎ 331914, fax 311423), and **Optimist Travel**, 237 Dagbitskaia Str (☎ 352942, fax 310589). Both can arrange homestays and assist with travel arrangements (see p22).

Money
The National Bank in the Hotel Samarkand changes travellers cheques. If you have problems here (with old banknotes, for example) ask to be directed to their main branch who have been known to swap old dollar bills for new – for no charge.

LOCAL TRANSPORT

Local transport is fairly good. Trolley-buses Nos 1 or 3 will take you from the railway station to the Registan. Bus No 10 is particularly useful, running from the airport to the train station, passing the bus station, the Registan and the Hotel Zarafshon en route. Bus No 1 will also take you to the bus station, and No 3 goes to the train station. There are numerous minibuses plying individual routes. All get very crowded at rush hour.

WHERE TO STAY

Excluding homestays (US$15-20; see agencies listed above) your best bet for budget accommodation is the **Hotel Zarafshon** (☎ 333372). It's basically clean, central and friendly. Singles are US$15 but you may get charged less than this (we paid US$8 for a double).

The **Hotel Samarkand** (☎ 358812) offers standard 'Intourist' fare for US$55 single, US$70 double. The top hotel town is **The Afrosiab** (☎ 312236, fax 311044) which is still more expensive, with singles at US$105 and doubles at US$140. There's a swimming pool being built.

There are several other hotels but all suffer from one drawback or another: the **Hotel Sayor** (☎ 214916) is difficult to find although it is fairly close to the railway station: take trolley-bus No 1 or bus No 6 and get off by the roundabout with the statue of a horse and rider (it's a few hundred metres west of the statue of Gagarin on the main road from the station). Singles are US$17, doubles US$28. The **Hotel Leningrad** (☎ 335225) is closer to town, but it's in a bad state. Singles are US$10, doubles US$20. Less dilapidated is the **Hotel Turist** (☎ 240704), a high-rise monster a fair way from the city centre – but what a depressing place! Singles are US$17, doubles US$30, which they may well demand in hard currency.

A new hotel, the **Watan** (☎ 337214) is a lot better. It's half a block past ulitsa Machmud Kashgari on University Blvd. Locals say that it's for military personnel only but they seem willing to take anyone. Singles are US$25, doubles US$50.

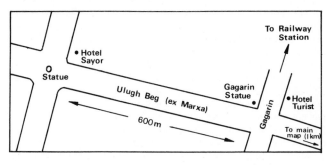

WHERE TO EAT

You are unlikely to get much more upmarket in Samarkand than the **Afrosiab Hotel** – or, if you can't get in there, the **Hotel Samarkand**. Otherwise, try the **Dilshod Restaurant** next to the Zarafshon Hotel. Note that it doesn't open until 7-7.30pm and that it is reasonably smart: you will be out of place in a sweaty t-shirt. The **Ramzes Restaurant** on ulitsa Amu Timur, a couple of blocks past ulitsa Machmud Kashgari has been recommended. In fact, the area around that end of ulitsa Machmud Kashgari is pretty well stocked with acceptable places to eat. The **Zarafshon Hotel** itself serves good, big meals at reasonable prices (breakfast is good) but evening meals are accompanied by an unusually atrocious (even for Uzbekistan) live band.

Most travellers end up eating in the **chaikhanas**. Anywhere in the market is good (but it's not a good place to wander alone at night). Food is usually shashlik, pilov or greasy meat soup but it's filling and very cheap. Opposite the bazaar, try the **Shark Restaurant**; you may need to buy the beers from the vendors outside on the pavement.

The chaikhana opposite the Registan is a good shady spot, and the corner of ulitsa Tashkent has a group of good places to sit and eat. If you want tea, you'll have to find some cups and wash them yourself.

WHAT TO SEE

✓ Registan Square

This square really constitutes the heart of the city. The Registan (literally 'sandy place') seems always to have been busy; originally it was the bazaar, with a caravanserai on the northern side. Skirting the square are three madrassahs and a mosque, and the effect of this combination is devastating. If you aren't impressed by this 'noblest of all squares' (Lord Curzon), then you might as well go home now.

The earliest of the three buildings is the **Ulugh Beg Madrassah** to the west (left as you face the central building). It is acknowledged to be the best of the three by Those Who Know. Built at the command of this great ruler between 1417-20, it housed up to two hundred students studying sciences, mathematics, astronomy, law, languages and theology. Ulugh Beg himself taught here. The fact that it has been restored is most easily seen by looking at the minarets, which were leaning precariously until fairly recently. Soviet engineers were called in and in 1938 the right hand minaret was rotated through 180° (no mean feat considering its size). The left hand minaret was straightened in 1965. To see the curve, look along the right hand wall. Inside the madrassah there's a small art gallery.

Directly opposite Ulugh Beg is the **Shir Dor Madrassah**. Built at the order of 'Little Timur' Amir Yalangtush Bahadir between 1619 and 1636, this was meant to be the mirror image of the Ulugh Beg Madrassah. Clearly it is not identical but apparently if you were to tip the frontals of the two madrassahs towards each other they would just touch along the centreline of the Registan. Shir Dor means 'lion-bearing'; the lions (that look more like tigers) above the entrance represent the rising sun, thus exempting themselves from the Islamic prohibition of animal images.

Between the two are the **Tillya Kari Mosque** and **Madrassah**. The name means 'decorated with gold' and they date from 1646-60. The inside of the mosque itself is recently restored (1979), and it is breathtaking (see p96-7). Note, however, the patches of water rising up the walls already, taking the colours as they go.

Entry to the Registan costs US$0.60.

✓ Shakh-i-Zindah

This necropolis, in its original location (Genghis Khan's troops refused to touch it) is one of Samarkand's highlights. Legend has it that Qutham ibn Abbas, either the cousin or the nephew of the Prophet Mohammed, was beheaded here by infidels. Instead of dying, he picked up his severed head and disappeared into the depths of a well, where he still lives today. Since then aristocrats have clamoured to be buried near the grave of this saint, resulting in a narrow alley of highly decorated mausoleums nicknamed 'City of the Dead'.

Abbas's tomb is at the top end on the right and although excavations reveal that there is actually no body here, the gravestone (which can be seen through a lattice grille) is original, listing his death as occurring in 676/7. The inscription above the door reads, 'The gates of paradise are open wide for the believer'. Modern legends linger as to his survival, and there are numerous rumours telling of a city of catacombs beneath the site.

Most other tombs date to within a century or so of Timur's time. The second mausoleum on the left (Timur's niece, 1372) is regarded as the best. Keep an eye out for the architects' signatures on the portals of the tombs. Remember that this spot is considered sacred by many (you are likely to see people praying in Abbas's tomb) so dress and act appropriately. Entry is US$0.80.

Gur Emir Mausoleum

This is the mausoleum of many of the key members of the Timur line including the Big Man himself, and despite its mediocre size it is breathtaking. Originally built for a favourite grandson, Mohammed Sultan, Timur was laid here because he died unexpectedly in 1405, while his real tomb in Shakrisabz (see p151) was not yet complete. He lies at the foot of his spiritual guide, Sheikh Mirsaid Bereke, and grandson Ulugh Beg is beside him. The entrance is marked by a long pole sticking out of a tomb opposite. While digging the mausoleum's foundations, workmen found human remains. Not willing either to find a new site or to desecrate the grave they reburied the individual as a holy man in the crypt of the king

The tombs were opened in 1941 and it was confirmed that Timur was lame (and he had had tuberculosis) and that Ulugh Beg had been murdered (beheaded by his own son). A time capsule was included when the tombs were closed. The jade stone over Timur's grave was originally one slab, brought back from Mongolia by Ulugh Beg, but it was stolen by Persian invaders under Nadir Shah. They took it to Messhed, only to return it, in two pieces, because it had brought them bad luck. Numerous modern myths surround the unsealing of Timur's tomb. An inscription was said to have been found warning that the opening of the crypt would release the spirit of war. Germany marched on Russia the day after the opening.

Gur Emir has been undergoing restoration for some time now and, judging by the amount of activity going on in 1996, it will remain closed for some time. If you do get in, beware of the extra camera charge as it is dark inside and pictures are unlikely to come out unless you have a very high powered flash. It is sometimes possible to get into the crypt beneath the building.

There is a large slab of carved marble in the courtyard outside the mausoleum which is supposed to be Kok Tash, the stone upon which Timur's throne sat. This is unlikely, but it has certainly been used for coronations since. The large stone bowl beside it was part of Timur's pre-battle ritual: he would have it filled with pomegranate juice (dark red) and then his army would file past, each man taking a swig of the 'blood' of the enemy.

✓Bibi Khanum Mosque

Designed to accommodate over 10,000 people, this mosque was to have been Timur's pièce de résistance. Unfortunately, it started to collapse; some say it was just too big, others too hurriedly built, still others blame seismic activity. Whatever the cause, shortly after it was finished in 1404 cracks started appearing. The huge stone lectern you see in the courtyard was placed in the mosque by Ulugh Beg but was moved outside in 1855 when it became clear that the building was no longer safe. It collapsed in an earthquake in 1887. Restoration started in 1974 and was supposed to be completed in 1985. It is still dragging on, however, and consequently the area is hemmed in with rusty scaffolding and the odd crane or two.

Legend has it that the head architect working on the mosque fell in love with Timur's wife, Bibi Khanum (hence the name). He beseeched her for a kiss but that fabled kiss left a permanent scar on her lips. Timur was not at all happy when he discovered this and called for the executioner, whereupon the architect promptly climbed to the top of a minaret, sprouted wings, and flew home to Persia. Entry is US$1 and there's an extra camera fee of US$1, so hide the camera unless you enjoy taking pictures of scaffolding.

✓Ulugh Beg's Observatory

Ulugh Beg, Timur's grandson, was one of the greatest intellectuals of his time. Although a noted theologian, mathematician and poet, his real passion was for astronomy. The remains of his observatory lie a couple of kilometres north of the bazaar (take minibuses Nos 1, 17, or 45 from the bazaar. Ask for 'Ulugh Beg').

The observatory was a circular three-storeyed building containing a sextant which stood 55 metres tall. In 1437, using this unique instrument he compiled the world's first star atlas and calculated the length of a year to within one minute of what we now know it to be. Unfortunately his great passion for science was out of kilter with the religious authorities of the day and, in league with his son, they organised a coup: Ulugh Beg was beheaded and his observatory torn down by a mob of dervishes. Legend holds that his extensive library was saved and lies hidden to this day. All that remains of the observatory is an 11 metre sextant arc which was discovered by a Soviet archaeologist in 1908. It's probably not wildly exciting unless you're an astronomy nut. Beware of extortionate camera charges. There is a small Ulugh Beg museum, too.

Museum of Culture & Art of the Peoples of Uzbekistan
The contents of this museum do not live up to its grand name. It's so close to the Registan, however, that it's worth a look – and there are toilets here if you need them. When I visited I had the whole place to myself, apart from the curators who were busy trying to sell me the exhibits. It is open daily (except Wednesday) from 9am-5pm. Entry is US$0.80.

Excursions from Samarkand
• **Shakrisabz** This small town, the birthplace of Timur, is well worth a day trip although the sites are mostly in ruins. It is a quiet, pleasant city and the ride through the mountains alone makes the journey worthwhile.

To the south of the city, there's the **Kok Gumbaz Mosque** (1435-6). A small entry fee is charged but the place is rather decrepit. Not far from here is the **mausoleum of Jehangir** (Timur's grandson) and behind this is the **original site of Timur's mausoleum**: look for the small, sunken, whitewashed building with the green door. It is unlikely to be open unless you are in a tour group. All that remains of Timur's **Ak Sarai Palace** is the huge wreck of an arched doorway but it's excellent for those arty 'crumbling relic' photos. Shakrisabz is famous for its embroidery and if you know what you are looking for you may be able to pick up something really valuable. If you don't, be careful. The bazaar is good; try the wonderful black figs, but caution is advised since too many can lead to stomach upsets of China Syndrome proportions.

If you want to try to stay here, the **Hotel Shakrisabz** (☎ 4 16 28, fax 4 11 80) is quite reasonable. It's at ulitsa Ipak Yulei, 26 (formerly ulitsa Lenina). Singles are US$30, doubles US$42. Cheaper **homestays** can be arranged.

You will have trouble getting a bus here and if you do it will be a slow one, so take a taxi from near the museum (see map). Look for one with the letters 'КФ' or 'КФА' on the numberplate and it should be about US$30 for the 1½-hour ride). Getting away from Shakrisabz is harder than getting there. Taxis back to Samarkand are extremely difficult to find, so you may have to take a public bus to Kitop (20 mins), where you will be able to pick one up.

• **Penzhikent** Uzbektourism ships tourists here to look at the excavations of this 'ancient city'. Reports of the site are not glowing, however. It is dusty and dreary, although this might get better as it is cleaned up.

• **Al Bukhari Mosque** Trips are often made out here to visit the shrine of Ismail Al Bukhari (810-70), author of the most famous compilation of the Hadith (the book of teachings and sayings of Mohammed). There is not much to see, however, and what there is is fairly modern. Visitors should wear long trousers and women should also ensure that their arms and head are covered. There are no buses here, so you'll have to take a taxi for the 20-30km journey. This can be very expensive, as it's not a regular taxi route and drivers charge you as much as they possibly can.

WHAT TO BUY

Though there isn't much in the way of good souvenirs in Samarkand one of the most interesting places to browse around is the small art gallery in the Ulugh Beg Madrassah. The pictures and sculptures here are by local artists and although quite expensive, if you're looking for one really special souvenir of your trip this might be the place to get it.

The bazaar is good to wander around or for a cheap meal although there isn't much that a tourist would want to buy here apart from food. Postcards and maps are available from the stall in the Hotel Samarkand. Samarkand is famous for its embroidery and carpets but if you want to buy one of the ornate knives, you would do better to wait until Kashgar.

MOVING ON

There are currently only two trains daily to Tashkent. These are No 53 (21.10) and No 61 (00.58).

Buses depart every hour until 16.15 to Tashkent; departures to Bukhara are at 07.15, 10.00, 11.15, 13.15, 17.10 and 15.15. Two buses go to Urgench per day, at 18.00 and 19.00; the journey takes 15 hours.

There are flights to Tashkent, Urgench, Bukhara and Moscow.

Samarkand and science

Samarkand has been home to the greatest scientific minds on the planet. And if they didn't live in the city, they certainly lectured here. Although their names are unfamiliar in the West today, the mark they left on science is not.

Head of the tweed jacket brigade was **Mohammed Ibn Musa Al Khorezmi** in the 9th century. His early work was released in the West (centuries later) under the name 'Al Gorismi'. The result? Modern mathematicians solve problems using algorithms, not alkhorezms. His book was to become a classic: 'Al Jabr' – or, as we spell it, 'algebra'. And who could forget **Al Biruni**, the first man ever to study the solar corona? Or **Ulugh Beg**, Tamerlane's grandson? In the 14th century he compiled the first star atlas since the Greek astronomer, Hipparchus. Ulugh Beg's tables were a massive improvement, covering over 1000 stars. One of the few pieces of his library to have escaped destruction, the tables eventually found their way to Istanbul, where, discovered by an English academic, they became the basis for 17th century navigational charts.

Tashkent

Of the cities in this guide, the Uzbek capital is one of the least histori-
cally interesting. There is enough here, however, to make it worth stopping off for a day or two, and since rail links inevitably centre on the city,
you'll have to spend some time here, anyway. Tashkent is a good starting
point for treks in the nearby mountains, too, and either Uzbektourism or
any of the private agencies listed on p22 may be able to help with organising excursions.

Many travellers find Tashkent a rather bland (and expensive) city, and
there is no denying its modern character and Soviet pedigree – the street
layout and huge civic buildings are hallmarks of Russian city planning.
Tashkent grows on you though, particularly if you're visiting in spring or
summer, and along with some good places to wander in the 'new' city,
enough of the old town and markets remain to make a brief stay here
enjoyable.

HISTORY

Tashkent is in fact a fairly ancient city, dating back at least to the second
or third century BC. Over the years it has known a number of names,
including Dzhadzh, Chachkent, Shashkent and Binkent, its fortune coming mainly from traders passing through on their ways to and from the
Orient. The history of the settlement is, like that of other Uzbek towns,
difficult to trace since there have been numerous invasions and annexa-
tions. What we can say is that, like the others, it was taken by the Arabs
in the eighth century; that they brought Islam and a largely civilised outlook with them; that the Mongols arrived in 1220 (it is probably fairly
safe to assume that they left very little standing); that with the decline of
their power the Timurids took over followed by the Sheibanids, and that
Tashkent was ruled independently by the Uzbeks and the Kazakhs following this period until the Russians arrived in 1865, following 51 years
of rule by the khanate of Kokand.

The Soviet era

Under Russian rule Tashkent was destined for great things: in 1867 it was
made capital of Turkestan, and with the arrival of the Trans-Caspian railway on 1 May 1899 it became the administrative centre of Uzbekistan
(except for the brief period between 1925-30 when Samarkand was the
capital). During the Great Patriotic War it served as a host for thousands
of refugees, among them such Soviet luminaries as Ivanov and Pogodin.

Although the city has been growing fast throughout the 20th century, its only moment of real fame occurred in the winter of 1965, when, through the mediation of Soviet Premier Alexei Kosygin, Pakistani and Indian Prime Ministers Lal Bahadir Shastri and Mohammed Ayub Khan signed a treaty here that ended their 17-day old war over Kashmir. Shortly after this, on 26 April 1966, it was in the news under wholly less pleasant circumstances: an earthquake ripped the city in two, leaving over 300,000 people homeless. Reconstruction was necessary on such a grand scale that virtually nothing of any real antiquity remains.

Tashkent today

Tashkent is still very much at the heart of Uzbekistan, and rightly so; it was the fourth largest city after Moscow, Leningrad and Kiev in the USSR. It is a big, sprawling Westernised urbanisation with very little feel to it and a population of over two million. Still, while it is developing fast (the first metro lines were completed in 1977) the underdeveloped areas stay poor and thus the old town is increasingly cramped and squalid.

ORIENTATION AND SERVICES

In a town this size it is a good idea to buy the biggest map you can find, – the shop in the Hotel Uzbekistan sells an excellent map with English labels, or try the bookshop on Pushkin St; get a map with a metro plan and with the bus routes marked on it.

Basically, the modern heart of the city is in the east, with the Amir Temur statue at the centre. The old town is to the west. Note that there are **two railway stations**. Trains to/from the north (eg Moscow and Almaty) use the main station (Sevirny Vokzal), whilst those from Samarkand and the west stop at the more distant south station (Yuzhny Vokzal). The north railway station (Sevirny) is next to metro stop 'Tashkent', while the easiest way to get to the south station is by taxi.

The main post office is to the north of Amir Temur Square on Tolstoy St, and international phone calls can be made from here too. If you want to phone in more comfort, you can do so from the Business Centre in the Hotel Uzbekistan, but it will cost you twice as much.

The people at the exchange counter in the Hotel Uzbekistan are pretty good about changing cash and travellers' cheques, even for non residents. If you have trouble here, though, try the National Bank for Foreign

---

Changing street names

As Uzbekistan strives to wipe out linguistic traces of the Russian occupiers confusion reigns on the streets. Many street names have been changed in the last few years; we've used the name that's best known, even if it's the old Soviet one. In Uzbek the word 'street' is *kuchasi* (as opposed to ulitsa in Russian).

Economic Activities which is at 23 Yuldosh Okhunboboev Street, a short distance south east of Amir Temur Square.

Uzbek visas and extensions

The Ministry of Tourism (Independence Square) has taken over the issuing of visas but recent reports of this newly-formed ministry are not good and there are already stories of rampant overcharging. You may even need to bargain. Previously, OVIR (5 Navoi prospekti, and 87 Jukovsky) could sometimes be persuaded to help. There is also a visa office (OVIR) in the international terminal of Tashkent airport, but there are reports of visitors being kept waiting for several hours before a visa was issued. The office is tucked away on the third floor of the building.

Foreign consulates

China, 79 Gogol St, (☎ 338088, 331396)
Kazakhstan 20 Samatovoi St (☎ 333705, metro: Khamid Olimdjon)
Pakistan, 25 Chilonzor St (☎ 771003, 776687)
Russia, 83 Nukus St (☎ 552948, 557954)
UK, 67 Gogol St, (☎ 345652, 347658)
USA, 82 Chilonzor St (☎ 776986, 771407, 771081)

LOCAL TRANSPORT

Public transport in Tashkent is generally very good. There's a modern metro system as well as buses, trams and trolley-buses.

If you are interested in taking a tour you are best off contacting either your hotel's travel agency or enquiring at the Hotel Uzbekistan. Their guides department has tour guides who speak several languages; tours (around Tashkent or as far afield as Samarkand) can usually be arranged at short notice.

WHERE TO STAY

Hotel prices in Tashkent seem to have gone up across the board in the last few years, and this, combined with the problem of having to stay in 'approved' accommodation, can make it an expensive city to visit if you're on a tight budget. Possible solutions are to stay for a short time only, or to make contact with the local travel services (see p22) and see what they can offer in the way of homestays. Alternatively, resign yourself to spending a bit more than usual and enjoy your stay.

The most expensive hotel in the city is the newly opened **Hotel Tatar** which is a short way east of Amir Temur Square. A joint Uzbek-Indian venture, a room here will cost you in the order of US$100. More established as a tourist hangout is the **Hotel Uzbekistan** (☎ 337786, 367991) which is expensive, at US$70 for a single and US$90 for a double. Its location, however, is ideal, and it has some excellent facilities, including an efficient business centre, exchange counter, and a translator/guide service. It's even rumoured that you can get a cold drink in here.

Next down the line is the **Hotel Tashkent** (☎ 332735, 332741), a lovely old place right in the centre of the city, on the same square as the opera house. Be extremely polite to the staff here: they appear to make up the prices as they go along. When we arrived, in the early hours of the morning the cheapest room was US$50, but we later met two American travellers who had stayed for US$25, and remembered the Tashkent as one of the nicest places they'd stayed in throughout their trip across Central Asia.

A big step down in standard is the **Hotel Chorsu** (☎ 428231, 428002), which is about 4km west of the city centre. If you ask at the front desk you will be told that the cheapest rooms here cost US$40, but pay a visit to the tourist office on the second floor, and they can get you a room for US$26. Expect the worst: the reception is alternately chaotic and deserted, the staff are distinctly dodgy, and the food in the 'breakfast room' (this meal is included in the room price) is inedible. On the plus side, there's an excellent restaurant just opposite the hotel and you are also next to the colourful old town if you stay here.

Other hotels to try include the **Hotel Russia** (☎ 562874) at 2 Kunaev and the **Hotel Dustlik** (☎ 347358) at 7 Navoi prospekti; both of these have in the past taken foreigners but said they didn't have a licence to do so, when we visited. Likewise the **Hotel Yoshlick** at 5 Pakhtakor St, was one of the cheaper places to stay in 1993, but was closed for renovations in 1996.

Finally, next to the north station is the **Hotel Locomotiv** where a single room costs US$20.

KEY

1 Alaysky Market
2 Hotel Dustilik
3 Post Office
4 Book/Map Shop
5 Tion Restaurant
6 Hotel Uzbekistan
7 Amir Temur Square
8 Hotel Tatar
9 Café
10 National Bank for Economic Affairs
11 Local Bus Station
12 Bakhor Restaurant
13 Cafés and Restaurants
14 Opera House
15 Hotel Tashkent
16 Courage Monument
17 Pakhtakor Stadium
18 Kazakh Embassy
19 Sevirny Railway Station
20 Foreigners' Rail Booking Office
21 Fine Arts Museum
22 State Museum of the History of Uzbekistan
23 Ankhor Café
24 Hotel Yoshlick
25 Hotel Chorsu
26 Madrassah
27 Turkish Restaurant
28 Navoi Literary Museum

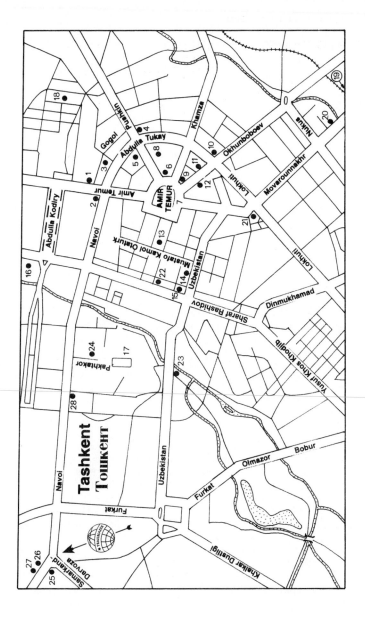

WHERE TO EAT

In the centre of town there are cafes and food vendors all over the place, so the cheapest way to eat is probably on the street. Head for the area around Mustafo Kamol Otaturk St (one block west of Amir Temur Square), where there's a variety of places for a snack and also for a proper meal. In summer, Sailgokh St becomes a big meeting place for locals, and the cafes here serve shashlik, cold drinks and ice creams. Nearby, however, you can also find the large (and fairly costly) **Zerefshan Restaurant** and several trendy fast food places including the **Turkish Café** and **American Food**.

For truly excellent shashlik and the breakfast of a lifetime, head for the Chigatai district of the **old town** (get there by 9am) where there is a very small, but busy, 'morning breakfast market'. Even if barbecued lamb isn't your idea of a perfect breakfast it's worth it; expect to be physically assaulted by numerous large ladies all trying to persuade you to buy their kebabs. Take a camera.

In the same area, and directly opposite the Hotel Chorsu, is another place not to be missed. The **Turkish Restaurant** is friendly, unbelievably clean (for Uzbekistan), and dishes up heaps of great food for a reasonable price. They even serve fresh baguettes with the meals.

Another excellent spot, for an evening meal in particular, can be found on Uzbekistan St, where the road crosses the Ankhor Canal. The **Ankhor Café** is cheap, has good food and has a pleasant setting next to the canal – it seems to be a favourite spot for well-heeled Uzbek government officials and businessmen after they finish work.

The **Tion**, on Pushkin St, is generally acknowledged to be one of the best places in town. If you're planning on an evening meal here book in advance. A degree of formality is expected, so don't wear shorts.

WHAT TO SEE

Old Tashkent

Definitely not the place to visit if you're planning on doing anything else that day, the old town is Tashkent the way it used to be before the Russians arrived – ie a maze. The streets are cramped and dirty but it's full of character. There isn't any point whatsoever in trying to find your way around the place – the only way you might conceivably find the way out is by trying specifically to get lost. Go early in the morning so that you have plenty of time on your hands.

One item worthy of note here is the oldest Koran in Tashkent. It's in a mosque on Zarkainar St; everyone knows where this street is although they'll all disagree on how to get there. The Koran is in building No 114, opposite a pleasant 16th century madrassah. Entry is free, although someone might try to charge you. The mighty tome (each page is a metre across) is in the building directly ahead of the entrance with the wooden door. Other Islamic texts decorate the room. Don't bother going before 9am but you might be turned away at any time.

To get to the old town, take virtually any bus going west along Navoi prospekti.

Alaysky Market
Not particularly exciting, but quite fun, and as good a place as any to buy fruit. Each stall boasts an elaborate display and if you watch closely you can actually catch the vendors polishing the fruit for this. It's probably not a good idea to buy the really shiny ones, as they are likely have been scrubbed with saliva and grotty handkerchiefs. It is up Amir Temur St.

Amir Temur Public Garden
There isn't much to see here but it's pleasant enough to wander among the food stalls and sit in the garden around the statue of Uzbekistan's national figurehead. This park used to be called Revolution Garden until recently, and a statue of Marx had pride of place. Now the huge statue of Timur dominates the place, with 'Strength in Justice' inscribed on the plinth.

The Courage Monument
This monument on Sharaf Rashidov prospekti commemorates the courage of Tashkent's citizens following the earthquake which devastated the city in 1966. An impressive statue stands alongside a block of stone that was supposedly shattered by the earthquake, and the monument itself stands at what's believed to have been the epicentre.

Museums
Tashkent museums are generally of a high standard. By now, however, you may have spent enough time looking at items and trying to work out what they are.
• **State Museum of the History of Uzbekistan** This museum is housed in an impressive new building on Matbuotchilar St, directly opposite Mustakillik (Independence) Square. It is open daily (except Monday) 10.00-18.00.
• **Fine Arts Museum** The exhibits here are drawn from, among other places, a collection formerly owned by a member of the Romanov family. It is at 6 Movarounnakr St and is open daily 10.00-17.00 (except Tues – closed, Monday 10.00-14.00). Entry is US$0.3.
• **Railway Museum** A small railway museum has been opened next to the north station, and locomotives from Russia, Czechoslovakia, USA, Germany and Hungary are on display. Entry is US$0.10, and the museum is open daily (except Monday and Tuesday) 09.00-17.00.
• **Navoi Literary Museum** Manuscripts, paintings and heaps of books by the man himself but since this 15th century Afghan writer is virtually

unknown in the West and labelling is in Cyrillic, this museum might be a bit boring for some. It's open 10am to 5pm, and located on Navoi prospekti, just after the intersection with Pakhtakor. Navoi's main work, *Mahakamat-al-Lugatayn (The Trial of the Two Languages)*, is available in translation.

• **The Applied and Decorative Art Museum** This place has been recommended, although we didn't visit it. It's open 10.00-18.00 daily and is near metro Kosmonavtlar.

WHAT TO DO IN THE EVENING
Opera
The Alisher Navoi Opera House, just south west of Amir Temur Square, was built in 1947 by the same architect who built Kazinsky station and Lenin's mausoleum in Moscow. There is a regular programme of music, opera and ballet here, and tickets (US$1-8) can be bought on the day of the performance from the ticket windows at the front of the building.

Nightclubs
If that's what you want, the **Asian Nightclub**, opposite the Yoshlick Hotel is the best bet. It is modern, obviously considered quite exclusive and patronised by a mixture of foreign businessmen and wealthy young locals. Entry is US $10-15. There is also a nightclub in the basement of the **Hotel Uzbekistan**.

WHAT TO BUY

Very little, really. If your stomach has recovered from the black figs you scoffed in Shakrisabz, why not try some more? Otherwise, sample some of the superb melons from the Alaysky market – quality here is good. Try to remember the taste so that you will be able to compare them with the 'world-famous' Hami melons in China.

MOVING ON
By rail
The **foreigners' booking office** is a short distance from the north railway station, on Movarounnakhr St. Tickets can be bought here for trains departing from either station, although you shouldn't be surprised if the staff, who are generally helpful, refer you to the police in the main station building (so that your visa and hotel vouchers can be checked) before they will sell you a ticket. It's open daily 08.00-12.00 and 13.00-17.00.

(**Opposite**) **Top:** S^u ($C_{\cdot}^y$) 250-65, built around 1949 and now plinthed at Kagan station (Bukhara). First versions of this locomotive were derived from the S^v introduced in 1915 and it was once commonly used throughout the USSR to haul passenger trains. **Bottom:** 'Hard Seat' is the cheapest class of rail travel in China.

Tickets to **Almaty** can be hard to come by and you would be wise to book as early as possible. There are two trains which ply the route on a schedule that seems so illogical it may well change. Train No T373 runs on odd days of the month (eg the 1st, 3rd etc) and leaves Tashkent at 13.55. Train No T199 runs on Monday, Wednesday and Friday and departs at 05.35. According to this scheme of things there will be days when there is no service at all, and other days when there are two trains, which seems ridiculous. Check the timetables at the foreigners' booking office. The journey to **Almaty** takes about 20 hours, and a second class ticket costs US$38. Trains leave from the north railway station.

Trains heading west depart from the south railway station but you should buy your tickets at the foreigners' ticket office by the north railway station. If you're planning to visit all the Silk Route cities to the west, it's probably worth working out a schedule and booking all your tickets before you go. Trains west run as follows: **Urgench** (No T54, departs 17.45, US$40 second class), **Bukhara** (No T62, 20.20, US$31 second class), **Samarkand** (No T80, 16.20, US$25 second class). The **Moscow** train, No T85 departs at 11.55 daily, and a second class ticket costs US$93.

At either station you may find that as soon as you set foot on the platform the police will want to check your visa, passport, hotel vouchers or train ticket.

By bus The bus station is on the metro, at Sabir Rahimov. From here there are buses to many destinations including Chimkent (3hrs), Samarkand (6hrs), Bishkek (13hrs) and Marghilian (9hrs).

By air

The airport is to the south of Tashkent and bus No 67 runs out there from the city centre (you can catch it just south of Amir Temur Square, on Movarounnakhr St). A taxi to the airport should cost the equivalent of about US$4. There are two terminals – the international terminal is a depressing three-storey concrete monstrosity, while the domestic terminal is an older, porticoed building, some 500m to the north. Buses to Tashkent run from in front of the domestic terminal.

There are flights to Urgench, Bukhara, Samarkand and Moscow. Domestic flights can be booked, among other places, in the Hotel Uzbekistan. Among the airlines offering international flights from Tashkent, Turkish Airlines has its office on Mustafo Kamol Otaturk St.

(Opposite) Food available from platform vendors includes such delicacies as snake fish.

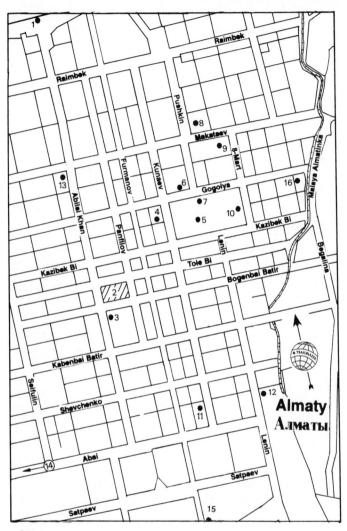

KEY

1 Almaty II Railway Station
2 Main Square & Government Buildings
3 Post Office
4 Public Baths
5 Panfilov Park, Cathedral, Memorial
6 Hotel Otrar
7 Zhulgyz Restaurant
8 Koreiskoi Kukni Restaurant

9 Food Market
10 Texaca Bank, Musical
   Instruments Museum
11 Hotel Dostyk
12 Hotel Kazakhstan & Shaggies
13 Hotel Zhetysu
14 To Hotel Rachat
15 State Museum

Almaty

The final stop on this route through the CIS, Almaty (formerly known as Alma Ata) is currently the capital of Kazakhstan and the starting-point of the Kazakh-Chinese rail link. It is a tidy, organised city whose graph paper street layout means that getting yourself lost requires quite some feat of ineptitude. It is also a classic example of the Soviet ethic, putting impersonal rationality above human diversity. While it is easily the largest and most developed city in Kazakhstan, there are plans to transfer the capital to a more central location, possibly to Akmola 1000km to the north.

Almaty is flourishing as European and American businesses rush in for a slice of the Kazakh pie. This means that facilities and attitudes here are relaxed and Western: there are embassies, there are at least two really top-whack hotels, and there's a local business guide published in English. Flights are available to cities around the world, visas are readily extended and people speak English. This doesn't make it a great holiday destination but it certainly makes life easier.

If you haven't already arranged your ticket to China don't bank on arriving in Almaty in the morning and being able to leave the same day as tickets for the twice-weekly passenger service (Monday and Saturday evenings) may take a while to arrange (see p169). There is not a great deal to see while you're doing this but it is certainly worth staying for a day or two, if only to admire the splendid wooden cathedral and the snow-capped peaks of the Tien Shan Mountains to the south.

HISTORY

There have been human settlements in the Almaty region since at least the second century BC, the inhabitants being the Saki, forefathers of the modern Kazakhs. Certainly this area played a part in the merchant routes across Central Asia but its people were mainly nomadic, so large towns were never really on the cards. The immediate region was known as Almaty ('apples') because of the fruit that grew so well here and main settlements centred on the location of present-day Almaty. Development really started in 1853 with the arrival of the Russians, who built Vernyi fortress here. By 1867 Vernyi had grown sufficiently to be called, officially, a city, and records relate that all householders were instructed to plant two rows of trees in front of their houses or face prosecution.

Vernyi's location in the foothills of the Tien Shan was a mixed blessing: whilst it ensured fertile soil and a temperate climate, it also put the city at the risk of flashfloods and earthquakes, natural phenomena which were to plague it for some time. The first major earthquake to hit the city was in 1887 but it took another one in 1911 to teach the Russians a real lesson; buildings are now designed to withstand the shocks of seismic activity. Yet Almaty, 'Father of Apples', as it was renamed in 1921, had more to learn about the elements that year, when a catastrophic mudslide destroyed many of the buildings, leaving $1\frac{1}{2}$ million cubic metres of mud and stones in their place. The arrival of the Turkestan-Siberia railway in 1930 really put the new Kazakh capital (since 1929) on the map, although its reputation for being simply remote possibly did as much as anything else. Leon Trotsky, among others, was exiled here in 1928.

Almaty today

The hazards of nature have been overcome to some extent; construction of the high-rise Hotel Kazakhstan is evidence of the progress of safe architecture research in earthquake zones, and the development of the huge dam in the Maloalmatinsky Gorge in 1966 has virtually eliminated the threat of mudslides. It proved its worth in the slide of July 1973.

There are two reasons why Almaty may be familiar to Westerners: the first involves a series of civil disturbances which took place here on 17-18 December 1986. It is difficult to know the truth behind these events; no foreign journalists were present, so information has been available only through the gleaning of Soviet press reports and rumours. It appears that a couple of hundred students staged a protest rally which, for some reason (it has been suggested that free alcohol was distributed by black market racketeers), rapidly escalated into violence. *The Sunday Times* claimed that 300,000 young Kazakhs were involved but this seems unlikely bearing in mind that the Kazakh population of the entire region was under 320,000 in 1979. The protests were essentially nationalist, and there were some casualties, although no one knows quite how many. The second reason, more dramatic, is that the USSR was officially dissolved here in 1991.

ORIENTATION AND SERVICES

Street names in this city are subject to constant review so you'll find that most of the guide books and city maps you consult will have different spellings of the same name or different names altogether when some Russian hero has been replaced by a Kazakh. Because the grid pattern layout of the city is so regular you're unlikely to get lost but using maps to route find does occasionally require a bit of lateral thinking.

Almaty has two railway stations, Almaty I and Almaty II. Trains may terminate at either. Almaty I is about 6km north of Almaty II, which is right on the northern edge of town. The train to Urumqi starts from Almaty II, which is where most people get on, but does stop briefly at

Almaty I. Since Almaty II is much easier to get to, you would do well to use it. See p169 for information on the Almaty to Urumqi train.

Embassies
China: 137 Furmanov St (☎ 634966)
France: 173 Furmanov St (☎ 506236)
Germany: 173 Furmanov St (☎ 506155)
Pakistan: 25Tulebaev St (☎ 333548)
Russia: 4 Zhandosov St (☎ 448222)
UK: 173 Furmanov St (☎ 506191)
USA: 99 Furmanov St (☎ 631770)
Uzbekistan: 36 Baribaev St (☎ 610235, 618316). Visas cost US$50 and take 10 days to arrange.

Tourist information
Intourist is based at the Hotel Otrar (☎ 330076), and they'll help with tours or buying tickets. You might do better, however, to contact a private travel agency, who may offer better value and assist with visa extensions, too. Intourist charge US$10 per hour for a personal guide, and since it doesn't take too long to see the main sights in Almaty, you may feel that this is worth it. They can also provide a car at US$8 per hour.

Money
Even some of the more expensive hotels in Almaty will accept only cash so you may have to visit a bank to change travellers' cheques. There are two or three large international banks in Almaty who can change them for you, and they should be able to give you a cash advance on a credit card as well. If you are lucky they will even exchange old US$ for new notes, – a lifesaver if people are refusing your dollar bills because they are battered or old.

Banks for foreign exchange include: Kramds Bank, on Rosibakiev St; Alem Bank, south of Panfilov Park at the junction of Lenin prospekt and Vinogradov (between Bogenbai Batir and Kabenbai); and the Bank of Texas and Kazakhstan (Texaca Bank) on the east side of Panfilov Park.

LOCAL TRANSPORT

Getting around is no problem. From Almaty II railway station, trolley-bus Nos 4, 5, or 6 will take you south down Abilai-Khan to the centre of town. To get from Almaty I railway station to Almaty II, take bus 79 or trolley-bus 13, which will also drop you right behind the market, in Pushkin St. Buses 92 and 97 are express to the airport, running from behind the Hotel Zhetysu. The long distance bus station is a couple of kilometres to the west of town, along Tole Bi St.

WHERE TO STAY

There are a lot of hotels in Almaty, but unfortunately there are few, if any, really cheap places to stay. The old Intourist **Hotel Otrar** (☎ 33 00 76) is pretty reasonable – though expensive – a single here is US$90, a double US$100. Much cheaper, try the **Hotel Kazakhstan** (☎ 61 99 06), at the southern end of town. It's an uglier than average high-rise beast but singles start at US$25 and doubles US$50. In the same price range, and easier to get to, the **Hotel Zhetysu** is not noted for its courteous service (not by foreigners, anyway). They don't seem to suffer from this, though: the hotel is always packed with local businessmen. Rooms start from around US$45.

Your cheapest option is to find a **homestay**, and the Zhetysu may be the place to do it. This hotel has a reputation as a first stopping place for foreign travellers needing somewhere to stay and private homeowners have tended to hang around here looking for punters to whom to rent out their front rooms.

Finding a place to stay is simple, though, if money is no object. You can't do better than the **Marco Polo Rachat Hotel** at 29/6 Akademik Satpaev (☎ 81 16 20). Rooms start at US$330 single for really top class accommodation. Next best is the **Hotel Dostyk** (☎ 63 64 01), an old Communist Party hotel, with a surprisingly pleasant old-world atmosphere. Among the luxuries here are cable TV, and an American restaurant which reputedly serves excellent food. Aircon singles are US$135, doubles are US$160 and suites go for US$300.

WHERE TO EAT

Good restaurants don't seem to last long in Almaty. The more expensive hotels thus remain the best places to get reasonable food. At the top of the range here, it will be hard to beat the restaurants in the **Marco Polo Rachat Hotel**, where excellent food will cost suitably high prices.

Good for a binge, though still not cheap, is the **Hotel Dostyk's** American restaurant where a meal will cost you upwards of US$20. Brunch here has been particularly recommended.

In the same price range, the two restaurants in the **Hotel Otrar** might be worth a look; the newly opened Indian restaurant here looked particularly good.

Opposite the Otrar, the **Café Zhulgyz** is on the edge of Panfilov Park near the cathedral; the food's as good as the Otrar, and the setting is infinitely better.

The **Café Cosmos**, on the 26th floor of the Hotel Kazakhstan isn't bad either; it's pretty cheap, and the view is good on a clear day. Downstairs, near the entrance of the hotel is one of Almaty's landmarks: **Shaggies'**

Burger Bar. It seems to have been rather left behind, not quite the happening place it once was. It's still not a bad place to stop for a break, though, and a burger (of sorts), fries and Coke clock in at around the US$5 mark.

Back in the market the situation is a bit better: shashlik and fried pancakes are hawked from the entrance all day. Also, on the corner of Makataev Mukaga and Pushkin St (behind, and to the north of, the bazaar) is the Korean restaurant **Koreiskoi Kukni**. While the service is atrocious the noodle soup is quite good.

There are **cafés** scattered fairly liberally around the rest of town, lots of which are better places for a drink than a meal. A new one that has been recommended is the **Café Light**, just a couple of blocks south of Panfilov Park on Lenin prospekt.

WHAT TO SEE

Zenkhov Cathedral and 28 Panfilov Guardsmen Park

In the middle of this park is the magnificent, wooden **Zenkhov Cathedral** which stands 56m high, laying claim to the title of tallest wooden structure in the CIS. It is commonly believed to have been constructed without the use of nails – very impressive if true. It was built between 1907 and 1911 and despite a long stint under Communism as a concert hall, it's a church again now, beautifully restored inside.

Just behind the trees to the east is the **war memorial**, hewn in a typically Soviet style. This one seems much more impressive than the one in Moscow; built along similar lines, it has 13 marble cubes, each representing a 'Hero City' (see if you can spot the extra one here), and each containing a shellcase full of earth from that city. The flowers on the memorial are usually left by newly-weds who visit immediately after their wedding ceremony for the obligatory photo session.

The park itself is small but leafy and cool on a hot day. Its rather unuser-friendly name comes from the heroism of 28 local soldiers who, under one General Panfilov, managed to hold off 50 German tanks in the battle for Moscow in Nov 1941. Most were killed. Marijuana grows wild here but the harvesting of it is not advised. Quite apart from its poor quality, it's illegal.

Museums

• **National Musical Instruments** On the eastern side of Panfilov Park in a rather wacky wooden building is the best kind of museum: one in which there are buttons to press. Each glass case contains a musical instrument of some sort. Press the button underneath the front panel for a demonstration of how the instruments sound. It's open daily (except Monday) from 9.30am to 6.00pm.

• **Museum of Art** This is a large, high quality museum featuring displays both of fine art and of more practical Kazakh applications like embroidery and weaving. There is also an open-plan model revealing the workings of a yurt. It is open from 9am to 6pm (last entry 5.30pm), closed on Monday. Trolley-bus No 16 stops right outside.

• **State Museum** Just off Republic Square in the far south of the town, this the most professional of the three museum. You can pretty much ignore the (well laid-out, nevertheless) prehistory section of dinosaur bones and flint arrowheads all labelled in Russian, and move on past the yurt display to the 'miscellaneous' department, which is packed with all sorts of goodies: there's plenty of Yuri Gagarin memorabilia and various other astronauts' equipment, Soviet Olympic medals and trophies, and more. Best is the section on Soviet-American relations, including tents used in combined sponsored walks and letters to 'The Russians' from American schoolchildren ('Dear friends, let's don't have any more wars. I am four years old. I love kittens' etc). It is open from 10am-6pm daily, except Tuesday. Bus Nos 2 or 61 or trolley-bus No 4 will take you there.

Public baths
The Almaty baths are immediately to the west of Panfilov Park and are considered to be of an extremely high standard. Sweat, show off your bod, and get thoroughly clean between 8am and 10pm daily.

Bazaar
The small bazaar is just to the north of the Hotel Otrar, but it's all a bit too modern to be really exciting. Watch out for the dried apricot salesmen, who will shovel low grade apricots into your bag, cover the surface with beautiful fruit, and then double the price. Koumiss (fermented mare's milk) is easy to find here but be warned that the old women who sell it are likely to bully you into finishing the whole glass.

Excursion to Medeo
Some 15-20km north of Almaty, at 1700m above sea level is the famous Medeo skating rink and sports centre, wedged uncomfortably against the Maloalmatinsky Dam. It is possible to take a bus up here for the day (No 6, departs every half hour from the market behind Hotel Otrar) and if the mountain air really agrees with you, you can stay in one of a number of hotels here.

Trekking
The mountains around Almaty contain some of the finest unspoilt natural scenery in the world, and for those who have the time Almaty is a great base from which to try some trekking. At its simplest, you can start walking from Medeo, although you'll need to get local advice about routes. If you're feeling more ambitious and have some spare cash, there's a range

of activities on offer, including hunting, fishing, horse riding and guided treks into the wilderness.

There are several companies which specialise in custom travel arrangements but one to try is **Kramds Mountain Firm Ltd** (☎ 537211 or 536850, fax 696753 for user no 1065), 164 Kabanbai St.

MOVING ON

By rail – the train to China
Buying a ticket If you have not already bought a ticket through your travel agent at home, the most important thing to do when you arrive in Almaty is to make arrangements to leave. The passenger service between Almaty and Urumqi (No 14 Ghengis Khan) currently operates twice a week, departing from Almaty II station on Saturday and Monday evenings at 21.45 local time, 18.45pm (Moscow Time).

Second class tickets cost US$65, first class US$120 on the Chinese train (it has been reported by travellers that the Russian train is cheaper, at US$46/US$90). You may also be required to pay a US$10 advance booking fee and a US$5 service charge. Tickets go on sale on the Tuesday before the departures. Note that you must have a Chinese visa in your passport before you can buy one. At the time of writing, tickets could be bought from Window 14, on the second floor of the station – above the window is a sign saying simply 'Urumqi'. There was considerable work taking place in the station, however, so they may well move to another ticket window.

You just cannot tell how long you will have to wait for tickets for this train. You might get a ticket at one day's notice or you might have to wait a week – it all depends on the demand that week. Having said this, the train appears not to have been as popular with tourists as expected, making late bookings easier. Booking problems can be alleviated to a large extent by getting a local travel agency to do it for you. The Hotel Otrar will do this for a fee, as will the other companies listed above. Note that you are likely to be bought a first class ticket automatically unless you state otherwise.

The only way to be sure of getting a ticket is to book as soon as they go on sale, or to book from abroad. It is possible to get tickets on the black market but be very careful, because this will almost certainly involve giving your passport to a complete stranger while he sorts things out. One way to approach the problem might be to arrive, book the ticket in advance, and then disappear off travelling for that time. A week-long stay in Almaty would be excruciatingly boring and without the right visa stamps on your passport visiting other places in the CIS can be tricky. Note that if you haven't got a ticket you stand very little chance of sneaking or bribing your way onto this heavily guarded train.

Departure Get to the station at least an hour in advance (remember that Moscow time is three hours behind Kazakhstan time). Although there are no longer passport checks before boarding the train, it's worth having time in hand as the train could leave early (up to half an hour early has been reported). Even if the train is already waiting, you will not be allowed onto it until shortly before its departure time. There is a waiting room but if you use it, keep a close eye on the train – just in case. Don't play it cool when people start boarding. Get on.

By bus
The long distance bus station (a 15 minute drive west along ulitsa Tole) serves many cities including Bishkek, Dzambul, Panfilov and Chimkent.

By air
Several major airlines fly in and out of Almaty, including KLM (who have an office next to Hotel Otrar), Lufthansa, Turkish Airlines and Air China. There are flights to **Moscow** (Trans-Aero, daily) at US$330, and **Urumqi** (Kazair's weekly flight to Urumqi costs US$141, and Air China also provide a twice weekly service).

Express buses Nos 92 and 97 will take you out to the airport from behind the Hotel Zhetysu.

Urumqi

For centuries travellers have been coming to Urumqi to visit beautiful Tianchi, the 'Lake of Heaven', and they probably will for centuries to come; it's the great tourist attraction of the area. The arrival of the railway line from Almaty was expected to boost tourist numbers. In fact, other areas have been expanding so fast that this effect of the new railway line is less apparent. Joint venture hotels are springing up all over the place as Central Asia suddenly becomes The Place To Be; and drab, grey Urumqi has done well for itself.

The city is a confused tangle of streets and back alleys and is certainly worth exploring for a couple of days, if only for the food. After the privations of the CIS, the last thing you'll want to see is shashlik, so the countless excellent noodle bars are where you ought to be. Forget the sights: Urumqi's real attractions are great food and cold beer.

HISTORY

Situated right at the foot of the Tien Shan Mountains, Urumqi's position at the end of the gap leading from the Tarim into the Dzungarian basins meant that it would always be a stopover for any caravan heading west; the fact that most people were just passing through ensured that it never really developed much. The Chinese first arrived in the 7th and 8th centuries, setting up a protectorate general near Chi-mu-su-ern 80km to the east. This was eventually transferred to Urumqi to be closer to the main trade routes. After the Tang withdrawal around 750AD, Urumqi came back under local rule.

Uprising and political intrigue
In 1760 the Chinese returned to set up the city of Dihua, whose population was artificially boosted by shipping in thousands of Han immigrants. The balance of power between the Han and the local Muslims has never been stable, though (as Cable and French note: 'there is a commonly accepted tradition in the Gobi that once every 30 years they' (the Muslims) 'must rise...'). As one would expect of the capital of the province, Urumqi has been at the heart of many of these uprisings. The constant intrigue associated with corruption and fear of popular uprising has led to a number of visitors commenting on the eerie feel of the place: Teichman, in 1935, said 'That there is something gloomy, dark and sinister about the Urumqi atmosphere no-one who has resided there is likely to deny', while Cable and French wrote that 'no-one leaves the town with

regret, and it is full of people who are only there because they cannot get permission to leave, and may not leave without permission'. In fact Teichman witnessed first hand the suspicion of the powers that be, writing of a banquet that 'waiters, dressed in white overalls, betrayed only by the bulgings of hidden automatics their military character...'

He had good cause to be worried, for banquets here have often been the scene of one altercation or another. In one notorious case in 1916, Chinese governor Yang Tseng Hsin, having discovered a plot to kill him, had the conspirators beheaded at the table one by one while he ate. He got his just des(s)erts eventually, however – gunned down over dinner by his minister of foreign affairs in 1928.

Political intrigue and suspicion are so closely woven into Urumqi's past that it is almost impossible to find the truth in its history. It was, naturally, heavily shaken by the major Islamic uprisings both in 1860 and in 1930 and until 1944 the city and its environs were under the control of the Chinese warlord, Sheng Shih-Ts'ai.

Urumqi today
Since 1949 Urumqi has developed rapidly and although still under Chinese rule, increased prosperity has had a calming effect. About a quarter of the population is still Uighur, and unless you're visiting Kashgar this is the only place where you will encounter this Islamic ethnic minority in any numbers.

The area is rich in mineral deposits and coal and in 1955 the Karamai oilfield, now one of China's leading oil producers, was discovered nearby. The arrival of the Xinjiang railway line in the early 1960s, the construction of better roads and the new Almaty rail link have facilitated greater communications and helped Urumqi to bury its shady past.

ORIENTATION AND SERVICES

Arrival in Urumqi
The station and its surroundings used to be utterly chaotic but people here have more or less got used to the idea of foreigners arriving from Kazakhstan. Still, it is as well to be careful as this would be the ideal place to get ripped off. Keep your rail ticket, as you'll need it to get out of the station.

Unless you've managed to change or borrow some money on the train you'll have to walk to the bank – about half an hour away, or you could try changing money in the Xinjiang Hotel. Changing money at the station is now quite difficult: locals aren't especially interested.

Orientation
The main offices, banks and hotels are mostly situated within walking distance of the post office. Urumqi is a lot of fun to explore but as with other large cities it's a good idea to get hold of a map; it's easy to get lost.

CITS give away copies of a good map with bus routes marked on it but other cheap, reasonable maps are available all over the city, in particular in front of the train station.

Services

CITS are based in the building next to the Holiday Inn but they are not very helpful and you may prefer to use the private travel service in the Hong Shan Guesthouse instead. They call themselves CTTS, have an office in Room 128 of the guesthouse, and will organise tours and tickets. Unlike CITS, they are more than willing to help with information, too.

The post office is on the large traffic circle to the north east of the train station. This is where any Post Restante is held, and the service seems to work well here.

The PSB have their main offices to the east of the Hong Shan Guesthouse. Renewing a visa here was, at the time of writing, relatively easy, taking only a few minutes and costing Y95.

Money

The Bank of China is your best bet for changing travellers' cheques; the main branch is south of the Hong Shan Guesthouse in the city centre, but there's also a branch opposite the Xin Qiao Restaurant, and a small service counter in the CAAC office. The Holiday Inn and Bogeda Hotel will change US$ cash, but both claim that they cannot change cheques for non-residents.

LOCAL TRANSPORT

The public bus system is good but thefts have been reported (usually when buses are really crowded), so keep an eye on your gear. The map available from CITS has the bus routes marked on it. Bus Nos 2 or 52 from right opposite the railway station will take you to the post office in 5-10 minutes and you can walk to most hotels from there. To get to the long distance bus station, take bus No 2 from outside the post office and ask for 'Nan tse go'. It's about two stops (look for the big Mercedes Benz-type sign). There is a CAAC bus to take you to the airport.

Other buses that are useful include Nos 7 and 17, both of which run from south of the Hong Shan Guesthouse up to the central roundabout by the post office. Bus No 7 is particularly useful: it runs south to north passing close to the main Bank of China, by the Hong Shan Guesthouse and the post office, and stopping outside the provincial museum.

There are several places to rent a bicycle (the staff at John's Information Café may be able to help). Urumqi is easily small enough to cycle around and this will save you the hassle of struggling on to crowded public buses.

WHERE TO STAY

There are a few really good quality hotels in Urumqi but the standard upmarket place is the **Holiday Inn** (☎ 2818788), where singles go for Y835 and doubles Y960 (also subject to 15% service charge). For those who can't afford to stay here the building is a useful orientation point; less than 400m from it is the backpackers' haunt, the **Hong Shan Guesthouse** (☎ 2824761). This is basic, clean and reasonable value at Y40 for a bed in a three-bed room, or Y32 for a bed in a five-bed room. You deserve a free Blue Peter badge and glass of orange squash if you manage to find the showers behind the building without any assistance. CTTS is in Room 128.

Cheaper than the Hong Shan, and correspondingly more basic, is the **Xinjiang Hotel** (☎ 5852511). It's further from the city centre but much closer to the train station, which may be an advantage. Accommodation in the dormitories costs Y25 in a six-bed dormitory, Y37 in a five-bed, Y40 in a three-bed and Y50 in a two-bed. They have a travel service on the second floor but prices quoted from here seem inflated.

Other hotels are more expensive. You might want to try the **Bogeda Hotel** (☎ 2823910), which was under renovation at the time of writing. Prices are likely to go up after the work is complete, but doubles are currently Y318. Their previously cheap dormitory may not reopen. Much further to the south, the **Overseas Chinese Guesthouse** (☎ 2863239), on Xin Hua Nanlu is cheaper, but is a ridiculously long way out. Bus No 7 (south-bound) from the post office will take you there. Look for the highrise pink and white building on the east side of the road. Singles here go for Y150, double rooms start at Y200.

Just north of the post office, the **Peafowl Hotel** (☎ 4522988) seems reasonably pleasant and has doubles at Y178. A lot further to the north on Youhao Road and Beijing Rd you can find a cluster of more expensive business hotels. The **Kunlun Hotel** (☎ 4840411) is extremely large and very smart but seems to have a problem drumming up custom; a double here is Y450. To the north of this the **Hotel World Plaza** (☎ 8522577) which easily rivals the Holiday Inn for comfort and price: singles are Y800.

WHERE TO EAT

After the food in the CIS you definitely owe yourself a treat and you can't beat breakfast at the **Holiday Inn** for that. Served between 7am and 11am, it is expensive at Y90 but you get all you can eat from a choice of every single breakfast food ever invented including real coffee and fruit juice. Waitresses smile at you as they trip over each other trying to get to your coffee cup to top it up. Get there as early as possible to facilitate

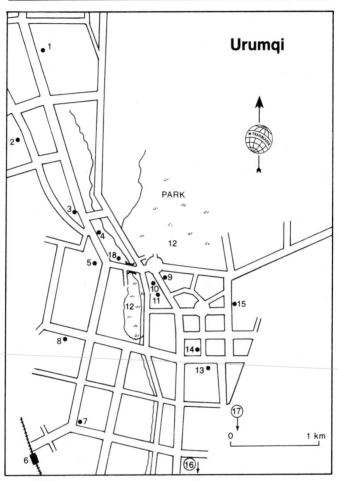

1 Kunlun Hotel
2 Provincial Museum
3 Peafowl Hotel
4 CAAC
5 Post Office
6 Railway Hotel
7 Xinjiang Hotel
8 Long Distance Bus Station
9 Hong Shan Guesthouse

10 John's Information Café
11 CITS/Holiday Inn
12 Renmin Park
13 Bank of China
14 Market
15 PSB
16 To Overseas Chinese Guesthouse
17 To Main Market
18 Xin Qiao Restaurant

maximum calorific intake. You can buy foreign newspapers here, and the toilets are lemon-scented and simply wonderful. Don't miss it.

The number one travellers' hangout in Urumqi is **John's Information Café** directly opposite the Hong Shan Guesthouse. This is the fourth branch of this banana-pancake serving, cool beer sipping, Western music playing joint. It's well worth a visit, if only to meet like-minded souls, arrange travel tickets, and get some good advice; or just to sit in a shady spot and write postcards. John himself may well be available but busy – next stops for his cafés are Xi'an, Xiahe and Lanzhou.

In comparison to the CIS all the food in Urumqi seems delicious, although there are very few real restaurants as such. What there are, by the thousand, are fast **food stalls** and street vendors serving a range of dishes including steamed dumplings, noodles, noodle soup and shashlik. The best area for these is some way from the centre of town but the journey is worth it; take bus No 1 north to the end of the line (about 15 mins). The street by the bus terminal is packed with good eating places, each charging only a couple of yuan for a meal. It is also a good place to meet Chinese students as the medical school is very close by. Other recommended places include the market next to the post office, which is good for shashlik; the noodle shops outside the bus station; or the stalls in the main market (to the south).

If you want a more civilised meal, try the **Xin Qiao Restaurant** which seems to be permanently empty but has a fridge full of beer and can rustle up some pretty good rice dishes.

WHAT TO SEE

In Urumqi
• **Xinjiang Provincial Museum** This large museum is only spoiled by its erratic opening hours, as it seems to shut for prolonged periods with little or no warning. It's supposed to be open from 10.00-18.00 daily (Sat and Sun 11.00-17.00; closed weekends in winter). Definitely worth the gamble, though, as it's full of interesting relics relating to the area's five ethnic minorities. A fascinating new display, the Xinjiang Ancient Corpse Exhibition, now has about 12 bodies and English captions explaining where they came from. Bus No 7 stops right outside this green-domed building. Entry is Y20.

• **Pagoda** Looking north from the Hong Shan Guesthouse you can see the pagoda. Climbing the hill is quite fun, and the view from the top is pleasant enough. There's a separate entrance fee to see the red pavilion at the top.

• **Renmin Park** This beautiful garden is a lovely place for a stroll; best in the early morning when it is filled with locals going through their Tai-Chi routines, or late evening. Entry is Y2.

• **Markets** There are numerous little street markets throughout Urumqi, and while there is probably not much that you will want to buy here, they are great fun to explore. Particularly worthy of note is the tiny, cramped one next to the post office, which seems to specialise in fish, offering the new arrival to China a startling insight into the way the Chinese keep their livestock. Russian goods, notably watches, are popular.

Tianchi

Literally translated, Tianchi means 'Lake of Heaven', and visitors tend to agree, most drawing analogies between it and Switzerland or Canada. It is a beautiful place to visit if it's hot but if it's either cold or foggy in Urumqi don't bother going, as conditions will be much worse in the mountains. It is possible to stay overnight here in a hotel, or the more adventurous can spend a night, or even a week, in a yurt, hiking by day and relishing the warm smell of camel by night.

Buses leave early for the $2^1/_2$-3 hour journey, at around 09.00, (you should aim to get there half an hour early, as there is only one bus, and if you miss it you'll have to wait till the next day). Bus tickets (Y20) are sold at the entrance to Renmin Park, on the left.

If you want to take a tour, operators will contact you at the Hong Shan but they usually charge Y50 just for putting you on the right bus. They will arrange a special tour for groups at Y120 per person. Other hotels arrange their own tours.

WHAT TO BUY

After the CIS, the main things you will probably want to buy will be food and beer. If you are going to visit Kashgar, then the ornamental knives, hats and other ethnic paraphernalia you see for sale in the markets in Urumqi will be better value there, so it's better to wait. It's worth browsing through the main department store though, (across the street from the

German archaeologist Albert von Le Coq, on his 1904 expedition, found the Urumqi authorities a touch harsh with the locals (which perhaps goes some way towards explaining why there have been so many uprisings). The Chinese were heavy-handed but the Russians from the local consulate were worse. He recounts that the consul used to thunder through the narrow streets in an open carriage with an escort of 20 Cossacks. Any individual in his way or simply within reach would be whipped 'on his face, shoulders, or wherever it happened, in the most inconsiderate fashion'. When he protested, he was told brusquely that he 'did not know how these people had to be treated'. Immediately following this anecdote he describes the traditional method of execution – 'a cage in which a condemned man was fixed on a movable footboard. His head was fixed between planks and every day the footboard was moved down a little so that the man's neck was slowly dragged out more and more until in the end – eight days it was said to last – death arrived'. 'The sight...' he relates '...made a very unpleasant impression on me'.

post office), just to see what's on offer. Here you can buy virtually any-thing from an alto saxophone (Y1470) or a guitar of sorts (Y100), to cheap stationery and a trendy ghetto-blaster with built-in disco lights.

MOVING ON

To Kazakhstan

• **Visas** If you have followed the advice in Part 1 of this book you will already have obtained your Kazakh visa. If you still need to get one, you can try the Kazakhstan Airlines office but you may well be disappointed. They issue tourist visas on production of booking vouchers from a tour company, or transit visas if you can prove that you will be leaving Kazakhstan within three days. If you don't have a Kazakh visa, this is your best bet...or you'll be heading back to Beijing. You should note that visas are **not** issued on the train.

The **Kazakhstan Airlines office** (☎ 3815796, fax 3821203) at 31 Kunming Lu, isn't easy to find. It's a long way up Beijing Lu, at the back of an industrial estate that changes its appearance almost daily. Probably the easiest way to locate it is to get to the Hotel World Plaza by bus or taxi and walk from there. The estate is 20 minutes' walk north of the World Plaza, on the right hand side of the road, and the airline's office is about 300m into the estate, straight down the access road. The office is open weekdays (except Wed) 10.00-13.00.

• **By rail** The Kazakhstan train (No 13) is easily booked from Urumqi though, as usual, your best bet may be to get someone to buy the ticket for you. The train leaves Urumqi on Saturday and Monday at 23.00 Beijing time. Tickets are sold in the main station.

• **By bus** There is a bus service to Almaty from Urumqi via the Khorgos Pass although occasionally the service is suspended when the pass is closed. There are usually one or two buses a week, and the journey costs Y460 and takes 36 hours. The best people to advise on this service are either CTTS or the staff in John's Café. Kazakh visas are **not** issued at the pass.

Into China

• **By rail** It can be tricky to buy train tickets for journeys east (CITS may tell you that it is impossible) but if you hang in there you'll get one in the end. Train times and numbers are: 15.45 (No ll4), 18.20 (No 70), 19.00 (No 244), 20.20 (No 54), 22.50 (No 98), 23.30 (No 144) and 17.25 (No 6). Turfan is only three hours away.

Some travellers head south-west to Korla on their way to Kashgar – there's a railway line from Turfan that goes this far, and then you can take a bus. The advantage is that the journey is broken up into more manage-able portions (the bus from Korla to Kashgar takes around 24 hours). The disadvantage is that there's not a great deal to see on the way. If you do this, try to make time for the 'lost cities' at Korla and Kuqa (further to the west).

• **By bus** The long distance bus station is on Heilongjiang Lu, which is a side road off Yangzijiang Lu – the main road running from the train station to the post office. Buses from here will take you to Turfan or further. Unlike trains, tickets are easy to get hold of and the journey to Turfan is actually quite short. CITS will book for you – for a 30% commission. There are extra services for both Kashgar and to Turfan, the former departing from near the train station, the latter from the Erdaoqiao market area. Better to stick to the main services, though.

• **By air** Cities linked to Urumqi by air include Almaty, Beijing, Kashgar, Lanzhou and Xi'an. CAAC quote the following: Beijing (daily) Y2530; Kashgar (daily) Y1220; Almaty (Sundays and Fridays) Y1660.

To Kashgar

There are two ways of getting to Kashgar: bus or plane, or you could go part of the way by train (see above). Flying is expensive, most budget travellers take the bus. It's a seriously long way, however. The journey takes '30-36 hours' – more like 40 actually – non-stop (on a 'deluxe' sleeper coach with reclining seats) or three days if you stop at night. Both types of bus depart daily. In the sleeper coach it costs Y187 for a top bunk or Y215 for a lower bunk – and since the only difference between the two is having to climb a couple of steps most people go for the former. The standard local bus, which stops every night, costs Y130. CITS or CTTS will book bus tickets for you, for a commission, of course. For some reason the bus ticket from Kashgar back to Urumqi is more expensive than the outward journey.

Make sure that you stock up on bread, biscuits and fruit for the journey, especially if the prospect if eating in grotty noodle shops along the way appals you. Rucksacks over a certain size will go on the roof of the bus; you can chain them there if you want to. Take a good pile of books with you and, if you have a walkman, plenty of batteries and restrict your fellow passengers to, say, half an hour each.

Kashgar

Located at the western end of the Taklamakan Desert, Kashgar is further inland than any other city on earth. It was from here that most Silk Road travellers crossed the Pamirs heading west. It was also from here that an important part of the Great Game (see p280) was played, as Russian and British diplomats collected information and ran spies to monitor each other's progress.

Today Kashgar is still more Central Asian than Chinese, making this the best city in China to wander around aimlessly. It's a wonderful place to lose yourself, or simply to sit and relax; most come for a couple of days and end up staying a week. The fact that Kashgar is so inaccessible means that it is still pretty much unspoiled by tourism. As one recent visitor put it, 'People who have been here belong to the most élite travellers' club in China'. Times are changing, however, and Kashgar is finding its way onto the itinerary of more and more tours so the chance to see this wonderful oasis city before it becomes too crowded with foreigners should not be missed.

HISTORY

Kashgar, owing to its strategic position at the crossroads of northern and southern routes (see p161), was one of the major stops on the Silk Road. The Chinese first arrived here in the 2nd century BC, when they drove out the Yueh Chin tribes but they were themselves driven out by those same tribes a century later. At the time, Kashgar was probably not known to the West at all, but Ptolemy (2nd century AD) writes of a 'Scythia beyond the Imaus', a 'kasia regio', and this may be where the name comes from; little more than this is know about its ancient history. It is clear, at least, that Kashgar was the victim of a number of invasions by semi-nomadic tribes. The Chinese then returned in the late 7th century under the Tang dynasty to install a military garrison but the sheer distance between the Tang capital of Chang'an and Kashgar meant that communications were difficult. They withdrew in 752AD, leaving it again to the wandering tribes. It was then taken and occupied successively by the Turks (10th century), the Uighurs (11th) and the Karakitais (12th). During these three centuries Islam became firmly entrenched in the region.

Marco Polo – life under the Mongols

In 1219 the Mongols arrived, yet the initial destruction wreaked by them was only short-lived, for the later unification of the Mongol kingdom under Kubilai Khan (1215-1294) meant that travel was safe, and thus that trade centres flourished. Marco Polo, who visited in 1275, said, 'The inhabitants live by trade and industry. They have very fine orchards and vineyards and flourishing estates. Cotton grows here in plenty, beside flax and hemp. The soil is fruitful and productive of all the means of life. This country is the starting-point from which many merchants set out to market their wares all over the world. The folk here are very close-fisted and live very poorly, neither eating well nor drinking well. There are some Nestorian Christians in this country, having their own church and observing their own religion'.

The Mongol rule was not to last for long, however, weakened by internal strife. In 1389-90 Timur arrived to sack Kashgar, heralding an age of unrest for it until the Chinese returned en masse in 1755. Reports state that they effected 'wholesale massacres' of the locals before installing Chinese settlers and traders to govern the place. In fact the balance of power has never been stable, for the local people believe, and not without good reason, that their land is under foreign occupation.

Yakub Beg

There have been several open rebellions and revolts. One particularly successful attempt to wrest power from the Chinese took place in 1862 with a movement which originally started in Gansu Province. It spread west rapidly and on 10 August 1863 Yarkand (200km southeast of Kashgar) witnessed a struggle that resulted in the deaths of at least 7000 Chinese settlers. The leader to emerge from this movement was Yakub Beg, who seized control by some rather underhand tactics and then proceeded to set up the independent Islamic state of 'Kashgaria'. In a well-publicised attempt to gain credibility for his 'state', he sent his brother to Great Britain as an ambassador (he made an extremely favourable impression wherever he was received). Meanwhile the Russians, keen to advance in the area, signed a commercial pact with Beg in 1872 and were thus able to occupy parts of Xinjiang province. The British, worried at this Great Game development, signed a similar treaty to try to halt Russian expansion towards India. The shrewd Yakub Beg had managed to gain international recognition for his state.

Not that it did him much good. A Chinese army under General Tso Tsung-T'ang advanced westwards at speed and managed to take Yakub's capital city of Turfan on 6 May, 1877. Beg committed suicide shortly afterwards. Defeat spelled the end of the revolt but the Muslims' desire for independence had not died, and there have been numerous altercations since. A notable one took place in 1928, with the Chinese only really regaining control in 1943. Throughout this period Kashgar was a key city for Great Game 'players': a Russian consulate was set up here in 1882, shortly to be followed by a British 'listening-post' in 1890.

Kashgar today

Chinese influence on Kashgar is plain for all to see (how could anyone miss that vast Mao statue?). While this annoys the Muslims, the last serious confrontations taking place only in 1990, it does mean that the city has developed fairly rapidly. There is still a unique feel to the place, though. The opening of the Karakoram Highway to foreigners in 1986 spelled out a part of Kashgar's destiny, for the majority of travellers here at any one time now seem to be either waiting to cross to Pakistan or to have just arrived from there.

ORIENTATION AND SERVICES

The main bus station is 400m east of Jiefang Rd, down a side street off Renmin St. Most people walk or take a rickshaw from here to the hotels.

Don't bother contacting the CITS office (at the entrance to the Qiniwake Hotel) for assistance. The office is peopled entirely by space cadets. They do claim to be able to book tickets, though: two days notice is required for buses, four for flights. A rather uninformative map from here will cost you Y3.

TOURS

There are no standard tours in Kashgar but virtually anything can be arranged if you are willing to pay for it. The best places to find out what's on offer are John's Café, and the Seman Hotel; in both you can set up any of the usual visits or arrange for a jeep and a driver to take you wherever you want to go. CITS also offer trips to Tashkurgan, Karakuli Lake, Hanoi and a landcruiser renting service.

LOCAL TRANSPORT

There is very little public transport in Kashgar and thus by far the best way to get around is by bicycle – which is all right because the only distant site is the Abak Khoja mausoleum 3km away. There's a bike hire place in the front courtyard of the Qiniwake Hotel.

There are motor rickshaws (haggle for prices), and many visitors enjoy going by donkey cart to the market. The CAAC bus will take you the 11km to the airport.

WHERE TO STAY

The top hotel is the **Kashgar Guesthouse** (☎ 222367), to the east of town. Rooms with bathroom attached are Y300, Y150 without. Although it is good, its location is highly inconvenient especially as no public buses go by this way.

The **Qian Hai Hotel** (☎ 222922) is a large new place right on Renmin St just east of the Bank of China. It's pretty swish but no English is spoken; you won't have the space of KGH, either, but then it is very central. Doubles here are Y320.

Streaks ahead of everything else in the popularity stakes is the **Seman Hotel** (☎ 222129), which was the old Russian consulate. Prices are Y120 for a double with attached bathroom, Y60 for a double with common bathroom and Y15 for a bed in the three-bed dormitory. It's a vast place and virtually everything can be arranged from here; the only drawback is the shortage of showers (get there early and queue).

The **Qiniwake Hotel** (☎ 222103 ext 3001) is on the site of the old British consulate but nothing is recognisable now. A double is Y160, a bed in a three-bed room Y40, and it's Y30 in a four-bed room. The dorms (10 beds in each) are Y20 per person. The bike rental stall just outside the hotel charges Y2 per hour.

Confusingly, sharing the same entrance gate, courtyard and telephone number as the Qiniwake is the **International Hotel** (☎ 222103 ext 4004). It's only a year old and no-one seems to have found it yet; consequently the staff are all really friendly. Doubles are Y240, and clean, tasteful suites go for Y700. It's not a bad place but the prices are quite high.

Two others that you might want to consider are the **People's (Renmin) Hotel** (☎ 223373), which charges Y16 for a dorm bed, Y20

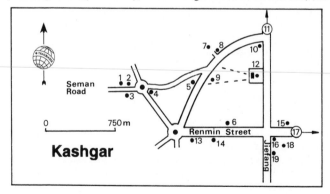

1 Limin Restaurant	8 CITS]	16 People's Hotel
2 Seman Road Restnt	9 Small Pond	17 To Sunday Market,
3 Seman Hotel	10 Spiral Tower	Abak Khoja Mauso-
4 John's Info Café	11 To Airport	leum (4km), Kash-
5 PSB	12 Id Kah Mosque	gar GH, Bus
6 Post Office	13 Bank of China	Station (400m)
7 Qiniwake &	14 Qian Hai Hotel	18 Renmin Park
International Hotels	15 Mao Statue	19 CAAC

each in a four bed room, and Y93 for a double room, but few foreigners stay here; or the **Tianan Hotel** right next to the bus station (☎ 224023 ext 8010). A bed in a double room costs Y30, it's Y20 in a triple, Y16 in a four bed room and Y10 in a dormitory.

WHERE TO EAT

Kashgar's restaurants tend to cater for travellers. This means you can order in English and expect the sort of 'Lonely Planetised' food consumed only in Western-clone bars in the middle of nowhere (ie banana pancakes). Still, it makes Kashgar an excellent place for a rest. For a more authentic atmosphere, head for the bazaar and its environs.

Number one of all the travellers' haunts is still **John's Information Café** opposite the Seman Hotel. This really is the lap of luxury: comfortable chairs, 60's music and cold beer. John flits between here and his other three branches in Urumqi, Dunhuang and Turfan. Either he or his manager are the best people to talk to about excursions, plane tickets, hiring cars etc.

Immediately opposite the entrance to the Seman are two small restaurants, the **Seman Road** and the **Limin**, which are giving John a run for his money. While they are not as luxurious, and rather spoiled by the din from the video bar next door, many reckon that the food is better here. Certainly they are always packed.

Another Western-style restaurant is **Le Bistro**, very close to the Qiniwake Hotel. It's slightly more expensive than the others but they make a valiant effort at hamburger and chips; the breakfast here is good. Alternatively, try the **Western Dynasty Great Hotel** on Renmin St.

WHAT TO SEE

The Sunday Market

This is not simply 'another' market, it is superlative in every way (hottest, most crowded, most colourful and biggest) – a real assault on the senses. People from all around Kashgar bring their wares for sale on Sunday morning, so you can buy any number of items here from clothing, cotton, wool or boots, to sheep or even a camel. It's hard work fighting your way through the crowds, so you might want to take a break in the mid-morning sometime.

Keep a very close eye on your valuables as this must be one of the best places in China for pick-pockets. You can cycle here (not for the faint of heart, as the streets all around are swarming) and park your bike in front of the big trade building. Or you can take a donkey-cart from outside the Seman Hotel. Typically Y2 per person is enough but be sure to agree on your destination because drivers often go to the market area behind the mosque and stop there (only two-thirds the distance).

Id Kah Mosque and Bazaar

This mosque was built in the late 18th century, and although it is considered big by Chinese standards (room for 5000), it seems pretty insignificant to those coming from Uzbekistan.

More interesting by far is the bazaar, just to its west, which is always
guaranteed to be humming with activity. Once you enter this maze you
are unlikely to resurface for a while, so it's lucky that there are numerous
food stalls here. This is a wonderful place just to wander and absorb the
atmosphere. Popular items for sale include carpets, embroidery and hats.
Don't miss it out because you have seen the Sunday Market or don't want
to buy anything; it really is one of the high points of the town.

Renmin Park

This is another good place to wander around, although it offers a stark
contrast to the hustle and bustle of the bazaar. The shady gardens are just
opposite the Mao statue. Unfortunately the soft drink sellers have
acquired ghetto blasters recently but the further you get into the park, the
quieter it gets. It's an excellent place for a picnic or an afternoon nap.
There is a zoo here, too – ideal for those who enjoy seeing large animals
stuck in small cages. Entry to the park is Y1, to the zoo is Y1.5.

Abak Khoja Mausoleum

This is quite hard to find (the otherwise useless CITS map comes into its
own here) but it is intrinsically the most interesting construction in
Kashgar: a square, domed building covered in green majolica tiling. It's
not known if Abak Khoja (whose real name was Hidayatilla and who is
now revered as a saint) is actually buried here. The mausoleum is also
named the 'Tomb of the Fragrant Concubine' after a local girl who was
abducted by Emperor Qianlong's officials and taken to Beijing to be a
concubine. Her fragrance worked on Qianlong who fell hopelessly in
love with her and the episode ended, as do all great love stories, tragical-
ly, with her death. In fact it is highly unlikely that she is buried here, if
she ever existed at all. More plausible is the rumour that this is the tomb
of rebel leader Yakub Beg (see p181).

The mausoleum has been repaired a number of times and around it are
several attractive buildings. There is an impressive graveyard next door,
with an entrance around the other side (don't climb over the wall).
Particularly interesting is the notice 'A Brief Interduction to Abak
Khoja's Tomb' (sic), which makes challenging reading unless you're
dyslexic.

It is best to cycle the few kilometres here if possible as the scenery is
attractive. Basically you want to head east from the Id Kah Mosque and
keep asking directions. The mausoleum is open daily until 6pm. Entry is
Y10, entry to the mosque is Y5 and there's a Y2 camera charge.

Excursions from Kashgar

There are a few things to see within a 50km radius of Kashgar but general consensus seems to be that they aren't really worth the effort.

The best of the bunch is probably **Karakuli Lake**, and trips can be arranged here for virtually any length of time. Expect close contact with yaks, oxen and camels, and to stay in a yurt; this could be fun if you are in a group.

Two places which are less worthwhile unless you have a special interest in them are the 'deserted ancient city' of **Hanoi**, and the **Caves of the Three Immortals**. A trip to the former involves a 1-2 hour rickshaw ride to the site, whereupon you discover that the stupa you saw in the postcards is all that there is to see here. The latter involves a trip of about the same length to see the three caves, situated on a cliff-face. Take plenty to drink for both trips. You can expect to be totally covered with dust by the time you get back.

WHAT TO BUY

Kashgar is just the place to make up for lost time in the souvenir stakes, especially if you are here for the Sunday market. Particularly popular are ornamental knives (a large knife may cause problems either within China or at customs on departure), hats, shiny metal boxes, skins and boots. You will certainly see pelts of endangered species like the snow leopard for sale. Don't buy them. Woven cloth, silk and rugs are all good here, but be wary of shelling out a fortune unless you really know what you are looking for.

MOVING ON

As well as buses back to Urumqi (see p179), it's possible to get buses from Kashgar to other destinations including Turfan. If you're planning on heading this way, though, it may be better to take an Urumqi bus and get them to drop you at Toksun, about three hours outside Urumqi and one hour from Turfan. (The reason for this is that the buses plying the route to and from Urumqi are more comfortable and more reliable than those running to Turfan). You are likely to be dropped outside the bus station in Toksun, from where you can get a local bus to cover the one hour journey to Turfan. Minibuses also go from outside the bus station and cost Y14 (or Y7 for locals). Note that it takes about 35 hours to get to Toksun, and you should time your departure from Kashgar to avoid arriving there in the middle of the night.

Turfan

Thirty-two kilometres south of Daheyan, and surrounded by fascinating relics including traces of lost cities, burial grounds and an impressive 37m high minaret, Turfan is a small, pleasant place with a slow, naturally relaxed pace of life. The fact that it's one of the most laid-back places in the country may have something to do with the weather: it's the hottest city in China. Luckily for those who don't like the idea of heatstroke, a simple tour of the main sights is easy to arrange and takes only a day by minibus. The rest of the time you should spend underneath the vine trellises sipping a cool beer and trying not to expire.

HISTORY

Turfan's history is neither well-documented nor particularly interesting, which is rather ironic because the area around the town is loaded with archaeological sites of immense significance. The region's early history is characterised by the ongoing struggle in the Han dynasty between the Chinese and the Xiong-Nu tribesmen – often cited, incorrectly, as the forefathers of the Huns who were later to ravage Europe. The Xiong-Nu wanted Turfan because it was their nearest link with the lands to the south, while the Chinese needed it as a necessary stepping-stone for their policies of westward expansion. Thus we have records of China attacking and taking Turfan in 108BC but of struggles continuing until 90BC when there was a formal submission. This 'submission' did not stop the Xiong-Nu, though, so the area had to be retaken by the Chinese in 67BC. In fact this mutual tug of war continued until 126AD, when China was finally able to claim total control of the Turfan depression.

Gaochang and Jiaohe

Whenever the controlling Chinese dynasty was in an expansionist mood Turfan was a rung on the ladder west, hence after losing and regaining it twice, military garrisons were stationed here at Karakhoto (Gaochang) and Yarkhoto (Jiaohe). Both of these towns were later mysteriously abandoned, a fact which has thrown up as many question marks for modern historians as it has archaeological treasures for the professional diggers who were later to descend on the place. Part of the explanation for their desertion may be linked to the arrival of the Mongols in the 13th century, for they were sure to decimate everything if any resistance was offered. Certainly it would not have been the first time they had been responsible for a city's change of location (see Samarkand, p143). Yet the Turfan region came into its own during the ensuing Yuan dynasty, for this was the Silk Route's swansong and oases along the Taklamakan became boomtowns.

The hottest city in China

Turfan's classification as an oasis is another bone of contention. Situated in the deepest depression in China (the surface of Aydingkul Lake sits 156m below sea level), it is actually the hottest, driest place in the whole country. Average summer temperatures of 38°C (100°F), a highest recorded temperature of 49.3°C (121°F) and the fact that it rains 'once every ten years' (Stein) would combine to make this an extremely scorched patch of bare earth, were it not for an ingenious irrigation system which harnesses water from the snows of the Tien Shan to the north. The midday heat still drives all but the hardiest locals indoors, where they sit trying to keep cool. All Western visitors have noted this intimidating heat, while a few have written of another problem which goes hand in hand with it: the local wildlife. Albert von Le Coq notes that:

'insect pests are very much in evidence here. There are scorpions whose sting is a very serious matter, and, in addition, a kind of great spider that, in spite of a hairy body the size of a pigeon's egg, can take mighty jumps with its long, hairy legs. It makes a crunching noise with its jaws and is said to be poisonous, although I have never known any bitten by it...The cockroaches too, are a repulsive pest, in size quite as long as a man's thumb, with big red eyes and formidable feelers. It is enough to make a man uncontrollably sick to wake in the morning with such a creature on his nose, its big eyes staring down at him and its feelers trying to attack its victim's eyes. We used to seize the insect in terror and crush it, when it gave off an extremely disagreeable smell...'.

Luckily the insect problem is pretty much under control these days and life is dominated by the grape harvest and irrigation schemes; everything else is just too much effort in the heat.

GETTING THERE

Turfan's nearest railway station, Daheyan, is 32km to the north. It does not sound much until you check out the public transport; bank on anything up to a couple of hours. Taxis and minibuses, however, do this trip in about 45 minutes.

It's a good idea to arrive as early in the day as possible, and certainly before 6pm. The last bus from Daheyan departs, in theory, at 8pm, but don't hold your breath for it. If you arrive too late, ask around as someone is bound to be going that way.

Public buses are invariably horribly crowded, and have a nasty tendency to break down, giving occupants an opportunity to experience the delights of the Taklamakan first-hand. Generally the buses get fixed relatively quickly by the driver, who seems to be permanently carrying a tool kit with all the necessities – coathanger, elastic bands and chewing gum.

If he starts pounding the engine with a hammer for no apparent reason, it could be a sign that he doesn't really know what he is doing and this is possibly your cue to start hitching.

It may be wise to book your train ticket out of Daheyan before you take the bus to Turfan. See p195.

ORIENTATION AND SERVICES

Turfan itself is very small, and you can walk to the hotels from the bus station. CITS is in the Oasis Hotel and is open 9am-1pm, 3-8pm. They're actually very helpful here and sell maps for Y2.

LOCAL TRANSPORT

Most people hire a bicycle from their hotel to get around Turfan but as virtually all the sights are too far away to reach by bike, the best thing to do is to hire a minibus and arrange your own tour.

Try to get five or six people together to fill the bus and bank on paying about Y250-300 for it (this price won't include entry fees). Drivers generally hang out at 8am in front of the Turfan Hotel but it's a good idea to meet one the night before to arrange things. Decide what you want to see before you start bargaining and note that Aydingkul Lake is a fair way away in the other direction, so tours including it will be more expensive. Likewise don't include the Emin Minaret in your tour, as it's only a short bike ride from the town centre. Check whether the grapes in 'Grape Valley' will be in season before you visit. Finally, remember to take food and plenty to drink as there will probably be no stops for lunch – and the heat is fearsome.

If you can't arrange a tour through either your hotel or just by asking around, try CITS, who do a complete tour for Y250 (taxi), Y350 (air-con taxi) or Y300 (minibus for seven people).

WHERE TO STAY

Basically there are only three places to stay in Turfan – or only three hotels which will accept foreigners. The travellers' favourite is the **Oasis Hotel** (☎ 522478). It's a pleasant, clean place, and despite the occasional lack of water in the early mornings, the showers are excellent once they start working properly. Doubles are Y260 but cheaper accommodation is available in four bed dormitories at Y22. Bikes can be hired outside; they'll ask for Y5 but can be bargained down to Y2.

Next favourite is the **Turfan Hotel** (☎ 522562). It lacks the efficient feel of the Oasis and the dormitory buildings are vaguely reminiscent of Victorian cell blocks but the rooms themselves are clean and cool. Double rooms cost Y100-Y280, a bed in the four-bed dormitory is Y25, and Y40 in the three-bed dormitory. One advantage of staying here is that you're a comfortable crawling distance from John's Information Café.

If both the above are full, go to the **Jiaotong Hotel** (☎ 523238). It's easy to find – right next to the bus station – but rather dark and basic. A dorm-bed is Y15 and a double Y80, though prices tend to vary depending on how much they think you're worth and how gullible you look.

WHERE TO EAT

In this heat the most important things are fruit drinks, cold beer and somewhere to sip them, preferably through a long straw so that you don't even have to move your head. **John's Information Café**, conveniently located opposite the Turfan Hotel, is that place. It's pleasantly shady and peaceful, the only thing which occasionally shatters the atmosphere being the mid-morning exercise sessions which take place in the large yard behind the café; for about half an hour you may find yourself treated to loud Chinese pop music and mass aerobics.

Inside the **Turfan Hotel** are a couple of patio-type restaurants. Both have been recommended and there is occasionally a local dance revue at

1 PSB	6 Gaochang Market	12 Bank of China
2 Museum	7 Post Office	(Main Branch)
3 Bank of China	8 Bus Station	13 Small Cafés &
(Branch)	9 Jiatong Hotel	Restaurants
4 Oasis Hotel	10 Cinema	14 John's Info Café
5 Silk Rd Restaurant	11 Bazaar	15 Turfan Hotel

the bigger one. The best bet, however, if you're up to browsing, is the street to the east of the Jiaotong Hotel (see map), where there's a line of good restaurants, most of them with English menus and friendly service. Otherwise you could try the **Pearl Restaurant** just north of the Turfan Hotel, on the opposite side of the road from John's. Alternatively, the **Silk Road Restaurant** (reopening shortly following renovations), serves great fried crispy duck.

There's cheap food in the Gaochang Market: corn on the cob, meat soup, noodles or huge portions of spare ribs. In the street opposite there's a food market at night, the ideal setting for a shashlik feast.

WHAT TO SEE

Emin Minaret
Despite its shape you might be forgiven for wondering whether you have seen this 37m high minaret somewhere before (its fourteen different patterns of brickwork certainly do seem reminiscent of the Kalyan Minaret in Bukhara). It was erected in 1778-9 by Uighur architects on the order of local leader, Emin Khoja, at a cost of 7000 liang (350kg of silver). He died six months after its completion. The mosque behind it is no longer functioning. Scattered around the buildings are graves littered with broken bottles and bleached human bones – rather eerie.

Compare the minaret with the remains of the one just east of the main city mosque (to the west of the town). Although the latter was clearly a lot smaller, the style of brickwork is similar. No one knows much about it, except that it was a victim of the Cultural Revolution; also a victim was the nearby city mosque, which is why it is so new.

To get to the Emin Minaret, cycle east from the Turfan Hotel along the small dirt road for about 10 minutes. Just when you think you must have taken a wrong turning you'll come to a field with the minaret in the middle. There's an entry charge of Y8 but you could wander through the fields and photograph it from a distance; there's not much to see inside.

Karez
Turfan's furnace-like climate means that water here evaporates fast. Obviously in this heat conservation is essential. Water is channelled through the region in subterranean canals called *karez* which are thought to have originated 2000 years ago in Iran. The underground network consists of 11,000 different canals, all interlinked, covering a distance of over 3000km. Water flows down from the mountains and is tapped by means of wells spaced at regular intervals, with tunnels linking them. The people are very proud of this system, claiming that it's one of the wonders of the world. A visit to see a canal will doubtless be included in any tour. Entry to the main site (which has a newly built and rather uninspiring exhibition hall) is Y8.

Flaming Mountains

Another staple tour sight (on the way to Gaochang, so it's hardly an effort to see them), these mountains extend for 100km and are so called because, in the intense heat of the day, they look as if they are on fire. Legend relates that they came from heaven when the Monkey King, enraged at having been locked inside a stove for a week (!) kicked it over, whereupon the heated bricks supporting it fell to earth. In the Chinese classic *Journey to the West*, silk roadster Xuan Xang was here when they were still actually burning, and he had to fan the flames with a magic fan so that he could pass unharmed.

Grape Valley

The rare combination of extreme heat and constant irrigation means that local fruit is particularly sweet, hence Turfan raisins are renowned throughout China. They are dried in the square, aerated brick buildings you can see everywhere; because they are shielded from the bright rays of the sun they retain their green colour. Grape Valley is simply one ten kilometre long vineyard. It is very beautiful – a good place to sit, and perhaps to sample some of the local wine. Although most is sweet, there is dry wine around. Quality varies considerably.

Gaochang

The history of this deserted walled city, 45km east of Turfan, is steeped in mystery. Originally known as Karakhoja, it was set up as a garrison town by the Chinese in the 2nd or 1st century BC. With the arrival of Buddhism it became a religious centre and was visited in 630AD by monk Xuan Xang, who was made so welcome that he had to go on hunger-strike in order to persuade the king to allow him to leave. By the start of the 15th century it had been abandoned but whether this was due to war or shortage of water no-one knows. Not much remains on this very large impressive site, so an active imagination helps when you get here.

It was here, in 1904, that German archaeologist Albert von Le Coq unearthed a life-size mural of Manes, founder of the heretical Christian sect of Manicheism. This find was particularly exciting because persecution of the sect had been so harsh that virtually nothing was known of it except from manifestos written against it. The majority of extant Manicheist documents come from this region. It was also here that von Le Coq noted the widespread destruction of priceless relics: he relates that one of his hired assistants had previously found 'cartloads' of ancient documents perfectly preserved, yet had disposed of them in the river for fear of divine retribution. He himself found a secret library, whose documents had all been destroyed by water as a direct result of the local farmers' irrigation schemes. It's a fascinating place to explore. Entry is Y13.

(**Opposite**) Built at the command of Emin Khoja in 1778 for 350kg of silver coins, Turfan's Emin Minaret stands 37m high.

Evidence of the Tang persecutions
While conducting his excavation of Goachang in 1904, von Le Coq stumbled upon a grisly scene in the north-eastern part of the city: 'after we had examined everything we broke open the floor, found the remains of the old domed roof, and then came suddenly upon confused heaps of the piled up corpses of at least some hundred murdered men. Judging from their clothing they were Buddhist monks. The top layer was all intact – skin, hair, dried-up eyes, and the frightful wounds which had caused their death, were in many cases intact and recognisable. One skull especially had been split from the top of the head to the teeth with a frightful sabre cut...'. The killings had taken place in the mid-9th century, when all monks were instructed to return to civil life. Any who refused were killed.

Astana Graves

The burial sites near Gaochang date from the 3rd century right up to the 13th. The area was investigated by European archaeologists (notably Stein) around the turn of the century but they stopped short of removing the bodies. There may be hundreds of chambers here but only three are open, so a visit lasts about 10-15 minutes. The bodies inside the tombs are not mummified but have been perfectly preserved by the arid climate. The mural inside the empty tomb reflects the Confucian ethic of Metal, Jade and Stone Man – illustrations of the depths of human knowledge and degrees of its self-display. The tombs are badly lit and the glass cases are very dusty, making it difficult to see the bodies. If you've seen the display in Urumqi nothing here is especially impressive. Entry is Y10.

Bezeklik – 'place where there are paintings'

The 'Thousand Buddha' cave complex at Bezeklik consists of over a hundred caves but only a handful of them are actually open. The caves, hewn and decorated between the 6th and the 9th centuries, were deserted at the same time as Gaochang. Monks used to live inside them and the frescoes here clearly represent the life work of generations of devotees. Many caves are closed because they are 'not interesting' but it is possible to peep through the shutters and see that they are in even worse condition than the rest. Entry to the complex is Y18 and photography is not permitted.

Bezeklik was visited by most of the early Western archaeologists. It was von Le Coq, however, who was responsible for the wholesale removal of murals and sculptures (to Berlin). You can clearly see the cuts he made around the frescoes so that he could insert saws behind them.

Almost without exception the remaining frescoes are in dreadful condition. Faces and eyes have all been picked out, and the walls and roofs of each cave have all been smeared with mud by Muslims (for whom the

---

(**Opposite**) **Top:** Bezeklik, the Thousand Buddha Caves. **Bottom:** Views from the train between Turfan and Urumqi are particularly impressive.

depiction of humans or animals is sacrilege). Guides may tell you that this took place in the 14th or 15th centuries but that's rubbish: the frescoes removed by Von le Coq (that survived the bombing of Berlin) are in perfect condition, and there are photographs of these in one of the caves. (Even the guides admit that they are in 'lovely' condition).

Just around the corner you will drive past a series of modern statues. These are characters from the Chinese classic, *Journey to the West*. You will have to pay for any photographs you take here. If you're on a tour, beware: minibus drivers tend to offload passengers here and say 'Bezeklik'. Everyone pays a Y10 entry fee to find that Bezeklik is a kilometre away and that they've just paid to visit a group of tacky statues.

Jiaohe

What makes Jiaohe so interesting is that although it was abandoned in the Yuan dynasty it is still largely intact. Whereas in Gaochang you can recognise the odd archway or two and little else, here you can see each building, and browse along what was clearly the main street.

Stein noted that this 'lost city', known to early archaeologists as Yarkhoto, marked 'the capital of Turfan down to Tang times' but that, because it was never totally deserted or buried, most of the really valuable items had already been removed or destroyed by the time he arrived. The town housed a garrison of Chinese soldiers in the Han dynasty, hence its safe location between two rivers (and thus its name, which means literally 'where two rivers meet'). No one knows exactly why the inhabitants moved out in the 14th century; perhaps there was a fire or that the water supplies failed. Or this could be the work of the Mongols, who arrived in the 13th century.

It is a fascinating place to explore, having been cleared up by the Chinese in the 1950s. Jiaohe is 18km west of Turfan; entry is Y13.

Aydingkul Lake

This salty lake is probably only of interest to geographers; at 156m below sea level it is the lowest lake in China and the second lowest in the world after the Dead Sea. Most people can't really be bothered, but tour drivers are happy enough to take you there.

Turfan Museum

The museum contains a lot of written material, both tablets and early paper, unearthed in the region and, in a display which is infinitely better than the one at Astana, there are five perfectly preserved corpses (still no match for Urumqi's exhibition, though). Sadly there is no evidence of the notorious fossilised dumpling which is supposed to prove that pasta was invented in China and not brought over by Marco Polo, as the Italians claim. Entry is expensive at Y12 and displays tend to be closed for no apparent reason.

Bazaar

This is one of the better bazaars in China, for while small, it is so incredibly crowded and bustling that there is a very intense feel to it. Cable and French wrote that it 'has a much more oriental look than that of Hami. In summer the whole street is covered with red matting and boughs of trees...the earth beneath is always damp, for the young shop assistants are responsible for scattering water many times a day in front of each stall..'. Not much has changed. Try it for food and photography – this is an excellent place for taking people's portraits (ask first, though). It's just opposite the post office and Jiaotong Hotel.

WHAT TO BUY

If you've come from Kashgar there won't be much here that you haven't already seen. Cable and French mention shiny, metal-covered boxes for sale here and these are still to be found today; they originated because Muslims couldn't use the Chinese pigskin bags. Most of them tend to be huge (trunk size) but it's worth keeping an eye out for smaller ones. Also in the bazaar is a wide selection of varied materials, often very brightly coloured; it might be fun to buy a length of this and create something outrageous when you get home. The department store sells cheap stationery.

MOVING ON

By bus from Turfan

Buses from Turfan to Daheyan go regularly from the bus station, 8am-6pm. The journey costs Y10. A **taxi** will charge you Y100.

Buses go to Kashgar three times a week 'if there's a demand'. They usually run on Tuesday, Thursday and Saturday. Tickets cost Y120 for the three-day journey. If you want a sleeper you'll have to go to Urumqi.

By rail from Daheyan

There are five trains east daily (as from Urumqi). They are No 54 (23.10), No 70 (21.06), No 98 (01.36), No 114 (18.06), No 244 (21.56) and No 144 (02.31). No 6, a tourist train, departs at 20.07, but only runs as far as Liuyuan (for Dunhuang). The journey to Dunhuang takes about 14 hours.

Arranging a train ticket from Daheyan onwards can be tricky unless you're happy travelling Hard Seat. Hard Sleeper tickets are particularly scarce because the trains all originate in Urumqi and so will be sold out well before they get anywhere near Daheyan. There's no rail booking office in Turfan, which means that, to save yourself the long trek to Daheyan and back, you will either have to make your booking out as soon as you arrive in Daheyan (ie on the way to Turfan) or get CITS to do it for you from Turfan. CITS here are reasonably competent but charge Y60 commission, and you'll need to give them two full days' warning to get a Hard Sleeper ticket. They won't book Hard Seat tickets.

Dunhuang

A major stop along the Chinese leg of the Silk Route, Dunhuang is the setting for the Mogao Thousand Buddha cave complex, arguably the most spectacular in China.

A two-hour bus ride south of Liuyuan station, Dunhuang itself is surprisingly small but there are a number of other interesting sights around it, including the huge sand dunes surrounding Crescent Moon Lake (great fun to climb). It's a pleasant place just to relax and explore slowly, and the numerous guesthouses here mean that finding accommodation is no problem.

HISTORY

The name Dunhuang means literally 'blazing beacon', and refers to the time when this small town was at the extreme western point of the Chinese empire. The Great Wall, although ending at Jiayuguan, exerted some influence here, as its watchtowers reached up to this point (hence the name 'beacon'). Dunhuang's other traditional name, Sha-Chou ('City of Sands'), is also apt, as it was sometimes the crossroads for the Northern and Southern Routes, and thus the last outpost for west-bound traders before they reached the dreaded desert of Lop. The vast dunes here feature in every traveller's account, including that of Marco Polo, who wrote of the 'Rumbling Sands'.

The Mogao Caves

Dunhuang's famous Mogao Caves ('The Caves of the Thousand Buddhas') thrived on the fear produced by the notorious Lop Desert; patronage was never short when traders were around, as everyone wanted divine protection and was willing to pay for it. The survival of the caves in their pristine condition is more surprising. Historians put their longevity down to the fact that this region was taken by the Tibetans in 781AD, thus the ruthless persecution of Buddhists which took place throughout China in the 9th century passed it by. Even the Mongol arrival in 1227 had no effect on these caves, although construction stopped under the ensuing Yuan dynasty.

Western treasure-hunters

The greatest threat to these 1000-year-old caves came recently, with the arrival of treasure-seeking archaeologists. Langdon Warner, an American who visited in 1923, saw some of the damage caused by Russian refugees fleeing the Revolution and decided to 'save' as many of the artefacts as possible by shipping them to the USA. Other archaeologists were more reserved, perhaps because the complex was never quite deserted, and thus the caves survived in remarkably good condition. History relates a rather different story concerning the documents discovered in the cave complex, of course; and one which the Chinese recall bitterly (see p200). Now virtually all lost to China, they are displayed in a handful of museums around the world.

GETTING THERE

To visit Dunhuang you will have to get off the train at Liuyuan station and take a bus (about $2^1/_2$ hours). Minibuses tend to be waiting just outside the station when trains pull in. If there isn't one, head for the bus station: walk straight up the main street, adjacent to the railway track, for 200m and it's on your left. The fare is Y10.

Be prepared for a problem here, however, because now that you are in Gansu Province you should have **special travel insurance** in order to be able to use public transport (see p84 for details). They could demand to see this policy before they sell you a ticket. Obviously, having just arrived in Gansu, you can't possibly have the necessary documentation yet: consequently they will refuse to take you to Dunhuang. CITS claim that insurance can now be bought at the bus station itself, so ask around, but if this fails, the next nearest place you can get it is...Dunhuang. If this happens there isn't much that you can do except beg, plead, lose your temper, whimper and finally try to find a driver of a private minibus who will take you. A taxi is a last, rather expensive, option. This little Catch-22 has been amusing travellers for some time now and is a prime example of the kind of absence of logic that can render travel in China so utterly soul-destroying at times.

ORIENTATION AND SERVICES

Dunhuang is so small that a half-hour cycle ride would be quite enough to acquaint yourself with all its streets. Bikes can be hired from street vendors everywhere.

There are three CITS offices here. The first two, virtually useless, are to be found in the Feitian and the Solar Energy hotels. The third, the only one where English is spoken, is on the ground floor of the building with the mural just to the left of the main street as you head south. It's open 7.30am-9pm in summer. Well, that's what they say; actually don't go between 12 noon and 3pm (or early, or late).

Tours of all the sights around the town can be arranged from the reception desks in most hotels; the more expensive the hotel, the higher the tour price. Alternatively, CITS offer a comprehensive tour for Y500.

The best way to get around the regular sights, however, is by public transport or bicycle. The exceptions are the Yumen and Yangwan Passes and the old film set. If you want to see these either take a taxi (expensive) or tag along with a tour group; tours are advertised in most hotels.

WHERE TO STAY

Because of the caves, Dunhuang has learnt to accommodate large numbers of tourists and thus boasts quite a few reasonable hotels. Dunhuang airport is currently being upgraded to take international flights, and as more and more tourists flood in, standards are set to rise yet further. Prices for budget rooms are remarkably similar, and as Dunhuang is a very small town, even the farthest hotel from the bus station is within easy walking distance.

The most upmarket place is the **Dunhuang Hotel** (☎ 8822008) where a really good double is Y400. Prices do get lower, though: in the adjoining block there are three- and four-bed rooms for Y30 per person. Across the road in the north building prices are the same but the standard is slightly higher. A **new hotel** may be about to challenge the Dunhuang's top spot, however. Located just south of the Feitian Hotel, it has yet to open its doors but will be be top of the range when it is completed, and is likely to have rooms starting from Y400.

To confuse matters, there is a second **Dunhuang Hotel** (☎ 8822413) a 10-minute walk west of the main hotel. Its location is good and it is not as expensive but it's nothing to write home about. Doubles are Y140, triples Y90, and a bed in a four-bed room is Y15-20. Within spitting distance is the **Mingshan Hotel** (☎ 8822130), with rooms of the same standard at similar prices: doubles Y120 and a bed in a four-bed room is Y20.

Further south, near the bus station, is the popular **Western Region Hotel** (☎ 8823017), which is probably the cheapest place in town, and currently rates as the backpackers' favourite: triple rooms cost Y120, and beds in the dormitory go for Y15. Nearly opposite the Western Region is another favourite, the **Feitian Hotel** (☎ 8822726), which is slightly better than the rest of the budget places, for marginally higher prices. A bed in a three-bed room costs Y20. Don't stay here in early spring or autumn when the nights are cold, as the bedding isn't up to much. Bikes can be hired here for Y2 per hour.

If you arrive in peak season and these places are all full, or if you just want to stay away from the crowds as much as possible, there are two other options. If you like the sound of the Dunhuang Hotel but don't want to pay top whack, the **Solar Energy Hotel** (☎ 8822306) could be for you: doubles are Y305. It looks great externally but has some ferociously unhelpful staff. The **Silk Road Hotel** (☎ 8823807) directly to the south of the Dunhuang Hotel, has a nice central lawn and helpful staff. Doubles here are reasonable at Y200. The **Nung King Hotel** (☎ 8822962) is nearby; look for the big 'Welcome to Our Hotel' sign. Although not quite as good as the Silk Road Hotel, it's reasonably cheap at Y48 per person in a double and Y30 per person in a triple.

WHERE TO EAT

Just as there are many hotels of a similar standard, so it is with restaurants. Nice, clean, expensive food can be had at the **Dunhuang Hotel**, as you might expect but it is possible to eat cheap food virtually anywhere. All the way up the street running north from the bus station are cheap restaurants with menus in English. The **market** is a great place to try local food, although in the evening you may have to put up with some terrible karaoke wailing. The night market is a good place for a drink. There's also **John's Information Café** in the grounds of Feitian Hotel, worth a visit but it seems to be rather suffering from the competition.

The **Café Manhattan** is a popular place just to west of the museum. Its relatively high prices (Y30-50 for a main course) are offset by its character, the good food and the fact that it's probably the only place in the west of China where you'll be able to pick up a pint of Guinness.

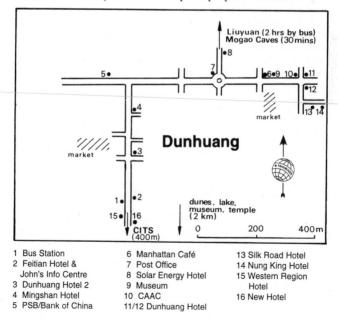

1 Bus Station
2 Feitian Hotel &
   John's Info Centre
3 Dunhuang Hotel 2
4 Mingshan Hotel
5 PSB/Bank of China

6 Manhattan Café
7 Post Office
8 Solar Energy Hotel
9 Museum
10 CAAC
11/12 Dunhuang Hotel

13 Silk Road Hotel
14 Nung King Hotel
15 Western Region
   Hotel
16 New Hotel

WHAT TO SEE

Mogao Caves

These caves are probably the finest in China, so you would be foolish to miss them. They were carved between the 4th century and the 14th, the best work taking place during the Tang dynasty (618-907). The caves were abandoned for a number of reasons, among them the decline of the Tang dynasty and the repeated threats of nomadic marauders.

They appear to have been rediscovered by one Wang Yuan Lu, or 'Abbot Wang', as Western visitors called him, who set himself up as their custodian. During his time here he discovered a sealed chamber in cave No 17 which contained a library of ancient documents, hidden for safety. British archaeologist Sir Marc Aurel Stein, hearing of this discovery on his 1907 expedition, went to investigate. After prolonged negotiations he was permitted to view the chamber and thus wrote himself into the history books, for inside was a hoard of documents so great that its discovery is now held to be on a par with Carter's opening of Tutankhamen's tomb. Stein then earned himself the perpetual hatred of the Chinese by purchasing over 5000 scrolls and paintings for the measly sum of £130, although French and Cable reckoned that 'the business transaction with the old priest was done honourably...'.

So big was the find that when French sinologist Paul Pelliot arrived at the caves one year later he didn't even realise that any manuscripts had already been taken. Among Stein's crateloads of documents was the *Diamond Sutra* which, printed in AD868, qualifies as the oldest known printed document in the world. It is still on display in the British Museum.

Visiting the caves Entry to the caves is a hefty Y80 but don't let this put you off. For their protection, strict rules have been laid down concerning tourists: you must be accompanied by a guide and cameras must be left outside. Try to get a group of foreigners together and then lobby for a guide who speaks English (there are some) otherwise your commentary will be in Chinese. Guided tours are free and generally excellent. They last about two hours. Don't bother staying on for a second tour to see more: it will be substantially identical to the first, as only a few caves are actually open to the public. It's not really worth bringing a flashlight unless you happen to have a high-powered one, as pocket torches aren't nearly bright enough; better to hire one when you get to the caves. The ticket office is in the small booth just before the bridge; staff will appear to wave you past but what they are half-heartedly trying to tell you is that the foreigners' window is around the corner. The Mogao Caves conform with a universal trend at all China's major tourist sights: namely that of putting the ticket office in an obscure spot a long way away from the actual entrance itself.

Characters you will encounter inside the Mogao Caves include:

The Buddha Everything you hear about his life is probably speculation. He was born sometime between the 6th and 4th centuries BC (arguments for specific birth dates come and go). After a period of experimentation with religions, notably self-mortification and yoga, he attained some sort of higher spiritual insight which he termed 'Nirvana', or 'The Blowing Out'. The crux of this state was the banishment of craving and desires, all of which bound him to the suffering which led to the cycle of transmigration, or reincarnation. Thus he became The Buddha; 'buddha' is not a name, it is a term of recognition ('the Enlightened One'). In fact he is referred to by a number of names, another popular one being 'Shakyamuni', literally 'Sage of the Clan Shakya'.

He then went out to teach the world what he had discovered, in the form of the 'Four Noble Truths'. Since his death, numerous myths have sprung up, many of which are allegorical. Subsequent followers have disagreed as to his 'message' and thus any number of stories will tell you different 'facts' about him. These myths are often the subject of paintings here.

Bodhisattva The major split within Buddhism is between the Mahayana and Theravada traditions. Mahayana probably originated in the early centuries AD as a revivalist tradition. One of its pretexts is that an individual's search for enlightenment actually assists other mortals in their own personal quests; monks termed 'bodhisattvas' are from this tradition, and their quest is thus centred on compassion for others rather than the selfish urge for personal escape.

Amida/Amitabha One Mahayana tradition dictates that Amida was a monk so good that he managed to create a 'Western Paradise'. This paradise was so elevated that the step into enlightenment from here was comparatively easy. Popular religion quickly developed this into a kind of 'heaven' and Amida became the centre of a devotional movement.

Maitreya It is generally held that Buddhism can never die – it simply fades away throughout the centuries until one person (the last was the Buddha, Shakyamuni) stumbles upon its truths and advocates it again. Maitreya is the Buddha of the future, who will rediscover the eternal truths when they have all been forgotten.

Ananda, Kashyapa and **Vairocana** The Buddha attracted many followers, of whom these first two are the most famous. Ananda was his closest friend; Vairocana is another follower, in the Mahayana tradition.

Other figures It is a mistake to divorce Buddhism from other traditions, as the situation is seldom this simple. The numerous other figures around the caves are the result of a meshwork of different traditions and influences. Thus you should be prepared to find demons and monsters guarding doorways, apsara ('angels') on the ceilings, and other weird permutations of paradise.

On your way out it's well worth stopping by the **Research and Exhibition Centre**, which is in the modern building next to the car park. Tickets are Y20 – which undoubtedly discourages many people but the exhibition really shouldn't be missed. The building contains all sorts of interesting relics from the caves (including documents not stolen by Stein and Pelliot from the Cave 17 cache). There are sections detailing how the caves were made, and full sized reproductions of some of the caves themselves, showing dates so that you can compare the different styles of art inside them. The displays are all beautifully laid out and labelled with clear explanations in English. This is one of the best museums you are likely to see in China.

Buses to the Mogao Caves trawl along Dunhuang's main street picking up punters and charging about Y10 for a return ticket. The journey takes about 40 minutes. It is possible to catch the morning bus and then return on the evening one but there's not much point as the caves are closed between 11am and 2pm.

Sand Dunes and the Crescent Moon Lake

Cable and French report that "'The skill of man made the Caves of the Thousand Buddhas, but the hand of God fashioned the Lake of the Crescent Moon'". The lake is pretty small and insignificant but its setting is wonderful. It is surrounded by rolling sand dunes which give the area an air of looking – well – as a desert ought to look. Unfortunately, those killjoys at CITS got here first so you'll have to pay Y20 as an entrance fee. The area is crowded with tourist stalls but the dunes themselves are untouched. On entry you are likely to be mauled by camel drivers who want to hire their animals. Don't bother: the lake is only a short walk away.

Climbing the dunes is extraordinarily hard work but well worth the effort. Note that the signs reading 'Sighty Stop' (sic) mean that you shouldn't proceed further in that direction. Coming down is wholly more enjoyable than going up, and you may even manage to make the sands 'sing' (see below). Be careful with your camera here as fine dust and intricate mechanisms don't mix, and note that this place ranks right up there with the Pacific Ocean in the 'bad places to lose a contact lens' stakes.

The Singing Sands

Cable and French stayed the night beside the lake and were woken by a strange noise of thunder. They were told that this was caused by the movement of the sands ('when the whole valley echoes and re-echoes with a noise like that of rolling drums, and when the sand, moved by vibration, starts rolling and continues to roll for hours on end') and that this noise explained the site's name 'the door of thunder'. Later they climbed a dune and, as they slid down it on their backs, experienced a strange sensation of vibrant sands, for as we slid, a loud noise came from the depths of the hill on which we were, and simultaneously a strong vibration shook the dune as though the strings of some gigantic musical instrument were twanged beneath us..'. This 'singing' phenomenon has been noted in other deserts. Try it, but be warned that the chances of getting the dunes to sing are slim. The chances, on the other hand, of filling your underwear with sand and having a painful, gritty bike ride home are considerably greater.

Dunhuang County Museum The museum is set in the fine Chinese-style building to the right just before the dunes. The entry ticket boasts that it exhibits 'more than twenty different items' but this seems unlikely unless you include the tourist shops. It's quite tricky to tell which is shop and which is museum – you will find yourself wandering around what seems to be a mock-up of a typical Chinese house until you realise that everything has a price-tag on it. Bona fide exhibits include a couple of millstones, a plough and two large stone oxen. Entry is Y10. It's not really worth the effort unless you're extremely bored or looking for souvenirs.

Buddhist temple Just before the museum, on the left, is a Buddhist temple, erected in 1991. The building is very beautiful and worth a stop but there's some debate as to whether it was built for tourists. CITS claim that it's a functioning monastery though there don't seem to be many monks around, and there's a Y10 admission fee.

Getting there To reach the sand dunes and Crescent Moon Lake cycle south down the main street past the bus station and simply follow the tarmac road (the road has been blocked at the southern end, so you will have to follow a zig-zag route, left and then right, before the road starts heading out of town). As long as you keep on the road, you can't go wrong. The scenery is lovely; in the autumn you can find huge bales of marijuana lying around to dry in the sun. Just before you reach the dunes there's the County Museum and temple. Take suntan cream.

Dunhuang Museum
Big signs in English advertise the displays on offer in this museum but inside the English disappears. Still, it's mostly self-explanatory, displaying coins, combs and weaponry, all unearthed in the region. It's OK for a browse but hardly riveting. Again, perhaps they should oust the tourist shops and add more exhibits for your Y15. Where did they unearth the Mig jet fighter parked outside?

Excursions from Dunhuang
There are a few possibilities here but none is really worthwhile. Trips will have to be arranged either by taxi or by joining in with another tour.

The **Yumen and Yangwan Passes** are over 70km away from the town, in opposite directions, and there's not much to see when you eventually get there. Yumen is the famous 'Jade Gate' (of Cable and French's *Through Jade Gate and Central Asia*), through which travellers heading west across the Lop Desert would pass after leaving Dunhuang.

The **film set** where the Japanese movie *Dunhuang* was made attracts truckloads of Nikon-toting tourists from Tokyo. Not exciting, say the reports.

WHAT TO BUY

Dunhuang is well prepared for tourists: every other store in the street is a tourist gift-shop. As well as the usual China trinkets, things to buy here include local specialities: 'Luminous Cups' which aren't actually luminous (apparently they used to be in the good old days). They are fragile, expensive and occasionally quite attractive. Jade and stone carvings are also popular.

MOVING ON

By bus from Dunhuang

To get back to Liuyuan you will have to take the bus again. Buses run regularly from 07.00-20.00, departing when full. The fare is Y10 but this may go up to Y15 in the evening after 18.00.

It's easy to get to Jiayuguan by bus, the journey takes seven hours and costs Y52. Not only will taking a bus save you the hassle of getting to Liuyuan station and queuing for a train ticket, but it will save you the time, too. In all, it probably takes up to five hours longer to travel to Liuyuan, buy your ticket and go by train, than it would do to catch a direct bus.

By rail from Liuyuan

Six trains head eastwards: No 98 (14.09), No 70 (09.48), No 144 (16.46), No 244 (11.01), No 54 (11.43) and No 114 (07.22). CITS will book Hard Sleeper tickets for you for Y50 (you'll be doing very well to get them without their help). If you are going to Jiayuguan you won't really be needing one anyway, as the journey takes only seven hours.

By air

There are flights from Dunhuang to Beijing, Jiayuguan and Lanzhou.

Jiayuguan

The termination point of the Great Wall proper, Jiayuguan was the gateway to the Chinese empire from the west, a remote, desolate outpost on the edge of the wilderness. There are a couple of important sights here: the western end of the Wall, now restored, is just outside the town, as is the ancient fort which once marked China's western entrance. In addition, there are countless tombs scattered around the area dating back to the 4th century AD, and more of these should soon be open. Entry fees for sights here are high but you can see all you want in a full day.

HISTORY

Jiayuguan owes its existence purely to its strategic position. Located towards the western end of the Hexi Corridor, sandwiched between the Qilian Mountains to the south and the Black Mountains of the Mazong Range to the north, it acts rather like a gate for travellers passing in and out of China from the west. This position has been exploited through the ages. We know that settlements here date back to the 2nd century BC and beyond, and that tolls on travellers were taken as early as the Han dynasty. The current fort was constructed in the late 14th century, although it has been altered since (most recently during the extensive renovations of the 1980s). During this period it marked the end of the Chinese world, a boundary between civilisation and the barbarians beyond. Although the Great Wall extended beyond here, this was its last real outpost.

The pass marked the border between the known and unknown, a desolate spot particularly for the those heading west. Yet at the same time it must have been a triumphant sight for travellers coming home from the deserts beyond. As Cable and French note, even the approach to this unappealing city was a joyous one: 'Only those who have crossed the Gobi roads can possibly understand the thrill and excitement of the traveller when the first tower of Kiayukwan comes into sight, about three miles before the town is reached. Drivers and passengers always raise a shout at the prospect of once more passing the portal of China'.

The fact that many of its occupants were in a celebratory mood does not seem to have made this remote spot any more lively: 'There is nothing to do here all day but sit and listen to the howling wind'. Some consolation was available, though: '...there was constant entertainment for the carters in watching the dosing of desert-tried (sic) beasts, the ramming of needles into the tongue of a sick mule, and the more delicate operation of cutting the cartilage of the nostril to cure spasms.'

ORIENTATION AND SERVICES

Four km south-west of the town, the railway station is too far to walk from any hotel. There are minibuses and taxis – or you use one of the motorbike taxis (see p209). The public bus station is to the west of the town (look for the modern clock tower). The airport is 14km to the north-east.

CITS, at 2 Shen Li Road, is pretty good: there are some excellent English speakers here and the office is generally one of the better ones in China. It's open 08.30-12.30, and 14.30-18.30 but they claim that there's someone here 24 hours a day in case of emergencies. Both the Jiayuguan and the Chang Chen hotels run their own tourist services.

LOCAL TRANSPORT

Private minibuses from the railway station take about 12 minutes and cost Y1.5. Getting back to the station isn't a problem – buses cruise past the hotels and tend to wait outside them.

Getting around Jiayuguan is easy: hire a bike for the exploring you want to do around town and then either a taxi or a motorbike taxi (see p209) for more distant attractions. It is possible to cycle to the Overhanging Great Wall and the Fort.

All major hotels offer tours. Trips usually cover the Fort, the Great Wall, the Underground Art Gallery and the Great Wall Museum for around Y250 for a car of three or four. A guide tells you what's what but you still have to pay your own entrance fees to the sights. CITS also offer tours but theirs are more expensive. Generally, you'd do much better to hire a bike.

WHERE TO STAY

The classiest hotel in Jiayuguan is the **Chang Cheng** (☎ 6225288). A double here costs Y398 and triples are available for Y240. There are two restaurants and all the facilities you are likely to need, including bike hire.

The standard travellers' haunt, however, is the **Jiayuguan Hotel** (☎ 6225804), which has rather poky four-bed rooms at Y25 per bed, three-bed rooms at Y37 per bed and doubles with attached bathrooms at Y200 for the room. Bike hire is Y2 per hour (Y200 deposit).

Better for cheap accommodation is the **Magnificent Great Wall** (Xiong Guan),(☎ 6225115). It's a bit more basic than the Jiayuguan Hotel but is cheaper (Y16 for a bed in a three-bed room; doubles for Y100). Several travellers have managed to stay at the **Youth Hotel** (☎ 6224671), which is also cheaper than the Jiayuguan Hotel. A double with bathroom is Y100 and in a three-bed room it's Y30 per bed.

If you are arriving late or catching a really early train you might also want to consider the **Railway Hotel** right in front of the station. They are not used to foreigners but are friendly. Doubles are from Y100 and a bed in a three-bed room costs Y30.

WHERE TO EAT

Jiayuguan's eating facilities are a bit thin on the ground, so if you want a proper sit-down meal you would do best to eat in one of the hotels. The Jiayuguan Hotel has a good restaurant with an English menu, reasonable prices and extraordinarily cold beer. Recommended! The **Coffee Shop**

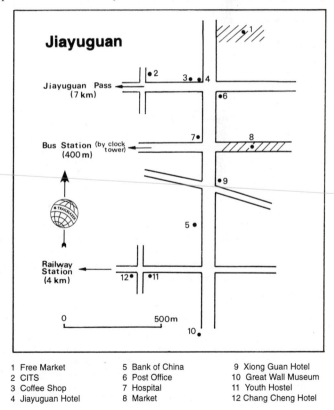

1 Free Market	5 Bank of China	9 Xiong Guan Hotel
2 CITS	6 Post Office	10 Great Wall Museum
3 Coffee Shop	7 Hospital	11 Youth Hostel
4 Jiayuguan Hotel	8 Market	12 Chang Cheng Hotel

next to the Jiayuguan Hotel is not bad at all. They don't have a menu in English, so the best way to choose a dish is just to wander into the open kitchen and point at what you want.

Better and cheaper, though less civilised, are the **bazaars** (see map). The southern one is better for noodle dishes and fresh fruit, while the northern one is good for shashlik and barbecued foods. Particularly good here is *malatang*, satays of meat or vegetables broiled, Sichuan-style. The chilli paint which they daub liberally all over them is particularly fiery, so extreme caution is advised. Each stick should cost about Y0.75-Y1.

According to CITS, the local speciality is 'Snow with Camel', the centrepiece of which is a large slice of camel's hump. It sounds revolting but our Chinese adviser assured us that 'it's even better than eating bear'. The Chang Cheng Hotel should be able to oblige.

WHAT TO SEE

Jiayuguan Pass

The fort itself dates back at least to the Han dynasty, when it was the final stage before traders left the protection of the Great Wall. Dangers to be faced outside were numerous, so travellers were never too keen to leave. Cable and French write that the West Gate was known as the 'Gate of Sighs', and that it was common for miscreants to be forcibly ejected through it – cast out into the wilderness, as it were. This expulsion was termed *kow wai*, or 'without the mouth', the image called to mind being that of China having 'spued (sic) an unwanted national from her mouth'. The portal used to be covered with mournful graffiti, to which they added some suitably evangelical trimmings. Tradition dictated, so they say, that travellers heading west through this gate throw a pebble at the wall beside it. If the pebble failed to bounce back to its thrower, the journey would end in tragedy.

Despite its long and venerable history, there is not much to see here apart from the walls and the gates themselves, as the pass is largely empty now. For Y20 it's worth a visit, though. There is a large map inside the main gate, and a short historical overview just outside it. Open 8.30am-6.30pm daily, it's about 7km west of the centre of town.

Overhanging Great Wall

In order to mark the official 'Other End' of the Great Wall, the Chinese tourist boffins have overseen the restoration of an impressive stretch some 5km north of the Jiayuguan Pass (along the new tarmac road). It's certainly worth a visit, if only so you can say 'I preferred the other end' when you get to Beijing. As you go from the Pass to the Wall you can clearly see the remains of the original wall, much dilapidated; thus it is a surprise to find that the 'overhanging' part of it is in pristine condition. Obviously this wasn't so much a case of renovation as it was of complete rebuilding. It is fun to climb the wall but hard work and for the energetic only; from the top you get a superlative view of Jiayuguan's smokestacks and factories to the east. It would seem by the smell that it is a Chinese custom to defecate when you get to the top. Entry is Y10.

The Underground Art Gallery/Cave Tombs
Discovered by a farmer in 1972 these tombs, some 20 km east of the city centre, date back to the Wei dynasty (4th century AD). No one knows how many tombs there are here as excavation is still underway. Only one is open to the public.

The paintings in the open tomb (No 6) are perfectly preserved. They are very small and simple: several depict everyday activities such as ploughing and hunting but some are little more than doodles. Quite a few seem simply to be attempts to draw perfect circles freehand. The cave is interesting to visit but expensive at Y30, although this may become better value as more tombs are opened. It can be visited at virtually any time, as the custodians live here. If you are not part of a group you will first be taken to the gift shop where it is a good idea to buy the pamphlet on the tombs' history, as no English is spoken at all.

Motorbike taxis
Outside the gates of the Jiayuguan Hotel is a permanent encampment of locals with motorcycles, all desperate for you to pay them to take you somewhere. It is cheap but also fairly dangerous, particularly since travel insurance doesn't usually cover motorbike accidents. To make matters worse, most of these guys are cowboys and don't seem to have a clue what's going on. In the course of the six hour trip I took we crashed twice – once into a flock of sheep and once into a river. Even CITS admits that it's only a matter of time before the first tourist gets killed this way, so it's wise to be wary of the service.

If you do accept a ride, check the machine – does it look as if it's in good condition? And the rider – does he look like the kind of guy you'd like to be responsible for your life? Insist on a crash helmet. Before you get on the bike, agree exactly what you want to see and how long you'll spend there. Make sure he understands that you would like to be brought home at the end of the day because standard policy is to double the price because 'no say want going home'...etc. It might also help to write down exactly what you want to see and the price you have agreed as proof of your agreement, because by the time he starts arguing when you get back you will be surrounded by a bevy of his biker pals, and this can be intimidating.

Finally, if possible, try to work out whether he really does know where you want to go, as the majority will happily agree to your itinerary and then deliver you straight to the Jiayuguan Pass. Many don't seem to know the way to any other sights, and they'll try to charge you for the time they spend looking for them. Ask for a lift to Tooting Broadway and they'll all agree to take you.

You will need sunglasses or some sort of eye protection, and suncream is a good idea. If you feel unsafe at any time, tell your driver to stop, get off and walk home. The walk will be dreary but probably considerably more fun than having gravel combed out of your face later.

Black Mountain Cave Paintings

These paintings, considerably older and less sophisticated than those at the Wei tombs, are more difficult to find. Very few people go to see them, since they are little more than primitive scratchings on the rocks dating from the Warring States period (up to 221BC). If you want to go, take a photograph of what they look like with you (pick up a postcard or a brochure from CITS), and show it to your driver before you agree on a price.

Great Wall Museum

The town museum, located at the southern end of Xinhua Rd just before it disappears into the desert, is rather disappointing. It is in a modern replica of an old Chinese fort, and although the display is reasonably well laid out, it is extremely small. Exhibits here include inscribed bamboo strips, miscellaneous metal and wooden tools and other ancient Chinese relics, all of which you will have seen before. There are a couple of paintings from the underground galleries and lots of photos. Look out for the military dress and early firearms, particularly the spears and arrows with explosive charges. Nothing is labelled in English. Entry is Y10.

WHAT TO BUY

The best places for souvenirs in Jiayuguan are the shops in the museum and the Chang Cheng Hotel. Luminous cups are popular here (see Dunhuang) but there is little else that you won't have seen before. The local artists seem to spend their time either copying other area's works or making the small stone sculptures which they rather grandly call 'Gobi Art'.

MOVING ON

Both CITS and the Jiayuguan Hotel have ticket booking services but getting hold of Hard Sleeper tickets to Lanzhou can be a problem. However the slow train (No 502) which departs at 08.33 and takes an extra five hours is sometimes underbooked. Soft Sleeper tickets are easier to get hold of, and are not too expensive. Hard Seats will always be available, of course, but the journey is over 20 hours and most will find this too much.

Heading east, train numbers and departure times are: No 70 (15.32), No 244 (18.48), No 144 (23.56), No 54 (17.34), No 98 (20.08), No 502 (08.33) and No 114 (13.37). There is an X-ray machine at the station which is probably best avoided: just walk past. No one tried to stop us.

If Hard Seat on the train doesn't appeal, there are at least two buses to Lanzhou daily (Y175 for a sleeper through CITS); and you can fly from here to several cities including Beijing, Lanzhou, Xi'an and Dunhuang.

Lanzhou

The spectacular scenery around Lanzhou's Bingling Si Buddhist cave complex makes this city well worth a stop. The caves are cut into cliffs high above the Yellow River, and you are unlikely to find a more isolated attraction anywhere. In addition to Bingling Si, the best museum you are likely to have seen since leaving Moscow makes a visit doubly worthwhile. Add to this a day exploring the city itself and an afternoon lounging around in one of the parks, you will probably end up staying for at least a couple of days. Lanzhou is also the nearest major city to Xiahe, or 'Little Tibet', a laid-back village that some travellers rate as their best visit in all China.

HISTORY

Situated at the eastern end of the Gansu (Hexi) Corridor, Lanzhou is another town which owes its historical significance to its geographical location. Its strategic position at the foot of the corridor has meant that throughout the years it has controlled traffic to Xi'an from the west and vice versa. It was the standard Yellow River crossing point for those heading to Jiayuguan.

Lanzhou has been inhabited since at least the 6th century BC but only really became prominent in 81BC during the Han dynasty, when it was established as the seat of power for the surrounding area. This role as the centre of local government was occasionally lost and regained as time went by until 763AD, when invasion by the Tibetans forced radical change. It was recovered by the Tang dynasty in 843, only to be lost again until 1041, when the Song dynasty stepped in. In fact every new dynasty that passed by this way invaded, and established prefectures here, until 1666, when Gansu was made a separate province and Lanzhou was declared the capital, as it still is.

From 1864-75 it was badly damaged in the Islamic rebellion which catapulted Yakub Beg into the limelight (see p181). Repairs proved temporary, however, as the town was devastated by a huge earthquake in 1920.

Recovery was swift, and by the time the Sino-Japanese War (1937-45) broke out, Lanzhou was the major distribution centre for all ammunition and supplies shipped in to China from the Soviet Union. The strategic significance of this town near the terminus of the Sino-Soviet Highway was not lost on the Japanese who bombed it heavily.

Lanzhou today

This is a large, modern city which plays a major role in China's petro-chemical industry; oil from the Yumen oilfield is refined here. It also lies at the heart of the Chinese nuclear industry. With a population of around two million, this is the largest Chinese city you will have encountered on the way east but while the modern side of the place ('The East is Red' Square, for example) can be a touch 'grey', there is still a lot of charm here. A good way to discover this lighter side is simply to wander through the streets to the north of the Victory Hotel. The Hezheng Lu Market is a good spot.

ORIENTATION

Though a large city Lanzhou is surprisingly easy to get around. It sprawls along the Yellow River from east to west, with railway stations at each end. Not many trains stop at the west station, but, given the chance, it's worth getting off here if you're after budget accommodation. Most things that are of interest to budget travellers are, in fact, at the west end of the city (a colourful night market, the bus station, museum etc), whereas the more expensive hotels, better restaurants and department stores are nearer the main railway station on the east side of the city. Getting from one side to the other is not difficult, just time consuming. Good maps are readily available at most hotels; CITS can certainly give you copies.

SERVICES

CITS main office is on the second floor of a building in the grounds of the Jincheng Guesthouse, but the 'front of house' is actually on the small lane running between the Jincheng Guesthouse and the Lanzhou Hotel. Their shop has 'Travel Service' prominently displayed over the door, so it's hard to miss, and the staff are fairly capable.

Just as good, however, and offering the same services at the same prices is the **West Asia Travel Service** in the Hua Yi Hotel. They are friendly and helpful and, if you are staying on the west side of town, a visit here will save you the trek of getting across to see CITS. They also have good maps with some street names in English, and are about the only people who can help to find bikes for hire.

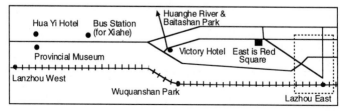

Both CITS and WATS will sell you Gansu Province travel insurance for Y35 (two weeks); you will need it if you are planning to take a public bus to Xiahe. It's slightly cheaper (Y30) to buy the insurance direct from the **PIC** office (People's Insurance Company) on Qinyang Lu, just west of The East is Red Square. **Don't** buy insurance from touts outside the railway station: they usually charge Y50 for the same policy.

Extending a visa in Lanzhou is particularly easy at the PSB which is on Qingyang Lu, by The East is Red Square. The main post office is to the south of this square, a short way down Pingliang Lu.

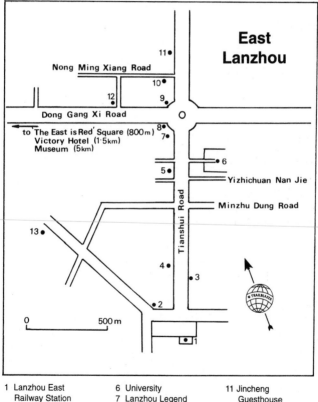

1 Lanzhou East
  Railway Station
2 Lanzhou Mansion
3 Lanshan Hotel
4 Yingbing Hotel
5 Bank of China

6 University
7 Lanzhou Legend
  Hotel
8 Department Store
9 Lanzhou Hotel
10 CITS

11 Jincheng
  Guesthouse
12 CAAC
13 Post Office

LOCAL TRANSPORT

The main bus to look out for is No 1, which goes east-west and back. From the main railway station, it runs past the Lanzhou Hotel, The East is Red Square, the Victory Hotel and the bus station, ending up by the provincial museum, the Hua Yi Hotel and the west railway station.

The best way to get around is by bike but there are few rental places, and the West Asia Travel Service is one of the few remaining places that can help out. If you keep your eyes open you may be able to rent one on the street; don't look for a great line-up of machines, as they've often only got one and just sit beside it in a fold-up chair.

TOURS

As well as CITS, the travel services in all the larger hotels run tours. They'll all tell you that it's impossible to get to the Bingling Si caves and back by public transport in a day, and they're probably right. There's a chance that you might be able to make it alone but this is not advised (see p217 for how it ended up when we tried it). The problem with a tour is that unless you're with a group,it's expensive: CITS and West Asia Travel offer tours for about the same price – Y130-140 per person including bus, boat and guide; on the other hand at least you can be certain of getting there and back in the same day. Xiahe is a different matter: the public bus journey is long and bumpy, but most people plan to stay in Xiahe for at least a couple of days, and it's easy to get there by yourself.

If you have Gansu travel insurance of your own (see p84), check that the cost of insurance isn't included in any tour prices, as travel services tend to add it anyway, unless you tell them you don't want it.

WHERE TO STAY

East Lanzhou: near the main station

Hotels in the east of town, near the main train station are, for the most part, fairly expensive (with one notable exception). Top of the pile is undoubtedly the **Lanzhou Legend Hotel** (☎ 8882876) where the cheapest rooms go for Y800. Opposite, the **Lanzhou Hotel** (☎ 8416321), is smart and well located and has doubles for Y320.

The **Lanzhou Mansion,** virtually opposite the station, has doubles at Y180 and a dormitory on the 19th floor for Y56 per person. This may be a problem to use, however, because the lift seems permanently stuck somewhere between floors 9 and 21. In this area, too, others worth trying include the **Lanshan Hotel** (☎ 8617211), unused to foreigners but friendly, if a bit dingy – Y112 a double; or the **Heping Hotel** (☎ 8611874) which is in better condition but is more difficult to find (look up the side street beneath the hotel sign). The pick of the bunch around here, (and probably in the whole of Lanzhou, if there are two of you) is the **Yingbing Hotel** (☎ 8886552), which is a short way north of the station. Prices for clean comfortable double rooms start at Y80; unfortunately there is no dormitory.

Central and West Lanzhou

The cheapest place in town, for single travellers at least, is the **Hua Yi Hotel** (formerly the Friendship Hotel). The rooms aren't great and the showers only work in the evenings (and only then if you can find an attendant to unlock them for you) but it's cheap for Lanzhou: Y37 for a bed in a double room. Although this place is a hassle to get to from the main railway station, it's conveniently close to several other things: a night market, the bus station, and west train station, and the Provincial Museum. Also worth a look is the **Victory Hotel** (☎ 8465221), although its location at the centre of the shopping district makes a trip from either train station rather time consuming. A double room costs Y150. To get here, take bus No1 and ask to be let off at 'Shung Cheng Men'.

WHERE TO EAT

Tianshui Lu, leading north from the main railway station, has several smart, clean and attractive restaurants, and in the same area, the road behind the Lanzhou Hotel (by the CITS office) has a number of small, friendly cafés and stalls.

In west of the city, near the Hua Yi Hotel there are several good places. The **fast food restaurant** next door to the Hua Yi Hotel is OK, although a bit overpriced when you compare it to the market. Next door is **First Beef Noodle**, which is clean, fast and excellent value (although it serves only beef noodles). Across the road from First Beef Noodle, there is a row of good eateries, although you can expect to pay reasonably high prices here, say Y15-20 per dish. About 50m west of here, the night market has all the shashlik and fried food stalls you could possibly hope for. Finally, in the centre of the city, there's a great restaurant next to the Victory Hotel. Very popular with locals, it's usually packed.

WHAT TO SEE

Bingling Si Buddhist Caves

These caves are some of the most impressive in China and alone justify a visit to Lanzhou. They are reached by bus and boat, but unfortunately you can only spend 1-2 hours at the caves themselves, as the journey is a long one: the round trip from Lanzhou takes about 12 hours.

Not only are the caves themselves (there are some 180 of them) in good condition, but the setting is truly spectacular, as they are stuck on a sheer cliff face above the Yellow River. In fact, it's the setting and the river journey that makes the day worthwhile: if you've been to Dunhuang you will have seen better caves already.

The oldest cave is allegedly No 169, which features an inscription dating it to the early 5th century. Most were carved out later, peak construction period being the Song and Ming dynasties (c960AD onwards). The construction of the Buddha figures is fairly typical: because the rock is not suitable for sculpture, they were built around wooden frames and it is possible to see, as at Mogao, broken limbs displaying their straw and clay contents. The centrepiece of the ensemble is a stunning 27m high Maitreya (see p201) figure, which is the first thing that comes into view as you approach by boat.

Getting there The best way is to take a tour, as the trip to the caves is fairly long and involved. The journey itself takes two hours on a bus to get to the Liujiaxia Dam and hydroelectric plant and then three to four hours on a boat up the Yellow River to the caves. Make sure that you bring food and drink (flasks of boiling water are provided, so dried noodles are a good choice), warm clothing and a good book: you will be sitting doing nothing for seven hours or so hours on a boat, which can get quite chilly. Entry to the caves is Y12 but this should be included in the tour price. It will allow you to see the caves at ground level but no further. Better access (eg entry to cave 169) is really costly: Y250.

According to staff at the site it is possible to stay the night at Bingling Si: there is a hostel opposite the 27m Buddha. This would make using public transport more feasible and Bingling Si would be a mellow place to stay for a night. Check with West Asia Travel Service first, however, to see if they can confirm whether the hostel is still open, and be prepared for some hard bargaining with the boat drivers. Finally, bring some food with you: the guesthouse may be open, but there's no guarantee that there'll be any food available.

Gansu Provincial Museum

One of the best museums in China, this is the first one with proper labelling in English. Among numerous displays is a large exhibition of 'Historical Finds of Gansu' which includes some impressive wood carvings, the famous bronze 'heavenly' horse of Ferghana, and paintings from tombs in the Jiayuguan area. There are also some of the handwritten sutras from Dunhuang (careless of foreign archaeologists to let these fall into Chinese hands) and, surprisingly, the complete skeleton of a woolly mammoth. Other sections include 'Chinese Art and Economics' and 'Produce of Gansu Province'. The museum is directly opposite the Hua Yi Hotel in the western part of the town, on Dong Gang Xi. It is open 9-11.30am, and 2.30-5.00pm (not Sunday). Entry is Y25 or Y5 if you can produce something that resembles a student card.

Parks

Baitashan Park, laid out across a steep hillside, is small and fairly attractive, but tends to get crowded and noisy at weekends, when the tea shops fill up and the fairground-type games are running at full capacity. If you find a quiet spot, it's a good place for a break, however, and there's a fine view of Lanzhou from the top. Entry is Y6 and the entrance is just across Sun Zhong Shan bridge.

Wuquanshan Park, on the south-western side of the city centre, makes a lovely place to while away an afternoon. Much bigger than Baitashan, its buildings are far more intricate and there's a large Buddhist temple in the centre. Art exhibitions are held here, too. Entry is Y5 and trolley-buses Nos 31 or 33 stop nearby.

A Lesson In Chinese Method

Travel in China can be a nightmare. The problems faced by Westerners usually stem from one common source – the people. My first attempt to visit Bingling Si drove this forcibly home to me: having got up at 6am to catch the first public bus, I had breakfast. After a 10 minute argument (which got me nowhere) in the Yunfeng restaurant, I eventually paid my bill: four times what it should have been. Then I found the right bus but the conductress wouldn't let me on. Why? 'No travel insurance'. Aha! But I had travel insurance from CITS in Dunhuang, valid 'throughout Gansu Province'. This was not valid, apparently, because I had not bought it in Lanzhou. I would have to buy more travel insurance. Naturally, the idea of paying another Y30 for another worthless insurance policy when I had already paid £100 for a real policy in England (and of wasting another day) didn't appeal to me. I argued. Twenty minutes later, in bad humour, she let me onto the bus. She then proceeded to charge me five times the regular bus fare ('or get out'). What could I do? I paid. She agreed to let me know when we got to the stop for Bingling Si. I greeted my fellow passengers, who all agreed that I was going to Bingling Si. Of course, they said, they would not mind telling me when to get off the bus.

Two and a half hours later we arrive at the bus terminal. 'Bingling Si?' I ask hopefully. 'Ha-ha' says the conductress, pointing back up the hill we have just descended. 'Bingling Si. It's a long way back. Ha-ha'. My fellow passengers grin at me. 'Ha-ha' they say. 'Ha-ha-ha'. It takes me two hours to get a bus back to the dam.

Once there I encounter the boat drivers: 'Bingling Si. Very far', they say gravely. 'Y200'. I wait for another group so that I can share a boat with them. When they arrive, they agree – but they are Chinese, so are paying a Chinese price; I will only have to pay Y5. Great. Of course, it is not to be. The boat drivers argue, shout, bicker and try every conceivable trick to get me to step off the boat for a second so that it can depart without me. Finally they refuse point blank to take even the Chinese passengers if I am on board. My fellow tourists give up, apologise, and ask me to go alone. As the boat pulls away, the other drivers surround me, triumphant. 'Where you want go. Ha-ha', they shout. 'Bingling Si' I sigh. 'Oh, Bingling Si. Very far. Y400. Ha-ha'. I take the bus back to Lanzhou without seeing the caves. The bus ticket costs me five times the regular price.

WHAT TO BUY

Lanzhou is a good place to buy clothing, particularly warm down jackets in winter. The main market area is just to the north-east of the Victory Hotel but better quality items can be had from the huge department stores in town (marked on most maps). Keep an eye out for the alternative medicine shops in which it's common to find window displays of armadillos or huge insects, dried and ready to be ground up for use as remedies of some sort. Particularly sordid are the street vendors around the railway station who specialise in tigers' claws.

MOVING ON

By rail
Several trains head east towards Tianshui, eight of which actually originate here, and tickets for these are easier to come by. They are: No 74 (19.08 every other day), No 76 (20.29), No 188 (10.38), No 128 (11.26), No 148 (13.28), No 178 (21.14), No 204 (14.12), and No 276 (15.28). These all depart from the main (east) station. The journey to Tianshui takes about seven hours

Back in 1992, in honour of the International Silk Road Festival here, the station and its surroundings were declared 'no spit' areas. There are still Gob Police patrolling who delight in fining foreigners for spitting or dropping litter.

By air
There are flights to Beijing, Xi'an, Dunhuang, Jiayuguan and Urumqi but the airport is 70km from Lanzhou and departures can be delayed by the wind.

EXCURSION TO XIAHE

A stay in Xiahe is the next best thing to a trip to Tibet. It's a small town in the mountains at an altitude of 3000m, some 250km from Lanzhou. Travellers and pilgrims alike come here to visit the **Labrang Monastery**, one of the six most important centres of the Yellow Hat Buddhist sect. Most Western visitors plan on spending a couple of days here but then get into the swing of things and end up staying for a week. It's a mellow, slightly backward town, in beautiful surroundings. Bring lots of film: this place is seriously photogenic.

Getting there
The local bus for Xiahe leaves Lanzhou's west bus station daily at 07.30. The journey can be long, crowded and bumpy and takes about eight hours, but the scenery is wonderful, and there's a stop for lunch about halfway, in Lingxia. Tickets can be bought on the day of departure but it's

better to book in advance. If you miss the bus it's possible to get to Xiahe by travelling to Linxia and change there but you should still aim to leave by mid morning if you want to arrive in Xiahe at a reasonable hour. Should you get stuck in Lingxia there is at least one reasonable hotel which will take foreigners.

Where to stay

There's no problem finding accommodation in Xiahe. Probably the favourite budget place to stay is the **Tara Guesthouse** (☎ 09412-21274), where basic, clean double rooms cost Y40 and dormitory beds cost Y15. The woman who runs the place is extremely friendly and will help with everything from bike hire to advice about excursions. There are no showers here but the public showers (Y2) are next door.

The **Monastery Guesthouse**, directly opposite the monastery is run by monks, and is a simple, well organised establishment. Rooms are clean but beds (Y12 in a two-bed room) are very, very hard.

The top hotel in Xiahe, meanwhile is **La Bu Leng Hotel** (☎ 09412 21849). It's a fair way out of the village (1.5 km west of the monastery) and is peaceful and secluded, although it's frequented by visitors on tours so if you catch a tour group in residence it may be less so. The walk along the river to the hotel is lovely. Double rooms go for Y200, but beds in triple rooms (no bath) cost Y15 per person, or Y20 with a private bathroom. This has to be about the only place in Xiahe where you can pretty much guarantee getting a hot shower. Bike hire is available and costs Y2 per hour.

Where to eat

There are no big restaurants in Xiahe but there are lots of small places all over the village offering Chinese, Tibetan and Western food. Everyone soon finds their favourite place to eat.

Moving on

There is one bus back to Lanzhou daily. If you miss it, buy a ticket to Linxia and change.

Tianshui

A stop here is highly recommended for the excursion to Maijishan, 50km to the south of Tianshui, where the Buddhist carvings on Mount Maiji really have to be seen to be believed. The fact that not many people come here makes a visit all the more worthwhile. Maijishan is the only real attraction, however; there's not much of interest in Tianshui itself, so one day here is probably enough.

HISTORY

Tianshui was the main stopping point on the road from Xi'an to Lanzhou. Its history stretches back further than this, however, and a number of sources cite the banks of the Wei River as the 'cradle' of Chinese civilisation. This region has been inhabited since neolithic times and may be the heart of prehistoric China. Originally Tianshui was called Kuei but it has been renamed a number of times, the Han dynasty knowing it as Kuei Xien and the Song renaming it Cheng Chi Xien. Its strategic significance was not lost on either. As was the case with Lanzhou, the town was taken by invading Tibetans in 763AD and not recovered by the Chinese until 845AD. It was then taken by the Tanguts and the Juchen tribes before the arrival of the Mongols.

Despite Tianshui's reputation as a Buddhist centre, Islam gradually filtered in until the rebellion of 1864-75. This was one of the first cities to be retaken by the Chinese on their way west. They were particularly harsh, and the Muslim population has never recovered.

Tianshui today is a sprawling, drab, industrial town which specialises in producing consumer wares like textiles and furniture. There are sizeable gold deposits in the hills around the city.

ORIENTATION AND SERVICES

The city is spread out over a wide area, with accommodation available in two possible regions: the Bei Dao district, which is the small village around the railway station, or Qin Cheng, which is the large built-up area 20km to the west. The Maijishan Buddhist cave complex is some 50km to the south. Thus there is a choice: either stay near the railway station, in which case you are closer to the caves but a long way from the centre of town, or travel all the way to the centre so that you are near CITS and the other (mediocre) sights but twice as far from the caves and a long way from the station. To make matters worse, there is virtually no public transport apart from buses to and from the city. It's probably better to stay by the railway station (in Bei Dao) because there are more hotels and they are easier to find.

SERVICES

The CITS office (☎ 214463) is in the Qin Cheng District. To get to the office turn left out of the entrance of the Tianshui Hotel and walk up to the main road (100m). Then follow this road to the left for about one km. CITS is on Minshan Rd right next to the big food and fruit market. It's on the 4th floor of the corner building.

The staff here are charming but there can be a real language problem. They aren't really clued up to arranging tours – no-one seems to visit here at all – but say they can do it. The going rate is Y250, so unless you're part of a big group give it a miss. The Tianshui Hotel also arranges tours but it's unlikely they'll be able to get a group together, either.

LOCAL TRANSPORT

Getting to the caves is easy from the Long Lin Hotel and tricky from everywhere else: the only problem is that buses are labelled only in Chinese, so you may end up having to ask each driver until you hit the right one. Getting back is simple but can be time-consuming: drivers stay at the foot of the cliff until their bus is full, so be prepared for a wait.

Getting from Bei Dao to Qin Cheng and back is simple – take

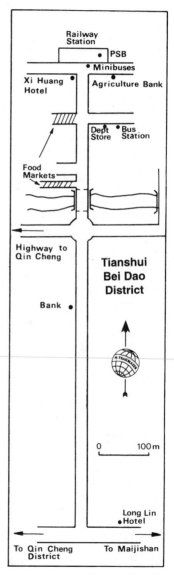

virtually any bus heading west from the train station (No1 is a good one). The journey takes about half an hour; keep an eye out for the military airstrip on the road there which is usually packed with Mig fighter planes. Probably not a wise photo choice, though.

WHERE TO STAY

In Bei Dao probably the best choice is the **Xi Huang Hotel** directly opposite the station. Foreigners are something of a novelty here but the place is excellent value: beds in a clean, modern, eight-bed dormitory are Y15 and the showers are great. Another cheapie near the station doesn't seem to have a name but can be found down the alley beside the Agriculture Bank of China. A bed in a four-bed room here is Y8. Much further upmarket, and a fair way from the station is the **Long Lin Hotel** (☎ 735541). It's a good 25-minute walk south of the station, but is probably the best hotel in the city. Few budget travellers stay here, however, and prices are pretty high: Y80 for a bed in a three-bed room or doubles for Y200.

In the Qin Cheng District, the **Tianshui Hotel** (☎ 212611) was designed to be an upmarket hotel, but is a bit faded and rather empty. The staff speak good English and appear prepared to bargain if business is slow. Doubles officially start at Y180.

WHERE TO EAT

As with hotels, you are hardly spoiled for choice. Currently the best food in town comes from the restaurant at the Xi Huang Hotel. Failing this, the restaurant in the Long Lin is all right, although overpriced. You'd probably do better to stay outside the front gate by the bus stop and eat at the noodle stand. There is also a small food market five minutes from the station which gets pretty busy at night.

If you're staying in Qin Cheng, the Tianshui Hotel is a good place to eat. For something cheaper get down to the main market square where stalls and noodle bars abound.

WHAT TO SEE

Maijishan

Mount Maiji (literally 'Wheat Stack Mountain', because it resembles one) is a top-heavy peak peppered with carvings, alcoves and caves. While the caves themselves are not as well-preserved as those you will have seen at Dunhuang, the setting is extraordinarily impressive. There are 200 caves and alcoves, dating back to the 4th century and as late as the 17th. Linking the caves is a high-rise walkway. The system itself is confused: you might not be allowed in without a guide, in which case you will be provided with one as at Dunhuang; try to get an English-speaker.

Alternatively you may be let in to wander as you please, in which case the caves will be locked and the only way to see their contents will be by squashing your face against the grilles. A torch won't help much in this situation but it is possible to get a fairly good view of what's inside each one as the caves themselves are shallow.

If you are afraid of heights, think carefully before paying the Y40 entry fee as some people get very nervous up there (half the fun comes from watching groups of Chinese women inching their way along the balconies, knuckles white on the handrails and eyes tight shut). Chinese tourists here seem to have an irrepressible urge to jettison their personal belongings whilst viewing the caves: money is rolled up into wafer-thin tubes and poked through the grilles, and on any free-standing statue (the 17m high Amidabha Buddha, for example) lies a heap of cigarettes, coins and general debris. Beware when you are walking underneath any of these.

Cameras and bags must be left at the entrance to the complex but this does not mean that there are no good pictures to be taken: across the main entry yard there is a flight of stone steps leading into the woods. In fact it follows an organised Maijishan Walk which is a bit commercial but may be worth it if you are feeling really energetic. Even if you are not, follow the steps, as they lead to the observation point from which all postcards of the mountain appear to have been shot. Very impressive.

To get to Maijishan, take a minibus from the railway station or the crossroads outside the Long Lin Hotel. The ride is about $1^{1}/_{2}$ hours and should cost Y5-10. Most buses wait at the foot of the hill, so to get back simply walk down the road to where you were dropped off.

Immortals' Cliff

CITS say that this site boasts three cliffs, six temples, 196 Buddha-figures and 83 square metres of murals. This is utter twaddle but there really are three cliffs. To get in, walk along the stream from the car park and then start climbing the hill. This is a seriously long flight of steps and is definitely not for the faint-hearted. Be wary of the Taoist masters who sit here telling fortunes, as it seems unlikely that anyone who is really at one with the universe will spend his life in a dingy shack hassling tourists and posing for photographs. Also beware of the joss-stick saleswomen, some of whom you may have to remove surgically.

The climb is well worth it, if only for the superb views from the top. The statues all seem to be modern but the setting really is lovely. The only authentically old Buddhist art appears to be on the third cliff, which is the lower one, towards the lake, but it is in a dreadful condition. There are mixed reports as to why this is so and if you believe them all you can only conclude that the Japanese sacked the place, whereupon it caught fire and then was wrecked during the Cultural Revolution. The largest figure, or what remains of it, dates from the Song dynasty and is interesting because it shows the Buddha with his son. Because of its dilapidated state only the head, the feet and the lotus flower that supports them survive. Below the cliff are two temples. The one on the right contains a statue of Guany Yin, who has 1000 arms and an eye in each hand.

If you have time, do visit this place as the views and the walking make it fun. The statues along the way are never very impressive but provide the excuse for the trip. Getting here can be a problem since it's 40km from the railway station; it's best either to get some friends together and hire a bus, or try for a taxi or motorbike taxi (ask for 'Xian Ren Ya'). Or you could combine a visit here with a stop at Maijishan. Entry is Y10.

Big Buddha Hill

The Big Buddha itself is impressive. Dating from the Tang dynasty and standing 26m tall, it is in good condition. It's at Gangsu, about 55km west of Tianshui, and the best way to get here is either by bus, or by train: any slow train heading west to Lanzhou should stop here.

Fu Xi

Fu Xi is considered a bit of a hero in these parts. A local creation myth recounts his role in history thus: once there was a great flood which was responsible for the deaths of all humans except Fu Xi and his sister. God spoke to Fu Xi and told him to marry the sister. He was not keen. One night God appeared to Fu Xi in a dream and told him to rely on fate: he was to roll a big boulder down a hill. If it hit a tree and cracked he was not to marry his sister, while if it made it to the bottom intact he was to marry her. Next day Fu Xi did as he'd been told; the rock survived. He married his sister and the result of their incestuous dalliances is the Chinese race.

Fu Xi Temple

Fu Xi is one of China's three mythical ancestors, and Tianshui was his hometown. Inside the gates here is a small local museum and the temple itself, which was originally constructed in the Ming dynasty. The statue of Fu Xi inside is the only one in China. Among other things he is credited with the creation of the Eight Diagrams which you can see on the ceiling and around the Ying and Yang symbols inside. These diagrams represent mathematical permutations and ultimate order. The temple is always open but the museum is supposed to be open 8.30-12am and 2.30-6pm; it tends to be closed about as often as it is open. Entry is Y2. To get here, take bus No 1 from the railway station to the free market (right at the heart of the Qin Cheng district – about a 30-45 minute ride). Walk west and you'll hit it.

(Opposite) Top: Mount Maiji (see p222), outside Maijishan, is honeycombed with caves and shrines dating back to the 4th century. Bottom: Keeping watch over the Yellow River, the 27m-tall Maitreya Buddha has been the centrepiece of the Bingling Si cave complex for more than ten centuries (see p215).

Jade Spring Temple

This is not far from the Fu Xi temple and is more impressive, containing a number of pleasant pavilions. In theory it dates back to the Yuan dynasty but actually it was rebuilt in the Ming. Many of the buildings were taken over or destroyed by the military during the Cultural Revolution, and there are still army barracks inside. The statue with eight arms in the temple at the top represents the Mother of the Stars. Just outside is the spring itself, which is covered but still provides water for the monks who live here.

The main pavilion houses a statue of the Jade Emperor, who sits at the highest level of heaven with a girl and a boy in attendance, one on either side. The flatulent-looking monsters on each side of the entrance are the guards: on the left is Ear with the Wind (who can hear noises as distant as the wind itself), while on the right is Thousand Li Eye, who can see things at a distance of – you guessed it – a thousand li. At the very top of the hill you can see the remains of the main temple, which was destroyed by the Red Guards; there is usually some incense burning here. Entrance to the temple is Y2. Directions are as for the Fu Xi temple. Ask for 'Yu Quan Guan'.

Nan-Guo Temple

This is small and rather remote but pleasant enough. It dates back to the early 5th century and is still very much 'active'. Inside are large statues of a Laughing Buddha and the poet Do Fu. The trees in the courtyard are very ancient, as we can tell from the signposts on each which read 'This is an ancient tree'. In fact only the temple design and the trees are original. It is situated at the top of the hill due south of the Tianshui Hotel, and to get here you will have to take a taxi or walk (about one hour). The least interesting of the city's attractions; entry is Y2. Ask for 'Nanguo Si'.

MOVING ON

Xi'an is only six hours away and there are a number of trains going east daily, so getting hold of a ticket is easy.

Train times and numbers are: No 178 (06.01), No 54 (16.35), No 70 (15.03), No 74 (01.56), No 76 (03.42), No 98 (19.56), No 128 (20.32), No 144 (01.17) and No 188 (17.50). A Hard Seat ticket to Xi'an costs Y24.

(Opposite) Standing 43m tall, Xi'an's Small Goose Pagoda is all that remains of the 8th-century Da Jianfu Buddhist temple.

Xi'an

Although it seems rather pedantic to speak of exact starting and finishing points in relation to the Silk Route, Xi'an does officially mark its eastern end. For the visitor China's ancient capital has a great number of attractions, the foremost undoubtedly being Emperor Shihuang's Terracotta Army.

When Xi'an was China's administrative centre in the Tang dynasty, it was subject to numerous foreign influences; it is currently more so than ever, thanks to a vast influx of money and interest from the West. The city lies at the heart of the Chinese tourist industry – perfect if your idea of travelling is a hotel suite the size of Milton Keynes with its own helicopter launch pad but something of a problem for budget travellers, because the appearance of wealthy foreign sightseers has prompted price increases across the board. You can end up spending a fortune on entry fees here: it now costs Y80 just to see the Terracotta Army.

Most visitors soon tire of this busy cosmopolitan city, two or three days being about as much as some can stand. Visit, see the sights on a tour, and then leave.

HISTORY

Xi'an was the nucleus of ancient China. Records show that there has been a major settlement here since at least the 11th century BC, one source dating it back to 2205 BC, when it was referred to as the Well-watered City. It was more than just another large city, however, for during a number of periods, notably the Zhou, Han, Sui and Tang dynasties it was the Chinese capital.

It has not retained its original site. In the 11th century BC the Zhou dynasty knew it as Fenghao, some 15km to the south-west of its present location. This site flourished until 771BC when the capital was moved east to Luoyang. By the time of the short-lived Qin dynasty it had moved back again, so that they ruled from Xien Yang, 12 miles west of present-day Xi'an. It was during this period that the elaborate tomb of Emperor Qin Shihuang was constructed, today a magnet for tourists from all over the world.

The greatest city in the world

The Han dynasty ruled from here after first rebuilding it on yet another site, just north of the present-day city. This one, Chang'an, was the greatest that China had ever seen, though that didn't stop the Han from deserting it for Luoyang again in 23AD. Following this the city went into a steady decline until its selection as capital by the Sui dynasty in the 7th century and thus Xi'an attained its present-day site, which was adopted and expanded by the succeeding Tang dynasty. The city swelled and was divided into three parts: a palace city for the emperor, the imperial city for the officials, and the outer city for the plebs. During this period, with a population of well over a million, it was not only the greatest city in China but almost certainly the greatest in the world. External influences flooded in and Chang'an nurtured a thriving foreign religious community, including sizeable colonies of Mazdean, Manichean and Nestorian missionaries. Evidence of this can be seen today with the Nestorian Stele (see p235), inscribed 781 AD.

Chang'an's decline
In 904 the Tang capital moved briefly to Luoyang again and in 907 the dynasty itself collapsed. Chang'an, although to remain a major Chinese city, was never to recover its status. It was still a thriving community, however, when Marco Polo visited in 1278. He called it Quengianfu and commented that, 'The people are idolaters and subject to the Great Khan and use paper money. They live by trade and industry. They have plenty of silk and make cloth of gold and silk of many varieties. There are merchants here of wealth and consequence. There is no lack of game, both beast and bird, and abundance of grain and foodstuffs. There are two churches here of Nestorian Christians'.

The Xi'an Incident
The world next heard of Xi'an some 650 years later, when General Chiang Kai Shek was the victim of a coup here in 1936. Following the aggressions of the Japanese, who had moved into Manchuria in 1931 and were to invade China proper in 1937, Communist chiefs tried repeatedly to make the KMT leader understand that his greatest threat was not from them but the Japanese. Chiang refused to acknowledge suggestions that the two warring factions unite to eject their common enemy and so, on 12 December, he was seized by his own men under Chang Xue-Liang. Communist Party leaders flew in to explain their views to him. On Christmas Day 1936 he was released and given full control of his men again. In fact, although he declared a truce in order to fight the Japanese, his efforts in this direction were minimal. All he really did during this period was to prepare for the civil war which he knew would restart when the Japanese were defeated. Chang Xue-Liang, for his efforts, was thrown into prison for 40 years.

Xi'an today
Until recently Xi'an was simply a large sized industrial city with a sound pedigree. All this changed with the discovery by some peasants of the

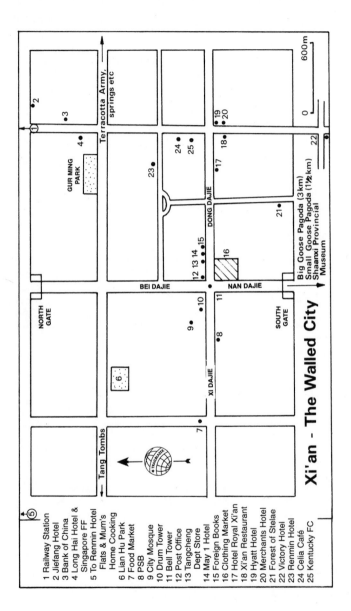

Xi'an - The Walled City

1 Railway Station
2 Jiefang Hotel
3 Bank of China
4 Long Hai Hotel &
  Singapore FF
5 To Renmin Hotel
  Flats & Mum's
  Home Cooking
6 Lian Hu Park
7 Food Market
8 PSB
9 City Mosque
10 Drum Tower
11 Bell Tower
12 Post Office
13 Tangcheng
   Dept Store
14 May 1 Hotel
15 Foreign Books
16 Clothing Market
17 Hotel Royal Xi'an
18 Xi'an Restaurant
19 Hyatt Hotel
20 Merchants Hotel
21 Forest of Stelae
22 Victory Hotel
23 Renmin Hotel
24 Celia Café
25 Kentucky FC

NORTH GATE

SOUTH GATE

BEI DAJIE

NAN DAJIE

XI DAJIE

DONG DAJIE

GUR MING PARK

Tang Tombs

Terracotta Army, springs etc

Big Goose Pagoda (3km)
Small Goose Pagoda (1½ km)
Shaanxi Provincial Museum

0   600m

long lost tomb of the Qin emperor Shihuangdi. The 'Terracotta Army' found inside has catapulted the city to superstardom in the tourist world; hotels, shops and restaurants here are now on a par with upmarket facilities anywhere else in the world.

ORIENTATION AND SERVICES

The railway station is right on the northern edge of the walled city itself, so getting to a hotel from here is simple. Xi'an is easy to explore, being rectangular with all streets running either east-west or north-south. Good maps are easily available.

There are CITS offices in both the Bell Tower Hotel and the Jiefang Hotel (rail tickets are booked from this office only), and the main CITS office is just to the south of the walled city, on the 5th floor of the building next to the Xi'an Hotel. None of the three is especially good news. Better but still not great is the FITS office (☎ 526 1454) in the lobby of the same building.

The best source for up to date information, in fact, is Stephanie, the owner of **Mum's Home Cooking** by the Renmin Hotel Flats. Her small restaurant has become the main travellers' hangout in the city, and she and her staff can help out with everything from train tickets to bike hire.

The post office is in the centre of the walled city next to the Bell Tower, and there are two branches of the Bank of China just south of the railway station on Heping Lu. The PSB can be found just to the west of the Bell Tower on Xi Dajie.

LOCAL TRANSPORT

The best way to get around is by bicycle: there are rental places scattered around the city – but Stephanie (see above) can help out if you get stuck. Although the main sights are just about within cycling distance most people take public buses or tours to get to them.

Public buses are good, although they become extremely overcrowded, particularly at rush hour: If you're using buses keep a close eye on your belongings. Good maps with the bus routes marked on them should be on sale outside the train station. Particularly useful is Bus No 9 which runs from just west of the railway station to the near the Renmin Hotel Flats, about 2-3km to the west.

TOURS

CITS are only too happy to take you on one of their over-priced tours, and wherever you are staying the hotel travel service will have similarly priced tours on offer. It's probably best to take a tour along the lines of the one organised by the Renmin Hotel Flats: for Y25 you get transport in a tour bus for the day – but that's all. Without costing a fortune this takes the hassle out of using the public transport system but leaves you fairly free to do what you like.

WHERE TO STAY

Budget accommodation
There are three main budget hotels in Xi'an, all of which are popular with backpackers. Currently 'in' is the **Renmin Hotel Flats**, although being 2km outside the walled city it's hardly convenient. It undoubtedly owes much of its popularity to Stephanie, the enterprising owner of Mum's Home Cooking, which is opposite. For some time now she has been arranging for all travellers to be met off the train and herded into a minibus that brings them straight here. (If you miss this transport, bus No 9 will get you to the Renmin Flats, or a taxi will cost about Y15). Accommodation is Y40 for a bed in a three-bed room, and the price includes breakfast.

Slightly cheaper and more central is the **Victory Hotel** (☎ 7893042). Rooms are a bit depressing but adequate, and the location is much better than the Renmin. Unfortunately, showers are available only from 18.00-22.00 and the staff aren't especially helpful, but it's the cheapest place in town, at Y35 for a bed in a triple room.

More expensive, but definitely worth considering if there are two of you, is the **May 1st Hotel** (☎ 7215932). Superbly located right next door to the Bell Tower, the rooms are clean and the staff are friendly. Doubles with attached bathroom start at Y132.

Mid-range accommodation
The **Jiefang Hotel** (☎ 7422219), right opposite the railway station, has double rooms for Y200. The **China Merchants Hotel** (☎ 7218988), on Heping Lu has doubles from Y410. The **Renmin Hotel** (☎ 7215111) on Dongxin Lu, is impressive from the outside but doesn't really live up to expectations once you get inside. There are doubles from Y470.

Upmarket accommodation
There's no shortage of top class hotels in Xi'an. A sample of the best includes: **The Long Hai Hotel** (☎ 7416091), just south of the station, at Y678 a double; the **Hyatt Hotel** (☎ 7231234), with doubles at US$110; the **Hotel Royal Xi'an** (☎ 7235311), near the Bell Tower, at Y700 a double; and, not quite as smart, the **Bell Tower Hotel** (☎ 7279200), which is next to the Bell Tower, at Y733 for a double.

WHERE TO EAT

There is good food to be had all over town, from high-class Chinese and Western food in the upmarket hotels to cheap dishes served in the lively atmosphere of the street markets. Current budget travellers' favourite in Xi'an is **Mum's Home Cooking**' opposite the Renmin Flats. The food is good but probably bears very little resemblance to your mum's home cooking.

The street running north from the Hyatt Hotel to the station is definitely the place to eat if you're homesick: it's notable for its cake shops. **Celia's Cafe and Bakery** is a bit overpriced but a brilliant place to spend a couple of dollars on coffee and sweet chocolate cake. There's also **Kentucky Fried Chicken** and **Singapore Fast Food**. If it's hot, head for the ice cream parlour 150m west of the Hyatt Hotel.

There is a multitude of great fast-food joints, if you are happy eating in less fancy surroundings. Take Nanguan Zhengjie south from the south gate for about 800m, and on the right is a **night market** lit by coloured lanterns where virtually every variety of noodle soup is served. The food is good, sometimes excellent, but watch out for occasional overpricing. This might be a good place to test out the local drink, *qiaou jiaou* – a warm, thick milky alcohol, made from rice, which tastes, strangely enough, rather like gluwein. In the Muslim quarter of town, try **San Jin Qiaou Rd** for any number of cheap, original dishes. Mind your wallet.

Finally, really cheap food can be had in some of the stalls around the clothing market immediately to the south of the Bell Tower. Head east from here and you'll hit the big money restaurants.

WHAT TO SEE

Tomb of Qin Shihuang (Terracotta Army)

Qin Shihuang, the 'First Emperor', whose reputation is that of a ruthless, ambitious tyrant, ascended the throne in 246BC at the age of only 13. Work on his mausoleum began immediately. The tomb itself, 30km east of present-day Xi'an, has yet to be excavated but has already created great excitement in the archaeological world as preliminary investigations suggest that the tomb has never been looted. According to a 1st century BC chronicle it took 700,000 workmen 36 years to complete, and contains a number of intriguing displays. Rivers of mercury were designed to flow perpetually throughout the mausoleum and the roof was depicted as heaven, studded with jewels. Most interesting is the assertion that the tomb is perpetually protected by mechanical booby traps, including crossbows set to fire upon intruders. It is said that, once complete, all workmen and designers who might be able to reveal the tomb's secrets were buried alive with their emperor. (And his wives, of course.) Archaeologists are unwilling to unseal the tomb for fear that its contents will crumble on exposure to the air.

In fact, although it sounds amazing, there's not a lot to see here as, obviously, you can't get in. Entry to the site is Y8. There is a separate entrance fee of Y6 for the small museum to the left of the front gate; it's a waste of money, but if you're really keen to see what's inside, try bargaining with the guys on the door.

The army itself What historical records did not reveal was that Qin Shihuang did not plan on going on alone; as well as wives and craftsmen he planned on taking an army along. The army was discovered by some farmers in the summer of 1974 while they were digging a well. It seems that the vaults containing the soldiers, some 6000 of them in all, were originally covered with a wooden roof but that General Xiang Yu, having plundered the tomb in the late 3rd century BC, set fire to it. It collapsed onto the army, burying it for 2000 years. Since the initial discovery in 1974 (Pit 1), another two vaults have been unearthed. All three are now open to the public.

Enough has been written about the Terracotta Army to render yet another list of superlatives unnecessary here. Suffice it to say that, with every soldier attired slightly differently, individually painted and perhaps modelled on real members of the imperial guard, this represents a feat of sculpture on an unprecedented scale.

The building housing the warriors is simply vast but that doesn't stop it becoming packed with tourists all the time. Note that you may not take photographs; you may pose for your picture with a terracotta warrior for Y150, though, but be prepared to queue. Y40 rents you the walkman tour or a private guide (they'll approach you near the entrance). Entry to the site is a hefty Y80.

Other terracotta attractions Outside the entrance are two small museums: one contains some miscellaneous objects unearthed during the excavations including, of course, a number of the warriors themselves. This gives a good impression of their size and of the detail which went into their construction. Entry is free and photographs may be taken inside.

Opposite this is the Chariot Museum which contains two beautiful bronze chariots unearthed in 1978, 20 metres to the west of the mausoleum's entrance. Entry to both these museums is included in the price of the main entry ticket.

Alongside the complex is a series of photographs of foreign dignitaries inspecting the warriors over the last 15 years, which provides a good general knowledge test for those who are into that kind of thing, while outside there are numerous stalls selling (surprise, surprise) miniature terracotta warriors. It is debatable whether there are more warriors outside the pits than in them. Still, prices are very cheap if you bargain.

Banpo neolithic site
Seven kilometres east of Xi'an is the Banpo neolithic village, which dates back to 4500BC and was discovered in 1953. The site is particularly

interesting for archaeologists because it is so well preserved, thus giving an accurate impression of what life was like for prehistoric man here. The village was home to some 300 people, for whom agriculture was the main source of food. They supplemented their diet with fish from the nearby Chan River (caught both with hooks and nets) and also kept pigs, dogs and fowl. While this is no doubt fascinating to the trained eye, it's not quite as fascinating to the untrained: it's certainly hard to work out, for example, what the photographic display of African tribesmen ('The Last Primitive Man') is doing there.

The village is included in most tours but you can get here on your own, either by bicycle or trolley-bus No 5 from the railway station. Entry is Y20, and for an extra Y40 (a total waste of money) you are allowed into the 'Banpo Matriarchal Clan Village', a Disney mock up of the way things might have been here all those years ago.

Huaqing hot springs and palace

The Huaqing springs have been channelled into royal bathing houses since the Zhou dynasty and it's still possible to bathe here. Royal palaces have been built and rebuilt on this spot since then, but most of the pavilions standing today date back only as far as the start of this century.

The palace was the site of the famous Xi'an Incident in which General Chiang Kai Shek was arrested by his own troops in 1936 (see p227) and if you follow the steps up the hill you will eventually get to the small pavilion where this arrest took place. To get up the hill there is a fee of Y5; there is no English sign but the view is pleasant enough and the walk is probably good for your heart. Chiang's office and bedroom are also open to the public. Most tours usually stop here for a couple of hours, and many complain that they get bored in this time but the palace is very picturesque, and is fun to explore – it's only a pity that it gets so crowded. Entry is Y30, and the stop is invariably included in tours to the Terracotta Warriors as the two sites are so close together.

Shaanxi History/Provincial Museum

Opened in September 1991, this museum is huge. Entry is Y38 but even cynics have to admit that it is a very good museum. All articles are well-lit, well-presented and labelled in English; it would be easy to spend a whole afternoon here. It contains a number of excellent murals removed from tombs to the west of Xi'an. Keep an eye out for the tomb display of Empress Chenguo of the Liao dynasty (907-1125) who was buried with some outstanding trinkets – including her husband. Particularly interesting are the silver wire suits in which the corpses were dressed before burial and the photographs of the way the tomb looked during excavation. The museum is to the south of the walled city, opposite the Small Goose Pagoda. You can cycle here, or take bus Nos 5 or 24 from the railway station. It is open from 8.30 to 6pm (last entry 5pm).

City walls and gates

Xi'an's walls and gates date back to the early Ming dynasty and are in remarkably good condition. Of the four gates, each at a point of the compass, only the south and west are open to visitors (the east gate is currently under repair, while the north gate is either 'too old and valuable', or 'badly repaired', depending on who you believe). Easily the most significant to us is the West Gate, for it was from here that travellers along the Silk Route began their westward trek. Inside there is an expensive art gallery where calligraphy and paintings range from Y80-10,000. The rafters of the ceiling are spectacular.

There is a Y10 entry fee to the two towers, which are open 8am-6pm daily. Beside each tower is a fascinating account of how they were built, which justifies your Y10 alone: 'the city wall's surface was built with three layers of big bricks. This technique was called 'very big surfacing with bricks' etc. It used to be possible to walk around the city on top of the walls, but now fences have been erected to stop people doing this.

Bell Tower

This tower is in the centre of the walled town. Dating back to the start of the Ming dynasty, it originally stood further to the west and was moved here in the late 16th century. It was renovated in 1986. According to local legend it was built on the advice of a local mystic: after a series of minor tremors and earthquakes, he diagnosed the cause of the problem as a dragon trapped beneath the soil of the city. The bell was to be pealed at regular intervals to scare it away. Inside the tower is a small, badly-lit display of Ming and Qing furniture which is unlabelled. The building's rafters are particularly ornate. Entry is Y15.

Drum Tower

The Drum Tower stands only a couple of hundred metres from the Bell Tower and it, too, was built in the Ming dynasty. It was used for military purposes, primarily for calling troops to duty. For Y5 you can get inside to see the occasional exhibitions here.

City Mosque

If you pass through the arch of the Drum Tower and follow the mass of tourist stalls, moneychangers and trinket shops to the left, you will shortly arrive at this beautiful, tranquil mosque. There has been a mosque on this site since at least the mid-8th century but the present buildings were erected at a much later date. In fact, although the layout you see dates back to the Ming dynasty, owing to successive renovations it is unlikely that any of the present construction dates from much before the 20th century. Still, it's certainly worth a visit and one of the few places in Xi'an where you are likely to get some peace and quiet. It's still in use and visitors are not admitted during prayer times. Entry is Y15.

Small Goose Pagoda

This pagoda, standing 43m tall, is all that remains of the Da Jianfu Buddhist temple, which was destroyed in the mid 9th century during the Tang purges. Originally built in the 8th century as a library for sutras brought back from India by Chinese monks, an earthquake destroyed its top two storeys, so that today it has only 13.

There's a Y10 entry charge for the park, plus Y10 to climb the pagoda, up what must be one of the world's narrowest and tightest staircases. It is probably best to cycle here, as it is a fair walk (south) from the town centre. Alternatively, take bus No 3.

Big Goose Pagoda

About three km further south than the Small Goose Pagoda, this one is slightly taller. It is in the grounds of the Da Xien Temple, which was established by the emperor Gazong in the mid-7th century in honour of his mother. The original pagoda was constructed of earth in 652AD at the request of legendary Silk Roadster Xuan Xang, who needed a comfortable pad in which to translate the sutras he had brought back from India. It collapsed a couple of times, to be replaced with this stone version in the Ming dynasty. There is a Y13 fee to get into the temple grounds and a further Y25 charge if you want to climb the pagoda for the excellent view of the city from the top. It gets quite crowded at weekends. To get here, either bicycle or take buses Nos 5, 41 or 501.

Forest of Stelae

Stelae are large inscribed stone tablets; these ones were created in order to preserve the integrity of the Chinese classics. The collection started in the 10th century but stones were being carved well before this, early productions including the *Book of Changes*, the *Book of Rites* and the *Analects of Confucius*. One stele is fairly famous in the West, recording the arrival of Nestorian Christianity and the foundation of a chapel here in 781. Not surprising then, that it is known as the Nestorian Stele; you will have to ask for it by name since there are over 1000 stelae here amongst which to get lost. Exhibits in the surrounding buildings include some high quality relics unearthed in the Shaanxi Province, as well as a number discovered further west along the Silk Road (Dunhuang, Maijishan etc). The museum is open 8.30-5.45pm daily. Entry is Y30.

Parks

Gur Ming Park, somewhat spoilt by litter, contains a couple of attractive pavilions but you may become the main exhibit if you visit. Entry is Y4. **Lian Hu** is cleaner: it is possible to hire rowing boats and pedalos here (even plastic duck boats), and one of the pools has an elaborate water slide – just the thing if you fancy a dose of bilharzia. The best, **Xing Qing Park**, is slightly further afield. It was the original garden of the Tang emperors' palace and is one of the few places where you will be able to get a little space for yourself in Xi'an. Open 6am-11pm, you can cycle here or take bus No 8 Entry is Y10.

Other tombs

It is perhaps not surprising, considering Xi'an's long and distinguished history, that there are a number of other royal tombs and mausoleums around the city. The majority of these are to the north-west and the best way to get to them is to organise a tour. CITS can advise.

WHAT TO BUY

As might be expected of a tourist mecca, there is an almost unlimited variety of souvenirs for sale. Miniature, or even life-sized, terracotta warriors are the most popular buys; many shops sell box-sets of them, with one standing, one kneeling etc.

Shaanxi local art is interesting. While every gift shop in China seems to be selling the standard calligraphy or watercolour hangings, this art is different: you will recognise it by its bright colours and slightly naïve quality. If you visit Banpo and like the sound of the groovy pan-pipe music played over the sound system, buy one of the neolithic flutes that made it: look for the black gourd-shaped objects sold at the entrance.

The cheapest buys are to be had in the narrow alleyway leading to the City Mosque (by the Drum Tower), where you are likely to be besieged by money buyers and black marketeers. Bargain hard, and don't believe them when they tell you what dynasty their antiques date from. Very popular here is Mao memorabilia: badges, pictures and copies of the *Little Red Book*, surely a must for every self-respecting student. Note that truly tacky Mao gear is available in Beijing, too (see p253). The Tang Cheng Department Store is excellent for life's necessities but be warned that if you leave your bicycle anywhere in its vicinity apart from the underground bike park just beside it, it will be confiscated.

MOVING ON

There are numerous trains running east to Luoyang daily, and there are five fast or express trains which stop in Luoyang and continue to Beijing. They are: No 8 (01.06), No 70 (21.47), No 76 (10.59), No 164 (08.20), and No 42 (18.35). There is also a special tourist train, No 6, which leaves Xi'an at 10.20 and arrives in Luoyang at 17.23. The journey to Luoyang takes eight hours, and it's 19 hours to Beijing.

Getting train tickets here can be difficult. There is a foreigners' ticket counter on the 2nd floor of the station but it is open only from 8.30-10.30, and 14.30-16.30. There is invariably a queue: arrive at least an hour early.

There are flights between Xi'an and many other cities including Beijing (US$120).

Luoyang

Luoyang is not really part of the Silk Route at all, but provides a convenient break in the journey from Xi'an to Beijing. It is the site of the first Buddhist temple in China and the setting for another set of spectacular Buddhist grottoes, the Longmen Caves. Both temple and caves are easy to reach from the centre of town and make a stop here well worthwhile. Luoyang itself is quiet and pleasant enough, particularly in April when the peonies are in bloom, and the old quarter has a charm all of its own. Martial arts fans will no doubt want to stop here to visit the famous Shaolin 'Kung Fu' monastery 85km to the north.

HISTORY

Like Xi'an, Luoyang is one of the truly ancient Chinese cities – its roots can be traced way back beyond the Neolithic era. The first major growth here took place in the 12th century BC when the Zhou dynasty, despite maintaining its capital at Fenghao (Xi'an) built a large city at Lo-i, to the west of modern Luoyang. The new city took on secondary capital status and was later to become the capital itself, replacing Fenghao in 771BC. It was to remain the capital throughout the reigns of 12 Zhou emperors. Emperor Qing (519-476) moved it 10km north-west to the banks of the River Luo, and the new city became known as Luoyang.

The influence of Buddhism

From the Zhou period the title of capital has swung back and forth between Xi'an and Luoyang, the latter being seen as easier to defend, and so adopted in times of trouble. It was during one of these swings, in 68AD, that Buddhism really arrived. Luoyang was the site of the first major Buddhist commune in China and it was here that many of the Indian sutras were originally translated and copied out for general circulation. The original White Horse Temple is located some 10km north-east of the present town, and this Buddhist connection provides the main reason for coming here today: the Caves. They were carved later on, however, after a prolonged period of strife, which ended only with the adoption of the city by a neighbouring warlord in 494AD.

Under the Tang dynasty Luoyang prospered, as it was declared their Eastern Capital – second only to Xi'an. Unfortunately, rebellions in the second half of the Tang's rule led to Luoyang's decline, and it was never really to recover its lost status. Since the foundation of the Republic in 1949, however, it has been making up for lost time. The most famous venture undertaken here was the Number One Tractor Plant which was set up with Russian assistance in 1959. Despite the fact that a tractor plant sounds monumentally boring, it is still one of the city's major attractions if you believe the tourist brochures.

ORIENTATION AND SERVICES

The city is spread out along one main road heading from north east to south west and nothing is particularly difficult to find. You are unlikely to get lost unless you wander into the Old Town, in which case you're sure to – but that's half the fun.

CITS are in their own building 200m east of the botanical gardens. This office certainly doesn't vie for the 'Best CITS in China' award – they're flabbergasted to see a foreigner and work doesn't come high on their agenda though some speak English here. Unless you speak Chinese you may not find the other CITS office, at the Peony Hotel, much use.

Only the main branch of the Bank of China will change travellers' cheques; it's in the high-rise block approximately 1km south-west of the roundabout (see map).

LOCAL TRANSPORT

Getting around is simple in Luoyang. It's fairly flat and the ideal way to see the city would be by bike. Public transport is very good; maps with bus routes marked on them are easily available and useful, even though they're not in English.

There simply isn't the market for tours in Luoyang that there is in Xi'an; consequently CITS are pretty expensive. You don't need to take a tour at all as you can catch a bus from in front of the train station to anywhere you are likely to want to visit. There are buses to Shaolin and minibuses to the Longmen Caves. Beware, however, of the touts here who will try to sell you bus tickets at three or four times the going rate.

WHERE TO STAY

Budget accommodation

Right opposite the station and also next to the stop for buses to the tourist sights is the **Luoyang Hotel**. It's certainly convenient but it's also noisy; the streets are always busy and the station clock has an especially loud electronic chime, the loos are pretty foul, and no English is spoken. It's OK for a night, though, and doubles are only Y50.

It might just be worth trying the **Tian Xiang Hotel** (☎ 3940600) just around the corner, although reports suggest it's gone downhill recently. They're not very helpful and will turn you away if you try to check in too early. A bed in a double room will cost you Y75.

The **cheapest hotel** in Luoyang is difficult to find and appears to have no name. It's on the opposite side of the railway line to virtually everything else (see map). They're pretty friendly but you'll need to be able to speak a bit of Chinese. A bed in the dormitory is Y15 and a double is Y35. To get here go down the underpass by the train station and turn left at the T-junction. Follow the road around the bend to the left and then right, and as the road starts to come out of the right-hand bend look down the tiny sidestreet on the left: there's a small level crossing. The hotel is in the building just beyond this; reception is at the near end. The walk from the train station will take 10-15 minutes.

Most expensive in this category is the **2nd Luoyang Hotel** (☎ 3938286, ext 3231), also opposite the train station. It's slightly quieter and reasonably friendly. Doubles here go for Y128.

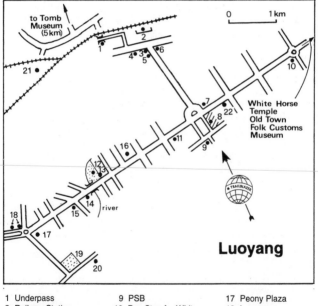

Luoyang

1 Underpass	9 PSB	17 Peony Plaza
2 Railway Station	10 Bus Stop for White	18 Luoyang
3 Luoyang Hotel	Horse Temple	Guesthouse
4 2nd Luoyang Hotel	11 Luoyang Restaurant	19 Botanical Gardens
(more expensive)	12 Wangsheng Park	20 CITS
5 Tian Xiang Hotel	13 Luoyang Museum	21 Cheap Hotel
6 Bus Station	14 Peony Hotel	22 Xuangong Hotel
7 Post Office	15 Friendship Store	
8 Food Market	16 Bank of China	

Other accommodation

The most upmarket place in town is the **Peony Hotel** which has some pretty plush facilities and some pretty plush prices, too. Doubles start at Y550, to which they then add a 5% service charge. Non-residents can change cash but not travellers' cheques here. There is a CITS desk for rail ticket booking but they're not keen on non-residents.

Somewhat cheaper is the **Luoyang Friendship Guesthouse** (☎ 4912780 ext 2002). It's a nice place with friendly staff and a good restaurant; what a shame it's so far from everything else. Singles are Y282 and doubles Y462. Bargaining may bring prices down by Y50 or so.

The **Xua Gong Hotel** (☎ 3931940) is on the main street just north of the food market. The staff aren't at all interested in foreigners, though, and there is an uncared-for, jaded feel to the place. Prices start at Y190. The swimming pool here should be opening soon.

A new hotel, the **Peony Plaza**, is set to open soon on the corner opposite the Friendship Guesthouse. Judging from the five stars stencilled on the front wall, it's unlikely to be cheap.

WHERE TO EAT

You are hardly spoiled for choice when it comes to eating in Luoyang. The best restaurants are, as might be expected, in the expensive hotels. Another top place, however, is the **HM Restaurant**, next door to the Peony Hotel. Specialities on the menu here include every snake dish you have ever heard of (and a number you haven't). This may be a good chance to try top class Chinese food, but it's not cheap: a meal will set you back around Y100 or more. Worth trying among the hotel restaurants is the one in the **Luoyang Friendship Guesthouse**, where reasonable prices and good food are combined with a friendly atmosphere.

The **Luoyang Restaurant** is definitely worth a try, although it will involve either a bus or a cycle ride from wherever you are staying. It's clean and pretty cheap – bank on spending around Y20 for a full meal and a beer. Better, though, if you don't mind less decorous surroundings, is

---

Peonies

Luoyang is famous throughout China for its peonies – as the travel guide so rightly states: 'Luoyang grows the best of peonies in China, just as people have often said "Luoyang's peonies are Number One"'. Luoyang's botanical fame has led to the **Peony Festival** which takes place in April and whose apparently international renown ensures that if you arrive at this time you'll be mobbed by gardeners, amateur botanists and photographers. The best place to see the peonies is at the Botanical Gardens, a lovely, well thought-out complex where you can hire a rowing boat or just wander around. Peonies can also be seen at the Wangsheng Park but the funfair and zoo mean that a visit here can be something of an ordeal.

the **market** two blocks away, which always seems to be busy and serves up all the usual noodle-based soups and dishes. You could also check out the area just to the east of the station, where there is a selection of filthy-looking-but-not-that-bad-really places to eat.

Standard travellers' haunts are the two or three small restaurants sandwiched between the Luoyang and the Tian Xiang hotels. There is not much between them; probably the best is the one nearest Tian Xiang, which is very friendly and has English menus.

WHAT TO SEE

Longmen Caves

These Buddhist grottoes stretch along the banks of the Yi River for nearly one km and are ranked among the top three cave complexes in China (Dunhuang's Mogao caves and Datong's Yungang caves being the other two). Work started in 494AD when the Northern Wei moved its capital here and most carving took place under the Tang dynasty, although some work was actually done as late as the Qing.

CITS claims there are over 3600 stone inscriptions, 2100 niches and 100,000 Buddha statues on display here and it's probably a good idea to take their word for it, as counting them would take forever. The rock here is ideally suited to carving; it is only a shame that so many visitors have chipped off pieces to take home with them. It is rare to find a small carving of the Buddha which hasn't had its face carved out but the larger statues are more or less intact, with the exception of the Emperor Xiaowen and Empress Wenzhao from the Bingyang Cave, who are now on display in New York and Kansas respectively.

Getting to the caves is easy: take bus No 81 from outside the railway station. Minibuses also go to the caves and a ticket should cost about Y1.50 (though they may try to charge up to Y10); the journey takes 30-40 minutes. The A4-sized entry ticket costs Y25.

The Ancestor Worship Cave The caves are not numbered, which makes it difficult to identify them. The one you will recognise instantly, however, is the Fengxiansi or Ancestor Worship grotto, which is the vast one located up a wide flight of steps. This cave is over 30m wide and dates back to the mid-7th century, when Empress Wu Zetian generously donated some of her cosmetics allowance to finance its construction. The central statue here is a 17m high Vairocana (see p201), flanked by disciples Ananda and Kashyapa and guarded by four heavenly guards, one of whom is depicted treading on the head of a demon. The carving in this cave is considered to represent the best of Tang sculpture.

Other caves Keep an eye out for the **Bingyang Caves**, virtually the first on the right as you enter. Of these three the middle one is the most notable, having taken 23 years to carve. Note the decapitated statues representing Emperor Xiaowen and Empress Wenzhao, the heads of which are currently on extended sabbatical in the USA. The **Lotus Flower Cave** (late Northern Wei) is located half way along the complex and is recognisable by the large flower on the ceiling. The **Wan Fo Cave** (Ten Thousand Buddhas Cave) immediately to its right, was built in 680 and is notable for the multitude of tiny Buddha sculptures on the walls. CITS says that there are 15,000 of them, which rather leaves us wondering why they didn't call it the Fifteen Thousand Buddha Cave.

In case you still haven't had enough after all these statues of the Buddha, there are more over the river. To get across the bridge you will have to leave the complex, so make sure that you will be readmitted without buying another ticket. If you want to buy anything from the numerous souvenir stalls, bargain hard; check the back covers of books for stickers pasted over their official price.

White Horse Temple

According to tradition, Buddhism first came to China at the request of Emperor Liu Zhuang of the Han dynasty. Having had a strange dream which he asked his courtiers to interpret, he was told that the figure in it was the Buddha. He immediately sent messengers on a fact-finding mission to Afghanistan with instructions to investigate this new religion. When they returned, they brought with them two friendly monks and a white horse laden with sutras. Liu Zhuang was pleased and built this temple in 68AD to show it, naming it after the horse.

Despite the temple's history, not much remains that is genuinely old, as large parts were restored in the Ming and Qing dynasties. It is still an interesting place to visit, though. About 400m from the entrance is the **Qiyun Pagoda** which was built in the Han dynasty and restored in 1175. Both pagoda and temple are maintained by a community of monks, members of which can be seen trooping in for meditation sessions from time to time. Obviously, if something is going on, don't interrupt.

The temple is 12km east of Luoyang. To get to the bus stop (see map) cycle or take a bus and ask for 'Xi Guan'. From here take bus No 56. Entry to the pagoda courtyard is Y5, and entry to the temple complex itself is Y23. It is open 8am-6pm.

Museum of Ancient Tombs

This museum is fascinating – most definitely not the sort of place where you would want to spend the night. Advertised as the 'first tombs museum in China' (snappy title or what?), it contains real vaults which have been taken to bits, shipped in from their original locations, and then lovingly reassembled. It was built so far from the town (a 20-minute bus ride) because it was important to rebuild the tombs in soil that wasn't too wet but judging by the condensation, damp spots and thick mould growing inside some of them the choice of venue was not ideal. The tombs themselves are dark and eerie, dating from the Han to the Northern Song dynasties. There are 22 of them in all, lining the corridors of this underground museum like cells. Entry to the museum is Y12.

Apart from the relocated tombs there are a number of other attractions. There are three original tombs in a separate area and it is possible to get into these but they are fairly simple and the Y15 entry charge makes them mediocre value. There is also a Funerary Objects Exhibition Hall (free entry) and a Madame Tussauds-style mock-up of a funeral procession: if the attendant is alive she will turn on the power and you can see the headman revolving and the musicians playing – kitsch city.

Bus No 83 from the station drops you at the end of the drive, or you can cycle (it's uphill all the way but easy going free-wheeling back).

Old Town

Luoyang itself isn't unpleasant, but could hardly be described as exciting. The old town is considerably better value; made up of narrow winding back streets and tiny shops, it is an ideal place to get thoroughly lost. You can cycle here, or take virtually any bus (No 5 will do) from the station to Xi Guan and walk (5-10 minutes).

Luoyang Museum

The area around Luoyang has been inhabited for at least 500,000 years. Since 1953 over 60 sites and 10,000 graves have been excavated so it's not surprising that some of the relics have remained here.

A new display, 'Archaeological Treasures of Luoyang', presents many of them clearly and with English labels. The display is split into four parts: bronzeware, ceramics, gold and silver, and jade. It's well worth a visit. Entry is Y12.

Folk Customs Museum

Though it's even more interesting than the Luoyang Museum, this museum is virtually unknown. It is right in the heart of the old town and is worth a visit just for the building itself, which is an early Qing temple. Displays inside represent different Chinese customs such as weddings and birthday parties, and are occasionally labelled in English. There is also a beautiful Qing wooden pagoda (6m tall), a display of paper cuttings and a shadow theatre.

Unfortunately the museum is extremely hard to find: about 1.5km east of Xi Guan, the main road through the old town crosses the River Chan. As you head east, take the last tiny sidestreet on the right immediately before the bridge. Follow this side-street for 500m from the main road and the museum is on a small turning to the left. It's open 0800-1200 and 1400-1730; entry is Y8.

Excursion to Shaolin

Eighty-five km to the east of Luoyang is the famous Shaolin Monastery where Kung Fu was nurtured. The monastery itself was founded in the late 5th century and is now entirely given over to teaching and tourism. If you are a martial arts nut this is **the** place to visit, and it's even possible to arrange to stay here and learn how to kill people with your toes just like Bruce Lee did.

Shaolin is very popular with Chinese tourists, although few Westerners get here, so the idyllic pictures you will see at CITS are a bit misleading. Better, or so they say, is the less visited Xung Yua Temple 10km from Shaolin, which is much more tranquil. To get to Shaolin you will have to take a bus. With CITS this will be expensive but you could arrange a minibus independently for a small group; you will have no problem finding drivers in the station area. Expect to pay Y30 per person.

WHAT TO BUY

The large Friendship Store towards the Luoyang Guesthouse has huge amounts of alcohol for sale, so this could be the place to pick up a bottle of your favourite tipple to take into the Botanical Gardens for a rowboat picnic. Alternatively, try the local brew, *dukang*. This spirit, which proves that nothing is capable of putting hair on a Chinaman's chest, is brewed only in Henan Province. Although it was invented 1500 years ago, it was not available this century until some was produced at the request of a Japanese premier in the 1970s. It caught on. Main ingredients are barley, *sorgan* (a local grain) and napalm. Luoyang is the best place to try it, but bear in mind that Liu Ling, the god of alcohol in the Western Jin dynasty, once overdid it on the dukang, downing three bowls; it took him three years to recover.

MOVING ON

By rail

It is easy to get a ticket to Beijing from here, unless you want a sleeper, in which case you're in for a challenge. For the sleeper, try No 232 (20.12) as it originates here. Otherwise, trains going to Beijing include: No 8 (07.06), No 70 (03.47), No 76 (17.10), No 164 (15.16) and No 42 (00.35). If you have no joy in the ticket office you can always ask CITS to book a ticket for you, but easier would be to plump for a day's travel in Hard Seat; No 8 only takes $10^1/_2$ hours, arriving in Beijing at 17.35.

By air

There is a small local airport, 30 minutes outside town, which handles flights to Beijing, Guangzhou, and Xi'an, among other places. For some destinations you may have to use the airport at Zhengzhou instead.

Beijing

Beijing, the end of the line. As with Luoyang, this city has never been part of the Silk Route but it would be a shame to come all this way and not to explore China's capital. The sights here are so numerous that no matter how long you stay you are unlikely to see them all. Most visitors wander around for three or four days, during which time they see the main sights: Tiananmen Square, the Great Wall, the Forbidden City and the Temple of Heaven.

It's a busy, hectic city and is the least relaxing stop along the route in this guide, but most travellers agree that it is also one of the highlights of their trip. As well as being at the cutting edge of the Chinese drive towards modernisation, it also represents the last major bastion of communism in the world today.

HISTORY

The earliest evidence of human settlement around Beijing was found at the Zhoukoudian site, 48km to the city's south-west, in 1921. The remains of this settlement and of its most famous occupant, Peking Man, are tentatively dated at around 500,000BC. The first Chinese records of the area, however, are considerably later than this, citing one Yen, a feudal state of the Zhou dynasty (12th century BC-771BC), as having its capital, Chi, on a site close to present-day Beijing. This was the first capital here.

The area thrived for 500 years until it was wiped out by Shihuang, the First Emperor, who was on his way to uniting China for the first time. Having destroyed the place, he immediately set about rebuilding it. By the time of the Han dynasty (206BC-220AD), the Beijing area had already been noted for its strategic significance owing to its proximity to the barbarian threat from the north. Thus in times of danger its importance grew, but it was never really adequately protected from invasion and consequently it was taken and retaken a number of times by the northern tribes, often becoming the capital of the invaders' kingdoms. The major invasion, of course, was perpetrated by the Mongols under Genghis Khan in 1215. Having torched the place they proceeded to build their own capital here, calling it Khanbalik (City of the Khan). The Chinese knew this city as Ta-Tu (Great Capital) and it was during the Mongol rule that the first Westerners entered the city – including Marco Polo, who described the Khan's palace: 'The palace itself has a very high roof. Inside, the walls of the halls and chambers are all covered with gold and silver and decorated with pictures of dragons and birds and horsemen and various breeds of beasts and scenes of battle. The ceiling is similarly adorned, so that there is nothing to be seen anywhere but gold and pictures. The hall is so vast and so wide that a meal might well be served there for more than six thousand men. The number of chambers is quite bewildering. The whole building is at once so immense and so well constructed that no man in the world, granted that he had the power to effect it, could imagine any improvement in design or execution...'.

The Ming dynasty and the Forbidden City
When the Mongols fell in 1368, Zhu Yuanzhang, founder of the Ming dynasty, moved the country's capital south to Nanjing. The old capital, Ta-Tu, was given to his son, Prince Yen. Yen immediately usurped the throne and moved the capital back there, renaming it Beijing (Northern Capital). It was during the Ming dynasty that most of the present Imperial City was designed. There have been a number of fires in the last 500 years and the old city of Ta-Tu has been demolished; only a couple of parts of the walls and the khan's wine bowl (see p262) remain today.

The Qing dynasty
The Ming move back to the city was partly political: Beijing was suitably close to the Great Wall, so possible invasions could be monitored from here, while reinforcements for the wall garrisons were close at hand. Not that it made much difference: following a series of civil uprisings, the Manchurians were invited across the Wall by a Ming general in 1644. They immediately stomped down to take Beijing and from here they ruled until the abdication of Pu Yi in 1912. In the meantime the capital suffered greatly at the hands of Western powers: following the Arrow War of 1856-60 the Summer Palace was looted and burnt to the ground by Anglo-French troops. European embassies began to spring up in 1860, and parts of the city were declared foreign areas; the Boxer rebellion of 1900 saw the siege of embassy officials and other foreigners inside the legation here for two months. When reinforcements finally arrived, punitive measures were taken, including the incineration of the recently rebuilt Summer Palace.

The Revolution and beyond
After the abdication of Pu Yi, Beijing remained at the heart of the country until the Kuomintang moved the capital to Nanjing in 1928. It was renamed Pei Ping (Northern Peace), as it had been during the first years of the Ming rule. The civil war led to the neglect of Pei Ping, so much so that the later efforts of both Communists and the KMT were not enough to stop the city being occupied by the Japanese in 1937. The civil war recommenced at the end of World War II, and it was only following the

retreat of the KMT to Taiwan (with huge hoards of treasure from the Forbidden City) that the city was renamed. In 1949, of course, the People's Republic of China was officially founded here. Since then it has weathered the stormiest excesses of the Chinese political system, including the vast mass gatherings of the Cultural Revolution and the Democracy Movement.

Beijing today
With a population of about 11 million it's hardly surprising that Beijing comes across as rather impersonal to the modern visitor, and the fact that the inner city itself is not actually that big means that it is difficult to avoid the crowds. The tourist sights are particularly busy most of the time: foreign visitors are herded on and off tour buses while hordes of Chinese take pictures of po-faced friends and relations standing rigidly in front of important monuments. For the budget traveller, Beijing is an excellent place to meet up with other visitors, and in a couple of hotels there is a massive population of rucksack-toting, beer-drinking travellers, all discussing the latest foreigner overpricing outrages.

ORIENTATION AND SERVICES

Finding your way around
Beijing is a large and confusing city to navigate around but, like Xi'an, things are made simpler by the fact that streets head either east-west or north-south. It is very difficult for a foreigner to understand street names because, as so often is the case in China, each street has a number of names. This is easily illustrated by the main east-west thoroughfare, Chang'an Ave, which passes directly between Tiananmen Square and the Forbidden City: this starts off in the west as Fuxing Lu, then becomes Fuxingmenwai Dajie, Fuxingmennei Dajie, Xi Chang'an Jie, Dong Chang'an Jie, Jianguomennei Dajie and then Jianguomenwai Dajie.

The best way to find your way around is to buy a large street map and to spend your first morning cycling up and down Chang'an Ave and then around the Forbidden City and Tiananmen Square, widening your route as things become progressively more familiar. Expensive hotels, of course, invariably have English-speaking receptionists who can help you out if you get really stuck.

Embassies
Australia (☎ 6532 2331) 21 Dongzhimenwai Dajie, San Li Tun
Austria (☎ 6532 2062) 5 Xiusui Nan Jie, Jianguomenwai
Belgium (☎ 6532 1736) 6 Sanlitun Lu
Canada (☎ 6532 3536) 19 Dongzhimenwai Da Jie, Chaoyang District
Denmark (☎ 6532 2431) 1 Dongwu Jie
France (☎ 6532 1331) 3 Dongsan Jie, Sanlitun

Germany (☎ 6532 2161) 5 Dongzhimenwai Dajie
Kazakhstan (☎ 6532 6182) Sanlitun
Mongolia (☎ 6532 1203) 2 Xiushui Beijie, Jianguomenwai
Netherlands (☎ 6532 1131) 4 Liang Ma He Nanlu
New Zealand (☎ 6532 2732) 1 Dong Er Jie, Ritan Lu
Norway (☎ 6532 1329) 1 Dong Yi Jie, Sanlitun
Pakistan (☎ 6532 6660) 1 Dongzhimenwai Dajie
Russian Federation (☎ 6532 2051) 4 Dongzhimen Bei Zhong Jie
Sweden (☎ 6532 3331) 3 Dongzhimenw Dajie
UK (☎ 6532 1961) 11 Guang Hua Lu
USA (☎ 6532 3831) 3 Xiushui Bei Jie, Jianguomenwai
Uzbekistan (☎ 6532 6854) 2-1-92, Ta Yuan Diplomatic Compound

Services

CITS staff can be found in many of the upmarket hotels, notably the Beijing Hotel. The two main offices, however, are at opposite ends of Chang'an Rd: **CITS head office** (for all China) is at 103 Fuxingmennei Dajie (☎ 6601 1122), while **CITS Beijing** is at 28 Jianguomenwai, in the building next to the Gloria Plaza Hotel. It's CITS Beijing that you are most useful, and they are fairly helpful. They can book air tickets (☎ 6515 8564) and train tickets (☎ 6515 8565), and also can advise on city tours and booking all aspects of a trip onwards through China. Both offices are open 08.30-17.00. **CITS ticketing offices** (☎ 6512 6688 ext 1751) deal with air tickets only, and are to be found in the Beijing International Hotel. The service here is surprisingly good and you may find that they can provide you with the cheapest air tickets in town. They are open: (weekdays) 08.30-11.30 and 13.30-17.00; (Saturdays) 08.30-12.00, and closed on Sundays.

The **Public Security Bureau** is immediately to the east of the Forbidden City on Beichizi Dajie and the visa office here is open 08.30-11.30 and 13.00-17.00 (closed Saturday afternoons and Sundays). Beijing, however, is not the place to extend your visa, if you can help it. Although the prices are cheap, the system here demands that you leave your passport for a week. There is an alternative, which is to go to the 'Beijing Consultation Centre for Private Overseas Trip'(sic), on Taiyanle Hutong, on the west side of the Forbidden City, where they will get you a visa extension in two working days – for an extremely hefty charge. If possible, extend you visa somewhere other than Beijing where it is bound to be much cheaper and quicker.

The **CAAC office** (☎ 6601 7755, open 08.00-20.00) is to the west of the Forbidden City, at 15 Fuxingmen Dajie, (on the north side of the road), and an excellent bus service runs to the airport from here.

The main **post office** is on Jianguomenbei Dajie, immediately to the east of the Beijing International Hotel. There is an efficient poste restante counter here. There's also a new post office almost directly opposite the Beijing International.

If you need **hard currency**, the CITIC Industrial Bank will change travellers' cheques into US$ and also allow you US$ withdrawals on major credit cards. They have a branch next to the Friendship Store on Jianguomenwai Dajie, which is open from 09.00-12.00 and 13.00- 16.00. This is also a good place to try if you need to have money wired from abroad.

If, after months on the road, you're desperate to read an English paper, pay a visit to the British Council (4th Floor, Landmark Building, 8 Dong San Huan Beilu, Chaoyang District) who have a reading area with papers and news magazines.

LOCAL TRANSPORT

Most travellers rent **bicycles** from their hotels and since the city is flat this is a good way to get around. In a city of this size, though, some sights are a long way apart.

Buses are generally very good but can be frighteningly overcrowded, so be very careful with your valuables. Don't even bother trying to get on at rush hour. One useful bus is No1, which runs east-west along Chang'an Ave from the west railway station (where trains from Xi'an and Luoyang arrive) to the city centre. You should have no problem spotting this one: it's a double decker.

The **underground** is simpler but won't take you back to your hotel unless you're staying right in the centre of town. Station names are also in English, and the set fee for any trip is Y2.

Taxis are easily available and drivers are usually good about using the meter though you may need to remind them. The price per km should be advertised on a sticker in the side window. Motor and bicycle **rickshaws** are another matter, and you'll have to bargain to get a reasonable price.

TOURS

Tours to virtually anywhere are available from the leading hotels and CITS. A lot of the main sights are not actually too far away though, so it's probably worth ignoring tours to, say, the Forbidden City, the Summer Palace or the Temple of Heaven, as a short trip by bike or on a public bus won't kill anyone.

It is worth taking a tour to see the Wall, however, and the Ming tombs (if you haven't had enough of tombs by now). The best place to organise the Wall trip is at the travel service in the Jing Hua Hotel, where a day trip to Simatai costs Y80. Likewise, Monkey Business (☎ 6329 2244), who specialise in Trans Siberian train travel, are worth contacting. They are at Beijing Commercial Business Complex, No 1 Building Yu Lin Li, Office

Room 406, 4th Floor, Youanmenwai. CITS tours are generally for package tourists, often incorporating a whole day's sightseeing, and consequently if you take one you may end up visiting places that you don't want to see, have already seen, or are capable of seeing on your own.

WHERE TO STAY

There are hundreds of hotels in Beijing. Here is a very brief selection:

Budget accommodation

Currently, there are only two main choices. South of Tian Tan Park, **Jingtai Hotel** (☎ 6722 4675) is reasonable: doubles go for Y90, (Y120 with bathroom), and the place seems clean and friendly. It's not too far from the city centre, and the market on Anlelin Lu at the top of the lane is particularly colourful.

The **Jing Hua Hotel** (☎ 6722 2211), on Nansanhuan Xi Lu (about 1¹/₂km south west of the Jingtai), is cheaper and consequently extremely popular with backpackers. It's the dormitories that are the best value here: a bed in the 30-bed dorm is Y26, in a six-bed dorm Y28, and in a four-bed dorm Y35. Doubles with bathrooms are unspectacular at Y150. Bikes can be hired from the restaurant next door for Y10 per day but there's a Y400 deposit required. There is a reasonable travel service on the second floor.

Mid-range hotels

The **Bei Wei Hotel** (☎ 6301 2266), 13 Xijing Lu (west of Tian Tan Park), is pretty central and good value at Y242 a double. In the same area the **Qianmen Hotel** (☎ 6301 6688), on Hufang Lu, charges Y630 a double. Single occupancy reduces this to Y580.

The **Long Tian Hotel** (☎ 6771 2244 ext 5888), Panjiayuan Nan Li, charges Y298 for a standard room and Y366 for a superior room but is much less conveniently located. The former backpackers' favourite, the **Qiao Yuan Hotel** (☎ 6303 8861) is also a fair way out from the city centre. Near Yongdingmen railway station, it has recently been refurbished and has double rooms for Y280.

Upmarket hotels

Lottery winners should head straight for the **Palace Hotel** (☎ 6512 8899), where the cheapest rooms start at US$260. A bar of chocolate from the foyer shop will set you back US$7.50. Just across the street are the **Peace Hotel** (☎ 6512 8833), with rooms from US$90, and the **Taiwan Hotel** (☎ 6513 6688), which has doubles for Y798. The **Beijing International Hotel** (☎ 6512 6688) charges from US$100 for a simple tourist room to US$1200 for a suite.

On Chang'an Ave, the **Beijing Hotel** (☎ 6513 7766), which is the closest hotel to Tiananmen Square has doubles for US$110. The **Minzhu**

Beijing

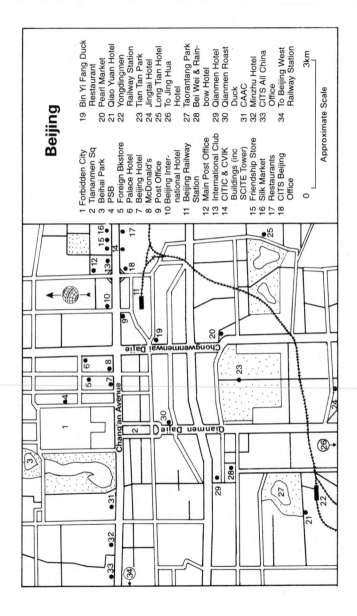

1 Forbidden City
2 Tiananmen Sq
3 Beihai Park
4 PSB
5 Foreign Bkstore
6 Palace Hotel
7 Beijing Hotel
8 McDonald's
9 Post Office
10 Beijing International Hotel
11 Beijing Railway Station
12 Main Post Office
13 International Club
14 CITIC & CVIK Buildings (inc SCITE Tower)
15 Friendship Store
16 Silk Market
17 Restaurants
18 CITS Beijing Office
19 Bin Yi Fang Duck Restaurant
20 Pearl Market
21 Qiao Yuan Hotel
22 Yongdingmen Railway Station
23 Tian Tan Park
24 Jingtai Hotel
25 Long Tian Hotel
26 To Jing Hua Hotel
27 Taorantang Park
28 Bei Wei & Rainbow Hotel
29 Qianmen Hotel
30 Qianmen Roast Duck
31 CAAC
32 Minzhu Hotel
33 CITS All China Office
34 To Beijing West Railway Station

Approximate Scale

0   3km

Hotel (☎ 6606 1579), further west on Chang'an Ave, charges US$85 for a single. All of the above, of course, will automatically add 10-15% to your bill as a service charge.

WHERE TO EAT

There are thousands of restaurants and food stalls in Beijing. It is as well to remember, however, that some of these close very early, although the larger places are more in tune with Western eating hours. The best way to work out where to eat is probably just to keep your eyes open as you wander around, and then come back later. Taxis are cheap, and are the easiest way to get from your hotel to the city centre in the evening.

Wherever you are staying, you will probably want to try the local speciality which is, of course, Peking Duck. Before partaking, however, you might do well to ruminate on some advice from Alexander Hamilton, who recounts 'The abominable Sin of Sodomy is tolerated here, and all over China, and so is Buggery, which they use both with beasts and fowls, in so much that Europeans do not care to eat duck...'. We can only hope that things have changed since 1727.

It is worthy of note that there is no one 'official' Peking Duck restaurant; what there are in abundance are restaurants whose name seems to imply that they are the original roast duck restaurant. Generally most of these are not bad at all. The **Bin Yi Fang Roast Duck Restaurant**, on Chongwenmenwai Dajie, is as good as any and is only a 10 minute walk from the railway station. Another favourite is the **Qianmen Roast Duck Restaurant** (☎ 6701 1379) at 32 Qianmen Dajie. Other duck restaurants are marked on most tourist maps.

For excellent contemporary Chinese food walk west along **Dongzhimennei Dajie** from Dongzhimen underground station and and you will find the street lined with small, cheap restaurants. All of them are good, although most people seem to end up with a favourite.

Another great spot is on a back street just off Jianguomenwai Dajie. To get here, go down Jianhua Lu, which is the small street leading south off Jianguomenwai, opposite the Friendship Store. Bear left at the first junction, and left again at the first opportunity into a quiet back street running parallel with Jianguomenwai. There are three or four excellent eateries here, and in the summer, with the trees strung with lights, it's a good spot for a long, beery dinner. The **vegetarian restaurant** at 158 Qianmen Dajie has also been recommended.

For Western food there is no end of choice, with more and more opening on a daily basis. For fast food there are now more than ten branches of **McDonald's**, and probably an equal number of **Kentucky Fried Chicken** places. The Friendship Store is flanked by **Pizza Hut** on one side, and **Vie de France**, a French bakery with delicious pastries and

freshly baked bread, on the other. If you fancy any sort of Western food, the best bet is simply to pick up a copy of *Beijing Scene* (see What to do in the evening, below) and head for one of the places in their listings.

An unusual option for eating out, if you have money to spare, is **Mr Lee's Restaurant**. Mr Lee specialises in dishes cooked in the same traditional way as they were for the last of the Imperial line at the turn of the century. Stories about how the Imperial household used to function are likely to accompany your meal. Phone for a reservation and directions to the restaurant (☎ 6618 0107). Unfortunately he's so much in demand that he's often booked for days in advance.

WHAT TO SEE

Tiananmen Square
The ideal starting place for a tour of Beijing. The square itself is vast (40 hectares) and has been the site of a number of important movements in 20th century Chinese history, from the declaration of the Chinese Republic in 1949, through the massive fanatical reviews of the Cultural Revolution to the massacre of the peace protestors in 1989. If you include the Forbidden City to the north, the numerous sights in and around the square will take at least a day.

Chairman Mao's Mausoleum
In the centre of the square, this is the best sight to visit first, as it is open only from 8.30-11.30am. It was completed in May 1977 and is still pulling the crowds in, with well over a million Chinese visitors coming each year. The mausoleum is hemmed in north and south by four statues, each representing historical struggles of the Chinese people (who have a distinctly Russian look to them here). Queues are astonishingly long, a testament either to the fact that Mao lives on in the hearts of the people, or that the Chinese just love to stare at things in groups. The line moves surprisingly fast, however, so you shouldn't have to wait for more than 20-30 minutes. Inside, guards bark at you if you slow down or look as if you are about to stop for a better view. It would be unwise to eat, drink, light a cigarette or attempt to take a photograph. Bags and cameras must be left in the booths on the east side of the mausoleum.

The mausoleum also contains memorial halls to statesmen Zhou Enlai, Liu Shaoqi and Zhu De but these may be closed. Do not rush to leave the complex, as there are some wonderfully tacky Mao souvenir stalls by the exit.

National Museum of Chinese History
On the eastern side of the square, this huge building also houses the Museum of the Chinese Revolution. It contains extensive relics from every period of China's history, with occasional English labelling, mak-

ing a visit here something of a guessing game. Easily recognisable are the prehistoric tools, early jewellery and terracotta warriors. Watch out for the gunpowder display featuring flying bombs, and the jade burial suit, complete with jade posing pouch.

The Museum of the Revolution contains many hundreds of relics from pre and post WWII struggles – everything from photographs, flags and cannons to a cloth cap once worn by Mao. Also in this building is a display of gifts given to the Chinese government by foreign dignitaries, which is less culturally exciting but still pretty interesting: check out the Brazilian teatray surfaced entirely with butterfly wings, and the fearsomely tacky Shakespeare plate from the UK.

Entry to each museum is Y10. They are open 8.30am-3.30pm, closed Monday.

Great Hall of the People
Covering an area of 170,000 square metres, this hall is used for meetings of the National People's Congress but is open to the public from 8.30am to 3.30pm when meetings are not being held. Unless you enjoy looking at vast, empty rooms it's probably best to give this a miss, saving yourself Y30. The impressive 10,000 seat auditorium would, however, make a truly wonderful venue for a *Rocky Horror* bash.

Qianmen Gate
This was the main entrance to the northern half of the city. It was built in 1419 and, at 42m, is the tallest of the old buildings here. It's possible to get inside for Y5 to see the photograph museum (no English labels). Continue climbing for a good view of the square and its surroundings, and to visit the huge souvenir shops; although items in here have price tags on them, prices are not necessarily fixed.

Other Sights in Tiananmen Square
The monument to the People's Heroes stands directly north of Mao's mausoleum; this was the centre of the wreath-laying protests in 1976 (see p75). It is decorated with Mao's and Zhou Enlai's calligraphy and the base contains carvings which illustrate suitably revolutionary events in Chinese history. Directly to the north of this flies the PRC flag from sunrise to sunset, and if you get here early or late enough you can catch the Colours ceremony. Finally, note that there are toilets and a bicycle park just to the east of the Tianan Gate.

Tiananmen (Gate of Heavenly Peace)
On the northern side of Tiananmen Square sits the entrance to the Imperial (Forbidden) City. This famous gate was also used as a podium from which imperial decrees were read and from here, on 1 October 1949 Mao proclaimed 'The People's Republic of China has now been founded. The Chinese People have now stood up'. The front is embellished with a

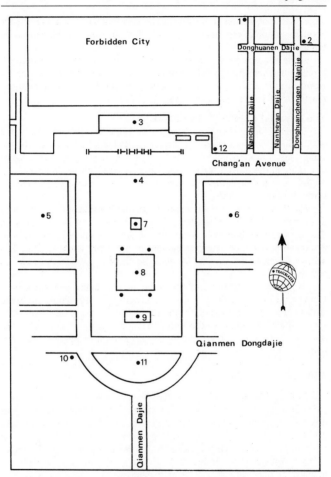

TIANANMEN SQUARE

1 PSB
2 Bank of China
3 Tianan Gate
4 Flagstaff
5 Great Hall of the People

6 Museums of Chinese History and the Revolution
7 Monument to the People's Heroes
8 Mao's Mausoleum

9 Qianmen Gate
10 Kentucky Fried Chicken
11 Arrow Castle
12 Bicycle Park and lavatories

huge picture of the man himself, and the inscriptions read 'Long live the Peoples' Republic of China', and 'Long live the unity of the peoples of the world'.

Inside is an exquisite ceiling, a couple of paintings of Mao and his acolytes and some dodgy 60's furniture. Open 0900-1700, it's not really worth visiting unless you are desperate to spend Y15 on an 'I mounted the Tower of Tiananmen' certificate.

The Imperial Palace (Forbidden City)

The Imperial Palace, comprising more than 178 acres, 1000 buildings and 9000 rooms, is so vast that it's difficult to know where to start. If you want to explore the whole thing be prepared to spend days inside; half a day is about the most a sane person can take. It would be impossible to do justice to it in a short guide such as this, so what follows is merely a brief overview.

The Palace itself, also known as the Purple Forbidden City, was built in the reign of the Ming emperor, Yong Le, between 1406-20, and since then has been the home of 24 emperors, right up until 1911. It has been destroyed by fire and rebuilt a number of times but reconstruction has always followed the original designs, so the integrity of the place is retained.

Maps of the Imperial City are common, and many city maps have them on the back. For those not taking private tours, it is worth hiring the cassette tour outside Meridian Gate: for Y30 you get a rather droll 'personal' guide around all of the sights below by Roger Moore. After the tour, of course, there's nothing to stop you exploring other areas on your own.

The Imperial Palace is open 8.30am-4.30pm but ticket offices close at 3.30pm. Entry is Y55.

• **Entering the city** There are five bridges over the Golden Waters River leading to Tianan Gate. The middle one and the central path throughout the city were reserved exclusively for the emperor's personal use. Emperors were not expected to soil their feet with the earth and so the central path through the palace was constructed entirely of marble; this was known as the Imperial Way. Just to be sure that no dirt ever touched the imperial feet, moreover, the emperor was carried everywhere in a sedan chair. Tianan Gate leads you to Duanmen (Upright) Gate and then to the Meridian Gate, which is the entrance to the Forbidden City proper. Ticket offices are on the right.

(Opposite): The Great Wall. Everyone sees the Wall outside Beijing (bottom left) but few make it as far as the western end in Jiayuguan (bottom right, see p208). The fort (top) marked the boundary between the Chinese Empire and the wilderness that was the rest of the world.

Although you cannot see the water from the Meridian Gate, you should be aware that you are crossing over the moat, which is fifty metres wide, and through the walls, which are seven metres thick. Emperors used to stand inside Meridian Gate to supervise the flogging of errant courtiers in the eastern half of the square inside; records tell of one such session in 1534 when 134 men were beaten here. Seventeen died.

• **Central halls** Heading north, you will pass through the Gate of Supreme Harmony, to face the largest structure inside the city, the **Palace of Supreme Harmony**. From the throne in this palace, the emperor surveyed the most important court pageants. Nearly 100,000 state officials could fit into this square, and they did on truly auspicious occasions: when he had a birthday party, for example. Passing on, you will come to the **Hall of Complete Harmony**, which was used as a preparation room for the emperor and for occasional state functions; there are two original sedan chairs in here today. Behind this is the **Hall of Preserving Harmony** which was used for less significant banquets and the final stage of the highest civil service examinations. Of the ten shortlisted candidates (drawn from all over China) three would be chosen by the emperor. These three were allowed to follow the Imperial Path through the city once. Behind the Hall of Preserving Harmony, note the vast carved marble slab decorating the **stairway**: this is the largest single piece of marble in the city, weighing in at over 200 tons. It is 16.5m long, 3m wide and 1.5m thick, and it was dragged to the palace in winter, when water was thrown over the roads to make them icy.

• **Inner court** To the north of this ramp lie the living quarters of the emperor – the élite part of the city – and there are three successive palaces here. The first, the **Palace of Heavenly Purity**, was the emperor's bedroom until the mid 18th century, when it was converted into a meeting room for foreign dignitaries. The second, the **Hall of Union**, was the empress's quarters, while the third, the **Palace of Earthly Peace**, was used, among other things, for the consummation of imperial marriages. It is worth noting the blocked up hole against the wall of this building, part of a charcoal underfloor heating system. Behind the palace you will find the **Imperial Garden**, which was laid out in the Ming dynasty. From here the path leads straight to the **Hall of Imperial Peace**, and then the Shenwumen Gate, the northern exit from the Forbidden City.

• **Other sights** It would be a mistake only to wander through the palace from south to north. Other sights of interest in the eastern part of the city include the **Museum of Clocks**, the **Dragon Screen**, the **Jewellery**

(Opposite) : If you can't make it to Tibet make sure you get to Xiahe (see p218), outside Lanzhou, one of the six key centres of Yellow Hat Buddhism.

Museum and **Qianlong's Garden** (which contains a tiny artificial river along which cups of wine were floated; whenever the cup stopped moving with the flow the individual nearest it would have to compose a poem or drink the contents). Also look out for the **Imperial Opera House** and the famous **well** in which Guangxi's favourite concubine, Zhen Fei, was drowned on the orders of his aunt, Ci Xi.

Immediately to the north of the Forbidden City is Jingshan Park, built on an artificial hill (made out of earth removed to create the palace moat). Most palace visitors go straight into the park after leaving the north gate, for the top of the hill affords a fine view of the city. If you are not totally overloaded with Forbidden City architecture, there are two interesting buildings on the northern side of the park, too. As Beijing's parks go, however, this is not one of the best, so try elsewhere if you fancy a quiet place to sit.

Excursions to the Great Wall

China's most famous tourist attraction has a long and venerable history. As far back as the Warring States period individual principalities were building walls to protect themselves. With the unification of China by Emperor Shihuang in 221 BC, however, it was decided to link the extant stretches of wall together in order to protect the Chinese against their one common enemy: the barbarians from the north. The building project embarked upon was immense, with hundreds of thousands of men, often convicts, forced to work under atrocious conditions.

The Wall has been periodically revamped, usually at times when the northern threat was particularly serious, notable examples being the Jin and Ming periods, the latter of which embarked on a vast renovation project that took over 100 years. In this case, however good walls didn't make good neighbours: Ghengis Khan had no problem at all wandering into China from the north in 1279, trashing the place, and setting up his own dynasty (the Yuan). Likewise, following the Ming renovations, the Manchurians were actually invited to invade in the 17th century, marching in to set up the Qing dynasty. While the Wall may be considered a failure for defensive purposes, though, it acted as a very effective means of communication, allowing envoys to travel through dangerous country safely, and messages to be quickly relayed across vast areas.

Visiting the Wall The Wall makes an easy day trip from Beijing, and the majority of tourists head for the stretches at either **Badaling** or **Mutianyu**. This in itself is an excellent reason for going somewhere else, a good choice being **Simatai**, which is harder to get to by yourself but is the destination for the reasonably priced tour run by the travel service at the Jing Hua Hotel. Most exclusive of all (at the moment) is the area around **Jinshanling**, not easily reached unless you have your own transport. You'll need to get a group together and hire a minivan.

Mutianyyu, Simatai and even Jinshanling get very busy in the summer but they are nothing compared to Badaling. Wherever you decide to go, allow a full day to give time for a good two to three hour wander when you get there (it's a two-hour drive to both Mutianyu and Badaling). Be prepared for some intensive stair climbing, although there are cable cars at Mutianyu and Badaling. Being lazy will cost you at least Y50. You'd do better to walk since there are excellent views and, as the Mutianyu sign says, 'You will have greater pleasure and be a true hero'. Quite so.

Bus tours to **Mutianyu** and **Badaling** run from virtually every hotel. CITS currently organise a day tour to Badaling and the Ming Tombs for Y320, and an afternoon tour to the Wall at Mutianyu for Y230. To get to Badaling on your own, you can take a train from Xizhimen (north) railway station. It's about a three-hour ride each way, so it's perfectly possible to catch an early morning train out and a late afternoon train back.

For **Simatai**, take the 7am bus from Dongzhimen station (don't miss it: it's the only one all day) or try the travel service in the Jing Hua Hotel, which will take you there and back for Y80.

While most visitors spend long enough at the Wall to have a walk and take some pictures, there is the scope here for longer excursions. If the weather is nice, radical student-types bring guitars, sleeping bags and noxious substances, and yomp off to the further reaches to camp; this has been highly recommended by some. The more energetic (and those with their own transport) recommend a **day hike** along the Wall between **Jinshanling** and **Simatai** – it's about five hours of hard walking and not for the faint-hearted. Bring lots of water, and good shoes.

Finally, check the listings guide, *Beijing Scene,* for occasional special events. These can be quite fun; 'Jazz on The Wall' and 'Hamlet on the Wall' were two recent examples.

Tian Tan – The Temple of Heaven

Tian Tan was the site at which the most auspicious imperial ceremonies were held; emperors have communicated with heaven from here since the early 15th century. Although there were altars on this site for centuries, the temple as we know it was built at the order of Yong Le (also, of course, responsible for the Forbidden City), in 1420, and since then emperors have visited regularly to pray for good harvests and to celebrate the winter solstice. Invariably the emperor would enter the complex from the eastern gate, spending at least one night fasting in the **Hall of Abstinence**. West of this hall stands the marble **circular altar**, constructed in 1530 and later rebuilt in 1740. It is worth noting of this altar, as of every building in the ensemble, that construction dwelt upon the sacred numbers three and nine, each being representative of heaven. Thus virtually any statistic you can think up about the buildings here (apart from their construction dates, of course), will be a multiple of three. Try counting the number of tiers, steps, or the posts around the edge. Just north of the altar is the **Imperial Vault of Heaven** which contained the sacred ancestral tablets, to be produced for each ceremony. The **circular wall** around this vault is said to have been designed for its acoustic properties, which should ensure that a whisper towards the surface of one side of the circle is clearly audible on the opposite side. What it actually ensures is that there is always a deafening ruckus here as everyone claps and bellows frantically at the wall. 'It doesn't work', they all shout. Perhaps the batteries are flat.

To the north is the **Hall of Prayer for Good Harvests**, whose name is self-explanatory: this is the most important building of the complex, and it is particularly impressive. When you look at it, remind yourself that it was built entirely without glue or nails.

The temple is very impressive, and the park which provides its setting is lovely, too. Try to get here as early as possible in the morning or late in the evening (preferably early) when the place will be more or less quiet, otherwise it will be swarming. It's a 10 minute cycle ride south of Tiananmen Square, and bus Nos 35 and 36, among others, run past the northern entrance. Entry to the park only is Y1.5 but tourists are pressed to take the sightseeing ticket, which gains you entry to all of the buildings and costs Y30; keep your ticket, as it is needed for access to different areas. The park is open from 6am-10pm, the temple from 8.30am-5pm.

The Summer Palace

The palace and its grounds together cover an expanse of 290 hectares – four times the size of the Forbidden City. This is another Beijing sight which could take days to explore if you have the time, though considering the fact that three-quarters of the park is underwater, you should bring an aqualung if you want to see everything. Kunming Lake, the Lake of Superior Brightness, was originally a small pond but was converted into a reservoir in 1292 to provide drinking water for the area. In 1750, Qianlong built a garden here to celebrate his mother's birthday and the lake was further dredged and expanded. Since that time the site has been used by the imperial households as a summer retreat. Following the Opium Wars the palace was sacked by Anglo-French troops in 1860. It was rebuilt on its present site by Empress Ci Xi just in time for it to be burned to the ground again in 1900 after the Boxer Rebellion.

As with the Forbidden City, there is far too much on display to cover adequately here but you should try to see the following:

From the East Palace Gate the visitor steps into the **royal residence** areas. Here, in the late 19th century, the Empress Dowager Ci Xi lived and received guests. Her unfortunate nephew, Guang Xu, was imprisoned here, despite the fact that he was the legitimate heir to the throne, and the wall she built to stop him from escaping can still be seen. In this area you will find Ci Xi's private theatre and a number of living quarters which have been converted into museums (Ci Xi's car, clothing, carriages and make-up are all on display). On the left as you reach the lake you will see the small **Perceiving of Spring Jetty/Island** – so called because the ice melts here first at the end of winter. Passing to the south along the shore you come to the beautiful 17-arch marble bridge leading to **South Lake Island**, which is the setting for the **Dragon King Temple**.

Heading north and west, meanwhile, you will be approaching **Longevity Hill**. Turning left around the lake you find the **Long Corridor**, which, measuring 730m from end to end, is the longest covered walkway in the world. It is very impressive, with unique artwork on every eave. This brings you to the main architectural structures of the complex, the **Cloud Dispelling Hall** and the **Tower of Buddhist Fragrance**, which at 41m high is the park's dominant non-fluid feature. In the former building Ci Xi used to celebrate her birthdays, and there are a number of museums here, each of which charges an entry fee; in one of them is the famous portrait of her in 1905 by Dutch artist Voss Hubert. Entry to the hall and tower is Y10.

Most visitors see about this much and then visit the famous **marble boat** further to the west, but there is a good deal more exploring to do if you have the time. It would be easy to spend a whole day here. Perhaps it might be fun to walk around the lake, or row across it, and find a quiet spot on the south-eastern side for a picnic.

To get to The Summer Palace take the metro to Xizhimen station. Walk west along Xizhimenwai Dajie towards the zoo. Then either take bus No 332 west to the end of the line or catch a minibus, whichever comes first; the terminal is right next to the entrance. There is a good, clear, aerial map of the complex on the right as you go in. Entry to the palace is Y45.

Beihai Park

Located just to the north-west of the Forbidden City, Beihai Park is another pleasant place in which to while away an afternoon, although it can get rather crowded, especially at weekends. Entry is Y10 and the boat to the island costs Y2.

Its history considerably predates the Imperial Palace, for it was on the southern side of the lake here that Kubilai Khan lived. Construction of the **lake**, which accounts for over half of the park's area, originally started in the 10th century, the rocks being piled up in the middle to form Qionghua (Jade Flower) Island. The Yuan dynasty remodelled the place, while the ever-busy Qianlong conducted major reconstructions here, too. The buildings were sacked and burned by foreigners in 1900 following the Boxer Uprising. Entering the park from the south you will find all that remains of Kubilai Khan's 'Stately Pleasure Dome': a huge carved **jade**

bowl from which, apparently, he used to drink wine (he must have been some drinker, because it's about three feet across). This bowl was lost for some time, but was rediscovered in 1749. Behind the bowl, in the **Chengguandian** (Hall for Receiving Light) is an impressive Buddha figure encrusted with jewels, hewn from a single piece of white jade. The figure originally came from Burma and was presented to Ci Xi in the late 19th century.

Crossing the Yong'an Bridge you come to the park's most famous construction, the 35m high **White Pagoda**, which was built in 1651 to commemorate the first official visit of a Dalai Lama to Beijing. In fact the top half of it only dates to 1977 and it had been rebuilt a number of times before this as a result of earthquake damage.

Other notable sights, both on the island and off it, include the dew collecting plate, which was used to gather pure dewdrops for the emperor's various potions, and a nine-dragon screen on the northern shore. The Five Dragon Pavilions which line the shore are so-called because their roofs look like the spine of a huge swimming serpent. There are also botanical gardens on the northern side, and it is possible to rent rowing boats in summer. In winter the lake becomes a huge ice-rink.

Museums

Apart from the museums in Tiananmen Square there are numerous other museums including the **Museum of Peking Man** (the skull here is a replica), Zhoukoudian, Fangshan District; the **Museum of Buddhist Sutras and Relics (Fayuansi Temple)**, Xuahwu District; **Cultural Palace for Nationalities on Fuxingmennai Dajie;Beijing Art Museum**, Wanshousi St, West District; **Beijing Stone Carving Museum**, Wutansi (Five Pagoda Temple), Xizhimenwai; **Memorial Hall of the Chinese People's Anti-Japanese War**, near Lugou Bridge, Fenghai District; **Observatory** (astronomical instruments dating back to 1442), Jianguomen; **National Art Gallery**, Wusi St, East District; **Natural History Museum**, Tianqiao St.

WHAT TO DO IN THE EVENING

Beijing is not renowned for its nightlife but it has opened up dramatically over the last year or two. If your budget will handle it there are plenty of places to go to in the evening. The best source as to what's on is the main expat news-sheet *Beijing Scene*, copies of which can be picked up from their office behind the Silk Market (Rm 168 Kindly Commercial Development Centre, 9 Xiushui Nanjie), or at most of the places listed here. Other sources of information are the tourist magazines *Beijing This Month* and *Beijing Weekend*, and the *China Daily*. There are plenty of Western style places to see everything from films to drama, and live music. For more traditional entertainment, there's opera or acrobatics.

Opera

Forget what the historians tell you about Chinese opera; if you enjoy elaborate costumes and ear-wrenching wailing, this is for you. Most head for the **Peking Opera Troupe** at Liyuan Theatre (☎ 1935 2045) at the Qianmen Hotel, 175 Yong'anlu. Another popular venue is the **Beijing Hu Guang Guild Hall** at No3, Hufangqiao, Xuanwu district. If you're Western, it's obligatory after sitting through an opera to comment on how wonderful the costumes were.

Acrobatics

You are unlikely to see better acrobatic displays than in China: leaping through hoops, throwing small children around, spinning plates on sticks and more – how could anyone fail to enjoy it? The best way to find venues is by checking the *China Daily*, but there are usually shows at the **Chaoyang Theatre** (☎ 6507 2421), 36 Dongsanhuan Beilu, Hujialou, at 7.15pm nightly. The travel service at the Jing Hua Hotel organises tickets and transport to see the acrobats, for Y60.

Bars and clubs

There are now innumerable Western bar-restaurants, among the most established being **Mexican Wave** on Dongdaqiao Lu, Jianguomenwai; **CD Cafe** (great jazz on Friday nights) on East Third Ring Rd, south of the Agriculture Centre; and **The Sunflower Club** on South Ritan Park Rd, Jianguomenwai. Big names such as **Hard Rock Cafe** and **TGIFriday's** are also to be found. The **Poachers' Inn** is the nightclub where most expats seem to go after everything else has closed; it has the atmosphere of a teenage disco, so you'll need to be in the right mood.

WHAT TO BUY

Lazy shoppers make for the large **Friendship Store** on Jianguomenwai Dajie, where shopping is straightforward, numerous Western luxuries are available (including books and newspapers), and prices are high. Still, it's very convenient. A good present from here might be one of the fragile silk or paper kites you'll have seen people flying at the Temple of Heaven.

If you're after books, go to the **Foreign Languages Bookstore** on Wangfujing Dajie, where choices are a bit limited but prices are cheap. Check out the CDs and tapes upstairs. The CVIC and Lufthansa Centres likewise offer upmarket goods (including Western designer names). Browsers often head off to the **Wangfujing** area directly east of the Forbidden City which is Beijing's Oxford Street, with high quality goods offered from the many stores here. Bargain hunters and shopping addicts favour the little streets to the south of Tiananmen Square in the **Qianmen District,** where almost anything seems to be available from small stalls and shops. The best place for souvenirs is the **Pearl Market** (Hongqiao), which is in a large multi storey building opposite the north-east corner of Tiantan Park. Bargain hard! Another great shopping spot is the **Silk Market** on Jianguomenwai Dajie, where clothing is the main thing on offer. It's a great place to look for designer and outdoor clothing, too, as many of the big names (Ralph Lauren, North Face, Karrimor etc) have their clothing made in China, and you can get the stuff at excellent prices.

MOVING ON

By air
Numerous airlines offer flights to major cities worldwide. A good place to start looking is in the SCITE Tower (confusingly spelt CVIK) opposite the Friendship Store on Jianguomenwai, where among others, you will find British Airways. Compare prices with the CITS Air Ticketing Centre in the Beijing International Hotel, who can sometimes offer the cheapest tickets of all. Sample fares, through CITS are: London Y5500 and Berlin Y5500, Hong Kong Y2310, Paris Y5500, Singapore Y3780 and Tokyo Y4390. Flights within China booked here include Xi'an Y980, Lanzhou 1120, Shanghai Y1100, Guilin Y1720 and Chengdu Y1570.

There's an airport bus from the CAAC office. The trip takes about an hour, depending on traffic. First buses go at 5.30am but it would be safer to get a taxi at this time.

By rail
• **Domestic** Tickets must be bought at the railway station from which you will be departing; thus westbound travellers (Luoyang, Xi'an, Lanzhou) should go to huge new West Station (take bus No 1 all the way west to its terminal), and most other travellers will need to go to the Central Station. Alternatively CITS will book for you, saving you the queuing – all for Y50. Note that there is a Foreigners' Ticket Office in Beijing Central Station, through the Soft Class waiting room.

• **International** To get a ticket for one of the international trains you will almost certainly need to go through CITS or a private ticket agency. Whoever you use, try to book as early as possible – most people book their tickets in advance and pick them up when they arrive in Beijing, to avoid being faced with a long wait. CITS currently charge between Y1600 and Y1800 for a ticket on the Trans-Siberian to Moscow. Otherwise, good people to contact are **Monkey Business** (see p249) who specialise in Trans-Siberian and Trans-Mongolian rail travel. For more information see *Trans-Siberian Handbook*, also from Trailblazer Publications.

PART 6: ROUTE GUIDE AND MAPS

Using this guide

This route guide highlights the places and points of interest on the rail journey from Moscow to Beijing. Station names are given in Cyrillic, Chinese and Roman script on the strip maps and identified in the text by a kilometre number.

Kilometre marker posts
These are usually situated on the right hand side of the track, often very close to it, so that sometimes you may have to press your face up against the window and squint downwards in order to see them.

Where something of interest appears on one side of the train only it is designated by the letter (R) or (L) for right or left. Obviously, if you are heading in the opposite direction to this guide, all sights will be on the other side. Diagrams correspond to the **key map** on the inside back cover. Note that some of the distances quoted in the text are approximations, so it is wise to be ready for a particular sight a couple of kilometres before it is due.

To make things more complicated the marker posts often appear not to be following any coherent system at all: numbers jump up and down at random as the kilometre post painter raises two bony, paint-stained fingers at rail authorities, standard mathematical practice and cosmic law in general. The trick to pin-pointing your location along the line lies in watching out for two or three markers in succession every now and then so you know which way the numbers are counting.

Stops
Trains generally stop at stations for anything between one and thirty minutes but it is worth noting that however long your train may be supposed to stop at a particular station, it will wait only as long as the driver feels like waiting. Consequently I have not indicated how long stops last, as this is impossible to predict. Take your cue from the carriage attendant if you want to get off for a wander but never go far from the train itself. There is sometimes a whistle in China to indicate when the train is about to pull away but there is no warning in the CIS. At smaller stations you may have to climb over the track in order to get to the platform; do not allow a different train to get between you and your carriage, or you won't be able to get back in.

Speed calculations

Using the kilometre posts and a watch, it's possible to calculate how quickly, or more usually how slowly, the train is going. Note the time that elapses between one post and the next and consult the table below.

Seconds	kph	mph	Seconds	kph	mph
24	150	93	52	69	43
26	138	86	54	66	41
28	129	80	56	64	40
30	120	75	60	60	37
32	113	70	64	56	35
34	106	66	68	53	33
36	100	62	72	50	31
38	95	59	78	46	28
40	90	56	84	43	27
42	86	53	92	39	24
44	82	51	100	36	22
46	78	49	120	30	18
48	75	47	150	24	15
50	72	45	180	20	12

Moscow to Kandagach

Moscow to the rail junction at Kandagach is 1880km, a journey of about 38 hours. For Kandagach to Tashkent and Almaty see p273, for Kandagach to Urgench see p275.

Km0: Moscow: Kazan Station (Kazanskii Vokzal)
The station for trains to and from Central Asia. Built between 1912 and 1921 in the old Russian style, this imposing building stands on the south side of Komsomol Square (metro: Komsomolskaya) and is not to be confused with the two other stations here (for trains to St Petersburg and Siberia). Make sure you arrive early as trains tend to leave right on time.

Km23: Perovo
An important rail junction, Perovo is noted for its locomotive repair shops. It was also the former country seat of the Sheremetyevo family, one of the wealthiest in tsarist Russia.

Km80: Voskresensk
Situated on the Moskva River, this city is a major fertiliser producer, processing minerals brought in from the Yegoryevsk phosphorite deposits to the north.

Km110: Golutvin In itself Golutvin is a fairly insignificant little town but here the line crosses the Oka River, whose source lies in the central Russian uplands. From here it flows north and east until it meets the Volga, 1480km away. It remains frozen for up to 250 days per year.

Km155: Alpatyevo Immediately after this station the train enters Ryazan *oblast* (province). This consists mainly of Oka/Don River lowlands including forested, swampy regions and large areas of wooded steppe; thus trees and vast sections of dark, damp earth are the principal views on this stretch. While it doesn't make particularly inspiring viewing, it does make the region suitable for the cultivation of potatoes, wheat and rye; industry revolves around the processing of these products.

Km200: Ryazan The city was founded in 1095, on a site some 30km to the south-east of its present-day location. Having been wrecked comprehensively by the Mongols in 1237, however, it was moved to its new position near the Oka river and was renamed Pereyaslavl Ryazanski. It quickly began to dominate the outlying region and is still the centre of Ryazan oblast today. Having been annexed by Moscow in 1520, it was rebuilt and renamed in 1778.

Ryazan witnessed some brutal pogroms (attacks on Jewish communities) at the turn of this century. Tsar Alexander II's assassination in 1881 sparked off bursts of militant anti-Semitism, which were particularly unjust, if only because his assassin was not actually Jewish. In fact public sentiment had been whipped up by authorities in the church and the government, both organisations fearing that the Jews were attempting to undermine their credibility. Provocative rumours circulated like wildfire, among them the accusation of 'Blood Libel': that the Jews indulged in ritual human sacrifice (this myth has been found elsewhere in Europe). Pogroms occurred here in 1881 and then reappeared in 1903-6. Some 200 other cities saw anti-Semitic violence like this. Ryazan's most

MAP 1

famous son is Ivan Pavlov (1849-1936), the Nobel prizewinning scientist who developed the concept of the conditioned reflex via his experiments on dogs. Today it is a large, sprawling city producing light bulbs, shoes, clothing and cash registers.

Km415: Yagodno Just east of this station the train passes into Tambovskaya oblast which, covering an area of 21,000 square kilometres, maintains the fertile Oka/Don lowlands at its heart. It was founded in 1937.

Km439: Morshansk A large city on the Tsna River, Morshansk was chartered in 1779 and produces tobacco, lumber, glass and wool; check out the stupendously ugly factories (R). Shortly after this station, at km445, note the palace/cathedral on the horizon (R), though it will be too far away to photograph unless you have a very high powered lens.

Km492: Vernadovka East of this station the line enters Penza oblast. From the train not much seems to change because the line is still largely hemmed in by trees but in fact the oblast is mostly agricultural, covering 26,000 square kilometres.

Km541: Bashmakovo The big sign (R) means 'Bon Voyage'.

Km691 On the approach to **Arbekovo** (km701) ramshackle houses line the tracks, all hemmed in by their rather pathetic-looking vegetable patches. Growing your own is still the easiest and cheapest way to get food around here, a fact which is highlighted by the plots which also crop up along the railway line itself, often apparently in the middle of nowhere.

Km710: Penza This city is renowned as a rail junction and an industrial centre (grain and timber). It was founded in 1663 as a fortress at the

---

Lenin – the making of a national icon

Vladimir Ilyich Ulyanov was born in Ulyanovsk in 1870. The fact that he came from a secure, warm family has rather baffled psychologists and historians; why (and when?) did he become so militant?

Two events in his early childhood have been pinpointed as having played key roles in his transition from gifted intellectual to revolutionary leader: his father, a school inspector, was threatened with the loss of his job in the late 19th century because the government greatly feared the effects of educating the masses; shortly after this, moreover, his brother Alexander was hanged for taking part in a student conspiracy to assassinate Emperor Alexander III in St Petersburg.

Coincidentally, help came from his high school principal, who pulled strings to get the ostracised young man into Kazan University. The principal's son, who shared a birthday with Lenin (22 April), was Alexander Kerensky, whose provisional government was later to be toppled by him in 1917.

edge of the Muscovite domain and chartered in 1682. There are a couple of old steam locomotives still in use here. Immediately after Penza the line crosses the Sura River, which rises north-east of Kuznetsk and heads off to flow into the Volga 870km away.

Km830: Kuznetsk Kuznetsk is a major commercial centre for wood and leather. It was founded in 1617 and chartered in 1780, developing a certain notoriety as a robbers' nest in that century. It enjoyed a brief period as Stalinsk (one of a number of them) until the 1960s. Now it thrives on industry, particularly pig iron, ferro alloy and chemical plants. As would seem logical, the huge Kuznetsk coalfield is close at hand.

Km856: Nikulino East of this town there is an attractive valley, at km864(L), just before the train passes into Ulyanovska oblast. The centre of this region is the manufacturing town of **Ulyanovsk**, which was formerly called Simbirsk. One might expect the names of both the town and the oblast to change now but in fact they seem likely to remain intact for the good reason that Ulyanov (Lenin to us) was actually born here, in 1870. Politician Alexander Kerensky must have been rather bitter about the naming, as he was also born here.

Km910: Novospasskoye This town lies on the Syzran River, which rises in the southern Urals, flowing 590km altogether. As you leave Novospasskoye you head into Kuibyshev oblast, which is laid out across nearly 56,000 square kilometres of the Volga valley. The soil is good for agriculture and extremely rich in minerals (asphalt, gypsum, phosphorite), although the area has earned itself a certain notoriety because of its droughts. Much industrial traffic still flows from here along the Volga.

Km955: Syzran The water tower here (R) marks the outskirts of the city; note the two attractive blue domed churches (also R). The city extends for 30km along the banks of the Volga, which can be

MAP 2

Соседка
SOSEDKA
Хутор
KHUTOR
Башмаково
BASHMAKOVO
Пачелма
PACHELMA
Титово
TITOVO
Адикаевка
ADIKAEVKA
Белинская
BELINSKAYA
Студенец
STUDENETS
Симанщина
SIMANSHCHINA
Рамзаи
RAMZAI
Арвеково
ARBEKOVO
ПЕНЗА Sura R
PENZA
Канаевка
KANAEVKA
Асеевская
ASEEVSKAYA
Чаадаевка
CHAADAYEVKA
Сюзюм
SYUZYUM
Кузнецк
KUZNETSK
Никулино
NIKULINO
Ключики
KLYUCHIKI
Прасковьино
PRASKOVINO
—N→
Новоспасское
NOVOSPASSKOYE
Ново-Образцовое
NOVO OBRAZTSOVOE
Сызраны SYZRAN

PENZA OBLAST

ULYANOVSKAYA OBLAST

MAP 3

seen on the right as you leave, the line curving around it. The islands you can see are actually artificial. There is an impressive view from the mile-long bridge as you cross the river. The **time zone changes to GMT+4**.

The Volga River

The Volga (in ancient times 'Ra') is Europe's longest river. It rises in the Valdai hills to the north-west of Moscow and from there its waters reach 3700km to the Caspian Sea. It drops from 224 metres above sea level to 29.4 below it during this time which, by my calculations, works out as an angle of 0.0039247°. (In case you are interested, I reckon it would take 9.37 years for Heinz ketchup, flowing at a velocity of 0.028 miles per hour, as it does, to make the journey from one end to the other – although it might conceivably speed up a bit as it gathered momentum).

The Volga hosts 200 tributaries, mostly from the west, and its basin occupies 1,360,000 square km, covering about one third of the former USSR's space. This ranges from the dense, temperate rainforest regions at its source to hot, dry semi-desert in the south. It remains frozen for four months every year. In former times passengers used to remove their hats as the train crossed 'Mother Volga'.

Syzran is an industrial centre specialising in petrol extraction and refining, oil being brought in from the two major fields near Stavropol. Locomotives, prefabricated homes and other goods, including shoes, are made here.

During the Great Patriotic War the city expanded very fast, growing some 15km to the south and 30km to the east, but its origins are fairly humble – it was originally founded in 1684 as a Rus military settlement. In fact the reason for Syzran's size is its oil, which was first exploited in 1936, explaining the boomtown era during the war. You can see the oil refineries on the horizon (R) as you cross the river.

Km1050: Chapaevsk On the Chapaevsk River, this town is noted for its chemical plants, which specialise in the production of explosives. Originally it was named Ivanschenkovo, although it was called Trotsk between 1919-27 (no prizes for guessing which revolutionary leader it was named after).

Km1090: Samara The city was founded in 1586 as a Muscovite stronghold and then fortified in 1591, only to be demolished by the Mongols in 1615. It was renamed Kuibyshev during the Soviet period, after the revolutionary politician and economist. Its main claim to fame derives from a brief period during the Great Patriotic War (1941-3), when it became the seat of Soviet power while the Germans threatened Moscow. Lenin would probably have approved of the move: having been expelled from Kazan, he moved to Samara University, where he graduated in law with a set of straight firsts in 1891.

The city is a major industrial centre; oil from the huge Pokhvistnevo and Zhiguli fields nearby is brought in by pipeline and refined here, and main products include aircraft, locomotives, ballbearings and movie projectors.

Km1190: Neprik East of this station the train moves into Orenburgskaya oblast (formerly Chkalov). Lying in the southern foothills of the Urals, this area is drained by the Ural, Samara (Kuibyshev), Greater Kinel and Ilek rivers and boasts a humid continental and steppe climate; you should be starting to notice the temperature rising by now. The soil is rich in minerals including copper, jasper, limestone, oil and gold.

Km1518: Orenburg This large city is the northern terminus of the Trans-Caspian railway and the centre of Orenburgskaya oblast. It was founded in 1735 on the site of present day Orsk and then moved here in 1743 (this site was originally a Russian stronghold called Berda). It was a major caravan centre on the route from Central Asia, although it suffered at the hands of rebel leader Yemelyan Pugachev in 1773. Real

Pugachev
Yemelyan Ivanovich Pugachev (1726-75) was the leader of a major Cossack uprising. Having returned injured to Russia from campaigns abroad, he began to hear rumours of the 1772 Cossack rebellion and of its cruel suppression. He immediately started to rally troops, and was promptly arrested and sentenced to be deported to Siberia. Having escaped, he claimed that he was Emperor Peter III (who had actually been deposed by Catherine the Great and then murdered) and demanded both birthright and the abolition of serfdom. The latter request made him very popular with the peasants, and he soon found himself at the head of an army. He stormed Orenburg in 1773, whereupon wealthy landowners in the vicinity fled to Moscow with stories of revolution; Catherine realised the gravity of the situation and despatched armies. After a protracted campaign Pugachev's forces were beaten at Volgograd. He escaped but was later betrayed by his accomplices, taken to Moscow and executed.

development started with the arrival of the railway in 1905 and soon after it was renamed after the Soviet aviator Valeri Chkalov. The city recovered its original name only recently.

The Ural River – the Europe/Asia border After the train leaves Orenburg (heading south) it crosses the Ural River (Orenburg is on the right bank). The Ural rises in the southern Ural mountains, flows 2500km to the Caspian Sea and is considered to be the border between Europe and Asia. From here the views from the train really begin to open up: great open spaces and huge skies. Trees still line the track, making the journey especially attractive in autumn.

Km1541: The train comes to a small river, and then, on the right, is what appears to be a lone piece of heavy artillery.

Km1687: Kos Aral Just after the town is an Islamic graveyard (R), which is worth looking out for. You will see plenty of these across the CIS: small groups of white buildings, occasionally with white domes, often apparently in the middle of nowhere.

KAZAKHSTAN

MAP 4

Km1690: Kazakhstan border Immediately south of Kos Aral the train crosses the border into Kazakhstan and you are most emphatically in Central Asia. There are currently no customs procedures but things may change. The **time zone is now GMT+5** (ie two hours ahead of Moscow time).

You are now in Aktyubinsk oblast, which is the region north of the Aral Sea. It comprises desert in the east and steppes in the west, and its soil is particularly rich in mineral resources including phosphates, oil and half the nickel reserves of the former USSR. The oblast is divided by the Irghiz and Emba rivers.

Km1737: Karatogai A remnant of Soviet rule, the sign (R) here reads 'Slava Trudu' – 'Praise work'.

Km1784: Aktyubinsk The centre of Aktyubinsk oblast, on the Ilek River. You are now 1610km west of Almaty.

Aktyubinsk lies at the heart of the Central Asian chemical extraction industry and specialises in nitrogen-based fertilisers. Architecture here is particularly uninspiring: occasionally the architect concerned has made a bold statement by placing blocks of flats at right angles to one another instead of adjacent. Testament to the industry are all the chemical-carrying wagons with the names of their contents crudely stencilled on the sides. Still, it's an excellent place to buy lunch, as there are a couple of good food stalls on the platform.

Km1880: Kandagach Junction for the lines to Tashkent and Almaty (below), and Urgench (turn to p275).

Drinking the water from the fountain on the platform here is not advised.

Kandagach to Tashkent

It takes 18-20 hours from Kandagach to Tashkent, a journey of 1498km.

Km2293: Sariulek Heading south-east, this is the first town in Kyzil-Ordinskaya oblast.

Km2370: Aralskoe More This city, also known as Aralsk, was once situated on the northern tip of the Aral Sea. This is now a major ecological disaster area (see p278).

Km2562: Bai Kozha To the east of this city the line curves around to the north as it skirts one of the former USSR's most mysterious non-towns. When Yuri Gagarin, the first ever human cosmonaut, made his maiden space flight on 12 April 1961 the Cold War was in full swing. The Soviets, unwilling to announce the location of the nucleus of their space programme, registered Vostok I's launch point as Baikonur in northern Kazakhstan. In fact, simple flight pattern prediction and subsequent surveillance indicated that Gagarin had been fired into space from a point on the Syr Darya River, some 300km to the south-west of Baikonur.

MAP 4A

MAP 4B

Бостандык
BOSTANDIK

Тюратам
TYURATAM

Белтакыр
BELTAKIR

Хор-Хут
KOR-KUT

Джусалы
DZHUSALI

Кизил-Там
KIZIL-TAM

Кара-Кеткен
KARA-KETKEN

Джалагаш
DZHALAGASH

Айтек
AITEK

Кара-Узяк
KARA-UZYAK

КЗЫЛ-ОРДА
KZIL-ORDA

Берказань
BERKAZAN

Керкелмес
KERKELMES

Тартугай
TARTUGAI

Коскаракум
KOSKARAKUM

Чиили
CHILI

Тюмень-Арбык
TYUMEN-ARIK

Яны-Курган
YANI-KURGAN

Аккум
AKKUM

Талап
TALAP

Беш-Арык
BESH-ARIK

Сауран
SAURAN

Туркестан
TURKESTAN

Куншагыр
KUNSHAGIR

Утрабат
UTRABAT

Акшокат
AKSHOKAT

Тимур (TIMUR)

Кара-Кунгур
KARA-KUNGUR

Акдала (AKDALA)

Арысь I (ARISI)

KYZIL ORDINSKAYA OBLAST

Syr Darya River

CHIMKENTSKAYA OBLAST

This point, just outside a city imaginatively named Leninsk, was the site of the vast majority of the USSR's space research.

Soviet planners claimed that this little discrepancy was hardly significant in real terms, as Baikonur is only 300km away from Leninsk (after all, what's a few hundred kilometres in a galaxy 100,000 light years across?). Western experts, however, held that in space research this was a significant distance and noted that Gagarin's rocket didn't even get 300km above the earth. The end of the Cold War has put a stop to this argument, leaving a rather embarrassing lie to be covered up: the space station at Leninsk is now officially called Baikonur.

Since Gagarin's 143,300km per hour, 89 minute jaunt, all subsequent rockets have been launched from here. Gagarin was declared a Hero of the Soviet Union and was turned into the Communist Party's media darling. He enjoyed fanatical popularity until his death in an air-crash in 1968.

Km2818: Kyzil Orda This is the capital of Kyzil Ordinskaya oblast.

Km3095: Turkestan This 10th century city was the home of the 12th century Islamic poet Khoja Akhmed Yassafi. Yassafi's mausoleum was built by Tamerlane in the 14th century at great expense; it incorporates what is reputed to be the largest intact dome in central Asia.

Km3205: Aris I Rail junction for the lines to Tashkent and Almaty (see p283). For the route map from Aris I to Tashkent see p282.

UZBEKISTAN

Km3338: Kazakhstan-Uzbekistan border The time zone remains the same (GMT + 6 = Moscow time + 3).

Km3378: Tashkent See p153.

Kandagach to Urgench

From Kandagach to Urgench is a journey of 1061km, which takes about 25 hours. Note that owing to cutbacks in the rail services of Russia and Uzbekistan, through trains from Moscow to Urgench run irregularly and are currently subject to revue.

Km0: Kandagach Note that at this station the kilometre markers reset themselves from km1880 back to km0.

Shortly after the station the train crosses the Ilek River, which winds its way 530km into the Ural.

Km21(R): There's an Islamic graveyard to the west (R) of the line. In this region, and from here on, it is possible to see the occasional Kazakh herdsman herding his goats or fat-tailed sheep across the steppe. You may even see the odd camel or two, or a yurt.

Km61: Kalmikargan By now, things are looking fairly desolate. The land is generally flat and peppered with coarse grass, and everything starts to look much more like a desert.

It is worth reflecting, as you cross all this bar-ren wasteland in comfort, on the lot of Bekovitch Cherkassky (see p125), who marched through this near-wilderness on his way to Khiva in 1717, only to be slaughtered along with his entire army when he eventually made it. Stations, you may notice, become less frequent as the landscape becomes progressively more barren.

MAP 5

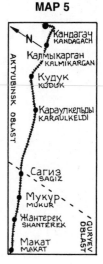

Km255: Sagiz This town marks the border of Guryev oblast, which holds the Emba oilfield – one of the largest in the CIS. It also has substantial natural gas reserves: small wonder the major oil companies are itching to get into the CIS.

Km375: Makat The train makes a 180° turn here as it veers sharply to the south. Note that kilometre markers are on the east side of the line (left if you're travelling south) after this.

The line crosses into Mangyschlakskaya oblast and passes through **Beinu** (km660).

MAP 6

Emba River
Кульсары
KULSARI

Опорная
OPORNAYA

KAZAKHSTAN

GURYEV OBLAST

N

Беинеу
BEINU

Каракалпакия
KARAKAL

Бостан
BOSTAN

Жаслык
SHASLIK

UZBEKISTAN
KARAL KALPAKIR
ASSR

Куаниж
KUANISH

Кырккыз
KIRKKIZ

ARAL
SEA

Раушан
RAUSHAN

TURKMENISTAN

Кунград
KUNGRAD
Алтинкул
ALTINKUL
Хатеп
KATEP
Тахиаташ
TAKIATASH
Лавак
LAVAK

Amu Darya R.

Ташауз
TASHAUZ

Ургенч
URGENCH

UZBEKISTAN

Km762/860: Kazakhstan-Uzbekistan border

The line enters Uzbekistan for the first time (here again there are currently no formal border procedures). The time zone remains GMT+5. From here, kilometre markers count down from km860.

You may have noticed that the horizon (R) appears to be getting lighter in colour. This is not a mirage, although you may see them here; in fact the white is caused by salt deposits left when the sea, which once covered the whole area, evaporated. It becomes more obvious as you travel on. In fact the earth is so salty along the Khiva oasis that fields have to be flooded with fresh water twice every year to wash them. While the land keeps producing, life downstream slowly gets more saline and poisonous. The 'inland sea' deposits become really obvious by km685, where the train is quite clearly skirting around a salty depression (L), with banks rising above it (R). The line gets a little greener from here on, with small bushes making an appearance; these are called *saksau* and produce purple flowers in the autumn.

Km627: Kungrad
The central town of the Karal Kalpakir Autonomous SSR, in the Amu Darya River delta. Huge amounts of fruit are sold here, particularly melons. The station is usually swarming with food sellers and the nearby river means that fish are available, making this is a good place to try *solenaya riba* (snake fish, see p161).

From here the track runs parallel to the Amu Darya River until Chardzhou (see p279). The Amu Darya is the Oxus of which the 19th century poet Matthew Arnold wrote:

> 'Oxus, forgetting the bright speed he had
> In his high mountain cradle in Pamere,
> A foiled circuitous wanderer – till at last
> The longed-for dash of waves is heard, and wide
> His luminous home of waters opens, bright
> And tranquil, from whose floor the new-bathed stars
> Emerge, and shine upon the Aral Sea'.

Km521: Takiatash This small town is the starting point for the Turkmen Canal which irrigates the cotton fields of the Karakum Desert. It is one of several canals (the Karakum Canal being the longest) which have diverted the waters of the Amu Darya from the Aral Sea with disastrous results (see p278).

TURKMENISTAN

Km506: Uzbekistan-Turkmenistan border For a brief spell (about 100km) the line crosses Tashauz oblast in Turkmenistan. There are no border controls and you probably won't notice you're in a different country since the landscape looks exactly the same.

Turkmenistan

The 488,110 square kilometres encompassed by Turkmenistan's borders comprise mostly the Karakum ('Black Sands') Desert, which stretches between the Caspian Sea and the Amu Darya River, bordering Iran and Afghanistan to the south.

Turkmenistan's inhabitants were traditionally termed Turkomen (although this name has been used of virtually all Central Asians at one time or another) and were particularly renowned for their fine horsemanship. They were subjugated by the Russians in 1881, however, and in 1924 the Turkmenia SSR was established.

Sovereignty was declared by premier Sapurmarad Niyazov in August 1990 and although the country is relatively sparsely populated (about 4.4 million people altogether, averaging out to 9 per square kilometre of land) it could well have a bright future, being phenomenally rich in oil and natural gas. Authority previously emanated from the 175 seat Supreme Soviet but this was replaced recently by the 50 seat Majilis.

The country's capital is Ashkabad and it is from here that the president organises periodic referenda and elections. Presumably he does this for his own personal amusement because the chances of his losing are negligible: his party, the Democratic Party, is the only political group allowed to stand. Results are correspondingly impressive: in 1992 Niyazov won 99.5% of the votes. Not satisfied with that, he did better on the next showing: in 1994 he voted himself back into office (until at least 2002) with a majority of 99.99%.

Km463: Tashauz The capital city of the oblast is a major cotton producing centre.

UZBEKISTAN

Km400: Urgench See p122. This is the stopping point for those visiting the historic walled city of Khiva (see p124).

The tragedy of the Aral Sea
In 1918 a Soviet decree authorised massive irrigation projects in Kazakhstan and Uzbekistan: water from the two main rivers, the Amu and Syr Darya, was to be diverted in order to transform vast areas of semi-desert into cotton fields. The theft of the rivers' water (55 cubic kilometres per year) left the Aral Sea in a vulnerable position and it has been shrinking ever since.

From 1973 to 1989 the sea lost a volume of water equivalent to 11 times the size of Lake Erie. Since 1960 some 40% of its surface area has evaporated, leaving 17,500 square kilometres of former seabed dry. Fishing ports on the Aral Sea's shores used to account for 10-15% of the Soviet Union's catch; now the water is too salty to support any marine life at all and the cities are abandoned, miles from any water supply. Ships lie up to 40km from the water's edge like great beached whales.

Perhaps more worrying are the 43 million tonnes of sand, salt and poisonous residues swept up from this man-made desert by the wind and dispersed annually. Throat cancer in local cities has risen by 500%. Nothing can grow in the area now and problems are accentuated by the effect of the sea's gradual disappearance on the climate: summers get hotter and winters colder; sand-storms are common. Traces of chemicals known to have been used on cotton crops here, including banned defoliants and pesticides (DDT is still used) have been found as far away as the Arctic.

Urgench to Bukhara

It takes 9-10hrs to cover the 520km between Urgench and Bukhara.

The line south of Urgench continues along parallel to the Amu Darya for the next 400km, until Chardzhou.

Km345: Uzbekistan-Turkmenistan border South of the rather insignificant town of Pitnyak (km350) the line crosses the Uzbek border into Turkmenistan again.

TURKMENISTAN

Km167(L) The Amu Darya River comes into view here, skirting in and out of sight for some time. As might be expected, the land around it is very fertile, and there are even some paddy fields.

You are now more or less in the centre of the Karakum and Kizylkum Deserts (the river constitutes the border between the two). Altogether the Amu Darya flows 1400km, making it the major river of Central Asia.

Km77 The large natural gas plants here are a testimony to the natural resources of the region.

Km58: Denev Lush green fields (courtesy of
Amu Darya irrigation, of course) surround this
town. Note that the kilometre markers change sides
for a while from here and are now on the left (east)
side of the line.

Km11 There is a large radar installation here (R).
It is probably unwise to photograph this. Kilometre
markers shift back to the right hand side (west).

Km0/4089: Chardzhou This is Turkmenistan's
second city after Ashkabad. After the city the train
crosses the two forks of the Amu Darya for the last
time and heads back towards Uzbekistan.

Km4069: Turkmenistan-Uzbekistan border
After passing through the small town of Farab
(km4082) the line crosses the border back into
Uzbekistan here.

UZBEKISTAN

Km4050: Alat Just east of this town the track
crosses the Zeravshan River. This rises in a glacier
in the Altai Mountains and then heads west into
Tajikistan and Uzbekistan, fizzling out in the
desert just short of the Amu Darya, near
Chardzhou. The valley around it is noted for its
early civilisations. Alexander the Great's men
knew the river as Polytinetus, meaning 'very pre-
cious', partly because water is an extremely valuable commodity in the desert but more specifically
because its bed was rich in gold. Its current name,
Zeravshan, means 'gold scattering river'.

Km4040: Karakul The town is not particularly
interesting itself but its name is: Karakul sheep are
the main livestock here and across Central Asia
generally. They are produced for their black wool
which is thin, tightly curled and glossy if taken
from young lambs. The demand for luxury pelts
means that lambs are slaughtered as young as possible, sometimes before they are even born.

Km3969: Bukhara I (Kagan) See p133.

MAPS 7 & 8

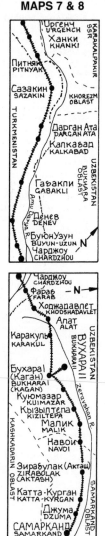

Stoddart, Connolly and the Great Game
In the early 19th century Russia began to toy with the idea of despatching troops south towards British India. Napoleon had made tenuous plans for a Russo-French alliance that would march through Persia and Afghanistan to wrest the Indian jewel from the British. While this specific threat never actually materialised, it gave the British a nasty shock and hammered home the fact that they knew very little of the territory north of the Karakoram and Pamir Mountains. How real was the Russian threat? Modern historians suggest that a Russian invasion of India was never a realistic option but, as Peter Hopkirk points out in *The Great Game*, in the course of 200 years the Russians closed the gap of no-man's land between theirs and the British Empire from some 2000 miles to as few as 20 in places.

Thus began the Great Game, a battle of espionage and intrigue played out across the deserts and mountains of Central Asia. While the Russians sent agents to prepare the way south and armies to travel it, the British sent spies to chart the territory, assess the risks and to attempt to forge allegiances with the local rulers. The spies themselves were generally young officers of exceptional bravery and linguistic ability. They travelled undercover for months disguised as holy men or traders, sure in the knowledge that if they were discovered they would die gruesome deaths. Some did.

Two great gamesters stand out as particularly notable for those visiting Bukhara: Colonel Charles Stoddart and Captain Arthur Connolly. Stoddart had been despatched to Bukhara in 1839 in order to foster good relations with the emir, the legendarily cruel Nasrullah. Nasrullah had not been at all impressed with the English officer, however, and had him incarcerated in the *zindan* (see p138). After the best part of three years as a prisoner his spirits must have received a great boost with the arrival of another emissary, Connolly, who had come by with the intention of persuading the emir to free his fellow officer. Unfortunately Connolly, as he had been warned by other local rulers, was thrown into jail too, and following the catastrophic British defeat in Afghanistan in 1842, Nasrullah had them both publicly executed.

Bukhara to Samarkand

Bukhara to Samarkand is 171km, a journey of about five hours.

Km3893: Navoi East of this city, named after the Afghan writer (see p159), the line crosses Samarkand oblast – all 19,800 square kilometres of it. At the heart of this is the Zeravshan River, along which the railway line passes, and which ensures irrigation for the extensive orchards and cotton fields. This oblast was formed in 1938 after the earlier, larger oblast of the same name was abolished in 1926.

Km3799: Katta Kurgan A large body of water appears at this town (R); this is the Katta Kurgan storage reservoir, known as the Uzbek Sea.

It was built to be fed by a canal from the Zeravshan River, and completed in 1948. The Kara Darya (L), is the Zeravshan's northern arm.

Km3722: Samarkand See p143 for details of the most celebrated Central Asian city of them all.

Samarkand to Tashkent

Samarkand to Tashkent is 335km, a journey of 7-8 hours.

Km3713 East of Samarkand the train leaves the Zeravshan River and heads through cotton fields, rich on the river's water.

Km3635: Gallya Aral A dusty industrial town, originally called Milyutinskaya. The land begins to get more hilly around this area and views become progressively more impressive until the line passes between narrow, steep cliffs. This is a canyon between the Nuratov Mountains (L), and the Turkestan Mountains (R). At km3624 the views are spectacular, with eagles soaring the thermals above the rocks on either side.

Km3609 The huge power station (R) is part of Dzhizak. Taken by the Russians in 1866, this town was a major caravan trading centre until the turn of the century when it declined with the arrival of the railway. Once the train has left the outskirts the landscape becomes flat again, peppered with coarse grass and the occasional hill in the distance.

Km3551: Ulyanovo One of a number of 'Ulyanovo's; perhaps the name has changed by now. The town is utterly nondescript and its only claim to fame is that it is about as close to Tajikistan as you are going to get on this leg of your journey (about 15km). It is also the last town before passing into Sirdarin oblast.

Km3487: Gulistan This station is the first within the eastern Uzbekistan time zone. **Local time is now GMT+6**.

Km3449: Sirdarinskaya This city was named Syr Novorossiysk until 1947 and is situated on the banks of the Syr Darya – the other great Central Asian river. Syr Darya (Jaxartes to the ancients) is formed by the junction of the Naryn and Kara Darya Rivers in the Ferghana Valley and flows west through Tajikistan. It then heads north back into Uzbekistan at Farkhad and from there it passes through a massive hydro-electric dam into Kazakhstan, forming the eastern and northern boundaries of the Kyzilkum Desert. It also marks the border of Tashkent oblast, which encompasses some 9500 square km. This area thrives on agriculture thanks to its water. The main crop is cotton but rice, wheat and various fruits are also grown. The railway arrived in Tashkent in 1898 and now bisects the oblast from north to south.

Km3421: Almazar Vast quantities of water provided by the Syr Darya make irrigation easy, hence this area produces consistently good harvests. The Almazar region's speciality is fruit, and here the train passes through some attractive apple orchards. It's picturesque in spring when the trees are in blossom. Just out of sight (L), is the vast Aydingkul Lake.

Km3378: Tashkent The Uzbek capital (see p153).

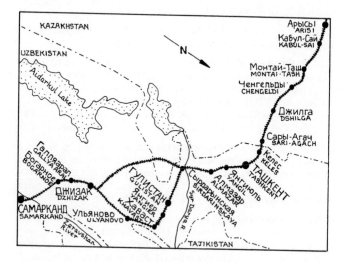

Tashkent to Almaty

Tashkent to Almaty is 908km, which takes about 20 hours.

After Tashkent you pass through **Keles** (km3341), a small wool-washing village, the last station before Kazakhstan.

KAZAKHSTAN

Km3338: Uzbekistan-Kazakhstan border You enter Chimkent-skaya oblast, Kazakhstan. Time zone stays the same (GMT+6 = Moscow time +3) because Kazakhstan is divided down the centre and you are now in the eastern half.

Km3291(L): Another sign like the one you may have seen at Km1737. It still means 'Praise Work'. From here the horizon becomes progressively flatter and bleaker, very dusty.

Km3205: Aris I As the train pulls away keep an eye out for the two old steam locomotives (L) facing each other, abandoned.

Km3202: Aris II Really rather dreary; there's what looks like a breeze-block storage facility on the left as you leave. Note that the kilometre marker posts switch to the right hand side (south of the line) and start counting up as the train makes a sharp (120°) turn towards Chimkent.

Km3250: Chimkent This large city lies at the heart of Chimkentskaya oblast and is a major industrial centre. It was ruled by the Arabs in the 8th and 9th centuries, when it was named Isfidzhab and was an important caravan trading centre. The Mongols saw to it that nothing remained when they trooped through in the 13th century. The Russians arrived in 1864 and were responsible for the reconstruction of the place; now it thrives on metalworks, chemicals, lead refineries and fruit preserving factories. It is on the Aris River, a tributary of the Amu Darya.

Km3340: Tilkubas East of this station the train passes into Dzhambul oblast (formerly Aulie Ata). Drained by the Chu, Talas and Assa rivers and bounded to the south by Kirghizstan, the greater part of this area consists of dry clay steppe and sandy desert, although in the south it has been heavily irrigated. Industry revolves around the phosphorite mines scattered throughout the region.

KIRGHIZSTAN

East of the small town of **Surum** the train passes through Kyrgyzstan for about 20km. There are no border formalities.

MAP 10

Kyrgyzstan

This Central Asian republic covers just under 200,000 square kilometres and boasts a population of 4.5 million. Its capital is Bishkek (called Frunze, after Soviet general Mikhail Frunze, until 1991) and its official language is Kyrghiz. Along with Kazakhstan, Kyrgyzstan was the only other Central Asian state to denounce the 1991 Russian coup instantly and to pledge immediate support to Boris Yeltsin. It declared its independence on 12 December 1990 and is now run by President Askar Akayev.

Akayev has had some trouble with his market reforms, however: in a situation rather like Yeltsin's, he was soon faced with a parliament that was unwilling to do anything that he wanted them to. Thus, in 1994 he did as Yeltsin had done: abolished parliament and called for national elections. A new parliament was set up, comprising of a 35-member Legislative Assembly and a 70 member People's Assembly. This system seems to be working: in an effort to stop the rapid emigration of ethnic Russians from the country, Akayev has seen to it that, although the main language of the country becomes Kyrghiz, all business is conducted in Russian. He has also installed a pro-Russian employment policy in his civil service. These sensible actions have lessened the ethnic tension in a region where tolerance is really quite rare.

The train travels for about 20km through Kyrgyzstan before crossing back into Kazakhstan.

KAZAKHSTAN

Km3530: Dzhambul Nothing much remains to remind the visitor that this was once a major Silk Road stop. It has been occupied since at least the 5th century AD when it was known as Taraz and, of course, was taken by the Arabs in the late 8th century. It was later renamed Yani, and then Aulie Ata by the local Kazakhs. It fell to the Russians in 1864 and they called it Mirzoyan. There is little to see here apart from the Talas River, which the train crosses immediately after leaving the city.

Km3765: Chu A small city, thriving on its cotton, metal and sugar industries. The line crosses the Chu River immediately north of Chu; this river rises in the desert and flows 950 kilometres into the huge salt lake Issy Kul in Kirghizstan. It is used as a major source of hydro-electric power and irrigation.

Km3840: Kulakshino As you head north-east the soil becomes progressively redder whilst the horizon becomes more mountainous. This is a sign that the train is approaching the foothills of the Tien Shan (see p286).

Km3895 After Otar station the line crosses into Almaty oblast, which measures 67,000 square km and incorporates a hefty stretch of the Kazakh-Chinese border. It ranges from mountains in the south to desert in the north-west. There is extensive agriculture among the foothills of the Tien Shan, particularly fruit (Almaty means 'Father of Apples').

Km 3941(R) More salt deposits indicate that this area was once covered with water.

Km4030/1656: Almaty All change here for China. See p163.

Almaty to Urumqi

It takes approximately 36 hours, including the border crossing, to cover the 1230km on this section.

Km1585: Kapchagay This nondescript town is situated on the large Kapchagay Lake. This is fed by the Ili River, which flows from the Tien Shan Mountains directly westwards (it also flows east from this range into China) to Lake Balkhash, for which it provides 75% of the water. The line crosses the river north-east of Kapchagay station.

Km1445: Aynabulak North of this town you cross the tributaries of the Karatal River, which rises in the Tien Shan to the east and, like the Ili, flows into Lake Balkhash. The line crosses the main branch of the Karatal just south of **Ushtobe** station. Ushtobe makes the most of its proximity to this river by irrigation schemes: water is so copious here that the main crop is rice.

Km1270: Aksu River This river also rises in the Tien Shan and flows into Lake Balkhash. The station just to the north of it is **Matay**.

Km1231: Lepsy River As the train approaches Lake Balkhash rivers abound; this one is 340km long and is, once again, formed in the Dzungarian Ala Tau (Tien Shan). Crossing the river you reach the town of **Lepsy** (km1227). Chinese characters make their first appearance on the station sign here.

MAP 11

Km1217(L): Keep an eye out for **Lake Balkhash**. You are now 160km west of the Chinese border and 960km east of the Aral Sea.

Balkhash itself is 603km long and between 24km and 89km wide, although this changes considerably with varying rainfall. Thus its area has been recorded as between 9660 and 11,750 square km. These fluctuations are accompanied by appropriate changes in depth of up to three metres.

The lake is interesting in that the western half is fresh and the eastern half salty. There seems to be little doubt that the lake was once completely saline and considerably bigger than it is today, covering the areas to the east and the west which are both now deserts. Similarities in wildlife indicate that as recently as 200 to 300 years ago Balkhash was joined to Alakul and Sasykul to the east (the line passes by them – see p287), and scientists believe that it once reached right up through the Dzungarian Gate, through which the train line now passes, linking up with lakes on the other side to form a vast sea which filled the Turfan Depression (Aydingkul Lake – see p194 – may be the last remnant of this).

Wildlife abounds both in and around Lake Balkhash; although only six species of fish are native to its waters, another fourteen have been introduced and now it is one of the major fisheries in the CIS. This fish cultivation does not reach as far as the Ili River delta, which is renowned for being shark infested. Other wildlife includes pelicans, wolves and wild boars. The last wild tiger here was killed in the 1940s.

The Tien Shan

The Tien Shan (Heavenly Mountains) range is vast. Stretching some 3000km across and up to 480km wide, it covers an area of nearly a million square kilometres, approximately six times the size of the UK. It is bounded to the north by both the Kazakh and Dzungarian plains (the train skirts around the south side of these), and to the south by the deep Tarim Basin.

Its highest peaks (the tallest is Pobeda – 'Victory' – at 7322m/24,406ft) are generally along the Kazakh-China border, whilst its lowest point is the surface of the Aydingkul Lake, at 156m/516ft below sea level. This means that there is a variation in contour, ie vertically up and down, of over 7 km, which is 23.3 times the height of the Eiffel Tower, or equivalent to 70,000 Mars Bars stacked one on top of the other. The mountains' importance for the towns on either side is immense: snows melting on the peaks (there are some 4000 miles of glaciers here) produce the water which flows down to create the oases that make life possible. The Tien Shan range was formed in the Late Palaeozoic era (225-570 million years ago) but major movement is still occurring, and shifts of the earth's crust along fault lines here regularly cause major earthquakes (Almaty 1887, Kashgar 1902 etc).

Animals at home in the Tien Shan include wolf, fox, the rare snow leopard (do not buy pelts when you see them for sale), wild boar and bear.

Km1137: Aktogay This town was once a sleepy little place known only for breeding sheep and camels. Now it provides the main rail junction for those heading east to China. It's also the junction of the Turk-Sib line which links Aktogay with the Siberian city of Novosibirsk.

From here the train makes a 180° turn so that the kilometre markers restart at km0 on the opposite side of the line. Between here and the next stop, **Koktuma**, the landscape changes; you are now heading south-east directly into the foot-hills (R) of the Tien Shan. If there has been heavy rain in the mountains, the large Sasykul lake might just be visible (L).

Km143: Beskol The sign (R) here says 'We wish bon voyage to all travellers on the international Almaty to Urumqi train'.

Km170(L): Alakul Lake Covering 1500 square km, this salt-water lake was presumably once part of Lake Balkhash. It is over 45m deep in places (twice as deep as any point in Balkhash, which is usually no deeper than 6m). The train passes by it for some 90km. East of **Koktuma** the lake slips out of sight on the left and the mountains (R) sweep in closer.

Km266(L) The wire fence marks the **Kazakh-Chinese border** as the train approaches the Dzungarian Gate.

Crossing the border

There are numerous horror stories about customs on this crossing, although most relate to the crossing from China into Kazakhstan: the guards, it seems, particularly enjoy rifling through Westerners' luggage, removing any low value items that may take their fancy (T-shirts, alcohol, cigarette lighters etc). If you are worried about this, you might want to try poking a couple of packets of Western cigarettes into your bag as decoys; at least then you won't have lost anything valuable. Fines levied (ie for overweight baggage) may have to be paid even if they are blatantly unfair though friendly bargaining might work, as long as you keep your cool. Customs officers tried to charge two travellers from Hong Kong US$60 for overweight luggage, even though the combined weight of both of their bags was less than 20kg. They managed to bargain this down to US$10 in the end.

Smuggling is rampant on the train: everyone, it seems, is bringing something into China illegally. Watches, jewellery and electrical goods are all popular, and most passengers will be carrying a few extras for the black market. Do not be surprised to hear puppies yapping all the way to Urumqi, as many carriage attendants increase their earnings by smuggling them out of Kazakhstan under their beds. Alongside the harmless contraband, more serious items may be changing hands, too: a Siberian I met was selling a couple of infra-red night sights he had 'borrowed' from the Red Army during his military service. He managed to offload one of them on the train and, in doing so, made four months' wages for himself in twenty minutes. You'd be remarkably foolish to try to smuggle anything at all across this border: although searches of foreigners are often little more than cursory, you can guarantee that if you get caught there will be serious trouble. Other passengers are likely to encourage you to put their stuff in your bags. Don't.

MAP 12

Km304: Druzhba: Kazakh border town

Bogie changing Since the rails in the CIS and China are of different gauges bogies must be changed at borders. Passports are collected and most passengers get off while the carriages are raised on hydraulic lifts. You can stay on board but be warned that the toilets will be locked throughout the process, which can take a couple of hours. It is possible to climb down onto the track to take photographs, although if the station hands see you, they'll probably give you an earful. Leave someone you trust holding the door open or it might be locked while you are outside the train, and don't go far away.

Kazakh customs and immigration While the bogie changing process is taking place Kazakh customs officials search berths at random. If they see foreigners the chances are that they will search their luggage, sometimes removing a couple of items for personal use. You must fill out a Kazakh customs form to prove that you are leaving the country. Make sure that you get your passport back at the same time as the others in your carriage.

There is a **foreign exchange counter** at this station but don't worry if you miss it, as you will have no problems changing money on arrival at Urumqi.

CHINA

Km2350: Alashenko: Chinese border

Customs and immigration Twelve kilometres on from Druzhba is Alashenko, where you will be required to handle the entry side of customs and immigration. There are two forms to fill in here: the first is a **health declaration** and you may also be asked for a health certificate. What the Chinese would really like is a document proving that you are healthy and don't have AIDS but since Europeans have no such document they tend to get confused. Any medical-type certificate will do (inoculation certificates are fine), because in fact no-one appears to be able to read English at all.

You will also have to fill in a **customs declaration form** noting any valuable items that you may be carrying (see p52). Make sure that you keep your copy of this in a safe place.

The customs building at Alashenko looks like a cross between a Holiday Inn and a night-club, and opinions vary with regard to treatment here: in summer 1992 the place was rather like Toytown, manned by young, excited guards with fresh faces and new, over-sized uniforms. Searches were not at all thorough and when they did find anything amiss (a large lady with a cache of watches from Moscow in my compartment, for example) they laughed it off and moved on. Things are different now and there's a less relaxed attitude, with foreigners' luggage being very thoroughly searched.

The train spends about two hours at Alashenko. Kilometre markers count down from here.

Continuing east you pass Ebinhur Hu (L). This lake is smaller than Koktuma but at 64 km by 24 km it is still fairly sizeable. It was originally, of course, part of Lake Balkhash.

You're now travelling through **Xinjiang province**, China's largest political unit. The area has been under Chinese rule periodically since the 3rd century BC. Its name reflects the fact that it was considered a late addition to the empire, meaning literally 'New Dominion'. It is vast, accounting for at least one sixth of China's entire landmass: some 1,646,700 square kilometres in all. The UK, whose population is six times greater, would fit into Xinjiang 11 times.

The province is so sparsely populated because of its geographical layout: Xinjiang is bordered by the Altai mountains to the north (forming the Mongolian border), the Pamirs to the west, and the Kunlun to the south. Within this semicircle lie two vast depressions separated from each other by the Tien Shan range, which runs from east to west. The northern depression is the Dzungarian Basin, which makes up 700,000 square km of near wilderness. To the south is the mighty Taklamakan Desert (see p160), almost exactly the same size but considerably more barren.

Xinjiang's layout of large open basins surrounded by mountains means that it becomes a furnace in the summer. The fact that it is so far inland ensures that rainfall is negligible; human life here is impossible outside the mountains' foothills and the oases which skirt the depressions. Only one of Xinjiang's rivers, the O'er Chi'ssu, reaches a sea at all.

The deserts are almost entirely bereft of life but the mountains and their highlands, some of which have never been explored by man, contain a great variety of wildlife, including wolves, bears, wild sheep, camels, yaks and leopards.

Km2066(R) Note the differences between the Chinese graveyard and the Kazakh/Uzbek ones you will have seen earlier on. The scenery has also changed now that you are on the Chinese side of the border: fields of cotton, sweetcorn and sunflowers tend to be in small strips, as opposed to the vast cultivated areas of the CIS. As you pass this way in the early morning it is common to see people doing their exercises (*tai chi*) beside the track, apparently miles from anywhere. If you are travelling in autumn every flat area in each of the villages you pass will be covered with corn and peppers left to dry in the sun. There are still good views of the Tien Shan to the right.

Km2014: Shihezi The high Tien Shan mountains on the right provide huge quantities of water, which forms streams and rivers that disappear into the Dzungarian basin to the north. Thus the train crosses a number of rivers on this stretch of the journey.

Km2000: Manas This city is situated on the Manas River, a tributary of the Telli Nor salt lake. There are a number of large oilwells nearby. Generally the buildings in this area are modern, but there are some old-style mud walled houses around.

Km1946: Hutube The centre of Hutube county, this city's specialities are cattle-raising, wheat, rye and fruit. It's also a leading gold town.

Km1895 Approaching Urumqi it is difficult not to notice the build up of industrial junk along the line: large factories belch fumes into the air here. Xinjiang contains many huge oilfields and at km1892 some of the storage facilities can be seen.

Once past these the approach is impressive as the train curls around to the right of the city. The landscape (R) heaves up and down violently in a series of valleys, falling away to the left to give a view of the very grey and smoggy-looking town. The mountains behind it constitute the Bogda Shan range. This stretch can be agonisingly slow as the train shudders along, labouring up the final hill to the station.

Km1872: Urumqi Welcome to China. See p171 for information about the town that 'no-one leaves with regret'.

Urumqi to Daheyan (Turfan)

Urumqi to Daheyan is 138km, which takes about three hours.

Km1839(R) There is a wind-power plant at this point (R). The landscape has become progressively less green, looking rather like grassy steppe-land. The Tien Shan still lies to the right and the Bogda Shan to the left (snowy peaks can be seen occasionally), and the ground is very rocky; the rail route had to be blasted through this area.

Km1827(R): Lake Caiwopu The large lake leads up to the town of the same name at km1817. Water flowing through the numerous irrigation channels here is heavily polluted with chemical fertiliser residues.

Km1785(L) The small green-domed mosque in the village here is a sign that you are in Xinjiang province and not Han China. The scenery is very impressive as the Tien Shan mountains reach up beside you, arching in all around the track. From this point the line actually passes through the range, making for an exciting ride. Views on both sides are outstanding, so try to get to a door that opens or a window that's not opaque. This is the most impressive scenery that you are likely to see from the train on any part of your trip east.

Km1734: Daheyan (Turfan) The hottest city in China. See p187.

Turfan to Liuyuan

It takes about 12 hours to cover the 688km from Turfan to Liuyuan.

After leaving Turfan the line arches slightly northeast, following the foothills of the Bogda Shan mountains, and there are vast tracts of literally nothing on either side. Some 270km to the south however, is Lop Nor. This salt lake has earned a certain notoriety for its ability to baffle explorers and geographers by apparently shifting its position from time to time. In 1876 the Russian explorer, Przewalski, noted that it was considerably to the east, and one whole degree south, of its recorded location, and that contrary to all reports its water was fresh. In doing so he launched a debate con-

MAP 13

cerning the lake's actual position that was to last 20 years. The solution came from Sven Hedin, arguably the greatest Central Asian explorer of them all. He proved that the streams of the Tarim water system empty into different areas, depending on climate and season. Thus in some years the lake was in one position and fresh, while in others it stood somewhere else altogether and was saturated with salt. Hardly surprising, then, that it has been dubbed the 'Wandering Lake'.

In fact Lop Nor has been drying up for some time now and all that remains of it is a small series of wandering pools surrounded by large areas of salty marshlands. These marshes support very little life, but in the course of the last 30 years they have become even more desolate owing to China's habit of detonating nuclear devices here. It's probably not worth visiting unless you fancy growing an extra head.

Km1324: Hami 480km east of Urumqi, Hami is renowned throughout China for the excellence of its fruit, particularly its melons.

It was here in 1905 that German archaeologist, Albert von Le Coq, was to make the worst decision of his professional career: whilst carrying out some rather disappointing research around the city he heard rumours of a massive find of manuscripts in a sealed grotto at Dunhuang. Naturally, he was extremely interested in this recent discovery and decided to pursue the opportunity immediately. Just before he was due to leave, however, a telegram arrived from his supervisor, Albert Grunwedel, announcing that he was on his way over from Germany, and that he expected to be met in Kashgar in six weeks time. Clearly von Le Coq did not have time both to visit Dunhuang and make the rendezvous. He recounts how he decided what to do: 'somewhat in despair, I left the decision to fate by tossing a Chinese dollar: heads win, tails lose! Tails, ie the inscription side, came uppermost, and so I had my horse saddled and began our journey to Kashgar'. In fact Grunwedel was seriously delayed and when he eventually did arrive the German contingent headed off to Kyzil. Two and a half years later Marc Aurel Stein followed up the Dunhuang rumours that von Le Coq had ignored and stumbled upon the richest haul of Oriental manuscripts in Central Asia (see p200).

Km1173: Wei Ya East of this small station the train passes into **Gansu province**, which reaches into the geographical heart of China. Measuring 616,000 square kilometres (5% of the country), it is bounded to the south by Shaanxi and Sichuan provinces and forms the wedge between Mongolia and Tibet (see p95 for Hexi Corridor). Gansu boasts a continental climate but its proximity to the Gobi Desert means that there is very little rain here. Originally the province was taken by the Chinese in the 2nd century BC (but the name Gansu dates from only the Yuan dynasty) and until 1911 it included the Xinjiang Autonomous Region to the west.

The province was at the heart of the Muslim uprisings in 1861-78 under Yakub Beg and as a consequence most of its cities were devastated by the Chinese when they regained control. The main industry in Gansu today is oil, centred around the Yumen oilfield, one of the world's biggest. Agriculture is important, too, as the Yellow River opens out through the province near Lanzhou, offering excellent irrigation opportunities. Eastern Gansu is the main earthquake zone in China, with minor movements every 10 years and major ones every 65. The last big one killed 250,000 people in 1920, so the next one is probably eight years overdue. Despite this threat, Gansu remains at the heart of China's nuclear industry.

Km1046: Liuyuan To get to the famous Mogao caves at Dunhuang, see p196.

Liuyuan to Jiayuguan

Liuyuan to Jiayuguan is 282km, which takes approximately five hours. This part of the rail journey sees the train entering the Gansu, or Hexi, Corridor, and thus you will see mountains gradually encroaching on either side. The ranges on the left are, respectively, the Mazong, Heli and Long Shoushan, while on the right there are the Tulai Nan Shan, Tulai Shan, Lenglong Lin and the Daban Shan. The Mongolian border is some 300km to the north; the 'corridor' itself is only 300km wide.

Km973: An Bei East of this station the line crosses the Shu Le River, which stretches across 483km from the Nan Shan mountains in northern Gansu to the salt lake Khara Nor near Dunhuang.

Km901: Shu Le He Presumably because Shu Le He is in a depression residents try to elevate their television aerials as much as possible, hence each house sports a long wooden pole with a heap of

MAP 14

electrical wiring at the top of it. East of this town the line crosses the Shu Le River again.

Km811: Yumen   The site of the famous Jade Gate (see p203) is itself looking a bit jaded these days. Since the discovery of the oilfield here in 1937 though, this city has been on a roll. The field has an estimated reserve of some 700 million barrels and the Yaer Xia field nearby has another 670 million tonnes waiting to be exploited.

Km768   Keep an eye out for Jiayuguan Fort (L), the western end of the Great Wall. This might make a good photograph from the train, despite the factories behind it.

Km764: Jiayuguan   If you want to explore what was traditionally the westernmost city in China, get off here. See p205 for more information.

Jiayuguan to Lanzhou

Jiayuguan to Lanzhou is 732km and takes about 18 hours.

Km740: Jiuquan   This was the first real stop inside the Wall after Jiayuguan for travellers heading east, and most Western visitors, including Marco Polo, seem to have spent some time here (the Polo family stayed here for a year). There isn't much to see from the train but there are some sights worth visiting here, notably some recently restored Buddhist caves.

Km670(L)   The vast expanse of sand dunes stretches on for at least another 30km before slipping over the horizon.

Km612: Gaotai   Just west of this station the train crosses the Hei River, which rises in the Nan Shan mountains to the south and flows more than 480km north-west to form the Etsin Gol lake. From here on the countryside gets greener and more hilly; note that this is still the Gansu Corridor, the easiest way to get from east to west.

Km295: Wuwei   This was another (possibly the) major stop for Silk Road travellers in the Gansu Corridor and, like Jiuquan, although there is little to see from the train there is a fair bit if you feel like stopping here. Wuwei was called Liangchow until 1913, and main industries today are wool and cotton weaving. In 1969 the famous 'flying horse' bronze sculpture, depicting a galloping steed, poised with one foot resting on the back of a swallow, was discovered here; it is now on display in the Gansu Provincial Museum in Lanzhou.

From Wuwei all the way to Lanzhou the line runs parallel to the Zhuanglang River and the remains of the Great Wall. Note the cave dwellings by the line on this stretch of your journey; about 1% of the Chinese population actually still lives in caves.

MAP 15

The Yellow River

This is China's second longest river, measuring 3011km from its source in Tibet all the way to the Yellow Sea. It drains an area of 745,000km and well over 100 million Chinese live in its basin. It is particularly prone to seasonal flooding and dykes have been built around its banks for thousands of years with varying degrees of success; in 1887 it burst its banks near Kaifeng and covered 48,000 square km. Two years later another flood injured over 1,000,000. The Chinese actually placed explosives charges on the banks in 1938 to slow the Japanese advance, causing the deaths of over 900,000 of those unfortunate enough to have built their homes in its path – all 34,000km of it.

The Yellow River is unusual for a number of reasons: firstly its course has changed substantially over the years, so much so that the point where it originally entered the Yellow Sea is now some 800km from the point where it does now. Second, it has a phenomenally high output (up to 48.2 cubic km of water every year), which is partly responsible for its tendency to flood. Finally the river is the world's muddiest, its waters being rich with the loess dust which is deposited all over China's plains, making them so fertile. Every cubic metre of water from this river contains 25kg of the silt and this figure can go up to 5400kg (ie 70% of the river by volume) when it is flooding. It is the presence of this silt which makes the river appear so murky, accounting for its name, Yellow.

Scenery is superb along this stretch. The countryside is lush and green, divided up in exactly the way that Westerners imagine Chinese fields ought to be – draped over obscure hilltops and cut into terraces along slopes to corner every useful millimetre of space. Farming these fields is still done manually and it is common to see families pulling wooden ploughs or women weeding by hand. The rolling landscape provides a wonderful backdrop.

Km37 Bridge over the Yellow River (Huang He).

Km11 From here the kilometre marker posts disappear, perhaps to conceal the fact that the Chinese timetable distances have been about 8km out all along.

Km1: Lanzhou Xi Lanzhou West station. If you're planning to stay at the Friendship Hotel in Lanzhou it's best to get off the train here.

Km0: Lanzhou The approach to this station is incredibly dreary. Train kilometre markers indicate that you have now come over 1872km from Urumqi and well over 2000km from the border. Here they reset themselves to km1745. For details of this city, and the spectacular Bingling Si caves nearby, see p211.

Lanzhou to Tianshui

It takes approximately 8 hours to cover the 343km between Lanzhou and Tianshui.

From Lanzhou to Xi'an the line runs parallel to the Wei River (R). This is the chief tributary of the Yellow River, rising in Gansu province and flowing some 870km from the Mawei Shan Mountains to join the Yellow River at Tung Kuan in Shaanxi province. Its valley is often cited as the cradle of Chinese civilisation.

Km1745: Leaving Lanzhou Kilometre markers begin with km1745, and this is the distance to Beijing, so the countdown starts here. Scenery once out of Lanzhou is very attractive: rolling green hills with farms dotted wherever possible and the Wei River slipping in and out of view from time to time, occasionally with steep cliffs on either side. Stations tend to alternate between either very attractive (eg Xianguanying, with its trees planted on the platform) or very ugly (Xu Jia Taia at km1705, which seems simply to be a huge pile of coal and rocks).

Km1669 At this point the train goes through the first major tunnel on this leg of the journey, the first of many, in fact. Each tunnel is some 400m long and construction dates are printed above their entrances. Generally these were blasted out in the early 1950s. Immediately afterwards note the especially dense agriculture on either side of the track; it would be tricky to find more than a couple of feet of earth here that isn't being used for something.

Km1665 The line passes an attractive gorge here. As you go through these hills there are some wonderful views, which rather make you appreciate how difficult it must have been to build this particular stretch of the railway. Hills on either side where cultivation appears to be even remotely possible look as if they have been peeled like fruit so as to create flat surfaces for crops to grow on. It seems the only things they haven't tried so far here are hanging baskets.

Km1553: Long Xi Keep an eye out for steam locomotives sitting around this station. As you leave, there's a small ornate pagoda (R).

Km1510: Wushan This is the largest town on the Lanzhou-Tianshui line and from here the scenery becomes very impressive. The Wei River valley is highly fertile, and in this region it opens out into a large, flat plain surrounded by hills. Agriculture is dense on both sides of the river and the fields are immaculately geometrical. The whole area is peppered with tunnels as the train skirts the river.

Km1402: Tianshui After the scenery along the way, the smoke-stacks and dust of Tianshui are rather depressing. Still, while the city itself is unattractive, the Maijishan Buddhist grottoes here are astonishing. See p220 for more information.

Tianshui to Xi'an

Tianshui to Xi'an is a distance of 323km, which takes 6-7 hours.

East of Tianshui the train crosses into Shaanxi province. This is a large area (195,800km) bordered by the Yellow River and Shanxi province to the east, Ningxia and Gansu provinces to the west, Inner Mongolia to the north, and Sichuan province to the south.

Shaanxi is the region which has probably been at the heart of China the longest. It was along the banks of the Wei River here that the distant ancestors of the modern Chinese originated, and the Chinese capital has often been here, at Xi'an. Yet Shaanxi seems to be particularly disaster-prone: it suffered particularly badly during the Muslim uprising of the mid-late 19th century, and although the ensuing Chinese clampdown was not as ruthless here as it was further west, some 600,000 were killed. This death toll was then pushed up considerably by a drought in the latter part of the rebellion; four to five million people died as a result of ineffectual relief work.

Following the end of the empire in 1911 there was more bloodshed as local lawlords fought each other; Shaanxi effectively fought a civil war, along with Gansu, and the climax of this was the siege of Xi'an in 1926. 100,000 died of starvation within the city walls. As if the people had not suffered enough, two years later there was another famine: three million died.

Shaanxi was at the heart of the Communists' anti-KMT struggle, its main centre being at Yan'an, from where both the civil war and the fight against the Japanese during World War II were conducted.

The province is divided into three geographical sections: the Wei River valley, the mountainous southlands, and the northern upland plateau. This journey hugs the Wei River all the way, producing some great views as the train passes in and out of the tunnel network through the cliffs on either side of the river. Scenery is particularly dramatic during the first half of the journey.

Km1324: Tuo Shi Although there have been a number of impressive tunnels before this station they multiply considerably after it and for a short period the train appears to spend as much time inside them as it does outside. While the views are spectacular, however, the tunnels complicate photography.

Km1316(R) The small footbridge over the Wei River at this point, with the high peaks in the background is good for a photo if you are quick enough.

Km1291 The scenery here is particularly attractive: there is a very beautiful island in the river (R), just a single green hill with a spectacular backdrop. From this point the number of tunnels and impressive views drops off sharply.

Km1251: Fu Lin Bao From here east, standard views on this journey alternate between flat, cultivated countryside and grotesque industrial developments. This is emphatically the case at this town, which could almost be a Russian city. Note the grotty blocks of flats (L) and the large communist monument with the huge red star on the top (R).

Km1247: Bao Ji Also unattractive, but you may want to look out for the three disused steam locomotives (L) as you leave. Once again, after this station the line passes through an industrial zone that is little more than storage space for rusting oil drums, piles of old steel and the occasional sooty factory, before reaching the countryside. The hills on either side have almost entirely faded away now, leaving very little to look at.

Km1100 The train crosses the Wei River, which is considerably bigger here than at earlier parts of this journey.

Km1082 The first glimpse of Xi'an. Peter Fleming, travelling in 1935, describes his initial view of the city from the train: 'It was very obvious that the Communist threat was being taken very seriously. Barbed wire entanglements surrounded not only the isolated station but the entire circumference of the city walls. The great gates had a strong guard on them and were kept ajar, so that not more than one person could enter or leave the city without a pass of some kind' (*News from Tartary*). While the barbed wire is gone now, the view cannot have changed much and the city walls are still the dominating feature here; note the large northern gate. The approach to the station itself skirts the northern side of the city and is distinctly dismal, passing some extremely squalid blocks of flats.

Km1079: Xi'an The discovery of the Terracotta Army here 20 years ago has transformed this ancient capital. For further information see p226.

Xi'an to Luoyang

Xi'an to Luoyang is a distance of 387km and takes 7-8 hours.

This is probably the least interesting part of the whole journey. There is next to nothing to see from the train and not much of any historical significance happened along the way, either. Scenery itself is pleasant enough but after a very short while it becomes monotonous and after this trip you may agree with Edgar Snow, who wrote that 'the farms of Shensi (Shaanxi) may be described as slanting... There are few genuine mountains, only endless broken hills, hills as interminable as a sentence by James Joyce, and even more tiresome'. (*Red Star over China*).

Km1040: Xin Feng Zhen There are a number of old steam locomotives in use here. East of this station the landscape becomes more hilly, with each hill often carved into huge terraces by the local farmers; presumably this is exactly the kind of landscape Snow was writing about.

Km966: Hua Xi'an The River Wei joins the Yellow River here and this station is the last one in Shaanxi province. You now enter Henan.

Henan is one of China's smaller provinces, measuring only 166,800 square km. The Yellow River divides it into two, about 80% being to its south, hence the province's name, meaning 'south of the river'. Henan was the home of one of the first Chinese dynasties, the Shang (c1600-1200BC) and it has been estimated that this culture moved its capital to Anyang in 1385BC. From then on Luoyang was pretty much the centre

of dynastic activity. It exchanged the role of capital periodically with Xi'an but never regained its lost status following the Mongol invasion in the 13th century, and has even been superseded as provincial capital by Zhengzhou, a modern industrial town which leapt to prominence because of its position at the junction of the main Chinese east-west and north-south railway lines.

Henan is one of the oldest silk manufacturing areas in China and it may even be that silk was invented here. Production has not always been easy, however: recent disruptions include the Japanese invasion (they held half the province) and recurrent plagues of locusts; in 1943 80% of all crops were destroyed.

Km914 The surroundings get progressively more rocky along this part of the journey and here the train starts passing through the hills instead of around them. There are a number of cave dwellings to be seen on either side.

Km834: Sanmenxia Xi (West) A pagoda and two small pavilions can be seen (R) as the train pulls away.

Km821: Sanmenxia The huge, bland blocks of flats give the city a rather Russian air. Sanmenxia was the cornerstone of the Staircase Plan in 1955, a vast undertaking designed to control the Yellow River once and for all. Forty-four major dams were to be built along the river's course, of which the largest was to be here, creating a reservoir which would hold 70 million cubic metres of water. It was due for completion in 1962 but after Russian assistance was withdrawn in 1961 it was abandoned.

Km692: Luoyang This city is the setting for one of China's most impressive cave complexes. See p237 for further information.

Luoyang to Beijing

Luoyang to Beijing is 792km, a journey of 11-12 hours.

This leg of the journey is more or less flat and stations become more numerous as you approach Beijing.

Km646(R) Note the two large stone horses, only a couple of metres from the track. Each is half buried and appears to be in excellent condition.

Km575: Zhengzhou Its strategic location at the crossroads of the Beijing-Canton and Shanghai-Urumqi railway lines makes Zhengzhou

MAP 17

the natural capital of Henan province. Since the railway made it here in 1903 (this was one of the very first major lines to be built in China) Zhengzhou is a comparatively modern city and there isn't a huge amount to see, even if you get off at this station and explore.

The train turns 180° here, so heading 'backwards' as it goes north to Beijing. Kilometre marker posts jump up by almost exactly 100km shortly afterwards and this now provides an accurate countdown to Beijing.

Km652 North of Huang Henan An the line crosses the Yellow River for the last time, in style: over a bridge several km long.

Km611: Qi Li Ying The town lies at the centre of a large cotton growing region, and this district was the first to be reorganised into a farming commune in April 1958 during the disastrous Great Leap Forward (see p74). By November of that year virtually 100% of the province's rural population was 'communalised'.

Km490: Anyang Despite its being one of China's former capital cities, there is little to see in Anyang. There are, however, numerous steam locomotives at the station.

North of Anyang the line crosses the Zhang River and enters **Hebei province**. Covering 192,000 square km, Hebei constitutes only 2% of China's total landmass but is still considerably bigger than the UK. Its capital since 1967 has been Shijiazhuang (particularly difficult to pronounce coherently after a few drinks). Beijing would be a part of Hebei if it were not for the fact that it is an Independent Municipality; likewise Tianjin, which was the province's capital until 1967.

Hebei has had a rough time this century: from 1937-45 it was almost entirely occupied by the Japanese, who were notoriously brutal to the civilian population. Having been liberated at the end of the war, the KMT stomped in and so the whole region saw another four years fighting in the civil war. It is one of the most densely populated Chinese provinces, with a higher population per square metre than either the UK or even New York State; bearing in mind that half of the province is mountainous and completely uninhabited this would suggest that the place is fairly crowded. Still, you are unlikely to be able to tell this from the train, as it all looks fairly similar to the rest of this part of the journey – flat and rather nondescript, with occasional rolling hills.

Km266: Shijiazhuang The capital of Hebei province is noticeably more modern than the other cities on this section of the route. With a population of about a million it's an important producer of cotton textiles, machinery and electronics.

Km9 On the final approach to Beijing the line crosses the Lugu Bridge, the scene of the first battle of the Sino-Japanese war on 7 July 1937. It all started with a Japanese 'military exercise' in which they 'lost' a soldier. They asked permission to cross this bridge in order to find him and the Chinese, having watched the Japanese advance through Chinese territory for a number of years, refused it. The motive for a battle was there, and it led to a war which lasted eight years.

Km0: Beijing See p245.

APPENDIX A: TIMETABLES

Since there is no through train along the Silk Route (as there is on the Trans-Siberian) you will need to take several different trains to cover all the places mentioned in this book. Trains in the CIS and China are identified by a number. There's a wide choice and the best options are mentioned in the 'Getting away' section at the end of each city guide and in the timetables below. Since these timetables are subject to change they are given for guidance only. Consult the Thomas Cook Overseas Timetable for the latest information. Note that the times below are all Moscow Time (see p58).

Table 1: Moscow – Tashkent – Almaty

	No86		No98*		No8		No24	
Moscow	11.44	05.35	00.24	17.04	22.15	15.38	14.16	05.30
Ryazan			04.07	11.12	02.05	12.08	18.10	01.45
Syzran	04.34	11.26	18.38	22.28				
Orenburg			06.05	11.10				
Aktyubinsk			12.20	03.15	08.43	06.40		
Kandagach			13.51	01.10	10.22	04.47		
Makat			21.08	16.19			05.27	11.53
Kungrad			11.05	02.57			21.21	22.22
Urgench			15.22	22.30			02.06	18.05
Chardzhou			23.50	14.40			09.15	11.10
Bukhara			02.20	11.44			12.32	08.26
Samarkand			07.22	06.20				No 23
Tashkent	04.40	11.55	No97*					
Aralsk	No85				19.00	20.16		
KyzilOrda					02.25	13.12		
Turkestan					07.40	08.43		
Chimkent					11.34	05.19		
Dzhambul					16.24	01.12		
Almaty					03.30	15.15		
					No 7			

* Service currently runs infrequently – confirm departure days and times

Table 2: Almaty - Urumqi

	No 14	
Almaty I	17.45	05.05
Aktogay	0415	19.05
Druzhba	15.00	12.50
Urumqi	09.30	23.00
	No 13	

Table 3: Urumqi - Beijing

	No 98 ▼		No 51/4 ▼		No 244 ▼		No 70 ▼	
Urumqi	21.31	10.23	18.30	14.56	15.25	07.19	16.49	17.41
Turfan	00.30	07.37	21.29	12.10	18.56	03.58	19.51	14.55
Hami	08.24	00.15	04.59	04.14	04.04	19.04	03.35	07.10
Liuyuan	14.05	19.08	10.48	23.16	11.33	12.45	09.09	01.58
Yumen	19.17	13.43	15.55	17.55	17.43	07.19	14.26	20.45
Jiayuguan	19.58	12.50	16.33	17.02	18.30	06.25	15.05	19.53
Wuwei	05.31	02.56	02.51	07.10	06.34	19.39	03.44	10.09
Lanzhou	12.50	19.22	10.14	23.53		11.35	08.18	02.31
Tianshui	19.56	12.08	16.35	17.20	▲		15.26	20.13
Xi'an	02.14	06.08	23.30	10.47	No 243		21.47	14.22
Luoyang	08.25	23.54	05.30	04.45			03.47	08.20
Zhengzhou	10.17	21.54	07.45	02.45			05.49	06.20
Shijiazhuang	▲		▲				11.20	00.51
Beijing	No 97		No 52/3				14.40	21.24
							▲ No 69	

APPENDIX B: PHRASE LISTS

Travel without languages is little more than a prolonged and elaborate game of charades. The route featured in this guide is not well travelled, and you should be prepared for the fact that virtually no-one you meet, either in the CIS or China, will be able to speak English. Travel in these areas is quite difficult enough without putting yourself at the disadvantage of not being able to state what you want or understand even the simplest statement. Not only will the short investment of time required to learn a few phrases before you leave repay you when you get there with less hassle, it will also demonstrate some degree of respect for the locals you meet along the way, and make you friends surprisingly fast. (This is particularly true in China where if you can say even 'hello, my name is.... I am from ...' you are likely to receive hearty handshakes and congratulations all round).

The sections here highlight only a few useful words. I would seriously recommend that you take along phrasebooks and learn as much as possible.

Russian

Although Uzbekistan and Kazakhstan have their own languages, for the time being Russian is the language which is understood by most people in the CIS.

CYRILLIC ALPHABET

First, acquaint yourself with the Cyrillic alphabet so that you will be able to read station and street names. Derived from the Greek, Cyrillic was introduced in Russia in the 10th century through a translation of the Bible made by two Greek bishops, Cyril (who gave his name to the new alphabet) and Methodius.

Cyrillic letters	Roman letter	Pronunciation*	Cyrillic letters	Roman letter	Pronunciation*
А а	a	(far)	П п	p	(Peter)
Б б	b	(bet)	Р р	r	(Russia)
В в	v	(vodka)	С с	s	(Samarkand)
Г г	g	(get)	Т т	t	(train)
Д д	d	(dog)	У у	u/oo	(rule)
Е е	e	(yet)	Ф ф	f/ph	(frost)
Ё ё	yo	(yoghurt)	Х х	kh	(loch)
Ж ж	zh	(treasure)	Ц ц	ts	(lots)
З з	z	(zebra)	Ч ч	ch	(chill)
И и	ee	(seek)	Ш ш	sh	(fish)
Й й	y	(ready)	Щ щ	shch	(fresh chicken)
К к	k	(Kiev)	Ы ы	i	(did)
Л л	l	(Lenin)	Э э	e/ih	(tent)
М м	m	(Moscow)	Ю ю	yu	(union)
Н н	n	(never)	Я я	ya	(yak)
О о	o	(over)	Ь ь		softens preceding letter

* pronunciation shown by underlined letter/s

KEY PHRASES

The following phrases in Cyrillic script may be useful to point to if you're having problems communicating:

Please write it down for me   **Запиши́те э́то для меня́, пожа́луйста**

Help me, please   **Помоги́те мне, пожа́луйста**

I need an interpreter   **Мне ну́жен перево́дчик с англи́йского**

CONVERSATIONAL RUSSIAN

Run the hyphenated syllables together as you speak and roll your 'R's:

General
Hello	*Zdrah-stvoo-iteh*
Good morning	*Dob-royeh-ootro*
Good afternoon/evening	*Dobree den/vecher*
Please	*Po-zhalsta*
Do you speak English?	*Gavar-iteh lee vy pa anglee-skee?*
No/Yes	*nyet/da*
thank you	*spasee-ba*
excuse me (sorry)	*izveen-iteh*
good/bad	*haroshaw/plahoy*
cheap/expensive	*deshoveey/daragoy*
Wait a minute!	*Adnoo meenoo-too!*
Please call a doctor	*Vi'zaveete, po-zhalsta, vracha*
Goodbye	*Das-vedahneya*

Directions
map	*karta/schema*
Where is …?	*G'dyeh …?*
hotel	*gastee-neetsoo*
airport	*aeroport/aerodrom*
bus-station	*stantsia afto-boosa*
metro/taxi	*metro/taksee*
tram/trolley-bus	*tramvai/trolleybus*
restaurant/cafe	*restarahn/kafay*
museum/shop	*moo-zyey/maga-zyeen*
bakery/grocer's	*boolach-naya/gastra-nohm*
box office (theatre)	*teatrahl-naya kassa*
lavatory (ladies/gents)	*too-alet (zhen-ski/moozh-skoy)*
open/closed	*at-krita/za-krita*
left/right	*na-prahva/na-leva*

Numerals/time
1 *adeen*; 2 *dvah*; 3 *tree*; 4 *chetir*; 5 *p'aht*; 6 *shest*; 7 *s'em*; 8 *vosem*; 9 *d'evat*; 10 *d'e'sat*; 11 *adeen-natsat*; 12 *dve-natsat*; 13 *tree-natsat*; 14 *chetir-natsat*; 15 *pyat-natsat*; 16 *shes-natsat*; 17 *sem-natsat*; 18 *va'sem-natsat*; 19 *d'evat-natsat*; 20 *dvatsat*; 30 *tree-tsat*; 40 *so'rok*; 50 *p'ad-desaht*; 60 *shez-desaht*; 70 *sem-desaht*; 80 *vosem-desaht*; 90 *d'even-osta*; 100 *sto*; 200 *dve-stee*; 300 *tree-sta*; 400 *chetir-esta*; 500 *p'at-sot*; 600 *shes-sot*; 700 *sem-sot*; 800 *vosem-sot*; 900 *devet-sot*; 1000 *tees-acha*.

How much/many?	*Skolka?*
rouble/roubles	*rooble/rooblah/roobley**
Please write down the price	*Nap'eesheet'eh, pazhalsta, tse-noo*
ticket	*beel-yet*
1st/2nd/3rd Class	*perviy/ftoroy/treteey class*
express	*express*
What time is it?	*Kato'riy chahs?*
hours/minutes	*chasof/meenoot*
today	*sevodna*
yesterday/tomorrow	*fcherah/zahftra*
Monday/Tuesday	*pani-dell-nik/ftor-nik*
Wednesday/Thursday	*sri-da/chit-virk*
Friday	*pyat-nit-sah*
Saturday	*sue-boat-ah*
Sunday	*vraski-sen-yah*

*1st word is for 1 unit, 2nd word for 2-4 units, 3rd word for 5 or more.

Food and drink

menu	*menoo*
mineral water	*meenerahl-noi vady*
fruit juice	*sokee*
vodka/whisky	*vodka/veeskee*
beer	*peeva*
wine/cognac	*veenah/kanya-koo*
champagne	*sham-pahn-skoya*
Cheers!	*Zah vasheh zdaro-vyeh!*
caviare	*eek-ry*
salmon/sturgeon	*lasa-seeny/aset-reeny*
chicken/duck	*tsy-plonka/oot-koo*
steak/roast beef	*beef-shteks/rost-beef*
pork	*svee-nooyoo*
veal	*atbeef-nooyoo telyah-choo*
ham/sausage	*vechina/kalba-soo*
bread/potatoes	*khlee-ep/kar-toshka*
butter/cheese	*mah-sla/sir*
eggs/omelette	*yait-sa/amlet*
salt/pepper	*sol/perets*
tea/coffee	*chai/koh-fee*
milk/sugar	*mala-ko/sahk-har*
bill	*shchot*

Questions and answers

What's your name?	*Kak vahs zavoot?*
My name is ...	*Menyah zavoot*
I'm from Britain/USA	*Yah preeyeh-khal eez Anglee-ee/S-Sh-Ah*
Canada/Australia	*Kanadah/Avstralee*
New Zealand/Japan	*Novee Zeelandee/Yaponee*
Sweden/Finland	*Shvetsee/Finlandee*
Norway/Denmark	*Norveggee/Danee*
Germany/Austria	*Germanee/Avstree*
France/Netherlands	*Frantsee/Gollandee*

Where are you going?	*Kudah vhee idyotyeh*
I'm going to ...	*Yah idoo ...*
Are you married?	*Vee zhyehnaht/zamoozhyem?**
Have you any children?	*Yest ly oo vas dety?*
boy/girl	*mahl-cheek/de-vooshka*
How old are you?	*Skolka vahm l'et*
What do you do?	*Shto vhee delayetyeh*
student/teacher	*stoo-dent/oochee-tel (-neetsa)**
doctor/nurse	*vrach/myeh-sestra*
actor/artist	*aktor/khoo-dozh-neek*
engineer/lawyer	*een-zheneer/advokaht*
office worker	*sloo-zhash-chey*
Where do you live?	*G'dyeh vhee zhuvyotyeh*

* (feminine form)

Uzbek

Hello	*Salaam alaykum*
Thank you	*Rakhmat*
Yes/No	*Ha/Yok*
How much is this?	*Bu kanda?*
It's very expensive	*Bu juda kimmat*
railway station	*temir yol stantsia*
restaurant/hotel	*awsxawna/musafirkhona*

Kazakh

Hello	*Salaam alaykum*
Thank you	*Rakhmat*
Yes/No	*Solai or eeya/Joq*
How much is this?	*Baharsi niche?*
It's very expensive	*Khambat*
railway station	*poryuz zhorle*
restaurant/hotel	*tamaq khana/khonaq khana*
Goodbye	*Bolenguz*

Uighur

Hello	*Salaam alaykum/Yakh shimusiz*
Thank you	*Rakhmat*
Yes/No	*Shundaq/Yaq*
How much is this?	*Baharsi neche?*
It's very expensive	*Bu nahaiti kemmet*
railway station	*poryuz yorle*
restaurant/hotel	*ashkana/mikhman khana*
Goodbye	*Heira hosh*

Chinese

Particularly tricky. The problem with Chinese is one of pronunciation - so much depends on your tone and emphasis that if you do not get the sound exactly right you will not be understood at all. The best way to learn in advance is either to take lessons, or to buy a cassette course (simple ones are under £10/US$15 and come with a useful phrasebook).

The country's main dialect is Mandarin, spoken by about three-quarters of the population. Mandarin has four tones: high tone (–), rising (ˊ) where the voice starts low and rises to the same level as the high tone, falling-rising (ˇ) where the voice starts with a middle tone, falls and then rises to just below a high tone; and falling (ˋ) which starts at the high tone and falls to a low one.

READING PINYIN CHINESE

Pinyin is the system of transliterating Chinese into the Roman alphabet. Pronunciation is indicated by the underlined letters below:

Vowels

a	as in f<u>ar</u>	e	as in w<u>e</u>re
i	as in tr<u>ee</u>	o	as in <u>or</u>
	or as in w<u>e</u>re	u	as in P<u>oo</u>h
	after c, r, s, z, ch, sh, zh	ü	as in c<u>ue</u>

Consonants

c	as in eat<u>s</u>	h	as in lo<u>ch</u> or the kh in an
q	as in <u>ch</u>eap		Arabic word, with the sound
r	as in t<u>r</u>ill		from the back of the throat.
x	as in <u>sh</u>eep	z	as in plod<u>s</u>
zh	as in <u>j</u>aw		

KEY PHRASES

The following phrases in Chinese characters may be useful to point to if you're having problems communicating:

Please write it down for me   请写下

Help me, please   请帮我

Please call a doctor   请你叫医生

USEFUL WORDS AND PHRASES

General

Hello	*Nǐ hǎo*
Please	*Qǐng*
Do you speak English?	*Nǐ huì shuō yīng yǔ ma?*
Yes/No	*Dùi/Bū dùi* (literally correct/ incorrect)
Thank you	*Xiè xie*

Excuse me (sorry)	*Duì bù qǐ*
Excuse me (may I have your attention?)	*Qǐng wèn*
good/bad	*hǎo/bu hǎo*
Wait	*Děng*
Goodbye	*Zài jiàn*
UK/USA	*Yīng guó/Měi guó*
Canada/Australia	*Jīa ná dà/Ao dà lia*
France/The Netherlands/Germany	*Fǎ guó/Hé lán/Dé guó*
I understand/do not understand	*Wǒ dǒng le/Wǒ bù dǒng*
Translator	*Fān yì*

Directions

Where is…?	*Zài nǎr…?*
toilet (ladies/gents)	*cè sǔo (nü/nan)*
airport	*jī chǎng*
bus station	*chē zhàn*
railway station	*hǔo chē zhàn*
taxi	*chū zū qì chē*
museum	*bó wù guǎn*
hotel/restaurant	*lǚ guǎn/fàn guǎn*
post office	*yóu*
PSB/CAAC office	*Gōng ān jú/Zhōng háng gōngsi*
What time will we arrive at…?	*Liè chē shénme shí jiān dào…?*
What station is this?	*Zhè shì nà yí zhàn?*

Numerals/time

1 *yī*, 2 *èr*, 3 *sān*, 4 *sì*, 5 *wǔ*, 6 *liù*, 7 *qī*, 8 *bā*, 9 *jiǔ*, 10 *shí*, 11 *shí yī*, 12 *shí èr*, 13 *shí sān*, 14 *shí sì*, 15 *shí wǔ*, 16 *shí liù*, 17 *shí qī*, 18 *shí bā*, 19 *shí jiǔ*, 20 *èr shí*, 21 *èr shí yī*, 30 *sān shí*, 40 *sì shí*, 50 *wǔ shí*, 100 *yì bǎi*, 101 *yì bǎi líng yī*, 110 *yì bǎi yī shí*, 150 *yì bǎi wǔ shí*, 200 *èr bǎi*, 500 *wǔ bǎi*, 1000 *yì qiān*, 10,000 *yí wàn*, 100,000 *shí wàn*, 1 million *yì bǎi wàn*,

Monday/Tuesday/Wednesday	*Xīng qī…yī/èr/sān*
Thursday/Friday/Saturday/Sunday	*Xīng qī…sì/wǔ/liù/rì*
How much?	*Duō shao?*
That's too expensive	*Tài guì le*
yesterday/tomorrow/today	*zuó tiān/míng tiān/jīn tiān*

Transport

ticket	*piào*
Hard Seat/Soft Seat	*Yìng Zuò/Luǎn Zuò*
Hard Sleeper/Soft Sleeper	*Yìng Wò/Luǎn Wò*
Please may I upgrade this ticket to….	*Qǐng nǐ huan gao yí ji de piào*

Food and drink

menu	*cài dān*
mineral water/tea/beer	*kuàng quán shuǐ/chá/pí jiǔ*
noodles/noodle soup	*miàn/tāng miàn*
(fried) rice	*(chǎo) fàn*
bread/egg	*miàn bāo/jī dàn*
pork/beef/lamb	*zhū ròu/niú ròu/yáng ròu*
chicken/duck/fish	*jī/yā/yú*
vegetables	*shū cài*
Do you have any vegetarian dishes?	*Nǐ zhèr yǒu sù-cài ma?*

INDEX

Abbreviations: (B) Bukhara; (K) Kashgar; (Kh) Khiva; (S) Samarkand